MEETING
THE
SHADOW

. . . .

This *New Consciousness Reader*
is part of a new series of original
and classic writing by renowned experts on
leading-edge concepts in personal development,
psychology, spiritual growth, and healing.

MEETING THE SHADOW

*The Hidden Power
of the Dark Side
of Human Nature*

. . . .

EDITED BY

JEREMIAH ABRAMS
AND
CONNIE ZWEIG

JEREMY P. TARCHER, INC.
Los Angeles

Library of Congress Cataloging-in-Publication Data

Meeting the shadow : hidden power of the dark side of human nature/edited by
    Connie Zweig and Jeremiah Abrams.—1st ed.
        p.   cm.
    Includes bibliographical references.
    ISBN 0-87477-618-X : $12.95
    1. Shadow (Psychoanalysis)   2. Good and evil—Psychological aspects.
I. Zweig, Connie.   II. Abrams, Jeremiah.
BF175.5.S55M44   1990   91-8168
150.19'5—dc20   CIP

Jeremy P. Tarcher, Inc.
5858 Wilshire Blvd., Suite 200
Los Angeles, CA 90036

Distributed by St. Martin's Press, New York

Manufactured in the United States of America
10 9 8 7 6 5 4 3 2 1

First Edition

The evil of our time is the loss of consciousness
of evil.

KRISHNAMURTI

Something we were withholding made us weak,
Until we found it was ourselves.

ROBERT FROST

If only it were all so simple! If only there were evil
people somewhere insidiously committing evil deeds,
and it were necessary only to separate them from the
rest of us and destroy them. But the line dividing
good and evil cuts through the heart of every human
being. And who is willing to destroy a piece of his
own heart?

ALEXANDER SOLZHENITSYN

That which we do not bring to consciousness appears
in our lives as fate.

C. G. JUNG

CONTENTS

. . . .

PART 7
Devils, Demons, and Scapegoats:
A Psychology of Evil

PART 8
Enemy-Making:
Us and Them in the Body Politic

PART 9

Shadow-Work:
Bringing Light to the Darkness
Through Therapy, Story, and Dreams

PART 10

Owning Your Dark Side
Through Insight, Art, and Ritual

ACKNOWLEDGMENTS

. . . .

Our deepest appreciation to the poets and artists whom we follow in exploring the dark side, especially those whose thoughts on the shadow have had a deep effect on this work and, as a result, on our lives: C. G. Jung, John A. Sanford, Adolf Guggenbühl-Craig, Marie-Louise von Franz, and Robert Bly.

For loving support and creative assistance, our thanks to Jeremy Tarcher, Barbara Shindell, Hank Stine, Daniel Malvin, Paul Murphy, Susan Shankin, Susan Deixler, Lisa Chadwick, Steve Wolf, Joel Covitz, Tom Rautenberg, Bob Stein, Suzanne Wagner, Linda Novack, Michael and Kathryn Jaliman, Peter Leavitt, Deena Metzger, Marsha de la O, and the women's writing circle, Bill and Vivienne Howe, Bruce Burman, Andrew Schultz, and the staffs of the Los Angeles and San Francisco C. G. Jung Institute Libraries.

Special mention to Connie's shadow sisters Jane, Marian, Susan, April; and lifelong gratitude to my wise mother and father. A twinkle in the eye for Jeremiah's patient children, Raybean and Pito.

A NOTE ON LANGUAGE

We recognize that our shared language creates as well as reflects our culture's unspoken attitudes. For this reason, we apologize for the archaic use of the masculine form *he,* which designates hypothetical individuals throughout these copyrighted excerpts. When read today, this usage seems jarring and dated. Unfortunately, even now we have not devised a better style. We hope that soon one will emerge.

THE EDITORS

. . . .

PROLOGUE

C O N N I E   Z W E I G

At midlife I met my devils. Much of what I had counted as blessing became curse. The wide road narrowed; the light grew dark. And in the darkness, the saint in me, so well nurtured and well coiffed, met the sinner.

My fascination with the Light, my eager optimism concerning outcomes, my implicit trust concerning others, my commitment to meditation and a path of enlightenment—all were no longer a saving grace, but a kind of subtle curse, a deeply etched habit of thinking and feeling that seemed to bring me face to face with its opposite, with the heartbreak of failed ideals, with the plague of my naiveté, with the dark side of God. At this time, I had the following shadow dream:

> I'm at the beach with my childhood sweetheart. People are swimming in the sea. A large black shark appears. There's fear everywhere. A child disappears. People panic. My boyfriend wants to follow the fish, a mythical creature. He can't understand the human danger.
>
> Somehow I contact the fish—and discover that it's plastic. I stick my finger through its end and puncture it—it deflates. My boyfriend is furious, like I killed God. He values the fish over human life. Walking up the beach, he leaves me. I wander off, up into the trees, where a blue blanket awaits.

In analyzing this dream, I realized that I had never taken the shadow seriously. I had believed, with a kind of spiritual hubris, that a deep and committed inner life would protect me from human suffering, that I could somehow deflate the power of the shadow with my metaphysical practices and beliefs. I had assumed, in effect, that it was managed, as I managed my moods or my diet, with the discipline of self-control.

But the dark side appears in many guises. My confrontation with it at midlife was shocking, uprooting, and terribly disillusioning. Intimate friendships of many years seemed to turn brittle and crack, bereft of lifeblood and its elasticity. My strengths began to feel like weaknesses, standing in the way of growth rather than promoting it. At the same time, dormant, unsuspected aptitudes awakened and arose rudely toward the surface, disrupting a self-image to which I had become accustomed.

My buoyant mood and balanced temperament gave way to deep drops into the valley of despair. At forty I descended into depression, living in what Hermann Hesse once called a "mud hell." At other times an unknown rage would storm out of me, leaving me feeling depleted and ashamed, as if I had been possessed momentarily by some archaic god of wrath.

My search for meaning, which had led earlier in life to intensive questioning, psychotherapy, and meditation practice, resurfaced with a vengeance. My emotional self-sufficiency and carefully cultivated ability to live without dependency on men gave way to a stinging vulnerability. Suddenly I was one of *those* women who is obsessed with intimate relationships.

Life seemed bankrupt. All that I had "known" as a fierce reality crumpled like a papier-mâché tiger in the wind. I felt as if I were becoming all that I was not. All that I had worked to develop, strived to create, came undone. The thread of my life pulled; the story unraveled. And the ones I had despised and disdained were born in me—like another life, yet my life, an invisible twin.

I could sense then why some people went mad, w torrid love affairs despite a strong marriage bond, why s nancial security began to steal or hoard money or give it why Goethe said that he had never heard of a crime of lieve himself capable. I was capable of anything.

I remembered a story I had read somewhere in whic murderer's eyes and recognizes the killing impulse in his moment he shifts back to his proper self, to be a judge, and condemns the murderer to death.

My dark and murderous self had revealed itself too, if just for a moment. Rather than condemn it to death, banishing it once more to invisible realms, I have tried slowly and tentatively to redirect my journey in an effort to face it. After a period of great despair, I am beginning to feel a more inclusive sense of self, an expansion of my nature, and a deeper connection to humankind.

My mother pointed out some twenty years ago, in the height of my spiritual grandiosity, that I was good at loving humanity but not so good at loving individual human beings. With the gradual acceptance of the darker impulses within me, I feel a more genuine compassion growing in my soul. To be an ordinary human being, full of longing and contradiction, was once anathema to me. Today it is extraordinary.

I have looked for a symbolic way to give birth to my shadow self so that my outer life would not be torn apart, so that I would not have to discard this creative lifestyle that I love so well. During the preparation of this book I traveled to Bali, where the battle between good and evil is the theme of every shadow puppet play and dance performance. There is even an initiation that the Balinese perform at age seventeen in which an individual's teeth are evenly filed so that the demons of anger, jealousy, pride, and greed are exorcised. Afterward, the initiate feels cleansed, baptized.

Alas, our culture offers no such initiation ceremonies. I have discovered that for me shaping this book has been a way to map the descent and carry a light into the darkness.

INTRODUCTION: THE SHADOW SIDE OF EVERYDAY LIFE

CONNIE ZWEIG AND JEREMIAH ABRAMS

> How could there be so much evil in the world?
> Knowing humanity, I wonder why there is not more
> of it.
>
> WOODY ALLEN, *Hannah and Her Sisters*

In 1886, more than a decade before Freud plumbed the depths of human darkness, Robert Louis Stevenson had a highly revealing dream: A male character, pursued for a crime, swallows a powder and undergoes a drastic change of character, so drastic that he is unrecognizable. The kind, hard-working scientist Dr. Jekyll is transformed into the violent and relentless Mr. Hyde, whose evil takes on greater and greater proportions as the dream story unfolds.

Stevenson developed the dream into the now-famous tale *The Strange Case of Dr. Jekyll and Mr. Hyde.* Its theme has become so much a part of popular culture that we may think of it when we hear someone say, "I was not myself," or "He was like a demon possessed," or "She became a shrew." As Jungian analyst John Sanford points out, when a story like this one touches the chord of our humanity in such a way that it rings true for many people, it must have an archetypal quality—it must speak to a place in us that is universal.

Each of us contains both a Dr. Jekyll and a Mr. Hyde, a more pleasant persona for everyday wear and a hiding, nighttime self that remains hushed up much of the time. Negative emotions and behaviors—rage, jealousy, shame, lying, resentment, lust, greed, suicidal and murderous tendencies—lie concealed just beneath the surface, masked by our more proper selves. Known together in psychology as the *personal shadow,* it remains untamed, unexplored territory to most of us.

INTRODUCING THE SHADOW

The personal shadow develops naturally in every young child. As we identify with ideal personality characteristics such as politeness and generosity, which are reinforced in our environments, we shape what W. Brugh Joy calls the New Year's Resolution Self. At the same time, we bury in the shadow those qualities that don't fit our self-image, such as rudeness and selfishness. The ego and the shadow, then, develop in tandem, creating each other out of the same life experience.

Carl Jung saw the inseparability of ego and shadow in himself in a dream that he describes in his autobiography, *Memories, Dreams, Reflections:*

> It was night in some unknown place, and I was making slow and painful headway against a mighty wind. Dense fog was flying along everywhere. I had my hands cupped around a tiny light which threatened to go out at any moment. Everything depended on my keeping this little light alive.
>
> Suddenly I had the feeling that something was coming up behind me. I looked back and saw a gigantic black figure following me. But at the same moment I was conscious in spite of my terror that I must keep my little light going through night and wind, regardless of all dangers.
>
> When I awoke I realized at once that the figure was my own shadow on the swirling mists, brought into being by the little light I was carrying. I knew too that this little light was my consciousness, the only light I have. Though infinitely small and fragile in comparison with the powers of darkness, it is still a light, my only light.

Many forces play a role in forming our shadow selves, ultimately determining what is permitted expression and what is not. Parents, siblings, teachers, clergy, and friends create a complex environment in which we learn what is kind, proper, moral behavior, and what is mean-spirited, shameful, and sinful.

The shadow acts like a psychic immune system, defining what is self and what is not-self. For different people, in different families and cultures, what falls into ego and what falls into shadow can vary. For instance, some permit anger or aggression to be expressed; most do not. Some permit sexuality, vulnerability, or strong emotions; many do not. Some permit financial ambition, or artistic expression, or intellectual development, while some do not.

All the feelings and capacities that are rejected by the ego and exiled into the shadow contribute to the hidden power of the dark side of human nature. However, not all of them are what we consider to be negative traits. According to Jungian analyst Liliane Frey-Rohn, this dark treasury includes our infantile parts, emotional attachments, neurotic symptoms, as well as our undeveloped talents and gifts. The shadow, she says, "retains contact with the lost depths of the soul, with life and vitality—the superior, the universally human, yes, even the creative can be sensed there."

DISOWNING THE SHADOW

We cannot look directly into this hidden domain. The shadow by nature is difficult to apprehend. It is dangerous, disorderly, and forever in hiding, as if the light of consciousness would steal its very life.

Prolific Jungian analyst James Hillman says: "The unconscious cannot be conscious; the moon has its dark side, the sun goes down and cannot shine everywhere at once, and even God has two hands. Attention and focus require some things to be out of the field of vision, to remain in the dark. One cannot look both ways."

For this reason, we see the shadow mostly indirectly, in the distasteful traits and actions of other people, *out there* where it is safer to observe it. When we react intensely to a quality in an individual or group—such as laziness or stupidity, sensuality, or spirituality—and our reaction overtakes us with great loathing or admiration, this may be our own shadow showing. We *project* by attributing this quality to the other person in an unconscious effort to banish it from ourselves, to keep ourselves from seeing it within.

Jungian analyst Marie-Louise von Franz suggests that projection is like shooting a magic arrow. If the receiver has a soft spot to receive the projection, it sticks. If we project our anger onto a dissatisfied mate, our seductive charms onto a good-looking stranger, or our spiritual attributes onto a guru, we hit the target and the projection holds. From then on the sender and receiver are linked in a mysterious alliance, like falling in love, discovering a perfect hero, or a perfect villain.

So the personal shadow contains undeveloped, unexpressed potentials of all kinds. It is that part of the unconscious that is complementary to the ego and represents those characteristics that the conscious personality does not wish to acknowledge and therefore neglects, forgets, and buries, only to discover them in uncomfortable confrontations with others.

MEETING THE SHADOW

Although we cannot gaze at it directly, the shadow does appear in daily life. For example, we meet it in humor—such as dirty jokes or slapstick antics—which express our hidden, inferior, or feared emotions. When we observe closely that which strikes us as funny—such as someone slipping on a banana peel or referring to a taboo body part—we discover that the shadow is active. John Sanford points out that people who lack a sense of humor probably have a very repressed shadow. It's usually the shadow self who laughs at jokes.

English psychoanalyst Molly Tuby suggests six other ways in which, even unknowingly, we meet the shadow every day:

- In our exaggerated feelings about others ("I just can't believe he would do that!" "I don't know how she could wear that outfit!")
- In negative feedback from others who serve as our mirrors ("This is the third time you arrived late without calling me.")
- In those interactions in whch we continually have the same troubling effect on several different people ("Sam and I both feel that you have not been straightforward with us.")
- In our impulsive and inadvertent acts ("Oops, I didn't mean to say that.")
- In situations in which we are humiliated ("I'm so ashamed about how he treats me.")

- In our exaggerated anger about other people's faults ("She just can't seem to do her work on time!" "Boy, he really let his weight get out of control!")

At moments like these, when we are possessed by strong feelings of shame or anger, or we find that our behavior is off the mark in some way, the shadow is erupting unexpectedly. Usually it recedes just as quickly, beause meeting the shadow can be a frightening and shocking experience to our self-image.

For this reason we may quickly shift into denial, hardly noticing the murderous fantasy, suicidal thought, or embarrassing envy that could reveal a bit of our own darkness. The late psychiatrist R. D. Laing poetically describes the mind's denial reflex:

> The range of what we think and do
> is limited by what we fail to notice.
> And because we fail to notice
> that we fail to notice
> there is little we can do
> to change
> until we notice
> how failing to notice
> shapes our thoughts and deeds.

failing to notice

If the denial holds, as Laing says, then we may not even notice that we fail to notice. For example, it's common to meet the shadow at midlife, when one's deeper needs and values tend to change direction, perhaps even making a 180-degree turn. This calls for breaking old habits and cultivating dormant talents. If we don't stop to heed the call and continue to move in the same life direction, we will remain unaware of what midlife has to teach.

Depression, too, can be a paralyzing confrontation with the dark side, a contemporary equivalent of the mystic's dark night of the soul. The inner demand for a descent into the underworld can be overridden by outer concerns, such as the need to work long hours, distractions by other people, or antidepressant drugs, which damp our feelings of despair. In this case, we fail to grasp the purpose of our melancholy.

Meeting the shadow calls for slowing the pace of life, listening to the body's cues, and allowing ourselves time to be alone in order to digest the cryptic messages from the hidden world.

THE COLLECTIVE SHADOW

Today we are confronted with the dark side of human nature each time we open a newspaper or watch the evening news. The more repugnant effects of the shadow are made visible to us in a daily prodigious media message that is broadcast globally throughout our modern electronic village. The world has become a stage for the *collective shadow*.

collective shadow

The collective shadow—human evil—is staring back at us virtually everywhere: It shouts from newsstand headlines; it wanders our streets, sleeping in doorways, homeless; it squats in X-rated neon-lit shops on the peripheries of our cities; it embezzles our monies from the local savings and loan; it corrupts power-hungry politicians and perverts our systems of justice; it drives invading armies through dense jungles and across desert sands; it sells arms to mad leaders and gives the profits to reactionary insurgents; it pours pollution through hidden pipes into our rivers and oceans, and poisons our food with invisible pesticides.

These observations are not some new fundamentalism, thumping on a biblical version of reality. Our era has made forced witnesses of us all. The whole world is watching. There is no way to avoid the frightening specter of satanic shadows acted out by conniving politicians, white-collar criminals, and fanatic terrorists. Our inner desire to be whole—now made manifest in the machinery of global communication—forces us to face the conflicting hypocrisy that is everywhere today.

While most individuals and groups live out the socially acceptable side of life, others seem to live out primarily the socially disowned parts. When they become the object of negative group projections, the collective shadow takes the form of scapegoating, racism, or enemy-making. To anti-Communist Americans, the USSR is the evil empire. To Moslems, America is the great Satan. To Nazis, the Jews are vermin Bolsheviks. To ascetic Christian monks, witches are in league with the devil. To South African advocates of apartheid or American members of the Ku Klux Klan, blacks are subhuman, undeserving of the rights and privileges of whites.

The hypnotic power and contagious nature of these strong emotions are evident in the universal pervasiveness of racial persecution, religious wars, and scapegoating tactics around the world. In these ways, human beings attempt to dehumanize others in an effort to ensure that *they* are wearing the white hats—and that killing the enemy does not mean killing human beings like themselves.

Throughout history the shadow has appeared via the human imagination as a monster, a dragon, a Frankenstein, a white whale, an extraterrestrial, or a man so vile that we cannot see ourselves in him; he is as removed from us as a gorgon. Revealing the dark side of human nature has been, then, one of the primary purposes of art and literature. As Nietzsche puts it: "We have art so that we shall not die of reality."

By using arts and media, including political propaganda, to imagine something as evil or demonic, we attempt to gain power over it, to break its spell. This may help explain why we are riveted to violent news stories of warmongers and religious fanatics. Repelled yet drawn to the violence and chaos of our world, in our minds we turn these *others* into the containers of evil, the enemies of civilization.

Projection also may help explain the immense popularity of horror novels and movies. Through a vicarious enactment of the shadow side, our evil impulses can be stimulated and perhaps relieved in the safety of the book or theater.

Children typically are introduced to shadow issues by listening to fairy tales that portray the war between good and evil forces, fairy godmothers and horrific demons. They, too, vicariously suffer the trials of their heroes and heroines, thereby learning the universal patterns of human fate.

In today's censorship battle in the arenas of media and music, those who would throttle the voice of darkness may not understand its urgent need to be heard. In an effort to protect the young, the censors rewrite Little Red Riding Hood so that she is no longer eaten by the wolf; and, in the end, the young are left unprepared to meet the evil they encounter.

Like a society, each family also has its built-in taboos, its forbidden arenas. The *family shadow* contains all that is rejected by a family's conscious awareness, those feelings and actions that are seen as too threatening to its self-image. In an upright Christian, conservative family this may mean getting drunk or marrying someone of another faith; in a liberal, atheistic family it may mean choosing a gay relationship. In our society, wife battering and child abuse used to be hidden away in the family shadow; today they have emerged in epidemic proportions into the light of day.

The dark side is not a recent evolutionary appearance, the result of civilization and education. It has its roots in a *biological shadow* that is based in our very cells. Our animal ancestors, after all, survived with tooth and claw. The beast in us is very much alive—just caged most of the time.

Many anthropologists and sociobiologists believe that human evil is a result of curbing our animal aggression, of choosing culture over nature and losing contact with our primitive wildness. Physician-anthropologist Melvin Konner tells the story in *The Tangled Wing* of going to a zoo and seeing a sign that reads: "The Most Dangerous Animal on Earth," only to discover that he is looking in the mirror.

KNOW THYSELF

In ancient times, human beings acknowledged the many dimensions of the shadow—the personal, collective, family, and biological. On the lintel pieces of the now-destroyed temple of Apollo at Delphi, which was built into the side of Mount Parnassus by the Greeks of the classical period, the temple priests set into stone two famous inscriptions, precepts that still hold great meaning for us today. The first of these, "Know thyself," applies broadly to our task. Know all of yourself, the priest of the god of light advised, which could be translated, know especially the dark side.

We are in direct lineage to the Greek mind. Our shadow self remains the great burden of self-knowledge, the disruptive element that does not want to be known. The Greeks understood this problem all too well, and their religion compensated for the underside of life. It was on the same mountainside above Delphi that the Greeks annually celebrated their famous bacchanal revels, orgies that glorified the forceful, creative presence of the nature god Dionysus in human beings.

Today, Dionysus exists for us only in degraded form in our cloven images of Satan, the devil, the personification of evil. No longer a god to be acknowledged and receive our tribute, he is banished to the world of fallen angels.

Marie-Louise von Franz acknowledges the relationship between the devil and the personal shadow when she says, "The principle of individuation is actually related to the devilish element, insofar as the latter represents a separation from the divine within the totality of nature. The devilish aspects are the disrupting elements—the affects, the autonomous power drive, and such things. They disrupt the unity of the personality."

NOTHING TO EXCESS

The other inscription at Delphi is perhaps more telling of the times in which we live. "Nothing to excess," the Greek god proclaims from his now-crumbled earthly shrine. The classicist E. R. Dodds suggests an interpretation of this motto: Only a people who knew excess, he says, could have lived by such a maxim. Only those who knew their capacity for lust, greed, rage, gluttony, and for all things excessive—who have understood and accepted their own potential for inappropriate extremes—can choose to regulate and humanize their actions.

We live in a time of critical excess: too many people, too much crime, too much exploitation, too much pollution, too many nuclear weapons. These are excesses that we can acknowledge and decry, though we may feel powerless to do anything about them.

Is there, in fact, anything we *can* do about them? For many people, the unacceptable qualities of excess go directly into the unconscious shadow, or they get expressed in shadowy behavior. In many of our lives these extremes take the form of symptoms: intensely negative feelings and actions, neurotic suffering, psychosomatic illnesses, depression, and substance abuse.

The scenarios might look like this: When we feel excessive desire, we push it into the shadow, then act it out without concern for others; when we feel excessive hunger, we push it into the shadow, then overeat, binge and purge, trashing our bodies; when we feel excessive longing for the high side of life, we push it into the shadow, then we seek it out through instant gratification or hedonistic activity such as drug and alcohol abuse. The list goes on. In our society, we see the growth of shadow excesses everywhere:

- In an uncontrolled power drive for knowledge and domination of nature (expressed in the amorality of the sciences and the unregulated marriage of business and technology).

- In a self-righteous compulsion to help and cure others (expressed in the distorted, codependent role of those in the helping professions and the greed of doctors and pharmaceutical companies).

- In a fast-paced, dehumanized workplace (expressed by the apathy of an alienated work force, the unplanned obsolescence produced by auto-mation, and the hubris of success).

- In the maximization of business growth and progress (expressed in le-veraged buyouts, profiteering, insider trading, and the savings and loan debacle).

- In a materialistic hedonism (expressed in conspicuous consumption, exploitative advertising, waste, and rampant pollution).

- In a desire to control our innately uncontrollable intimate lives (ex-pressed in widespread narcissism, personal exploitation, manipulation of others, and abuse of women and children).

- And in our everpresent fear of death (expressed in an obsession with health and fitness, diet, drugs, and longevity at any price).

These shadowy aspects run the width and breath of our society. How-ever, the tried solutions to our collective excess may be even more dangerous than the problem. Consider, for example, fascism and authoritarianism, the horrors that arose in reactionary attempts to contain social disorder and wide-spread decadence and permissiveness in Europe. More recently, the fervor of religious and political fundamentalism has reawakened on our own shores and across the seas in response to progressive ideas, encouraging, in W. B. Yeats's words, "mere anarchy to be loosed upon the world."

Jung understated the case when he said, "We have in all naiveté forgotten that beneath our world of reason another lies buried. I do not know what hu-manity will still have to undergo before it dares to admit this."

IF NOT NOW, WHEN?

History records from time immemorial the plagues of human evil. Entire na-tions have been susceptible to being pulled into mass hysterias of vast de-structive proportions. Today, with the apparent end of the cold war, there are some hopeful exceptions. For the first time, entire nations have become self-reflective and have tried to reverse direction. Consider this newspaper report, which speaks for itself (as cited by Jerome S. Bernstein in his book *Power and Politics*): The Soviet government announced that it was temporarily canceling all history examinations in the country. The *Philadelphia Inquirer* of June 11, 1988, reported:

> The Soviet Union, saying history textbooks had taught generations of Soviet children lies that poisoned their "minds and souls," announced yesterday that it had cancelled final history exams for more than 53 million students.
>   Reporting the cancellation, the government newspaper *Isvestia* said the ex-traordinary decision was intended to end the passing of lies from generation to generation, a process that has consolidated the Stalinist political and economic system that the current leadership wants to end.

. . . "The guilt of those who deluded one generation after another . . . is immeasurable," the paper said in a front-page commentary. "Today we are reaping the bitter fruits of our own moral laxity. We are paying for succumbing to conformity and thus to giving silent approval of everything that now brings the blush of shame to our faces and about which we do not know how to answer our children honestly."

This astounding confession by an entire nation could mark the end of an era. According to Sam Keen, author of *Faces of the Enemy*, "The only safe nations are those who systematically inoculate themselves by a free press and a vocal prophetic minority against the intoxication of 'divine destinies' and sanctified paranoia."

Today the world moves in two apparently opposing directions: Some leap away from fanatic, totalitarian regimes; others dig their feet in. We may feel helpless in the face of such great forces. Or, if we feel about such things at all, surely it must be the guilty conscience of unwitting complicity in our collective predicament. This bind was expressed accurately by Jung at mid-century: "The inner voice brings to consciousness whatever the whole— whether the nation to which we belong or humanity of which we are a part— suffers from. But it presents this evil in individual form, so that at first we would suppose all this evil to be only a trait of individual character."

To protect us from the human evil which these mass unconscious forces can enact, we have only one weapon: greater individual awareness. If we fail to learn or fail to act on what we learn from the spectacle of human behavior, we forfeit our power as individuals to alter ourselves, and thus to save our world. Yes, evil will always be with us. But the consequences of unchecked evil do not need to be tolerated.

"A great change of our psychological attitude is imminent," Jung said in 1959. "The only real danger that exists is man himself. He is the great danger, and we are pitifully unaware of it. We are the origin of all coming evil."

Cartoonist Walt Kelly's Pogo said it simply: "We have met the enemy and he is us." Today, we can give renewed psychological meaning to the idea of individual power. The frontier for action in confronting the shadow is—as it always has been—in the individual.

OWNING THE SHADOW

The aim of meeting the shadow is to develop an ongoing relationship with it, to expand our sense of self by balancing the one-sidedness of our conscious attitudes with our unconscious depths.

Novelist Tom Robbins says, "The purpose in encountering the shadow is to be in the right place in the right way." When we are in a proper relationship to it, the unconscious is not a demoniacal monster, as Jung points out. "It only becomes dangerous when our conscious attention to it is hopelessly wrong."

A right relationship with the shadow offers us a great gift: to lead us back to our buried potentials. Through *shadow-work,* a term we coined to refer to the continuing effort to develop a creative relationship with the shadow, we can:

- achieve a more genuine self-acceptance, based on a more complete knowledge of who we are;
- defuse the negative emotions that erupt unexpectedly in our daily lives;
- feel more free of the guilt and shame associated with our negative feelings and actions;
- recognize the projections that color our opinion of others;
- heal our relationships through more honest self-examination and direct communication;
- and use the creative imagination via dreams, drawing, writing, and rituals to own the disowned self.

Perhaps . . . perhaps we can also, in this way, refrain from adding our personal darkness to the density of the collective shadow.

British Jungian analyst and astrologer Liz Greene points to the paradoxical nature of the shadow as both the container of darkness and the beacon pointing toward the light: "It is the suffering, crippled side of the personality which is both the dark shadow that won't change and also the redeemer that transforms one's life and alters one's values. The redeemer can get the hidden treasure or win the princess or slay the dragon because he's marked in some way—he's abnormal. The shadow is both the awful thing that needs redemption, and the suffering redeemer who can provide it."

PART 1

. . . .

WHAT IS THE SHADOW?

Everyone carries a shadow, and the less it is embodied in the individual's conscious life, the blacker and denser it is. At all counts, it forms an unconscious snag, thwarting our most well-meant intentions.

C. G. JUNG

Yet there is a mystery here and it is not one that I understand: Without this sting of otherness, of—even—the vicious, without the terrible energies of the underside of health, sanity, sense, then nothing works or can work. I tell you that goodness—what we in our ordinary daylight selves call goodness: the ordinary, the decent—these are nothing without the hidden powers that pour forth continually from their shadow sides.

DORIS LESSING

Man's shadow, I thought, is his vanity.

FRIEDRICH NIETZSCHE

This thing of darkness I acknowledge mine.

WILLIAM SHAKESPEARE

INTRODUCTION

. . . .

Everything with substance casts a shadow. The ego stands to the shadow as light to shade. This is the quality that makes us human. Much as we would like to deny it, we are imperfect. And perhaps it is in what we don't accept about ourselves—our aggression and shame, our guilt and pain—that we discover our humanity.

The shadow goes by many familiar names: the disowned self, the lower self, the dark twin or brother in bible and myth, the double, repressed self, alter ego, id. When we come face-to-face with our darker side, we use metaphors to describe these shadow encounters: meeting our demons, wrestling with the devil, descent to the underworld, dark night of the soul, midlife crisis.

We all have a shadow. Or does our shadow have us? Carl Jung turned this question into a riddle when he asked: "How do you find a lion that has swallowed you?" Because the shadow is by definition unconscious, it is not always possible to know whether or not we are under the sway of some compelling part of our shadow's contents.

Jung said that intuitively each of us understands what is meant by the terms *shadow, inferior personality,* or *alter ego.* "And if he has forgotten," he joked about the average man, "his memory can easily be refreshed by a Sunday sermon, his wife, or the tax collector."

In order to be capable of meeting the shadow in our daily lives—admitting to it, and thus breaking its often compulsive hold on us—we need first of all a comprehensive understanding of the phenomenon. The shadow concept flows out of discoveries made by Sigmund Freud and Carl Jung. Paying due respect to his predecessor, Jung acknowledged Freud's breakthrough work as the most detailed and profound analysis of the split between the light and dark sides of the human psyche. According to Jung's former student and colleague, Liliane Frey-Rohn, "As early as 1912, while still under the influence of Freud's theories, Jung used the term 'shadow side of the psyche' to characterize 'not recognized desires' and 'repressed portions of the personality.' "

In 1917, in his essay "On the Psychology of the Unconscious," Jung speaks of the personal shadow as *the other* in us, the unconscious personality of the same sex, the reprehensible inferior, the other that embarrasses or shames us: "By shadow I mean the 'negative' side of the personality, the sum of all those unpleasant qualities we like to hide, together with the insufficiently developed functions and the content of the personal unconscious."

The shadow is negative only from the point of view of consciousness; it is not—as Freud insisted—totally immoral and incompatible with our conscious personalities. Rather, it potentially contains values of the highest

3

morality. This is particularly true, says Frey-Rohn, when there is a side hidden in the shadow personality which society values as positive, yet which is regarded by the individual as inferior.

The shadow most closely approaches what Freud understood as "the repressed." But in contrast to Freud's view, Jung's shadow is an inferior personality that has its own contents, such as autonomous thought, ideas, images, and value judgements, that are similar to the superior, conscious personality.

By 1945 Jung was referring to the shadow as simply the thing a person has no wish to be. "One does not become enlightened by imagining figures of light," he said, "but by making the darkness conscious. The latter procedure, however, is disagreeable and therefore not popular."

Today, shadow refers to that part of the unconscious psyche that is nearest to consciousness, even though it is not completely accepted by it. Because it is contrary to our chosen conscious attitude, the shadow personality is denied expression in life and coalesces into a relatively separate splinter personality in the unconscious, where it is isolated from exposure and discovery. This compensates for the one-sided identification we make with what is acceptable to our conscious minds.

For Jung and his followers, psychotherapy offers a ritual for renewal in which the shadow personality can be brought to awareness and assimilated, thus reducing its inhibiting or destructive potentials and releasing trapped, positive life energy. Jung continued to be concerned with the related problems of personal destructiveness and collective evil throughout a long and distinguished career. His investigations showed that dealing with shadow and evil is ultimately an "individual secret," equal to that of experiencing God, and so powerful an experience that it can transform the whole person.

Jung sought answers to the perplexing questions that trouble each of us, says Jungian scholar Andrew Samuels, and his life's work provides "a convincing explanation not only of personal antipathies but also the cruel prejudices and persecutions of our time." Jung saw his own destiny as that of an explorer, a man who creates new ways of conceptualizing age-old problems—psychological problems, as well as philosophical, spiritual, and religious ones. He said that he wanted to address those people who seek meaning in their lives, but for whom the traditional carriers of faith and religion no longer work. In the 1937 publication *Psychology and Religion,* Jung said, "Probably all that is left us today is the psychological approach. That is why I take these thought-forms that have become historically fixed, try to melt them down again and pour them into moulds of immediate experience."

Robert A. Johnson, a well-known author and lecturer whose writing is in the third generation of Jungian ideas, says that Jung's lasting contribution was the development of a magnificent vision of the human capacity for consciousness. "He posited a model of the unconscious so momentous that the Western world has still not fully caught up with its implications."

Perhaps Jung's greatest accomplishment was to reveal the unconscious to be the creative source of all that we eventually become as individuals. In fact, our conscious minds and personalities develop and mature *from* the raw material of the unconscious, in interactive play with life experiences.

Along with *self* (the psychological center of the human being) and *anima* and *animus* (the internalized ideal images of the opposite sex, the soul-image in each person), Jung classified the *shadow* as one of the major archetypes in the personal unconscious. Archetypes are innate, inherited structures in the unconscious—like psychological fingerprints—which contain preformed characteristics, personal qualities and traits shared with all other human beings. They are living psychic forces within the human psyche. According to the *Critical Dictionary of Jungian Analysis,* "Gods are metaphors of archetypal behaviors and myths are archetypal enactments." The course of Jungian analysis involves a growing awareness of this archetypal dimension of a person's life. ▢

To introduce and define the personal shadow in Part 1, we have chosen several outstanding examples from Jungian writers because it is in these formulations that the concept has become well known and useful as a tool for personal growth and therapeutic healing. The writers in this section address the essential issues that make it possible for us to perceive the shadow in everyday living. In later sections of this book, the concept is broadened from its personal to its collective manifestations in prejudice, war, and evil in essays chosen from a wide range of ideas.

In opening this section, poet Robert Bly uses a personal voice to narrate the story of the shadow in an excerpt from *A Little Book on the Human Shadow.* The disowned self, says Bly, becomes a holding buffer as we grow up—a "long bag we drag behind us"—that contains our unacceptable parts. Bly also links our personal *bags* to other kinds—our collective shadows.

Next, Jungian training analyst Edward C. Whitmont shows us the therapist's view of the shadow as it appears in patients' dreams and life experiences. This excerpt from *The Symbolic Quest* gives a sound definition to our theme.

"What the Shadow Knows," Chapter 3, is a 1989 conversation between San Diego–based analyst and Episcopal minister John A. Sanford and interviewer D. Patrick Miller, which originally appeared in the magazine *The Sun.* Throughout his career, Sanford has taken on the difficult questions of human evil. His psychological explication of the famous Robert Louis Stevenson story "Dr. Jekyll and Mr. Hyde" appears as Chapter 5 in this section.

"The Shadow in History and Literature" is an excerpt from *Archetypes: A Natural History of the Self* by British psychologist Anthony Stevens. Sandwiched between the two Sanford pieces, this article describes the shadow as it appears in works of the imagination.

Chapter 6, "The Realization of the Shadow in Dreams," is an essay by eminent psychoanalyst and dream scholar Marie-Louise von Franz, one of Jung's closest collaborators. It comes from *Man and His Symbols,* a popular book that Dr. von Franz helped to write and edit in concert with Jung and three other loyal disciples in the early 1960s. This source book was C. G. Jung's last living work, a compilations of ideas and images addressed to the broad reading public.

We end this section on a constructive note with therapist William A. Miller's piece, "Finding the Shadow in Daily Life," from his book *Your Golden Shadow.* Miller guides us into shadow phenomena by examining projections, slips of the tongue, and humor, and by showing how to discover the shadow in the ordinary events of life.

Jung once remarked, in a moment of exasperation about literal-minded pupils quoting his concepts out of context, that "the shadow is simply the whole unconscious!" Though he was not serious, his observation would be true only if a person were completely unaware of the unconscious in everyday life. Once we begin to develop awareness of parts of the unconscious personality, then the shadow takes on an identifiable personal form, which initiates the process of shadow-work. This procedure ultimately yields a profound awareness of who we are. According to analyst Erich Neumann: "The self lies hidden in the shadow; he is the keeper of the gate, the guardian of the threshold. The way to the self lies through him; behind the dark aspect that he represents there stands the aspect of wholeness, and only by making friends with the shadow do we gain the friendship of the self."

Wow

· · · · · · ·

1 · THE LONG BAG
WE DRAG BEHIND US

ROBERT BLY

It's an old Gnostic tradition that we don't invent things, we just remember. The Europeans I know of who remember the dark side best are Robert Louis Stevenson, Joseph Conrad, and Carl Jung. I'll call up a few of their ideas and add a few thoughts of my own.

Let's talk about the personal shadow first. When we were one or two years old we had what we might visualize as a 360-degree personality. Energy radiated out from all parts of our body and all parts of our psyche. A child running is a living globe of energy. We had a ball of energy, all right; but one day we noticed that our parents didn't like certain parts of that ball. They said things like: "Can't you be still?" Or "It isn't nice to try and kill your brother." Behind us we have an invisible bag, and the part of us our parents don't like, we, to keep our parents' love, put in the bag. By the time we go to school our bag is quite large. Then our teachers have their say: "Good children don't get angry over such little things." So we take our anger and put it in the bag. By the time my brother and I were twelve in Madison, Minnesota, we were known as "the nice Bly boys." Our bags were already a mile long.

Then we do a lot of bag-stuffing in high school. This time it's no longer the evil grownups that pressure us, but people our own age. So the student's paranoia about grownups can be misplaced. I lied all through high school automatically to try to be more like the basketball players. Any part of myself that was a little slow went into the bag. My sons are going through the process now; I watched my daughters, who were older, experience it. I noticed with dismay how much they put into the bag, but there was nothing their mother or I could do about it. Often my daughters seemed to make their decision on the issue of fashion and collective ideas of beauty, and they suffered as much damage from others girls as they did from men.

So I maintain that out of a round globe of energy the twenty-year-old ends up with a slice. We'll imagine a man who has a thin slice left—the rest is in the bag—and we'll imagine that he meets a woman; let's say they are both twenty-four. She has a thin, elegant slice left. They join each other in a ceremony, and this union of two slices is called marriage. Even together the two do not make up one person! Marriage when the bag is large entails loneliness during the honeymoon for that very reason. Of course we all lie about it. "How is your honeymoon?" "Wonderful, how's yours?"

Different cultures fill the bag with different contents. In Christian culture sexuality usually goes into the bag. With it goes much spontaneity. Marie-Louise von Franz warns us, on the other hand, not to sentimentalize primitive cultures by assuming that they have no bag at all. She says in effect that they have a different but sometimes even larger bag. They may put individuality into the bag, or inventiveness. What anthropologists know as "participation mystique," or "a mysterious communal mind," sounds lovely, but it can mean that tribal members all know exactly the same thing and no one knows anything else. It's possible that bags for all human beings are about the same size.

We spend our life until we're twenty deciding what parts of ourself to put into the bag, and we spend the rest of our lives trying to get them out again. Sometimes retrieving them feels impossible, as if the bag were sealed. Suppose the bag remains sealed—what happens then? A great nineteenth-century story has an idea about that. One night Robert Louis Stevenson woke up and told his wife a bit of a dream he'd just had. She urged him to write it down; he did, and it became "Dr. Jekyll and Mr. Hyde." The nice side of the personality becomes, in our idealistic culture, nicer and nicer. The Western man may be a liberal doctor, for example, always thinking about the good of others. Morally and ethically he is wonderful. But the substance in the bag takes on a personality of its own; it can't be ignored. The story says that the substance locked in the bag appears one day *somewhere else* in the city. The substance in the bag feels angry, and when you see it, it is shaped like an ape, and moves like an ape.

The story says then that when we put a part of ourselves in the bag it regresses. It de-evolves toward barbarism. Suppose a young man seals a bag at twenty and then waits fifteen or twenty years before he opens it again. What will he find? Sadly, the sexuality, the wildness, the impulsiveness, the anger, the freedom he put in have all regressed; they are not only primitive in mood, they are hostile to the person who opens the bag. The man who opens his bag at forty-five or the woman who opens her bag rightly feels fear. She glances up and sees the shadow of an ape passing along the alley wall; anyone seeing that would be frightened.

I think we could say that most males in our culture put their feminine side or interior woman into the bag. When they begin, perhaps around thirty-five or forty, trying to get in touch with their feminine side again, she may be by then truly hostile to them. The same man may experience in the meantime much hostility from women in the outer world. The rule seems to be: the outside has to be like the inside. That's the way it is on this globe. If a woman, wanting to be approved for her femininity, has put her masculine side or her internal male into the bag, she may find that twenty years later he will be hostile to her. Moreover he may be unfeeling and brutal in his criticism. She's in a spot. Finding a hostile man to live with would give her someone to blame, and take away the pressure, but that wouldn't help the problem of the closed bag. In the meantime, she is liable to sense a double rejection, from the male inside and the male outside. There's a lot of grief in this whole thing.

Every part of our personality that we do not love will become hostile to us. We could add that it may move to a distant place and begin a revolt against us as well. A lot of the trouble Shakespeare's kings experience blossoms in that sentence. Hotspur "in Wales" rebels against the King. Shakespeare's poetry is marvelously sensitive to the danger of these inner revolts. Always the king at the center is endangered.

When I visited Bali a few years ago, it became clear that their ancient Hindu culture works through mythology to bring shadow elements up into daily view. The temples put on plays virtually every day from the *Ramayana*. I saw some terrifying plays performed as a part of religious life, in a day by day way. Almost every Balinese house has standing outside it a fierce, toothy, aggressive, hostile figure carved in stone. This being doesn't plan to do good. I visited a mask maker, and noticed his nine- or ten-year-old son sitting outside the house, making with his chisel a hostile, angry figure. The person does not aim to act out the aggressive energies as we do in football or the Spanish in bull-fighting, but each person aims to bring them upward into art: that is the ideal. The Balinese can be violent and brutal in war, but in daily life they seem much less violent than we are. What can this mean? Southerners in the United States put figures of helpful little black men on the lawn, cast in iron, and we in the North do the same with serene deer. We ask for roses in the wallpaper. Renoir above the sofa, and John Denver on the stereo. Then the aggression escapes from the bag and attacks everyone.

We'll have to let this contrast between Balinese and American cultures lie there and go on. I want to talk about the connection between shadow energies and the moving picture projector. Let's suppose that we have miniaturized certain parts of ourselves, flattened them out, and put them inside a can, where it will be dark. Then one night—always at night—the shapes reappear, huge, and we can't take our eyes away from them. We drive at night in the country and see a man and woman on an enormous outdoor movie screen; we shut off the car and watch. Certain figures who have been rolled up inside a can, doubly invisible by being partially "developed" and by being kept always in the dark, exist during the day only as pale images on a thin gray strip of film. When a certain light is ignited in the back of our heads, ghostly pictures appear on a wall in front of us. They light cigarettes; they threaten others with guns. Our psyches then are natural projection machines; images that we stored in a can we can bring out while still rolled up, and run them for others, or on others. A man's anger, rolled up inside the can for twenty years, he may see one night on his wife's face. A wife might see a hero every night on her husband's face and then one night see a tyrant. Nora in *A Doll's House* saw the two images in turn.

The other day I found some of my old diaries, and I picked out one at random, from 1956. I had been struggling that year to write a poem describing the nature of advertising men. I remember that, and I recall that at that time the story of Midas was important in my mood. Everything that Midas touched turned to gold. I declared in my poem that every living thing an advertising man touches turns into some form of money, and that's why ad men have such starved souls. I kept in mind the ad men I'd known and was having a good time attacking them from my concealed position. As I read the old passages I felt a shock seeing the movie I was running. Between the time I wrote them and now I'd discovered that I had known for years how to eat in such a way as to keep me from taking in any kind of nourishment. Whatever food a friend offered me, or a woman, or a child, turned into metal on the way to my mouth. Is the image clear? No one can eat or drink metal. So Midas was a good image for me. But the film showing my interior Midas was rolled up in the can. Advertising men, evil and foolish, tended to appear at night on a large screen, and I was naturally fascinated. A year or two later I composed a book called *Poems for the Ascension of J. P. Morgan,* in which each poem I had written about business alternated with a culpable advertisement reproduced from magazines or newspapers. It is a lively book in its way. No one would publish it, but that was all right. It was mostly projection anyway. I'm going to read you a poem I wrote around that time. It's called "Unrest."

A strange unrest hovers over the nation:
This is the last dance, the wild tossing of Morgan's seas,
The division of spoils. A lassitude
Enters into the diamonds of the body.
In high school the explosion begins, the child is partly killed;
When the fight is over, and the land and the sea ruined,
Two shapes inside us rise, and move away.

But the baboon whistles on the shores of death—
Climbing and falling, tossing nuts and stones,
He gambols by the tree
Whose branches hold the expanses of cold,
The planets whirling and the black sun,
The cries of insects, and the tiny slaves
In the prisons of bark.
Charlemagne, we are approaching your islands!

We are returning now to the snowy trees,
And the depth of the darkness buried in snow, through
   which you rode all night

With stiff hands; now the darkness is falling
In which we sleep and awake—a darkness in which
Thieves shudder, and the insane have a hunger for snow,
In which bankers dream of being buried by black stones,
And businessmen fall on their knees in the dungeons of sleep.

About five years ago I began to be suspicious of this poem. Why are bankers and businessmen being singled out? If I had to rephrase "banker" what would I say? "Someone who plans very well." I plan very well. How would I rephrase "businessman?" "Someone with a stiff face." I looked in the mirror then. I'll read you the way the passage goes now, after I've rewritten it:

. . . a darkness in which
Thieves shudder, and the insane have a hunger for snow,
In which good planners dream of being buried by black stones,
And men with stiff faces like me fall on their knees in the
*   dungeons of sleep.*

Now when I go to a party I feel different from the way that I used to when I meet a businessman. I say to a man, "What do you do?" He says, "I'm a stockbroker." And he says it in a faintly apologetic way. I say to myself, "Look at this: something of me that was deep inside me is standing right next to me." I have a funny longing to hug him. Not all of them, of course.

But projection is a wonderful thing too. Marie-Louise von Franz remarked somewhere, "Why do we always assume projection is bad? 'You are projecting' becomes among Jungians an accusation. Sometimes projection is helpful and the right thing." Her remark is very wise. I know that I was starving myself to death, but the knowledge couldn't move directly from the bag to the conscious mind. It has to go out onto the world first. "How wicked advertising men are," I said to myself. Marie-Louise von Franz reminds us that if we didn't project, we might never connect with the world at all. Women sometimes complain that a man often takes his ideal feminine side and projects it onto a woman. But if he didn't, how could he get out of his mother's house or his bachelor room? The issue is not so much that we do project but how long we keep the projections out there. Projection without personal contact is dangerous. Thousands, even millions of American men projected their internal feminine onto Marilyn Monroe. If a million men do that, and leave it there, it's likely she will die. She died. Projections without personal contact can damage the person receiving them.

We have to also say that Marilyn Monroe called for these projections as a part of her power longing, and her disturbance must have gone back to victimization in childhood. But the process of projection and recall, done so delicately in tribal culture, face to face, goes out of whack when the mass media arrives. In the economy of the psyche her death was inevitable and even right. No single human being can carry so many projections—that is, so much unconsciousness—and survive. So it's infinitely important that each person bring back his or her own.

But why would we give away, or put into the bag, so much of ourselves? Why would we do it so young? And if we have put away so many of our angers, spontaneities, hungers, enthusiasms, our rowdy and unattractive parts, then how can we live? What holds us together? Alice Miller spoke to this point in her book *Prisoners of Childhood,* which in paperback form is called *The Drama of the Gifted Child.*

The drama is this. We came as infants "trailing clouds of glory," arriving from the farthest reaches of the universe, bringing with us appetites well preserved from our mammal inheritance, spontaneities wonderfully preserved from our 150,000 years of tree life, angers well preserved from our 5,000 years of tribal life—in short, with our 360-degree radiance—and we offered this gift to our parents. They didn't want it. They wanted a nice girl or a nice boy. That's the first act of the drama. It doesn't mean our parents were wicked; they needed us for something. My mother, as a second generation immigrant, needed my brother and me to help the family look more classy. We do the same thing to our children; it's a part of life on this planet. Our parents rejected who we were before we could talk, so the pain of rejection is probably stored in some pre-verbal place. ✓

When I read her book I fell into depression for three weeks. With so much gone, what can we do? We can construct a personality more acceptable to our parents. Alice Miller agrees that we have betrayed ourselves, but she says, "Don't blame yourself for that. There's nothing else you could have done." Children in ancient times who opposed their parents probably were set out to die. We did, as children, the only sensible thing under the circumstances. The proper attitude toward that, she says, is mourning. ✓

Let's talk now about the different sorts of bags. When we have put a lot in our private bag, we often have as a result little energy. The bigger the bag, the less the energy. Some people have by nature more energy than others, but we all have more than we can possibly use. Where did it go? If we put our sexuality into the bag as a child, obviously we lose a lot of energy. When a woman puts her masculinity into the bag, or rolls it up and puts it into the can, she loses energy with it. So we can think of our personal bag as containing energy now unavailable to us. If we identify ourselves as uncreative, it means we took our creativity and put it into the bag. What do you mean, "I am not creative"? "Let experts do it"—isn't that what such a person is saying? That's damn well what such people are saying. The audience wants a poet, a hired gun, to come in from out of town. Everybody in this audience should be writing their own poems.

We have talked of our personal bag, but each town or community also seems to have a bag. I lived for years near a small Minnesota farm town. Everyone in the town was expected to have the same objects in the bag; a small Greek town clearly would have different objects in the bag. It's as if the town, by collective psychic decision, puts certain energies in the bag, and tries to prevent anyone from getting them out. Towns interfere with our private process in this matter, so it's more dangerous to live in them than in nature. On the other hand, certain ferocious hatreds that one feels in a small town help one sometimes to see where the projections have gone. And the Jungian community, like the town, has its bag, and usually recommends that Jungians keep their vulgarity and love of money in the bag; and the Freudian community usually demands that Freudians keep their religious life in the bag.

There is also a national bag, and ours is quite long. Russia and China have noticeable faults, but if an American citizen is curious to know what is in our national bag at the moment, he can listen closely when a State Department official criticizes Russia. As Reagan says, we are noble; other nations have empires. Other nations endure stagnated leadership, treat miniorities brutally, brainwash their youth, and break treaties. A Russian can find out about his bag by reading a *Pravda* article on the United States. We're dealing with a network of shadows, a pattern of shadows projected by both sides, all meeting somewhere out in the air. I'm not saying anything new with this metaphor, but I do want to make the distinction clear between the personal shadow, the town shadow, and the national shadow.

I have used three metaphors here: the bag, the film can, and projection. Since the can or bag is closed and its images remain in the dark, we can only see the contents of our own bag by throwing them innocently, as we say, out into the world. Spiders then become evil, snakes cunning, goats oversexed; men become linear, women become weak, the Russians become unprincipled, and Chinese all look alike. Yet it is precisely through this expensive, damaging, wasteful, inaccurate form of mud-slinging that we eventually come in touch with the mud that the crow found on the bottom of its feet.

· · · · · · ·

2 · THE EVOLUTION OF THE SHADOW

EDWARD C. WHITMONT

The term *shadow* refers to that part of the personality which has been repressed for the sake of the ego ideal. Since everything unconscious is projected, we encounter the shadow in projection—in our view of "the other fellow." As a figure in dreams or fantasies the shadow represents the personal unconscious. It is like a composite of the personal shells of our complexes and is thus the doorway to all deeper transpersonal experiences.

Practically speaking, the shadow more often than not appears as an inferior personality. However, there can also be a positive shadow, which appears when we tend to identify with our negative qualities and repress the positive ones.

The following example of the shadow is a classical one from a familiar situation. A middle-aged patient complains repeatedly and bitterly about her mother-in-law. Her description seems by and large to be correct and adequate, for her husband, independently of his wife, has provided a description which is practically identical. Mother is seen by both as utterly domineering, never able to admit another person's viewpoint, in the habit of asking for advice and at once deprecating it, always feeling at a disadvantage, abused, martyred and, as a result of all this, almost impossible to reach. Our analysand, the daughter-in-law, feels that her mother-in-law stands between her and her husband; the son must constantly serve his mother, and the wife consequently feels eclipsed. Her marital situation seems to be in a hopeless impasse. She has the following dream:

> I am in a dark hallway. I attempt to reach my husband, but my way is barred by my mother-in-law. What is most frightening, however, is that my mother-in-law cannot see me, even though a spotlight shines brightly upon me. It is as if I did not exist at all as far as she is concerned.

Let us remember again that a dream always points to an unconscious situation. It is complementary and reveals that which is not sufficiently within the field of our awareness. A dream will not restate a situation which the dreamer already sees adequately and correctly. Where there is doubt in the conscious mind a dream may help to resolve that doubt by reiteration, but whenever a dream repeats something of which we feel utterly convinced, a challenge is thereby raised by the unconscious; our projections are held up to us. On the surface this dream seems to confirm the daughter-in-law's conscious complaint. But what does it say when we look for an unconscious projection? It tells the dreamer one thing quite clearly: The spotlight is upon *you* and not on your mother-in-law. It shows her the unconscious qualities which she projects upon her mother-in-law and which stand between her husband and herself. The mother-in-law in *her* prevents her from reaching her husband. It is *her own* necessity always to be right, *her* tendency to create obstacles and deprecate everything, and *her* tendency to be the great martyr, which stand in her way. The spotlight is upon her but the mother-in-law does not see her; she is so gripped by and identical with the qualities ascribed to the mother-in-law that she is unable to see herself as she is, to see her own real individuality. As a result her own individuality is as good as nonexistent, and since she cannot see herself truly she also cannot in real life see her mother-in-law as a human being and therefore cannot deal adequately with the obstructionist tactics which she indeed does use. This is a perfect vicious circle which inevitably occurs whenever we are caught in a shadow projection (or in an animus or anima projection). A projection invariably blurs our own view of the other person. Even when the projected qualities happen to be real qualities of the other person—as in this case—the affect reaction which marks the projection points to the affect-toned complex in *us* which blurs our vision and interferes with our capacity to see objectively and relate humanly.

Imagine an automobile driver who, unknowingly, wears spectacles of red glass. He would find it difficult to tell the difference between red, yellow or green traffic lights and he would be in constant danger of an accident. It is of no help to him that some or for that matter even most of the lights he perceives as red really happen to be red. The danger to him comes from the inability to differentiate and separate what his "red projection" imposes on him. Where a shadow projection occurs we are not able to differentiate between the actuality of the other person and our own complexes. We cannot tell fact from fancy. We cannot see where we begin and he ends. We cannot see him; neither can we see ourselves.

Ask someone to give a description of the personality type which he finds most despicable, most unbearable and hateful, and most impossible to get along with, and he will produce a description of his own repressed characteristics—a self-description which is utterly unconscious and which therefore always and everywhere tortures him as he receives its effect from the *other* person. These very qualities are so unacceptable to him precisely because they represent his own repressed side; only that which we cannot accept within ourselves do we find impossible to live with in others. Negative qualities which do not bother us so excessively, which we find relatively easy to forgive—if we have to forgive them at all—are not likely to pertain to our shadow.

The shadow is the archetypal experience of the "other fellow," who in his strangeness is always suspect. It is the archetypal urge for a scapegoat, for someone to blame and attack in order to vindicate oneself and be justified; it is the archetypal experience of *the enemy*, the experience of blameworthiness which always adheres to the other fellow, since we are under the illusion of knowing ourselves and of having already dealt adequately with our own problems. In other words, to the extent that I have to be right and good, *he, she,* or *they* become the carriers of all the evil which I fail to acknowledge within myself.

The reasons for this lie within the very nature of the ego itself; the development of the ego takes place as a result of the encounter between the Self—as a potential personality trend—and external reality, that is, between inner potential individuality and outer collectivity. On the first level of experience between right and wrong, which is the basis for self-acceptance, the beginnings of conscience are vested in and projected onto the outer collectivity. The child accepts himself in terms of fitting in. Harmony with the Self and thus with conscience appears at first to be dependent upon external acceptance—that is, upon collective and persona values, and those elements of the individuality which are too much at variance with accepted persona values cannot, seemingly, be consciously incorporated into the image which the ego has of itself. They therefore become subject to repression. They do not disappear however; they continue to function as an unseen alter ego which seems to be outside oneself—in other words, as the shadow. Ego development rests upon repressing the "wrong" or "evil" and furthering the "good." The ego cannot become strong unless we first learn collective taboos, accept superego and persona values and identify with collective moral standards.

It is most important to note that those qualities which at this point are repressed as incommensurable with persona ideals and general cultural values may be quite basic to our fundamental personality structures, but owing to the fact of their repression they will remain primitive and therefore negative. Unfortunately repression does not eliminate the qualities or drives or keep them from functioning. It merely removes them from ego awareness; they continue as complexes. By being removed from view they are also removed from supervision and can thereby continue their existence unchecked and in a disruptive way. The shadow, then, consists of complexes, of personal qualities resting on drives and behavior patterns which are a definite "dark" part of the personality structure. In most instances they are readily observable by others. Only we ourselves cannot see them. The shadow qualities are usually in glaring contrast to the ego's ideals and wishful efforts. The sensitive altruist may have a brutal egotist somewhere in himself; the shadow of the courageous fighter may be a whining coward; the everloving sweetheart may harbor a bitter shrew.

The existence of or necessity for a shadow is a general human archetypal fact, since the process of ego formation—the clash between collectivity and individuality—is a general human pattern. The shadow is projected in two forms: individually, in the shape of the people to whom we ascribe all the evil; and collectively, in its most general form, as the Enemy, the personification of evil. Its mythological representations are the devil, archenemy, tempter, fiend or double; or the dark or evil one of a pair of brothers or sisters.

The shadow is a constituent of ego development. It is a product of the split which comes about through establishing a center of awareness. It is that which we have measured and found wanting. It approximately coincides with what has been regarded as *the* unconscious, first by Freud and now rather generally, namely elements repressed from consciousness. In unconscious spontaneous representations the shadow is usually personified by a figure of the same sex as the dreamer.

Recognition of the shadow can bring about very marked effects on the conscious personality. The very notion that the other person's evil could be pointing at oneself carries shock effects of varying degrees, depending upon the strength of one's ethical and moral convictions. It takes nerve not to flinch from or be crushed by the sight of one's shadow, and it takes courage to accept responsibility for one's inferior self. When this shock seems almost too much to bear, the unconscious usually exerts its compensatory function and comes to our aid with a constructive view of the situation, as in the following dream:

> Somebody wanted to kill me with an apple. Then I saw that a neighbor of mine, whom I do not regard very highly, had managed to turn a rocky, arid plot of land, which I considered quite useless, into a beautiful garden.

This dream presents the shadow problem in two ways: first in archetypal terms and then in individual terms. To the apple the patient associated the notorious apple of the first chapter of Genesis—the devil's present. The unknown person treating him with the devil's or snake's gift constellates an archetypal form of the shadow, the general human fact that *everybody* has to deal with a shadow problem. The actual neighbor whom he looked down upon represents the personal shadow. The dream says in effect: You are afraid that the shadow—that in you which offers the apple, the discrimination between good and evil, hence the awareness of the temptation of the evil in you—will kill you. And indeed by eating the apple man came to know death (Genesis 3:19); but the apple also signifies the implication: "Ye shall be as gods, knowing good and evil" (Genesis 3:5). The dream therefore points to the fact that this personal problem which is so shocking to him is a general, fundamental, human—hence archetypal—problem. The confrontation of one's own evil can be a mortifying deathlike experience; but like death it points beyond the personal meaning of existence. It is important for the dreamer to realize this.

The second part of the dream says: It is your own shadow side—that in you which you find unacceptable, namely those qualities which you associate with the neighbor you despise—which takes an arid, unsatisfactory area and turns it into a paradise. The shadow, when it is realized, is the source of renewal; the new and productive impulse cannot come from established values of the ego. When there is an impasse, and sterile time in our lives—despite an adequate ego development—we must look to the dark, hitherto unacceptable side which has been at our conscious disposal. Goethe in his *Faust* has the devil say of himself when asked, "Who are you then?" that he is:

> *Part of that Power which would*
> *the Evil ever do, and ever does the Good.*

(The reverse of this statement is also true, that often enough the more we will the good, the more we create the evil—by overlooking our selfish intents or disregarding the evil, for instance, when we become professional do-gooders.)

This brings us to the fundamental fact that the shadow is the door to our individuality. In so far as the shadow renders us our first view of the unconscious part of our personality, it represents the first stage toward meeting the Self. There is, in fact, no access to the unconscious and to our own reality *but* through the shadow. Only when we realize that part of ourselves which we have not hitherto seen or preferred not to see can we proceed to question and find the sources from which it feeds and the basis on which it rests. Hence no progress or growth is possible until the shadow is adequately confronted—and confronting means more than merely knowing about it. It is not until we have truly been shocked into seeing ourselves as we really are, instead of as we wish or hopefully assume we are, that we can take the first step toward individual reality.

When one is unable to integrate one's positive potential and devalues oneself excessively, or if one is identical—for lack of moral stamina for instance—with one's negative side, then the positive potential becomes the characteristic of the shadow. In such a case the shadow is a positive shadow; it is then actually the lighter of the "two brothers." In such a case the dreams will also try to bring into consciousness that which has been unduly disregarded: the positive qualities. This, however, occurs less frequently than the too-hopeful, too-bright picture of oneself. We have this bright picture because we attempt to *will* ourselves into collectively acceptable patterns.

There are several kinds of possible reactions to the shadow. We can refuse to face it; or, once aware that it is part of us, we can try to eliminate it and set it straight immediately; we can refuse to accept responsibility for it and let it have its way; or we can "suffer" it in a constructive manner, as a part of our personality which can lead us to a salutary humility and humanness and eventually to new insights and expanded life horizons.

When we refuse to face the shadow or try to fight it with willpower alone, saying, "Get thee beind me, Satan," we merely relegate this energy to the unconscious, and from there it exerts its power in a negative, compulsive, projected form. Then our projections will transform our surrounding world into a setting which shows us our own faces, though we do not recognize them as our own. We become increasingly isolated; instead of a real relation to the surrounding world there is only an illusory one, for we relate not to the world as it is but to the "evil, wicked world" which our shadow projection shows us. The result is an inflated, autoerotic state of being, cut off from reality, which usually takes the well-known form of "If only so and so were such and such," or "When this will have happened," or "If I were properly understood" or "appreciated."

Such an impasse is seen by us, because of our projections, as the ill will of the environment, and thus a vicious circle is established, continuing *ad infinitum, ad nauseam*. These projections eventually so shape our own attitudes toward others that at last we literally bring about that which we project. We imagine ourselves so long pursued by ill will that ill will is eventually produced by others in response to our vitriolic defensiveness. Our fellow men see this as unprovoked hostility; this arouses their defensiveness and their shadow projections upon us, to which we in turn react with our defensiveness, thereby causing more ill will.

In order to protect its own control and sovereignty the ego instinctively puts up a great resistance to the confrontation with the shadow; when it catches a glimpse of the shadow the ego most often reacts with an attempt to eliminate it. Our will is mobilized and we decide, "I just won't be that way any more!" Then comes the final shattering shock, when we discover that, in part at least, this is impossible no matter how we try. For the shadow represents energically charged autonomous patterns of feeling and behavior. Their energy cannot simply be stopped by an act of will. What is needed is rechanneling or transformation. However, this task requires both an awareness and an acceptance of the shadow as something which cannot simply be gotten rid of.

Somehow, almost everyone has the feeling that a quality once acknowledged will of necessity have to be acted out, for the one state which we find more painful than facing the shadow is that of resisting our own feeling urges, of bearing the pressure of a drive, suffering the frustration or pain of not satisfying an urge. Hence in order to avoid having to resist our own feeling urges when we recognize them, we prefer not to see them at all, to convince ourselves that they are not there. Repression appears less painful than discipline. But unfortunately it is also more dangerous, for it makes us act without consciousness of our motives, hence irresponsibly. Even though we are not responsible for the way we *are* and feel, we have to take responsibility for the way we *act*. Therefore we have to learn to discipline ourselves. And discipline rests on the ability to act in a manner that is contrary to our feelings when necessary. This is an eminently human prerogative as well as a necessity.

Repression, on the other hand, simply looks the other way. When persisted in, repression always leads to psychopathology, but it is also indispensable to the first ego formation. This means that we all carry the germs of psychopathology within us. In this sense potential psychopathology is an integral part of our human structure.

The shadow has to have its place of legitimate expression somehow, sometime, somewhere. By confronting it we have a choice of when, how and where we may allow expression to its tendencies in a constructive context. And when it is not possible to restrain the expression of its negative side we may cushion its effect by a conscious effort to add a mitigating element or at least an apology. Where we cannot or must not refrain from hurting we may at least try to do it kindly and be ready to bear the consequences. When we virtuously look the other way we have no such possibility; then the shadow, left to its own devices, is likely to run away with us in a destructive or dangerous manner. Then it just "happens" to us, and usually when it is most awkward; since we do not know what is happening we can do nothing to mitigate its effect and we blame it all on the other fellow.

There are also of course social and collective implications of the shadow problem. They are staggering, for here lie the roots of social, racial, and national bias and discrimination. Every minority and every dissenting group carries the shadow projection of the majority, be it Negro, white, Gentile, Jew, Italian, Irish, Chinese or French. Moreover, since the shadow is the archetype of the enemy, its projection is likely to involve us in the bloodiest of wars precisely in times of the greatest complacency about peace and our own righteousness. The enemy and the conflict with the enemy are archetypal factors, projections of our own inner split, and cannot be legislated or wished away. They can be dealt with—if at all—only in terms of shadow confrontation and in the healing of our individual split. The most dangerous times, both collectively and individually, are those in which we assume that we have eliminated it.

The shadow cannot be eliminated. It is the ever-present dark brother or sister. Whenever we fail to see where it stands, there is likely to be trouble afoot. For then it is certain to be standing behind us. The adequate question therefore never is: Have I a shadow problem? Have I a negative side? But rather: Where does it happen to be right now? When we cannot see it, it is time to beware! And it is helpful to remember Jung's formulation that a complex is not pathological *per se*. It becomes pathological only when we assume that we do not have it; because then it has us.

· · · · · · ·

3 · WHAT THE SHADOW KNOWS: AN INTERVIEW WITH JOHN A. SANFORD

D. PATRICK MILLER

THE SUN:
Jung once said, "I would rather be whole than good," a statement that would probably mystify or disturb many people. Why do most people fail to recognize the relationship between evil and excessive "goodness"?

SANFORD:
This is really the problem of the ego and the shadow, a problem that's most sharply discernible in the Christian tradition. In the Bible the differences between good and evil are sharply drawn: there's God, who is good, and the Devil, who is evil. God desires human beings to be good, and evil is punished. The New Testament point of view is that if an individual gives in to evil and does evil things, then the soul is corrupted and destroyed; that is, a negative psychological process sets in. So there's always held up to the Christian the goal or model of "being a good person," and there's something to be said for that.

But originally the Christian tradition recognized that one carries the opposite within oneself. St. Paul said, "For the good that I would, I do not; but the evil which I would not, that I do." That's the statement of a depth psychologist; he knew he had the shadow, and he thought only God could save him from such a condition. But *knowing* what his condition was sort of held things together.

Later, that in-depth perspective was lost and people simply felt compelled to identify with good, or at least the pretense of being good. Doing that, you will quickly lose contact with the shadow. Also, somewhere along the line—it became obvious by the Middle Ages—the church made a very bad mistake. Now not only were some actions evil, but *fantasies* were evil, too. You were a bad person simply by having fantasies about evil; adultery was a sin, and thinking about adultery was a sin, too. Both had to be confessed and forgiven.

As a result, people began to deny and repress their fantasy life, and the shadow was driven even further underground. The split became greater.

THE SUN:
Did this process parallel the loss of the feminine element?

SANFORD:
Yes, I would say so. In feminine reality, contrasts are not so sharply seen and drawn. The masculine element sees things in bright sunlight; this is this and that is that. The feminine is like seeing in the moonlight; things kind of blend together, and they're not so distinct from one another. The whole matter of the shadow is very subtle and complex; it's not nearly as simple as the subject of good-and-evil may appear to be.

So the feminine element would have mitigated this complete split of the shadow and the ego. Early on, the church was the leader in a sort of feminist movement, but it later became quite patriarchal. The ego and the shadow became progressively farther apart, setting the stage for the Jekyll-and-Hyde phenomenon. If you study Christian history, you see the development quite clearly. Those people who professed to be doing very good things were leading the Inquisition, for instance.

Christians have no exclusive ownership of the shadow, of course. Everybody does horrible things. But the split is drawn quite starkly in the Christian tradition. The good thing that came out of all this was the return of depth psychology. Even though the church attempted to ban fantasies, it was obviously aware of the interior life and has always valued introspection.

THE SUN:
I grew up around religious fundamentalists, and I always noticed a kind of uptightness about them—as if they were literally trying not to have certain things enter their minds, much less be expressed openly. The internal split seems to require a great amount of energy to maintain.

SANFORD:
That's right, and it doesn't result in a really good person. Striving for a pure goodness results in a pose or a self-deception about goodness. It develops a persona—a face of goodness put on over the ego. Dr. Jekyll had a very big persona, and he believed in it completely, but he was never really a very good man. The connection between Jekyll and Hyde was Jekyll's secret yearning to *be* Hyde—but he never wanted to give up the face he had put on to society, and to himself. When he came up with the drug that changed him into his shadow, he thought he had the ideal answer. But then his own yearning to be Hyde took him over.

Here it's important to understand the crucial difference between the shadow and what's genuinely evil. As Fritz Kunkel once said, the secret is that *the ego is the devil*—not the shadow. He believed there is evil beyond the ego— an archetypal evil—but for most people, it's the ego that's really the problem.

The Jungian definition of the shadow was put well by Edward C. Whitmont, a New York analyst, who said that the shadow is "everything that has been rejected during the development of the personality because it did not fit into the *ego ideal.*" If you were raised a Christian with the ego ideal of being loving, morally upright, kind, and generous, then you'd have to repress any qualities you found in yourself that were antithetical to the ideal: anger, selfishness, crazy sexual fantasies, and so on. All these qualities that you split off would become the secondary personality called the shadow. And if that secondary personality became sufficiently isolated, you would become what's known as a multiple personality.

In every multiple personality case, you can always clearly identify the shadow. It's not always evil—it's just different than the ego. Jung said the truth of the matter is that the shadow is ninety percent pure gold. Whatever has been repressed holds a tremendous amount of energy, with a great positive potential. So the shadow, no matter how troublesome it may be, is not intrinsically evil. The ego, in its refusal of insight and its refusal to accept the entire personality, contributes much more to evil that the shadow.

THE SUN:
So the shadow gets a bad rap because the ego projects its own evil onto it.

SANFORD:
Exactly. If you go back to that psychological document we call the New Testament, you'll find that it says the devil is "the father of lies." Now the shadow never lies; it's the ego that lies about its real motives. That's why successful psychotherapy, and any genuine religious conversion, requires absolute honesty about oneself.

THE SUN:
The Jungian analyst Marie-Louise von Franz wrote: "The shadow plunges man into the immediacy of situations here and now, and thus creates the real biography of the human being, who is always inclined to assume he is only what he thinks he is. It is the biography created by the shadow that counts." This passage made me think about our society's tendency to become disillusioned with our politicians—because the biography they hand us while they're campaigning is never the biography that counts.

SANFORD:
The biography that the politician wants us to have—which has often been created by public relations people—is the persona, the mask. It's what hides the politician's true reality. But I think we can live with that reality pretty well, if we're allowed to. Owning up to the shadow is not nearly as damaging in the long run as denying it. What ruined Gary Hart, for instance, was not that he had affairs, but that he continued to lie about it when the truth was evident. Personally, that made me feel he simply wasn't too bright.

We certainly live in an era when elections are won and lost on the strength of the persona. Reagan is the example *par excellence,* because we know he never took a step or said a word that wasn't staged. I'm much more comfortable with President Bush, whether or not I approve of what he says, because I get the feeling that at least he's there—the real man is talking.

I think we were probably a little better in touch with politicians as real people in the days of whistlestop campaigning. The way that electronic media enhances the persona shows a monstrous side of our technology—it's very dangerous.

THE SUN:

The shadow certainly seems very present in our entertainment media these days—from Stephen King and Clive Barker stories, to horror films, to the overt satanism of some heavy-metal rock bands. I wonder if all this means we're moving toward recognition of the shadow—and integration—or are we just going down the tubes, as some social critics and censors seem to think?

SANFORD:

The question is when we cross the line from the shadow, which is a difficult but still human element, into the truly demonic. This brings up the matter of *archetypal* evil—is there a devil who's beyond the human ego? The Christians were not the only ones who worried about the devil, by the way—the early Persians thought about a divine agency that produced evil.

The holocaust of Nazi Germany and the pogroms of Stalin were not results of the individual human shadow. There, I think we're looking at an agency of evil in the collective psyche that is truly sinister, and that we do need to fear. A lot of people would deny that such evil exists, saying that all murderers are made by unfortunate childhoods and parental abuse. But my own feeling is that there is an archetypal agency of evil.

Some of those who would censor rock lyrics and so on may be partially right about the evil therein. I'll be frank in saying that when I occasionally come across such material I have a feeling of acute distaste. Some of it looks sinister to me. By no means should we assume that those who moralize about archetypal evil are free of it. In fact, moralizing about evil is a good way to succumb to it. It's a subtle matter. If you're attacking evil as a defense against insight into the self, you're making Dr. Jekyll's mistake.

THE SUN:

But how do we tell the difference between what looks sinister, and what *is* sinister?

SANFORD:

The question is well put, and not always readily answered. It depends a lot on the psychology of the person looking. The more rigid your psychological framework, the more things are going to look sinister to you. I can only say that when the archetypal level of evil is finally expressed, everyone is eventually shocked by it. But not always in time, of course. The world was very slow to recognize the evil of Nazi Germany.

What helps us tell the difference is what Jung called the feeling function—our inner means of ascertaining the value of something. The feeling function tells us what is desirable and not desirable, but it's not an ego judgment. The ego determines what's good and bad from the point of view of its own concerns: that which tends to support our egocentric defense system is what we deem to be good; that which is antithetical to it, we deem to be evil. When the Puritans infected the Native Americans with diseases that killed them, the Puritans saw it as a good thing, and preached sermons about how God was paving the way for them to settle the land. Of course, the Indians who were dying of smallpox would have had a very different judgment of the good and evil in the situation.

The feeling function is free of egocentric contamination. It is a pure feeling evaluation, but it's not always heard. The fact that the American public eventually turned against the Vietnam War was due to the rise of the feeling function—an increasing number of people came to a *feeling* judgment that the war was wrong and terrible, even if it supposedly served our political aims. And of course they were right. The value judgment of the feeling function is a reliable determiner of the good and evil in a situation—provided that it has the right information. If it doesn't have all the information, or sees only a part of the whole situation, the feeling function is perfectly capable of arriving at an erroneous conclusion.

THE SUN:
In your practice, what have you observed to be the process of integrating the shadow?

SANFORD:
When one first sees the shadow clearly, one is more or less aghast. Some of our egocentric defense systems then necessarily fall apart or melt away. The result can be a temporary depression, or clouding of consciousness. Jung compared the process of integration—which he called *individuation*—to the process of alchemy. One stage of alchemy is the *melanosis,* where everything turns black inside the vessel containing all the alchemical elements. But that black stage is absolutely essential. Jung said it represents the first contact with the unconscious, which is always the contact with the shadow. The ego takes that as a kind of defeat.

THE SUN:
Is it possible to get stuck there? Can we be doomed to one encounter with the shadow after another, with no integration following?

SANFORD:
I don't think so, because a genuine insight into the shadow also calls out what

Jung called the Self, the creative center. And then things begin to move, so the depression doesn't become permanent. A million and one changes can occur after that; it's different for every individual. What Kunkel called the "real center" of the personality begins to emerge, and gradually the ego is reoriented to a closer relationship with that real center. Then a person is much less likely to become affiliated with genuine evil, because the integration of the shadow is always concurrent with the dissolution of the false persona. One becomes much more realistic about oneself; seeing the truth about one's own nature always has very salutary effects. Honesty is the great defense against genuine evil. When we stop lying to ourselves about ourselves, that's the greatest protection we can have against evil.

THE SUN:

If the ego is not the "real center" of ourselves, then of what is it the center?

SANFORD:

What distinguishes Jungian psychology from practically all other psychologies is the idea that there are two centers of the personality. The ego is the center of consciousness; the Self is the center of the total personality, which includes consciousness, the unconscious, *and* the ego. The Self is both the whole and the center. The ego is a self-contained little circle off the center, but contained within the whole. So the ego might best be described as the lesser center of the personality; the Self is the greatest center.

We can see this relationship best in our dreams. In our waking life, the ego is like the sun—it illuminates everything but it also blocks out the stars. What we don't realize is that the contents of ego-consciousness are not our creation; they're given to us, they come up from somewhere. We're constantly influenced by the unconscious, but we're largely unaware of that. The ego prefers to believe it creates all its own thoughts. In our dreams, everything changes with the appearance of the dream ego. When we recall the dream, we automatically identify with the dream ego; we refer to it as "I," and say, "I met a bear, and we had a wrestling match, and then the dancing girl appeared," and so on. But the difference is that the dream ego knows things during the dream that the waking ego doesn't know. You may remember running very fast during the dream, for instance, and not remember why. But in the dream, you knew.

Most important, the dream ego is never more significant than any other figure in the dream. It may even find itself overpowered or overshadowed. When the sun goes down, the stars come out—and then you discover you're just one of the stars in a sky full of stars. That's the soulscape, which is invisible in our waking life.

THE SUN:

I've noticed that while I'm more or less comfortable with the *idea* of the shadow in waking life, the shadow in dreams is a lot more than an idea—it's completely real and very powerful. I sometimes become the shadow, as if *it's* integrating *me*.

SANFORD:

Yes, the shadow is an energy system in the dream that's at least as powerful as you are. In the psychic arena of the dream, all the elements of the psyche are less distinct from one another, and the dream ego may either observe them or become them, or something in between.

The shadow is always an aspect of the ego itself, the qualities of the shadow could have become part of the structure of the ego. You might say the shadow is like the ego's brother or sister, and not necessarily a sinister figure. And it's important to remember that the shadow always has a reason for anything it does, a reason related to those qualities excluded from the ego. To become the shadow in a dream is fairly unusual; it's more likely that the dream ego will observe the shadow changing forms during the dream.

THE SUN:

I suppose it's safer to become the shadow in a dream than in waking life.

SANFORD:

Well, we're up against the subtleties of the shadow again. My thinking in this arena follows Kunkel more than Jung. The idea is that the ego is originally quite close to the center of the Self. As it moves farther away, it develops an *egocentric* posture, which is often exacerbated by unfavorable childhood influences. The nature of those influences will determine the nature of one's egocentric defenses, and hence the nature of the shadow.

Let's say that a person experiences himself as weak and ineffectual against his environment, but he finds another way of getting through life, which is to become sort of a "clinging vine." He doesn't develop his own strength; he relies on other people who are strong, but he has to qualify for their support. So he strikes a pose of being both needy and very deserving. That's his egocentric posture for life; he's the kind of person who always needs your help, and who can cite all the reasons you should give it. If you don't help him, you're a bad person.

One thing about such a person is that he's very boring. People will stop supporting him when he's bored them thoroughly, and then he feels threatened and anxious. Now what he has repressed in order to maintain his egocentric posture of clinging are qualities of courage and forthrightness—very desirable qualities. But this clinging vine personality looks on these qualities as the devil, and is frightened to death of them. And in fact, those repressed qualities *can* become dangerous.

Take the example of a high school boy who has the egocentric defense of a turtle—he just wants to be left alone. He becomes the target of a gang of toughs whose egocentric propensity is to torment him, precisely because he's a loner. They harass the hell out of him, until one day his egocentric shell of withdrawal explodes and *bang*—out comes the shadow. Now he may just get into a fistfight, and even though he gets beat up, he comes out okay—and probably more integrated. On the other hand, he may go get his father's gun and shoot his tormenters, and a terrible thing has happened. If the energy has been too long and too deeply repressed, something of regrettable consequence can occur.

THE SUN:

Do you think that the boy calls his tormenters to him?

SANFORD:

Oh, absolutely. At the unconscious level, he's sending a message about what he needs for integration. Kunkel used to say about such a situation that the "archangels" are sent to complete the divine plan.

THE SUN:

But the archangels aren't necessarily going to take care of you.

SANFORD:

Thats right. They just set up the scenario. All we know is that when the archangels become involved, things won't stay the same. What happens next, nobody can predict. The release of the shadow is not to be taken lightly. Hence, it would be much better if the boy discovered his hostility in therapy, or some other caretaking situation where his shadow can come out gradually.

Kunkel made the mysterious statement that "in a showdown, God is always on the side of the shadow, not the ego." For all its difficulties, the shadow is closer to the creative source.

Now the ego that is not in an egocentric state is an entirely different matter; it has a healthy creative relationship to both the shadow and the Self. The ego is not really diminished in the process of integration; it simply becomes less rigid in its boundaries. There's a tremendous difference between a strong ego and an egocentric ego; the latter is always weak. Individuation, the attainment of one's real potential, can't take place without the strong ego.

THE SUN:

Does that mean that it's impossible just to be your "Self"?

SANFORD:

That's right. The ego is the necessary vehicle for the expression of the Self, but you have to be willing to put the ego on the line. It's like Moses confronting the voice of God in the burning bush, and then going down to lead the people of Israel out of Egypt. That's the action of the strong ego.

. . . .

4 · THE SHADOW IN HISTORY AND LITERATURE

ANTHONY   STEVENS

Fear of 'the fall' into iniquity has been expressed throughout the history of Christendom as terror of being 'possessed' by the powers of darkness. Stories of possession have always compelled fascination and horror, Bram Stoker's *Count Dracula* being but a recent instance of this genre. Tales of vampires and werewolves have probably always been with us.

Perhaps the most famous example of possession is provided by the legend of Faust, who, bored with his virtuous academic existence, enters into a compact with the devil. He was clearly suffering from a mid-life crisis. His single-minded pursuit of knowledge had led to a one-sided and over-intellectualized development of his personality, with far too much Self-potential unlived and 'locked away' in the unconscious. As usually happens in such cases, the repressed psychic energy demands attention. Unfortunately, Faust does not indulge in a patient self-analysis, holding dialogues with the figures arising from the unconscious in an effort to assimilate the Shadow; instead, he allows himself 'to fall into it' and be possessed.

The trouble is that Faust believes that the answer to his problem must lie in more of the same thing, in a more determined perseveration of the old neurotic pattern (i.e., he must acquire still more *knowledge*). Like Dr. Jekyll, another intellectual bachelor with a similar problem, he is intrigued by the numinosity of the Shadow when it 'personates' and, sacrificing his ego standpoint, he falls under its spell. As a result, it is all up with both of them and the outcome is the sort of thing that all dread: Faust becomes a drunk and a libertine, while Jekyll turns into the monstrous Mr. Hyde.

Our fascination with Faust and Mephisto and Jekyll and Hyde derives from the archetypal nature of the problem they crystallize. In a sense, both Faust and Jekyll are heroes because they dare to do what most of us shirk: we prefer to behave like Dorian Gray, putting on an innocent face (Persona) for the world, keeping our evil qualities hidden in the hope that no one will discover their existence; we entertain thoughts of 'losing' the Shadow, renouncing our moral duality, atoning for the sin of Adam, and, once more At One with God, re-entering the Garden of Eden. We invent Utopia, El Dorado or Shangri-la, where evil is unknown, and we take comfort in Marxist or Rousseauesque phantasies that evil resides not in our nature but in the 'corrupt' society that everywhere holds us in chains. But change the nature of society and the evil will disappear never to return.

The stories of Jekyll and Faust, like the Biblical story of Adam's fall, are cautionary tales that bring us down to earth and back to the eternal reality of our own evil. All three are variations on the same archetypal theme: a man, bored with his circumstances, decides to ignore the prohibitions of the super-ego in order to liberate the Shadow, encounter the Anima, 'know her' and *live*. All go too far: they commit *hubris*. And *nemesis* is the inexorable result. 'The wages of sin is death.'

The anxiety which haunts all such stories is not so much a fear of being caught as fear that the evil side will get out of control. The plots of science fiction are designed to create the same unease, as indeed was Mary Shelley's *Frankenstein*, the prototype of them all. That this is a universal anxiety of mankind was understood by Freud, as may be gathered from his account of the phenomenon in *Civilization and Its Discontents*. Because of the time and circumstances in which he lived (middle-class Vienna at the end of the nineteenth century), Freud believed that the repressed evil that men and women feared was entirely sexual. His systematic investigation of this aspect of the Shadow, combined with the coincidental decline in the power of the Judeo-Christian superego, did much to purge our culture of its erotic demons, enabling many previously repressed components of the Shadow to be integrated within the total personality of individual men and women without forcing them to suffer the concomitant guilt which would certainly have afflicted earlier generations. This affords an impressive example on a collective scale of the therapeutic value attributed by Jung to the analytic pro-cess of recognizing and integrating components of the Shadow.

However, an aspect of the Shadow that still remains to be exorcised—as powerful as sexual lust but far more disastrous in its consequences—is the lust for power and destruction. That Freud should so long have ignored this com-ponent, in spite of witnessing the First World War and the subsequent rise of fascism, is, to say the least, surprising. One suspects that it had much to do with his determination to make his sexual theory the foundation of psycho-analysis. ('My dear Jung, promise me never to abandon the sexual theory. That is the most essential thing of all. You see, we must make a dogma of it, an unshakable bulwark.') Anthony Storr makes the interesting suggestion that it may also have been due to Freud's ill-feeling over the defection of Al-fred Adler, who had pulled out of the psychoanalytic movement precisely be-cause of his conviction that the drive for power played a more important role in human psychopathology than the desire for sex.

The task of confronting the brutal, destructive elements of the Shadow has become in the twentieth century the inescapable destiny of our species: if we fail, we cannot hope to survive. With good cause this has become our 'uni-versal anxiety.' It is the Shadow problem of our time. 'We might just be in time to stop the apocalypse,' declares Konrad Lorenz. 'But it will be touch and go.'

At this very moment in the history of mankind, evolution has put us on the spot. If we are not to annihilate ourselves and most other species on the face of the earth, then ontogeny must triumph over phylogeny. There is an urgent *biological* imperative to make the Shadow conscious. The moral burden of this immense task is greater than any previous generation could have even conceived: the destiny of the planet and our entire solar system (since we now know that we are the only sentient beings in it) is in our hands. Alone among the great psychologists of our epoch, Jung provided a conceptual model which might help to make this ontological triumph possible. In the Shadow concept he synthesized the work of Adler and Freud, and in his demonstration of the actualizing propensities of the Self he transcended them. Only by coming consciously to terms with our *nature*—and in particular with the nature of the Shadow—can we hope to avert total catastrophe.

. . . .

5 · DR. JEKYLL AND MR. HYDE

J O H N   A .   S A N F O R D

We can begin by contrasting the description of Henry Jekyll with that of Edward Hyde. We are told that Jekyll was a "large, well-made, smooth-faced man of fifty, with something of a slyish cast perhaps, but every mark of capacity and kindness." So there is no reason to suppose that Jekyll did not have many good qualities. Only the hint of a "slyish cast" betrays the fact that hidden underneath the goodness of Henry Jekyll there was a person of more doubtful character. Later Jekyll describes himself in more detail as a man "fond of the respect of the wise and good among my fellow-men." This tells us that in addition to his natural store of goodness and kindness Henry Jekyll had a desire for approbation by his fellows and so struck a certain pose in front of mankind, that is, adopted a pleasing persona that would bring him the approval and respect of others.

Jekyll noted another side to his personality, however, which was at variance with this persona: "a certain impatient gaiety of disposition." This led him to seek certain pleasures in life which he found hard to reconcile with his "imperious desire" to carry his head high. Hence, Jekyll noted, he adopted a "more than commonly grave countenance before the public." In other words, the grave countenance Jekyll publicly struck was a mask to shield from others another side to his personality that Jekyll did not want anyone to see and which he regarded with "a morbid sense of shame." As a consequence, Jekyll wrote, "I concealed my pleasures" and "stood already committed to a profound duplicity of life."

Jekyll displayed psychological insight. He was aware of the duality of his own nature, and declared that "man is not truly one, but truly two." He could even hazard the conjecture that man is made up of a whole assortment of part-selves, that his personality is not single, but is like a village of people, an insight modern depth psychology corroborates. He saw this duality as "thorough" and "primitive," that is, archetypal and therefore present from the beginning as a fundamental aspect of man's basic psychological structure. Armed with this kind of psychological insight into himself, Jekyll might have gone on to great heights of conscious development but failed to do so because of a fundamental psychological error, as we shall see.

Hyde is described as young, full of hellish energy, small, and somehow deformed. He is a "Juggernaut," "not like a man," a person who evoked hatred in others at the very sight of him. He has a black sneering coldness, and is incapable of human feeling, and therefore is without any twinge of conscience and so is incapable of guilt. Hyde's youthfulness suggests that as the shadow personality of Jekyll, he contains unused energy. The Shadow, as we have seen, includes the unlived life, and to touch upon the shadow personality is to receive an infusion of new, that is, youthful energy. Hyde's small size and deformed appearance indicates that as the shadow personality Hyde has not lived very much in Jekyll's outer life. Having dwelt for the most part in the darkness of the unconscious he is deformed in appearance, like a tree forced to grow among the rocks and in the shadow of other trees. Hyde's lack of conscience, described by Jekyll as a "solution of the bonds of obligation," is also characteristic of the shadow personality. It is as though the Shadow leaves moral feelings and obligations up to the ego personality while he or she strives to live out of inner and forbidden impulses quite devoid of the mitigating effects of a sense of right or wrong.

But perhaps the most important thing we are told about Edward Hyde comes from Jekyll's comment that when he first was transformed by the drug into Hyde "I knew myself . . . to be more wicked, tenfold more wicked, sold a slave to my original evil . . ." At first Jekyll has only seen in himself a certain "gaiety of disposition," a pleasure-seeking side that might have led to mischief but nothing more, but once he has become Hyde he realizes he is far more evil than he ever supposed. From this description it appears that the shadow personality begins with our personal dark side, but at some point contacts a deeper, more archetypal level of evil which is so strong that Jekyll could say of Hyde that he alone among men was pure evil. In the hands of this archetypal evil the pleasure-seeking mischief in which Jekyll wanted to engage soon led to truly satanic activity, as exemplified in the hellish murder of Dr. Carew, which was done for the pure joy of evil and destruction. We can see this same satanic quality emerging in those situations in which a person cold-bloodedly kills others, either in war or crime, without evident remorse. It is an archetypal evil that both shocks and fascinates us and draws us with horrified absorption to the daily reading of our newspapers.

C. G. Jung once wrote that we become what we do. This helps us understand even more the reason for Jekyll's demise. Once he decides to *be* Hyde, even if only for a while, he tends to *become* Hyde. The deliberate decision to *do* evil leads to our becoming evil. This is why living out the darkest impulses of the Shadow cannot be a solution to the shadow problem, for we can easily become possessed by or absorbed into evil if we try such a thing. This attests to the archetypal nature of evil, for it is one of the qualities of the archetypes that they can possess the ego, which is like being devoured by or made identical with the archetype.

Jekyll himself becomes aware of this danger after he finds himself involuntarily turning into Hyde. This was an enormous shock to him. He had expected to be able to move from Jekyll to Hyde and back again at will, but now he finds that Hyde is taking over. His former confidence, which led him to say, "the moment I choose, I can be rid of Mr. Hyde," is now gone. This attitude shows a carelessness toward evil that predisposed Jekyll toward possession. It comes up again in the story in the scene in which Jekyll sits in the park and reflects that he is, after all, "like my neighbours," and compares himself favorably with other men, noting his active good will in contrast to the "lazy neglect" of others. Jekyll's careless disregard for the powers of evil, together with his desire to escape the tension of his dual nature, paves the way for his ultimate destruction.

So at this point in the story Jekyll resolves to have nothing more to do with the Hyde part of his personality and even declares to Utterson, "I swear to God, I swear to God I will never set eyes on him again. I bind my honour to you that I am done with him in this world. It is all at an end." And Jekyll does try to have done with Hyde. He renews his old life, becomes more dedicated than ever to doing good works, and also, for the first time, becomes devoted to religion as well.

We must assume that Jekyll's devotion to religion means that he went through formal religious observances, perhaps joining a Church of some kind. We know, of course, that Jekyll's religion is not sincere. He knows nothing of God, but is hoping to find in formalized religion and in his own religious pretensions a defense against being overcome by Hyde. No doubt many of us today are using religion in this way, especially those religious creeds that decry man's sins, threaten the sinful man with punishment, and encourage good deeds as the sign of salvation. This kind of religion tends to draw as members those persons who are consciously or unconsciously struggling to hold in check their shadow personalities.

But the attempt does not work with Dr. Jekyll, and Hyde has now grown stronger within him. Hyde as the shadow personality continues to exist in the unconscious and is now, more than ever, struggling to be free, that is, to possess Jekyll's personality so he can live as he wants to. The dark side has been strengthened too much, and the attempt to hold him in check and keep him locked in the basement of the psyche fails because Hyde is now stronger than Jekyll. So Stevenson is telling us that if living out the Shadow is not the answer, neither is the repression of the Shadow the answer, for both leave the personality split in two.

There is also Jekyll's insincerity and religious pretension. Both his religion and his desire to have nothing to do any longer with Hyde stem from his desire for self-preservation and not from his moral feelings. It is not for spiritual reasons, but because he fears destruction, that Jekyll wants Hyde contained. Underneath there still exists his unrecognized longing for evil, as is evidenced by the fact that even in the midst of this great resolve to have nothing to do with Hyde he did not destroy Hyde's clothes or give up the apartment in Soho. We could say that at this point the only way Jekyll could have kept from being overcome by evil was if his soul were filled with a spirit more powerful than that of evil; but in allowing himself to become Hyde, Jekyll emptied his soul and evil could take possession of him.

Henry Jekyll's fundamental mistake was his desire to escape the tension of the opposites within him. As we have seen, he was gifted with a modicum of psychological consciousness, more than most men, for he knew that he had a dual nature; he was aware that there was another one in him whose desires were counter to his more usual desires for the approbation of mankind. Had he enlarged this consciousness and carried the tension of the opposites within him, it would have led to the development of his personality; in the language we have been using, he would have individuated. But Jekyll chose instead to try to escape this tension by means of the transforming drug, so that he could be both Jekyll and Hyde and have the pleasures and benefits of living out both sides of his personality without guilt or tension. For as Jekyll, it is worth noting, he felt no responsibility for Hyde. "For it was Hyde, after all, and Hyde alone that was guilty," he once declared.

This gives us a clue to how the problem of the Shadow *can* be met. What was Jekyll's failure may tell us where to go if the conclusion of our drama with the Shadow is to be successful: success may lie in carrying that tension which Jekyll refused. Both repression of the knowledge of the Shadow, and identification with the Shadow, are attempts to escape the tension of the opposites within ourselves, attempts to "loose the bonds" that hold together within us a light and dark side. The motive, of course, is to escape the pain of the problem, but if escaping the pain leads to psychological disaster, carrying the pain may give the possibility for wholeness.

Carrying such a tension of the opposites is like a Crucifixion. We must be as one suspended between the opposites, a painful state to bear. But in such a state of suspension the grace of God is able to operate within us. The problem of our duality can never be resolved on the level of the ego; it permits no rational solution. But where there is consciousness of a problem, the Self, the *Imago Dei* within us can operate and bring about an irrational synthesis of the personality.

To put it another way, if we consciously carry the burden of the opposites in our nature, the secret, irrational, healing processes that go on in us unconsciously can operate to our benefit, and work toward the synthesis of the personality. This irrational healing process, which finds a way around seemingly insurmountable obstacles, has a particularly feminine quality to it. It is the rational, logical masculine mind that declares that opposites like ego and Shadow, light and dark, can never be united. However, the feminine spirit is capable of finding a synthesis where logic says none can be found. For this reason it is worth noting that in Stevenson's story the feminine figures are few and far between and when they do occur they are seen in an exclusively negative light. There is not one major character in the book who is a woman. Jekyll, Enfield, Utterson, Poole, the handwriting expert Mr. Guest, Dr.

Lanyon—all are men. The women figures have only brief mention. There is the woman who cared for Hyde's apartment, an "evil-faced" woman, cold and witchlike. There is a brief mention of the frightened maid whom Utterson meets when he goes to Jekyll's house on the final night, who is described as "hysterically whimpering." There is, of course, also the little girl who was trampled on, and the women who grouped around Hyde who were "wild as harpies." Even Hyde, in the laboratory that final night, is described as "weeping like a woman or a lost soul." The only vaguely positive allusion to a woman or to the feminine is the maid who witnessed the murder of Dr. Carew, but even she is said to have fainted at the sight.

In short, the feminine comes off badly in Stevenson's story. It is cold and witchlike, weak and ineffective, or is victimized, which suggests that the feminine spirit was rendered inoperative, and was unable to help in the situation. Translated into psychological language, we can say that when psychological consciousness is refused, as Jekyll had refused it, the feminine part of us, our very souls, weakens and languishes and falls into despair, a tragedy, for it is this very feminine power that can help find a way around what is otherwise an insoluble problem.

A comment on Mr. Utterson is in order. The portrayal of Utterson is a testimony to the skill of Stevenson as a storyteller, for while the majority of the narrative is told to us through his eyes and experiences, he himself never intrudes into the spotlight. His character is adroitly drawn. We like Utterson, we can picture him in our minds, we can follow his thoughts and feelings and reactions, yet the spotlight of the story always shines through him onto the central mystery of Jekyll and Hyde so that Utterson never takes over the center of the stage. Because of this we may be inclined simply to dismiss Utterson as a literary device, a necessary figure to have so that the story may be told, but not a character who is likely to have anything to teach us about the mystery of good and evil.

But in fact Utterson is more important than he seems, for he is the human figure whose sensibilities are aroused by evil and in whose consciousness the full story of good and evil, ego and Shadow, finally emerges. He represents the human being who has a sufficiently strong feeling function that he is shocked by evil and can therefore resist being overcome by it. It is exactly this feeling function, which enables a human being to react with horror at the depths of evil, that was weak in Jekyll and totally lacking in Hyde.

It is also necessary that evil eventually be known by someone. The doings of Jekyll and Hyde were a secret, but secrets have a way of trying to emerge. Every secret is propelled by hidden inner forces toward human consciousness, and for this reason evil deeds eventually emerge into the awareness of humanity in general, or someone in particular. Notice, for instance, that early in the story Utterson's mind is tortured by what he does not know, and he is unable to sleep. This is a sure sign that the unconscious is troubling Utterson, and is seeking to find a way to bring into his consciousness the dreadful and dark secret life to Jekyll and Hyde. So in the story it is Utterson whose consciousness becomes the container for the knowledge of evil, and thus he represents the ego at its most human and best, a kind of redemptive person whose dawning awareness of what is happening, and horrified feelings, provide a human safeguard against the takeover of human life by the powers of darkenss.

But how about Dr. Lanyon? He too came to see the nature of evil, but in the wrong way. Lanyon had not sought out the mystery of Jekyll and Hyde as did Utterson, and when the full extent of the evil broke in on him, it was too much for him. He saw evil too quickly, and looked into it too deeply, without the necessary preparation or the necessary human support. And that is the other side of becoming conscious of evil. We must become aware of it, but to look into it too deeply and naively may give us a shock from which we cannot recover.

The demonic drug that Jekyll concocted to achieve his transformation into Hyde is also worth a comment, especially in this present time of history when we are surrounded on all sides by drugs with mind-altering effects. I have often noted that, in some instances at least, alcohol seems to change people from a Jekyll to a Hyde personality. A person is one way until he or she takes a few drinks and then out comes the ugly side of the personality. In certain cases it may well be that at the bottom of the urge to drink is the struggle of the Shadow to assert itself, just as in our story Hyde yearned for Jekyll to take the drug so he could live out his own dark life.

We can also note that although the evil part of Jekyll's personality destroyed him, it also eventually destroyed itself. No sooner was Jekyll completely possessed by Hyde than Hyde himself died by suicide. This too is instructive, for it tells us that evil eventually overreaches itself and brings about its own destruction. Evidently evil cannot live on its own, but can exist only when there is something good upon which it can feed.

· · · · · · ·

6 · THE REALIZATION OF THE SHADOW IN DREAMS

MARIE-LOUISE VON FRANZ

The shadow is not the whole of the unconscious personality. It represents unknown or little-known attributes and qualities of the ego—aspects that mostly belong to the personal sphere and that could just as well be conscious. In some aspects, the shadow can also consist of collective factors that stem from a source outside the individual's personal life.

When an individual makes an attempt to see his shadow, he becomes aware of (and often ashamed of) those qualities and impulses he denies in himself but can plainly see in other people—such things as egotism, mental laziness, and sloppiness; unreal fantasies, schemes, and plots; carelessness and cowardice; inordinate love of money and possessions—in short, all the little sins about which he might previously have told himself: "That doesn't matter; nobody will notice it, and in any case other people do it too."

If you feel an overwhelming rage coming up in you when a friend reproaches you about a fault, you can be fairly sure that at this point you will find a part of your shadow, of which you are unconscious. It is, of course, natural to become annoyed when others who are "no better" criticize you because of shadow faults. But what can you say if your own dreams—an inner judge in your own being—reproach you? That is the moment when the ego gets caught, and the result is usually embarrassed silence. Afterward the pain and lengthy work of self-education begins—a work, we might say, that is the psychological equivalent of the labors of Hercules. This unfortunate hero's first task, you will remember, was to clean up in one day the Augean Stables, in which hundreds of cattle had dropped their dung for many decades—a task so enormous that the ordinary mortal would be overcome by discouragement at the mere thought of it.

The shadow does not consist only of omissions. It shows up just as often in an impulsive or inadvertent act. Before one has time to think, the evil remark pops out, the plot is hatched, the wrong decision is made, and one is confronted with results that were never intended or consciously wanted. Furthermore, the shadow is exposed to collective infections to a much greater extent than is the conscious personality. When a man is alone, for instance, he feels relatively all right; but as soon as "the others" do dark, primitive things he begins to fear that if he doesn't join in, he will be considered a fool. Thus he gives way to impulses that do not really belong to him at all. It is particularly in contacts with people of the same sex that one stumbles over both one's own shadow and those of other people. Although we do see the shadow in a person of the opposite sex, we are usually much less annoyed by it and can more easily pardon it.

In dreams and myths, therefore, the shadow appears as a person of the same sex as that of the dreamer. The following dream may serve as an example. The dreamer was a man of 48 who tried to live very much for and by himself, working hard and disciplining himself, repressing pleasure and spontaneity to a far greater extent than suited his real nature.

> I owned and inhabited a very big house in town, and I didn't yet know all its different parts. So I took a walk through it and discovered, mainly in the cellar, several rooms about which I knew nothing and even exits leading into other cellars or into subterranean streets. I felt uneasy when I found that several of these exits were not locked and some had no locks at all. Moreover, there were some laborers at work in the neighborhood who could have sneaked in. . . .
>
> When I came back up again to the ground floor, I passed a back yard where again I discovered different exits into the street or into other houses. When I tried to investigate them more closely, a man came up to me laughing loudly

and calling out that we were old pals from the elementary school. I remembered him too, and while he was telling me about his life, I walked along with him toward the exit and strolled with him through the streets.

There was a strange chiaroscuro in the air as we walked through an enormous circular street and arrived at a green lawn where three galloping horses suddenly passed us. They were beautiful, strong animals, wild but well-groomed, and they had no rider with them. (Had they run away from military service?)

The maze of strange passages, chambers, and unlocked exits in the cellar recalls the old Egyptian representation of the underworld, which is a well-known symbol of the unconscious with its unknown possibilities. It also shows how one is "open" to other influences in one's unconscious shadow side, and how uncanny and alien elements can break in. The cellar, one can say, is the basement of the dreamer's psyche. In the back yard of the strange building (which represents the still unperceived psychic scope of the dreamer's personality) an old school friend suddenly turns up. This person obviously personifies another aspect of the dreamer himself—an aspect that had been part of his life as a child but that he had forgotten and lost. It often happens that a person's childhood qualities (for instance, gaiety, irascibility, or perhaps trustfulness) suddenly disappear, and one does not know where or how they have gone. It is such a lost characteristic of the dreamer that now returns (from the back yard) and tries to make friends again. This figure probably stands for the dreamer's neglected capacity for enjoying life and for his extroverted shadow side.

But we soon learn why the dreamer feels "uneasy" just before meeting this seemingly harmless old friend. When he strolls with him in the street, the horses break loose. The dreamer thinks they may have escaped from military service (that is to say, from the conscious discipline that has hitherto characterized his life). The fact that the horses have no rider shows that instinctive drives can get away from conscious control. In this old friend, and in the horses, all the positive force reappears that was lacking before and that was badly needed by the dreamer.

This is a problem that often comes up when one meets one's "other side." The shadow usually contains values that are needed by consciousness, but that exist in a form that makes it difficult to integrate them into one's life. The passages and the large house in this dream also show that the dreamer does not yet know his own psychic dimensions and is not yet able to fill them out.

The shadow in this dream is typical for an introvert (a man who tends to retire too much from outer life). In the case of an extrovert, who is turned more toward outer objects and outer life, the shadow would look quite different.

A young man who had a very lively temperament embarked again and again on successful enterprises, while at the same time his dreams insisted that he should finish off a piece of private creative work he had begun. The following was one of those dreams:

A man is lying on a couch and has pulled the cover over his face. He is a Frenchman, a desperado who would take on any criminal job. An official is accompanying me downstairs, and I know that a plot has been made against me: namely, that the Frenchman should kill me as if by chance. (That is how it would look from the outside.) He actually sneaks up behind me when we approach the exit, but I am on my guard. A tall, portly man (rather rich and influential) suddenly leans against the wall beside me, feeling ill. I quickly grab the opportunity to kill the official by stabbing his heart. "One only notices a bit of moisture"—this is said like a comment. Now I am safe, for the Frenchman won't attack me since the man who gave him his orders is dead. (Probably the official and the successful portly man are the same person, the latter somehow replacing the former.)

The desperado represents the other side of the dreamer—his introversion—which has reached a completely destitute state. He lies on a couch (i.e., he is passive) and pulls the cover over his face because he wants to be left alone. The official, on the other hand, and the prosperous portly man (who are secretly the same person) personify the dreamer's successful outer responsibilities and activities. The sudden illness of the portly man is connected with the fact that this dreamer had in fact become ill several times when he had allowed his dynamic energy to explode too forcibly in his external life. But this successful man has no blood in his veins—only a sort of moisture—which means that these external ambitious activities of the dreamer contain no genuine life and no passion, but are bloodless mechanisms. Thus it would be no real loss if the portly man were killed. At the end of the dream, the Frenchman is satisfied; he obviously represents a positive shadow figure who had turned negative and dangerous only because the conscious attitude of the dreamer did not agree with him.

This dream shows us that the shadow can consist of many different elements—for instance, of unconscious ambition (the successful portly man) and of introversion (the Frenchman). This particular dreamer's association to the French, moreover, was that they know how to handle love affairs very well. Therefore the two shadow figures also represent two well-known drives: power and sex. The power drive appears momentarily in a double form, both as an official and as a successful man. The official, or civil servant, personifies collective adaptation, whereas the successful man denotes ambition; but naturally both serve the power drive. When the dreamer succeeds in stopping this dangerous inner force, the Frenchman is suddenly no longer hostile. In other words, the equally dangerous aspect of the sex drive has also surrendered.

Obviously, the problem of the shadow plays a great role in all political conflicts. If the man who had this dream had not been sensible about his shadow problem, he could easily have identified the desperate Frenchman with the "dangerous Communists" of outer life, or the official plus the prosperous man with the "grasping capitalists." In this way he would have avoided seeing that he had within him such warring elements. If people observe their own unconscious tendencies in other people, this is called a "projection." Political agitation in all countries is full of such projections, just as much as the back-yard gossip of little groups and individuals. Projections of all kinds obscure our view of our fellow men, spoiling its objectivity, and thus spoiling all possibility of genuine human relationships.

And there is an additional disadvantage in projecting our shadow. If we identify our own shadow with, say, the Communists or the capitalists, a part of our own personality remains on the opposing side. The result is that we shall constantly (though involuntarily) do things behind our own backs that support this other side, and thus we shall unwittingly help our enemy. If, on the contrary, we realize the projection and can discuss matters without fear or hostility, dealing with the other person sensibly, then there is a chance of mutual understanding—or at least a truce.

Whether the shadow becomes our friend or enemy depends largely upon ourselves. As the dreams of the unexplored house and the French desperado both show, the shadow is not necessarily always an opponent. In fact, he is exactly like any human being with whom one has to get along, sometimes by giving in, sometimes by resisting, sometimes by giving love—whatever the situation requires. The shadow becomes hostile only when he is ignored or misunderstood.

. . . .

7 · FINDING THE SHADOW IN DAILY LIFE

WILLIAM A. MILLER

There are at least five effective pathways for traveling inward to gain insight into the composition of our shadow: (1) soliciting feedback from others as to how they perceive us; (2) uncovering the content of our projections; (3) examining our "slips" of tongue and behavior, and investigating what is really occurring when we are perceived other than we intended to be perceived; (4) considering our humor and our identifications; and (5) studying our dreams, daydreams, and fantasies.

SOLICITING FEEDBACK FROM OTHERS

We may begin by looking *beyond* the mirror at our own reflection. Looking into a mirror we see only the reflection of ourselves as we choose to see it. Looking beyond the mirror we see ourselves *as we are seen*. If this seems impossible, begin with someone else.

Bring to mind the image of a person whom we know to live to some degree in self-delusion. This is not difficult, because we are all too familiar with the shadow dimensions of other people, and we are often amazed that they are so ignorant of what is so obvious.

Even though I may *want* to deny it, I am compelled to agree (at least in theory) that this matter is a two-way street. That is to say, if I can see clearly your shadow to which you are blind, then it must follow that you likewise can see clearly my shadow to which I am blind. If I would be more than happy to tell you what I see (in a nice way, of course), then you would probably be more than happy to tell me what you see (in a nice way, of course).

This is one of the most effective methods for gaining insight into our personal shadow—feedback from others as to how they perceive us. Unfortunately, the very thought of this is threatening to most of us. We would much rather continue to assume that others see us precisely as we see ourselves.

People who are in the best position to help us see our shadow elements are those who know us well. It could be our spouse, significant other, close friend, colleague, or fellow worker. Paradoxically, the people who are most likely to be helpful are those whom we are least likely to heed. We may accuse them of overt subjectivity, projection, or just plain fabrication. It would be less threatening to hear feedback from a stranger, but strangers are not in the position to give us the kind of authentic perceptions as are those who know us well. It is yet another indication of the difficulty of the journey.

Suppose I solicit your feedback, and you tell me that you have perceived me as a condescending person in several situations in which we have both been involved. I may accept that as your valid observation, even though it is difficult for me to hear. I want to say, "What on earth are you talking about? That is the *last* thing I want to be—condescending." But I hold my tongue.

This gives me a fairly substantial clue that I probably have just met a true shadow trait or characteristic. For anytime we overstate being "for" or "against," and press that position adamantly, we may just be in personal shadow territory, and we would do well to investigate.

I have heard your identification of my shadow trait, and even though I find it extremely hard to believe that I should appear to be condescending, I accept it as your perception. I then go to a close friend and explain to him what I am doing and tell him that another friend has told me that she sees me as a condescending person. I ask him to be honest and tell me if that is how he has perceived me. I may be satisfied with this second opinion, or I may want to repeat this process again. In any case, if I am sincere in my journey inward, I will want to know as best I can, one way or the other. When two or more people independently tell me they perceive in me a common shadow trait, I would do well to believe them and explore more deeply their observation.

EXAMINING OUR PROJECTIONS

A second pathway into the personal shadow is to examine our projections. Projection is an unconscious mechanism that is employed whenever a trait or characteristic of our personality that has no relationship to consciousness becomes activated. As a result of the unconscious projection, we observe and react to this unrecognized personal trait in other people. We see in them something that is a part of ourselves, but which we fail to see in ourselves.

We make both negative and positive projections. Most of the time, however, it is the undesirable dimensions of ourselves that we see in others. Therefore, to encounter the elements of the shadow, we need to examine what traits, characteristics, and attitudes we dislike in other people and how strongly we dislike them.

The simplest method is to list all the qualities we do not like in other people; for instance, conceit, short temper, selfishness, bad manners, greed, and others. When the list is finally complete (and it will probably be quite lengthy), we must extract those characteristics that we not only dislike in others, but hate, loathe, and despise. This shorter final list will be a fairly accurate picture of our personal shadow. This will probably be very hard to believe and even harder to accept.

If I list arrogance, for example, as one of those traits in others that I simply cannot stand, and if I adamantly criticize a person for arrogance in relating to people, I would do well to examine my own behavior to see if perhaps I, too, practice arrogance.

Certainly not all our criticisms of others are projections of our own undesirable shadow traits: but any time our response to another person involves excessive emotion or overreaction, we can be sure that something unconscious has been prodded and is being activated. As we said earlier, the people on whom we project must have "hooks" on which the projection can stick. If Jim is sometimes arrogant, for example, there is a certain degree of "reasonableness" about my offense at his behavior. But in true shadow projection my condemnation of Jim will far exceed his demonstration of the fault.

Conflict situations generate many issues and bring forth strong emotions; consequently, they provide an exceptional arena for possible shadow projections. In the experience of conflict we may be able to learn much about our shadow characteristics. What we decry in the "enemy" may be nothing less than a shadow projection of our own darkness.

We also project our positive shadow qualities onto others: We see in others those positive traits which are our very own, but which, for whatever reason, we refuse to allow entry into our consciousness and are undiscernible to us.

For example, we may perceive positive qualities in people without empirical evidence to support such perceptions. This often happens in romantic encounters and sometimes in personnel evaluations. Lovers, caught up in their desire for the other person, often project their own unconscious positive attributes onto that person. The trait projected may in fact be there in some form, else the projection will not stick. But frequently it is there nowhere to the degree that the other believes he or she sees it. For example, Susan, who possesses a very kind and generous dimension in her shadow, projects it onto Sam and lauds him for his great kindness, particularly to her. Friends may try to help Susan see that while Sam may not appear to be selfish and greedy, his demonstrations of kindness and generosity are more like "flashes in the pan." Susan, however, will hear none of this.

When one is once "hooked" by a positive quality in another person, one may project all sorts of other positive qualities onto that person. This happens occasionally in personnel interviews and is known as the "halo effect." The interviewee who thus hooks the interviewer can then do no wrong in the eyes of the interviewer. The interviewer's placing of personal positive qualities onto the interviewee may override strong evidence to the contrary.

These illustrations demonstrate undesirable situations but they nevertheless demonstrate the power of positive projection. Therefore we do well to realize the presence of potential positive dimensions of our shadow as well as negative. We need to list these qualities we admire and deeply admire in other people. Then when we hear ourselves saying, "Oh, but I could never be like that," we would do well to investigate those traits, for they are undoubtedly a part of our Golden Shadow.

EXAMINING OUR "SLIPS"

A third pathway into the personal shadow is to examine our slips of tongue, slips of behavior, and misperceived behaviors. Slips of tongue are those unintentional misstatements that cause us no end of embarrassment. When we say that among other things shadow is all that we would perhaps *like* to be, but wouldn't dare, we set the stage for shadow's appearance through these phenomena. "That is absolutely the last thing I wanted to say," or "I can't believe I said a thing like that," and similar "apologies" demonstrate that while consciousness proposes, shadow often disposes.

For example, Ann had been taught always to put the most charitable construction on all that others do. Therefore, when her friend Chris decided at age sixty to enter modeling school, Ann wanted to commend her, even though she privately thought it rather ludicrous. Her shadow told her just *how* ludicrous when Ann, wishing to be congratulatory of Chris's decision, told her: "I'm sure you will be an *outstanding* muddle." Of course she meant to say "model," but she was unaware of just how critical she was of Chris's decision. Instead, she said (or shadow said) "muddle," which was what Ann truly assessed the situation to be.

Slips of behavior are perhaps even more revealing. Sometimes there seems to be absolutely no explanation for a person's "aberrant" behavior. Someone will say, "I don't know what got into him; I've never seen him act this way!" The behavior seems totally alien to the generally perceived nature and disposition of the person and all (including the person) are dumbfounded by the experience.

Still another type of "slip" occurs when one is perceived other than as one intended to be perceived. For example, a speaker may intend to present herself quite congenially to her audience, only to be informed after her presentation that she "came across very sarcastically." A modest, shy woman may be offended by the "advances" of men at a party, being totally unaware of her sexually flirtatious manner. A man called on to deliver a brief speech honoring a colleague at an awards dinner was mystified when his spouse told him after the event how "nicely derogatory" he had been in his humorous remarks.

In all such situations (which certainly are common experiences to all of us) we are given the opportunity to journey inward to discover more of our selves, and benefit from that discovery. We can choose either to do it or not. It will do us no good to laugh off such "slips," or to become defensive, or to rationalize, or to sweep them under the rug. Boldly facing them will allow us to discern the darkness in our shadow, but will also profit us with the gold of deeper understanding of ourselves, which in turn may disallow these embarrassing, awkward, even destructive "slips."

CONSIDERING OUR HUMOR AND IDENTIFICATION

A fourth pathway into the personal shadow is the examination of our humor and our response to humor in general. Most of us know that humor is often much more than meets the eye; in fact, what is said in humor is often a manifestation of shadow truth. People who strongly deny and repress shadow generally lack a sense of humor and find very few things funny.

Consider, for example, the old story of the three clergy in a small town who got together weekly in a "support group" of sorts. The longer they met, the more intimate and trusting of each other they became. One day they decided that they had reached the level of trust where each could confess his gravest sin to the others and thus share his guilt. "I confess that I steal money from the offering," said the first. "That *is* bad," said the second, who then went on to confess, "My gravest sin is having an affair with a woman in the adjacent town." The third clergy, hearing the wretchedness of the other two declared, "Oh my brothers, I must confess to you that my most terrible sin is gossip; and I can't wait to get out of here!"

Most of us laugh at the conclusion of the story because it is funny, we say. But more than that, the story hooks our own shadow element of gossiping and we delight in identifying with the expected pleasures the third man will enjoy as he spreads the word around town about the sins of his two colleagues. Of course we *know* it is wrong, and we certainly wouldn't do such a thing; but remember, among other things, shadow is all that we wouldn't dare do, but would *like* to do. Finding the story funny actually enables us to perceive ourselves a little more clearly. On the other hand, the person who denies and represses shadow will find no humor in it, but will instead be judgmental of it all. Such a person will conclude that the story is not funny, but sad—it is yet another indictment of our times, they would say, and all three clergy should be punished.

We *know* that it is very bad taste to delight in another's pain or misfortune, and yet we find the antics of a person on ice skates for the first time to be exceedingly funny. Decades ago, one of the first scenes to delight viewers of the new "moving pictures" was the classic fall as a result of slipping on a banana skin. We howl at the exasperated comic who tells of the many misfortunes under which he or she suffers. The humor of these situations evokes laughter as the repressed sadism in us finds expression. Clearly, examining what we find to be humorous and especially funny will also help us to greater self-knowledge.

We may frequently observe the magnitude and intensity of shadow at a sports event, particularly a contact sport. Behavior that would probably result in fines and imprisonment in any other setting is appropriate, possibly encouraged, and even applauded in this one. Suggestions bordering on murder may be made by otherwise gentle people. I once encountered a group of elderly women while I was attending a professional wrestling match to do a sociological survey. I was so fascinated by their behavior that I forgot to do my survey. They were quite "normal," until the wrestlers stepped into the ring. But when the match began they stood up, shook their fists, and shouted, "Kill that no-good, lousy bum!" "Don't let him get away with that; break his arm!" Vicarious expression of shadow aggression was the order of the evening.

STUDYING OUR DREAMS, DAYDREAMS, AND FANTASIES

One final pathway into the personal shadow is the study of our dreams, daydreams, and fantasies. While we may wish to argue to the contrary, all of us dream, daydream, and fantasize. If we begin to pay attention to these experiences, we stand to learn a great deal about our shadow and its contents.

When shadow appears in our dreams it appears as a figure of the same sex as ourselves. In the dream we react to it in fear, dislike, or disgust, or as we would react to someone inferior to ourselves—a lesser kind of being. In the dream we often want to avoid it, frequently sensing that it is in pursuit of us, when it may or may not be. Shadow may also appear as an indistinguishable form we intuitively fear and want to escape.

Since the figure is our own shadow, or some representative part of our shadow, we need to face it and discover what it is and what it is about. We need to observe its actions, attitudes, and words (if any). Since it personifies dimensions of ourselves that could be conscious, it is a helpful resource to knowing ourselves. The usual tendency in the dream, however, is to avoid the shadow, just as it is for many of us in conscious life.

We may want to deny that we indulge ourselves in daydreams or fantasies, but the truth is that we spend more time at it than we care to realize. It is unbearable, if not impossible, for the conscious mind to be affixed on some concentrative function all its waking time. Therefore, what do we think about when there is nothing to think about? Where does our mind go; what images and fantasies invade our thoughts? Daydreams and fantasies can be so contrary to the persona we wear that they may even frighten us. We certainly do not intend to admit to others what these things are like, and many of us will not even admit them to ourselves.

But in denying their existence we miss yet another opportunity to know ourselves. For in our fantasies and daydreams we discover thoughts, plans, schemes, and dreams that we are unable to accept on a conscious level. These are often fantasies of violence, power, wealth, and sexual acting out. There are also fantasies of gold and daydreams of enrichment, wherein we see ourselves as achievers of the impossible. Once again, the shadow stands ready to share its gold if we will but encounter it and reflect on it.

We must conclude that entry into one's shadow is a very personal thing, and will be unique to each person who does it. Each of us must pursue our own path of entering and following through. Even though there can be no generalized procedure for this journey inward through shadow, the above recommendations can be helpful.

. . . .

THE OTHER

Why speak the names of gods, stars,
foams of a hidden sea,
pollen of the farthest gardens,
when what hurts us is life itself, when each new day
claws at our guts, when every night falls
writhing, murdered?
When we feel the pain in someone else,
a man we do not know but who is always
present and is the victim
and the enemy and love and everything
we'd need to be whole?
Never lay claim to the dark,
don't drain the cup of joy in a single sip.
Look around: there is someone else, always someone else.
What he breathes is your suffocation,
what he eats is your hunger.
Dying, he takes with him the purest half of your own death.

ROSARIO CASTELLANOS

PART 2

. . . .

SHADOW-MAKING: FORMING THE DISOWNED SELF IN THE FAMILY

Darkness, call me brother!
that I may not fear
which I seek.

ANONYMOUS

Shame, guilt, pride, fear, hate, envy, need, and greed
are inevitable byproducts of ego-building. They call
forth the polarity of inferiority feeling and power
drive. They are the shadow aspects of the first
emancipation of the ego.

EDWARD C. WHITMONT

We spend our life until we're twenty deciding what
parts of ourselves to put in the bag, and we spend the
rest of our lives trying to get them out again.

ROBERT BLY

INTRODUCTION

. . . .

Each of us has a psychological heritage that is no less real than our biological one. This inheritance includes a shadow legacy that is transmitted to us and absorbed by us in the psychic soup of our family environment. Here we are exposed to our parents' and siblings' values, temperaments, habits, and behavior. Often, the problems our parents have failed to work out in their own lives come home to us in the form of dysfunctional coping patterns.

"Home is where one starts from," said T. S. Eliot. And family is the theater in which we play out our individuality and our destiny. It is our emotional center of gravity, the place where we begin to achieve identity and develop character under the particular influences of those varied personalities that surround us.

In the psychological atmosphere created by parents, siblings, caretakers, and other important sources of love and approval, each child begins the necessary process of ego development. Human adaptation to the society requires the creation of an ego—an "I"—to serve as the organizing principle of our growing consciousness. Ego development depends upon our repressing what is "wrong" or "bad" in us, while we identify with what is perceived and reinforced as good. This gives the growing personality a strategic advantage in eliminating anxiety and winning positive regard. The process of growing an ego continues throughout the first half of life, modified by external influences and experiences as we move out into the world.

As ego comes, so goes the shadow: the disowned self is a natural by-product of the ego-building process, which eventually becomes a mirror image of the ego. We disown that which does not fit into our developing picture of who we are, thus creating a shadow. Because of the necessarily one-sided nature of ego development, the neglected, rejected, and unacceptable qualities in us accumulate in the unconscious psyche and take form as an inferior personality—the personal shadow.

However, what is disowned does not go away. It lives on within us—out of sight, out of mind, but nevertheless real—an unconscious alter ego hiding just below the threshold of awareness. It often erupts unexpectedly under extreme emotional circumstances. "The devil made me do it!" is the adult euphemism that explains our alter ego behavior.

Ego and shadow are thus in an age-old antagonism that is a well-known motif in mythology: the relationship of opposing twins or brothers—one good, the other evil—symbolic representations of the ego/alter ego in psychological development. Taken together, these sibling opposites form a whole. In the same way, when the ego assimilates the disowned self, we move toward wholeness.

In younger children the regulation of the threshold of conscious awareness is loose and ambiguous. In playgrounds we can witness the process of shadow formation in children and its reinforcement by adults. We marvel at the meanness and cruelty that emerges in children at play. When we feel the compunction to intervene, this is often a spontaneous reaction. Naturally, instinctually, we don't want children hurt. But we also want the child to disown the feelings and actions that we have disowned, so the child can fit a mature adult's ideal of appropriate play. In addition, we project or attribute to the "badly behaved" child that which we previously have rejected in ourselves. If the child gets the message, he or she will, in turn, disidentify with these impulses in order to satisfy the adult's expectations.

The shadows of others thus stimulate a continual moral effort in a child's ego- and shadow-making. We learn as children to cover up what is going on underneath ego awareness, so that we may look good and be acceptable to our important others. Projection—the involuntary transposition of unacceptable, unconscious tendencies into outer objects or people—serves as an aid to the fragile ego in its need to acquire positive feedback. According to Jungian analyst Jolande Jacobi, "No one likes to admit his own darkness. People who believe their ego represents the whole of their psyche, who neither know nor want to know all the other qualities that belong to it, are wont to project their unknown 'soul parts' into the surrounding world."

Of course, the opposite can occur. When the child feels he can never fulfill the expectations of others, he may act out unacceptable behavior and become a scapegoat for the shadow projections of others. The black sheep in a family is the designated recipient and carrier of the family shadow. According to psychoanalyst Sylvia Brinton Perera in *The Scapegoat Complex*, the scapegoat-identified adult is usually by nature especially sensitive to unconscious and emotional currents. This was the child who picked up and carried the family shadow.

British Jungian analyst A. I. Allensby recounts a story told to him by Jung about the family shadow (this story is drawn from John Conger's book, *Jung and Reich: The Body as Shadow*):

> [Jung] told me that he once met a distinguished man, a Quaker, who could not imagine that he had ever done anything wrong in his life. "And do you know what happened to his children?" Jung asked. "The son became a thief, and the daughter a prostitute. Because the father would not take on his shadow, his share in the imperfection of human nature, his children were compelled to live out the dark side which he had ignored."

Besides parent–child relationship patterns, other events add complexity to the shadow-making process. As the child's ego takes hold in awareness, a portion of it forms a mask—or *persona*—the face we exhibit to the world, which portrays what we and others think we are. Persona meets the demands of relating to our environment and culture, matching our ego-ideal to the expectations and values of the world in which we grow up. Underneath, the shadow does the work of containment. The entire process of ego and persona development is a natural response to our environment and is influenced by communication with our family, friends, teachers, and clergy through their approval and disapproval, acceptance and shame.

When we consider this scenario occurring in the family household, we can see how the alter ego develops. The shadows of other family members have a strong influence on the newly forming disowned self, especially when the dark elements are not recognized within the family group, or when the members collude to conceal the shadow of a powerful, weak, or beloved family member.

The essays in Part 2 give a context to shadow-making, discussing various aspects of the process in early life. In the first essay, which is from *Getting the Love You Want,* couples therapist and best-selling author Harville Hendrix discusses how repression produces the disowned self, while often fragmenting our coherent sense of identity.

When a family dynamic is extremely negative, abusive, or dysfunctional, guilt and shame become a troublesome core of our shadow legacy. Los Angeles Jungian analyst Robert M. Stein takes up the theme of parental rejection and betrayal and their lasting, contaminating effects on the child's psyche in Chapter 9, taken from his book *Incest and Human Love.*

Parents are a child's first teachers, and author Kim Chernin suggests in "The Underside of the Mother/Daughter Relationship" that their lessons are not always sweet. A mother's envy, rage, and guilt create a paradoxical circumstance for the woman coming of age today, says Chernin, who has written extensively on eating disorders among women. If left unacknowledged as shadow components, these feelings can have tragic, self-destructive consequences for the daughter.

Being a parent is a difficult and even dangerous responsibility. John A. Sanford's essay, "Parenting and Your Child's Shadow," brings clarity to the task of helping children develop a shadow that will not debilitate them by interfering with their natural and healthy psychological growth. This excerpt is from the book *Evil: The Shadow Side of Reality.*

Shadow-making is inevitable and universal. It makes us who we are and leads us to shadow-work, which makes us who we can be.

· · · · · · ·

8 · CREATING THE FALSE SELF

HARVILLE HENDRIX

In their attempts to repress certain thoughts, feelings, and behavior, parents use various techniques. Sometimes they issue clear-cut directives: "You don't really think that." "Big boys don't cry." "Don't touch yourself there!" "I never want to hear you say that again!" "We don't act like that in this family!" Or, like the mother in the department store, they scold, threaten, or spank. Much of the time, they mold their children through a subtler process of invalidation—they simply choose not to see or reward certain things. For example, if parents place little value on intellectual development, they give their children toys and sports equipment but no books or science kits. If they believe that girls should be quiet and feminine, and boys should be strong and assertive, they only reward their children for gender-appropriate behavior. For example, if their little boy comes into the room lugging a heavy toy, they might say, "What a strong little boy you are!" But if their daughter comes in carrying the same toy, they might caution, "Be careful of your pretty dress."

The way that parents influence their children most deeply, however, is by example. Children instinctively observe the choices their parents make, the freedoms and pleasures they allow themselves, the talents they develop, the abilities they ignore, and the rules they follow. All of this has a profound effect on children: "This is how to live. This is how to get through life." Whether children accept their parents' model or rebel against it, this early socialization plays a significant role in mate as well.

A child's reaction to society's edicts goes through a number of predictable stages. Typically, the first response is to hide forbidden behaviors from the parents. The child thinks angry thoughts but doesn't speak them out loud. He explores his body in the privacy of his room. He teases his younger sibling when his parents are away. Eventually the child comes to the conclusion that some thoughts and feelings are so unacceptable that they should be eliminated, so he constructs an imaginary parent in his head to police his thoughts and activities, a part of the mind that psychologists call the "superego." Now, whenever the child has a forbidden thought or indulges in an "unacceptable" behavior, he experiences a self-administered jolt of anxiety. This is so unpleasant that the child puts to sleep some of those forbidden parts of himself—in Freudian terms, he represses them. The ultimate price of his obedience is a loss of wholeness.

To fill the void, the child creates a "false self," a character structure that serves a double purpose: it camouflages those parts of his being that he has repressed and protects him from further injury. A child brought up by a sexually repressive, distant mother, for instance, may become a "tough guy." He tells himself, "I don't care if my mother isn't very affectionate. I don't need that mushy stuff. I can make it on my own. And another thing—I think sex is dirty!" Eventually he applies this patterned response to all situations. No matter who tries to get close to him, he erects the same barricade. In later years, when he overcomes his reluctance to getting involved in a love relationship, it is likely that he will criticize his partner for her desire for intimacy and her intact sexuality: "Why do you want so much contact and why are you so obsessed with sex? It's not normal!"

A different child might react to a similar upbringing in an opposite manner, exaggerating his problems in the hope that someone will come to his rescue: "Poor me. I am hurt. I am deeply wounded. I need someone to take care of me." Yet another child might become a hoarder, striving to hold on to every bit of love and food and material goods that comes his way out of the certain knowledge that there is never enough. But, whatever the nature of the false self, its purpose is the same: to minimize the pain of losing part of the child's original, God-given wholeness.

At some point in a child's life, however, this ingenious form of self-protection becomes the cause of further wounding as the child is criticized for having these negative traits. Others condemn him for being distant or needy or self-centered or fat or stingy. His attackers don't see the wound he is trying to protect, and they don't appreciate the clever nature of his defense: all they see is the neurotic side of his personality. He is deemed inferior; he is less than whole.

Now the child is caught in a bind. He needs to hold on to his adaptive character traits, because they serve a useful purpose, but he doesn't want to be rejected. What can he do? The solution is to deny or attack his critics: "I'm not cold and distant," he might say in self-defense, "what I really am is strong and independent." Or "I'm not weak and needy, I'm just sensitive." Or "I'm not greedy and selfish, I'm thrifty and prudent." In other words, "That's not me you're talking about. You're just seeing me in a negative light."

In a sense, he is right. His negative traits are not a part of his original nature. They are forged out of pain and become a part of an assumed identity, an alias that helps him maneuver in a complex and sometimes hostile world. This doesn't mean, however, that he doesn't have these negative traits; there are any number of witnesses who will attest that he does. But in order to maintain a positive self-image and enhance his chances for survival, he has to deny them. These negative traits became what is referred to as the "disowned self," those parts of the false self that are too painful to acknowledge.

Let's stop for a moment and sort out this proliferation of self parts. We have now succeeded in fracturing your original wholeness, the loving and unified nature that you were born with, into three separate entities:

1. Your "lost self," those parts of your being that you had to repress because of the demands of society.

2. Your "false self," the façade that you erected in order to fill the void created by this repression and by a lack of adequate nurturing.

3. Your "disowned self," the negative parts of your false self that met with disapproval and were therefore denied.

The only part of this complex collage that you were routinely aware of was the parts of your original being that were still intact and certain aspects of your false self. Together these elements formed your "personality," the way you would describe yourself to others. Your lost self was almost totally outside your awareness; you had severed nearly all connections with these repressed parts of your being. Your disowned self, the negative parts of your false self, hovered just below your level of awareness and was constantly threatening to emerge. To keep it hidden, you had to deny it actively or project it onto others: "I am *not* self-centered," you would say with great energy. Or "What do you mean, I'm lazy? *You're* lazy."

. . . .

9 · REJECTION AND BETRAYAL

ROBERT M. STEIN

Let us study more closely the mechanisms that are usually set into motion where one has been deeply wounded through a childhood experience of betrayal and disillusionment. The child experiences rejection and betrayal when the transition from the wholeness of the original archetypal situation to the more human personal relationship is missing or inadequate. This occurs, for example, when a mother continues to identify with the archetypal all-protective, all-nourishing Mother role even though other, quite opposite feelings and emotions are coming into her relationship with her child. The child needs to experience a more total picture of her true personality so that he, too, can begin to experience more of his own individuality.

When the mother identifies with the positive Mother archetype, the negative Mother will be strongly constellated in her unconscious. The child, instead of experiencing a transition from the archetypal Mother to the more human mother, with many shadings of feelings and emotions, finds himself caught between two opposing archetypal forces. This abruptly destroys his sense of wholeness, producing a large rent in his own personality, and his experience is one of rejection and betrayal. He resents being thrust out of the containment of the positive mother-child archetypal situation, but at the same time his impulse toward individuation urges him to move on. His choices are limited: either to remain a child or to evoke the wrath of the *absolute* rejecting and demanding Negative Mother. There is nothing in between. He is therefore faced with a dark power which destroys any sense of gratification or accomplishment even if he should move toward the goal of giving form and expression to his own individuality. This is how he has been betrayed.

To the same degree that the Positive Mother accepts and cherishes the child's nature with all its weaknesses and inadequacies, the Negative Mother rejects it and demands that its insufficiencies be overcome. This occurs on a very collective level, however, so that it amounts to a rejection of all that is unique and individual in the child; or all the factors that do not live up to an image the mother may have of how her child should be. The consequence of such an experience is that the child must hide or repress his own uniqueness, and these qualities become incorporated into the shadow. Since the shadow always contains many things which are really unacceptable, repugnant and destructive to others and to society, such contamination of individuality and shadow can be disastrous. The individual then experiences acceptance of the soul and shadow as identical. This makes it extremely difficult for him to establish or maintain a close human connection with anyone. Whenever one begins to get close to such a person, he will invariably do something to make one reject him. We need to try to understand more about this phenomenon since it is so common.

Why does someone suffering from the deep archetypal wound of betrayal seem to continually provoke rejection? It is almost as if something in him is asking for rejection. Such an individual often expresses just this view about himself. For some time I thought this was entirely owing to a fear of closeness, which exposes the old wound to further injury. This certainly made sense until I realized that although the wound may be exposed in the openness of a close human connection, it is the childhood experience of betrayal and rejection which caused the wound in the first place. Therefore, when a person both rejects and provokes rejection, the original wounding situation is repeated. Obviously he does not avoid suffering through these unconscious mechanisms. Let us look for other explanations.

The facts are better understood if they are seen as a consequence of a person's inability to distinguish between shadow and soul. This evokes deep feelings of shame, guilt and fear whenever such an individual enters into a communion with another soul. In other words, there are infantile and regressive elements in the shadow which should have been assimilated and integrated into the total personality, but this has not happened because of the experience of severe rejection by the internalized negative parental archetype. Whenever such a soul-shadow contamination exists, therefore, the individual still feels rejected even though there is a deep acceptance and love for him. He demands that the other person redeem him from the guilt he feels about the truly *unacceptable* and *destructive* aspects of his shadow, which he has not differentiated from the totality of his being. Such shadow elements as infantile demands and dependency needs, infantile or undifferentiated sexuality, greed, brutality, etc., though they belong to the human condition, must be generally contained or they do injury to others. Acceptance of these qualities in another goes along with the love and respect one person has for another's soul, but it does not mean that one is willing to be victimized by the shadow. But this is precisely what is sought by those individuals who provoke rejection. That is, that they should be allowed to give full expression to their shadow, and that they should be loved for the punishment which it inflicts— they feel that only then will they experience true acceptance and love. This throws a somewhat different light on the problem and points to a need to get closer rather than to a fear of being close. To put it another way, there is a deep need to rid oneself of the guilt and fear-provoking elements of the shadow, which is why it is continually being brought into those relationships which offer the possibility of a close human connection.

. . . .

10 · THE UNDERSIDE OF THE
MOTHER-DAUGHTER RELATIONSHIP

KIM   CHERNIN

We have arrived at the underside of the mother-daughter bond, the un-sweetened bitterness of it. To envy one's child, to want what she has, to feel that her having it has been at one's own expense—what a cruel and terrible irony it is to envy her the very opportunities one longed so urgently to give her.

As a mother, I came to an understanding of these women through my own introspection. And therefore I have allowed myself to observe some-thing even more difficult to acknowledge than the secret crisis of the mother's life. For the type of mother-daughter relationship most commonly brought into my consultation room is one in which the mother felt a keen and exas-perating envy of the daughter's opportunity, a resentment of the relative ease with which she seemed able to go off into this new world of opportunity opening around her before her eating problem developed and brought this movement to an end.

A mother's envy of a beloved child: As a mother there are few emotions more difficult to ponder. Naturally, we want the best for our daughters, ev-erything we were ourselves denied, and to this end we sacrifice ourselves un-stintingly. What, then, do we make of this exasperation we feel as we listen to them talk about the "new woman"? What, then, shall we say about this rancor rising in us, sometimes undeniably, when we overhear them gossiping about the future, planning to have three children and travel all over the world and become a painter and make a fortune on the stock market besides? And do we have to suppress a bitter laugh, a knowing sigh, a shake of the head that says of course we've heard it all before? A mother's envy.

Typically, the mother of the women who came to speak with me had known the possibilities of choice in her own life. She had received education, often higher education, and had frequently begun a career. She had chosen to renounce these as part of the self-sacrifice that seems to go along with moth-ering but was never able fully to embrace the sacrifice. She felt envy of her daughter, and she felt resentment.

This anger about sacrificing oneself for one's child is apparent also in women who attempt to combine career or vocation with maternity. Then, of course, the question becomes a matter of daily, repeated choices that call up uncertainty and anguish and rage. Whether to let the child watch television so that one can draw or paint. Whether to serve frozen spinach because it will not require washing and will therefore leave one free for that extra ten minutes of contemplation and absorption. Whether to leave her an hour or two longer at the kindergarten so that one can take a class. Sometimes one decides it one way, sometimes the other. One starts to meditate but then jumps to one's feet and rushes off late to pick up the child right after school, after all.

As daughters, we always knew about our mother's resentment, however heroically the older woman tried to disguise her trouble. And yet, for the mother's sake, the daughter doesn't want to know. She saw that her mother kept trying and failing; she heard her insist that it was woman's highest good to make sacrifices for her family. She listened to her deny in the next breath that what she was doing was a sacrifice. She saw her spend an entire day baking sourdough Swedish rye of the sort her grandmother used to bake. She felt the urgency with which the older woman looked around the table, watching her children's faces, trying to justify through their responses the day's expenditure of energy. She noticed the way the bowls of yeast and flour sat in the sink for a long time after that day, as if her mother could not bring herself to wash them out and put them away. It was the eldest daughter who washed them out and put them away, the same woman who a few years later began to starve herself. For she knew that the battle with the bread rising, on top of everything else, had enraged her mother.

She watched her mother go back and forth in the grocery store between the frozen food section and the fresh vegetables. She saw her pick up a package of frozen spinach, smiling with a strained expression as she told the daughter, who was still only a child, that this time it would be all right, did it matter if they had frozen food this one time for dinner? The daughters watched her suddenly turn and rush back over to the frozen foods and put the spinach away as if it were a filthy object. She followed her over to the vegetable counter, saw her mother pick up the fresh spinach and look tired suddenly, and sullen, and glance at her watch and put the spinach in the basket and then put it back on the counter. She went trooping behind her mother to the frozen foods, where again the mother picked up the package of frozen spinach and turned, says her daughter, with a "wild and hunted look." And so it went, back and forth, both of them trying to laugh at it, trying to pretend it was a game, this anguished journey from maternal obligation to free choice, through which the older woman was expressing her uncertainty and resentment about her role. The daughter remembers how her mother finally brought home the fresh spinach, which wilted in the refrigerator and was never cooked. She remembers knowing about her mother's anger from the way food was bought and stored and prepared.

As an adult, the daughter interprets. She says that her mother could no longer accept the limitations of her life. She acknowledges that her mother resented motherhood bitterly, often sabotaged it, felt envy of the daughter for being able to make other choices, was often competitive with her, and was in the end always defeated by her own ambivalence. And because the older woman was so deeply ashamed of these feelings, she often did not know she felt them at all, although the daughter sensed them.

Daughters raised in an atmosphere of mystification and ambivalence of this sort will inevitably be troubled as they go off into their own lives. They will be faced with a terrible inner division as they try to assure themselves that their mother was happy with the sacrifices she made for her daughter's sake, while at the same time they are telling themselves there was no sacrifice. Desperately, the daughter tries to banish her own anger and sense of emotional deprivation as she assures herself that there was no reason to feel deprived. And meanwhile these questions about her mother she dare not raise; this rage at the mother for having betrayed the female potential for development; this sense of infinite trouble that exists between mothers and daughters; these feelings she dare not acknowledge, all make it impossible for her to separate from the older woman, to go off into her own life and leave her behind. She stops, faltering before the possibilities of her own development, as she attempts frantically to unravel this complex knot that binds her energies and her ambitions.

This issue of surpassing the mother is not a simple question of doing with one's own life what the mother has not done. Rather, it is a matter of doing what the mother herself might have yearned to do and did not accomplish because of personal choice. If economic necessity or the belief in the unavoidable destiny of women shaped the mother's life, she would have had powerful aid in subduing her discontent and unhappiness with the institution of motherhood. But if the mother had alternatives and chose, nevertheless, to sacrifice herself for her daughter's sake; if she continued to feel ambivalent about this choice, yearning still for a life she did not have; if she convinced herself, now that the children had come, she could not have other forms of personal satisfaction and fulfillment, although she had already begun to doubt whether this was true; if her life continued to seethe with unacknowledged envy and resentment and muted yearning—then would her life raise for her daughter this problem of surpassing the mother that rests, I believe, at the heart of an eating problem. A daughter faces the issue of surpassing the mother when the older woman is no longer able to accept her oppression as inevitable or to efface herself as a persona and to live vicariously through her child. For then the daughter, if she seeks her own development, faces two intolerable possibilities. Suddenly, in coming of age and entering the world, she is in danger of calling up the older woman's envy and resentment. And even worse, more painful and disturbing to consider, she is now in a position to remind her mother of her own failure and lack.

Who, then, is there to blame? The wounded mother, who was once a daughter? The angry daughter, who may one day, as a mother herself, become the target of her own daughter's reproach?

We must progress beyond this tendency to blame the mothers. And we must at the same time become conscious of our anger and frustration, the sense of abandonment we have all known at times, daughters of women in crisis like ourselves. And then, having lived through the shock of acknowledging our rage at the mother, we must learn how to place it in a social context, taking the personal mother out of the home and setting her in that precise historic moment in which she gave birth to a child.

Most women manage to keep their breakdown and crisis hidden so long as they remain at home and persevere in the increasingly futile struggle to make a sacrifice of themselves to marriage and maternity. The underlying crisis, however, breaks through and becomes conspicuous as soon as a woman steps out to take advantage of those social opportunities made available in our time. Thus, a woman of any age becomes a modern mother, a woman in serious if hidden crisis, when she cannot efface and sacrifice and live through her children. But the same woman, at any age, becomes a daughter with an eating disorder the moment she steps out to seek her own development and must pause to brood upon her mother's life.

An eating disorder can be resolved only within this largest cultural context, which allows us to rage because of how terribly we have been mothered but including now in this rage our mothers as daughters with a right to their own despair. Then we shall have liberated an anger that indicts not the mothers but a social system that has never ceased to suppress women. And we shall be able finally to set free from the tangled knot of self-destruction and obsession the radical and healing knowledge that an eating disorder is a profoundly political act.

I am describing generations of women who suffer guilt: women who cannot mother their daughters because their legitimate dreams and ambitions have not been recognized; mothers who know they have failed and cannot forgive themselves for their failure; daughters who blame themselves for needing more than the mother was able to provide, who saw and experienced the full extent of the older woman's crisis, who cannot let themselves feel rage at their mother because they know how much she needs them to forgive her.

And what becomes of all this guilt felt by the daughters? How does it come to expression? Where do we find it breaking out in a disguised and symptomatic form?

But of course we know. We have by now the answer to this question, we know how the daughters of our time are turning against themselves. We have seen the way they break down at the moment they might prosper and develop; we have observed the way they torture themselves with starvation and make their bodies their enemies, the way they attack their female flesh. This futile attack upon the female body, through which we are attempting to free ourselves from the limitations of the female role, hides a bitter warfare against the mother. The characteristic traits of an eating disorder speak to us about the guilt we feel and the hidden anger we cannot express. For what is it a woman is likely to attack if she cannot directly express her anger toward her mother? Isn't she likely, in turning this anger against herself, to direct it toward the female body she shares with her mother? In a stunning act of symbolic substitution, the daughter aims her mother-rage at her own body, so like the one which fed her and through which she learned to know the mother during the first moments of her existence.

But the female body is not the problem here. It is the guilt and anguish derived from this symbolic attack against the mother that entraps the daughter's development. Hoping to master her rage, anxiety, and sense of loss at separating from the mother by directing these feelings toward her own female flesh, the woman coming of age today involves herself in an intensified act of self-destruction at the very moment she is seeking to evolve a new sense of self. This is the tragic paradox the new woman must resolve.

. . . .

11 · PARENTING AND YOUR CHILD'S SHADOW

JOHN A. SANFORD

It is certain that there will be the figure of the Shadow in our personality. In order to develop a conscious personality at all we must identify with something, and this means the inevitable exclusion of its opposite. It is important that children identify with the proper psychological attributes in the process of growing up, and not identify with the Shadow, for if there is too great an identification with the Shadow, the ego, so to speak, has a "crook" in it or a fatal flaw. Individuation and wholeness are only possible when the conscious personality has a certain moral attitude. If people are overly identified with their cheating, dishonest or violent side, and have no guilt or self-reflection, wholeness cannot emerge.

Helping children to develop correctly in this regard, however, is not a simple matter. Here moralistic preaching on the part of parents, Church, society, etc., is often ineffectual or even damaging. Of much more importance is the kind of life that the parents are actually leading, and the degree of psychological honesty they have. Moralistic preaching from hypocritical parents is worse than useless. Of even more fundamental importance to the development of the Shadow and the eventual working out of the problem of the Shadow is the "bonding" that must take place between parents and children. Early in a child's life he or she needs to be bonded by love to the mother and/or father, or to an appropriate mother or father substitute. In this way the necessary foundation is laid for a moral life, since the moral life, in the last analysis, comes down to a person's relatedness to people and a capacity for human feeling. In some children this bonding never takes place, and then the necessary emotional defenses against the darkest side of the Shadow are nonexistent or weak. This can lead to the development of criminal or sociopathic personalities, that is, to an identification of the ego with the Shadow.

But at the same time that parents encourage children to identify with their more positive characteristics, encouraging them to be honest, to have a certain regard for other people, and so forth, the parents must not split the child off too much from their dark side. For the Shadow is never more dangerous than when the conscious personality has lost touch with it. Take the case of anger. Of course children cannot be allowed to give way to angry impulses in ways that are destructive to others. At the same time, it is a loss to them if they lose touch entirely with anger, since anger, as we have seen, is often a healthy response. If a parent says, "You are a bad child to be angry at your sister," there is the danger that a sensitive child may repress his or her anger in order to win the parent's approval. This results in a split in the personality and a shadow personality that is autonomous and therefore dangerous, not to mention the loss of contact with the vital energy that anger provides. This is especially destructive if the parents allow *themselves* to be angry, but not the child. "I am allowed to get angry, but you are not," is often the *de facto* attitude that parents express. So the parent has a narrow path to tread. Perhaps when the child becomes furious with his or her sister the attitude must be something like, "It is understandable that you get angry at your sister, but you cannot throw rocks at her." This encourages the child to develop the necessary restraints on the more violent instincts and affects, without cutting him off from his dark side.

Because it is inevitable that we have a shadow personality, the Shadow is called an archetype. To say something is an archetype means it is an essential building block of the personality. Or, to use the word in its adjective form, to say that something is "archetypal" means that it is "typical" for all human beings. So it is typical for all human beings that as they develop a conscious personality there will also be its dark companion, the Shadow. Because the Shadow is an archetype, it has often been represented in myths, fairy tales, and great literature. One example of the latter is Robert Louis Stevenson's novelette *Dr. Jekyll and Mr. Hyde.*

It is also important that parents not punish children with rejection. Perhaps the best punishment parents can administer to children is that which is swift, and when it is over, it is over. The worst is certainly the withholding of affection and approval in order to control their behaviour. When that happens children get the message that they are bad; moreover, they are responsible for mother's or father's ill-humor, and this leads to feelings of guilt and self-rejection. To cope with such parents some children may then try desperately to conform to parent-pleasing forms of behaviour, which will result in a further splitting off of the Shadow.

If parents are to deal successfully with the shadow personality of a child, they need to accept and be in touch with their own Shadows. Parents who have difficulty accepting their own negative feelings and less than noble reactions will find it difficult to have a creative acceptance of the child's dark side. Notice, however, that by acceptance I do not mean permissiveness. It does not help a child to have parents who are permissive toward all kinds of behaviour. There are forms of behaviour that are not acceptable in human society and children have to learn this and have to establish their capacity to control these forms of behaviour from within. In a permissive atmosphere a child's capacity to develop his or her own behaviour monitoring system is blunted. The ego development will then be too weak to enable the child as an adult to cope with the Shadow.

It can be seen that being a parent calls for unusual finesse, consciousness, patience, and wisdom if the problem of the Shadow is to be dealt with creatively. One cannot go too far in the direction of permissiveness nor in the direction of being overly strict. The key throughout is the parents' own consciousness of their Shadow problem and their capacity to accept themselves, and, at the same time, to develop their own ego strength so they can cope with their own affects. Family life in general, and being a parent in particular, is a crucible in which the shadow problem can be met and worked upon, for in family life negative feelings are certain to be constellated. For instance, at times a parent will inevitably have negative feelings toward a child—when the child misbehaves, or is annoying, or interferes with the parents' independent life, or requires too much of a sacrifice of money, time, or energy. Under the duress of family life people are certain to experience divisions within themselves. Love for a child may be contradicted by at least a momentary hatred; a sincere desire to do the best for the child may be contradicted by powerful feelings of anger or rejection. In this way we experience what divided people we are and this self-confrontation generates psychological consciousness. In this lies one great value of the shadow personality: a confrontation with the Shadow is essential for the development of self-awareness.

. . . .

Only he whose bright lyre
has sounded in shadows
may, looking onward, restore
his infinite praise.

Only he who has eaten
poppies with the dead
will not lose ever again
the gentlest chord.

Though the image upon the pool
often grows dim:
Know and be still.

Inside the Double World
all voices become
eternally mild.

RAINER MARIA RILKE
The Sonnets to Orpheus

. . . .

PART 3

SHADOW-BOXING: THE DANCE OF ENVY, ANGER, AND DECEIT

Where love rules, there is no will to power; and where power predominates, there love is lacking. The one is the shadow of the other.

C. G. JUNG

Our shadow personality is often obvious to others, but unknown to us. Much greater is our ignorance of the masculine or feminine components within us. . . . For this reason Jung termed the integration of the shadow the "apprentice-piece" of becoming whole, and the integration of the anima or animus the "master-piece."

JOHN A. SANFORD

[Hate] has a lot in common with love, chiefly with that self-transcending aspect of love, the fixation on others, the dependence on them and in fact the delegation of a piece of one's own identity to them. . . . The hater longs for the object of his hatred.

VÁCLAV HAVEL

INTRODUCTION

. . . .

The deep bonds we feel for our same-sex siblings and intimate friends hold as deep a mystery as the bonds we feel for our opposite-sex fantasy lovers. Sister to sister, brother to brother, we see ourselves in a mirror reflection that reveals both a profound identity and a profound difference. Whether linked by blood or spirit, we can view in one another both shadow and self.

In many families, two sisters will appear to develop as opposites, like the two poles of one magnet. In *The Pregnant Virgin,* Jungian analyst Marion Woodman calls them "dream sisters." Like the mythological sisters Eve and Lilith, Psyche and Orual, or Inanna and Ereshkigal, each holds the counterpoint to the other's gifts: one is often drawn to the world of matter, nature, and food; the other is drawn to the world of spirit, culture, and mind. Forever separate, forever bound, in life these pairs often are torn apart by intense envy, jealousy, competition, and misunderstanding.

The theme of brothers or other male pairs who are superficially opposite yet complementarily linked also appears again and again: Cain and Abel, Jesus and Judas, Othello and Iago, Prospero and Caliban. In each pair, the dance between ego and shadow shifts so that as one appears, the other recedes. If for a crucial moment one sees the other man as shadow/enemy, that brother may die at his twin's hand. But in that same moment, a part of the murderer's self dies as well.

The key to healing these turbulent relationships is shadow-work. When a woman, who is very unlike her sister, asks herself in a difficult situation, "What would my sister do?" she calls on her invisible, undeveloped skills, which are visible in the other. When a man is able to value and integrate a trait in another man that is unfamiliar to him—wildness, quietness, or sensuality—he, too, enlarges his sense of self by including more of the other.

In our opposite-sex relationships, too, we are often troubled when meeting our own opposites. We fall in love with people who are as different from us as could be—passive and aggressive, introverted and extroverted, religious and atheistic, verbal and nonverbal. It's as if we are attracted to our intimate others because they have what we need. They can live out those qualities or aptitudes that remain latent within us: a shy woman permits her husband to speak for her; an uncreative man allows his wife's creativity to give him pleasure by association.

Perhaps this saying is true: If we don't develop it, we'll marry it. If we don't integrate our own anger, rigidity, thinking capacity, or emotional depth, we will be drawn to people who can compensate for those weaknesses and inferiorities, and we will risk never developing them ourselves.

This marriage of opposites happens frequently in our society for a cultural reason as well: the stated ego ideal of men—to be rational, dominant, unfeeling, and goal-oriented—is the shadow side of the ego-ideal of women—to be emotional, submissive, nurturing, and process-oriented. As a result, the shadow and the lover may share the same qualities.

Jungian analyst and astrologer Liz Greene explains: "That highly spiritualized, refined, ethical man may have a very primitive shadow, and he may also have a tendency to fall in love with very primitive women." However, Greene points out, when he encounters those qualities in shadow figures of his own sex, he will hate them. As a result, she says, "You get that curious dichotomy of idealizing and loathing the same thing."

Even though male-female stereotypes seem to be rapidly breaking down as we gain more social and economic options, the unconscious still has to catch up with the outer world. Imbalanced growth by a member of either gender can still lead us to complete ourselves by projecting and marrying our opposites.

This also explains why, at a later stage in a relationship, we may react with discomfort as our projections rattle and we discover our disowned selves in the beloved—and try to defend against our own forbidden impulses expressed by the other person. Anger, envy, and deceit often result. Without shadow-work, this distress may lead to a painful separation; with it, our discomfort may bring the rewards of a deeper self-awareness. James Baldwin expressed this poetically when he said.

> *One can only face in others*
> *What one can face in oneself.*

Any argument can be taken too far, of course, and end in oversimplification. There are those who would say that everything is projection and, therefore, that shadow-work in the inner world, taking responsibility for our own negative feelings, is all that we need do. However, we suggest that there are occasions for outrage that are real, valid reasons for negative feelings. Rape, murder, and genocide justify our rage and justify, too, social action that is liberated by that rage. In our personal relationships, the purpose of shadow-work is not to invalidate the inevitable negative thoughts and feelings that arise; rather, it seeks to shed light on what is projection, which we have a hand in creating and therefore in healing, and what is in the other person that is separate and may call forth a valid negative response.

This section explores shadow-boxing in adult relationships. In a piece from *Psyche's Sisters,* Christine Downing, a professor of religion and Jungian-style writer, explores the archetypes of brother and sister, which are typically neglected by psychology with its focus on parent-child issues and romantic love.

Chapter 13 is an excerpt from *The Survival Papers,* a book on midlife by Daryl Sharp, Toronto Jungian analyst and publisher of Inner City Books. He describes an encounter with a male friend/brother that exposed him to his own shadow qualities. After several years, the friends noticed that they had changed places, each becoming more like the other once had been.

With a reprint from the best-selling book *Intimate Partners,* we make the transition to opposite-sex relationships. Maggie Scarf describes a husband and wife who are caught in the trap of projective identification, each carrying the disowned aspects of the other spouse's self. Scarf explores the tension created by the initial attraction to these novel, unfamiliar traits and the later aversion, which causes crisis in many marriages.

Los Angeles columnist Michael Ventura, in a piece from *Shadow Dancing in the USA,* tells of meeting his own "horrors" as they emerged from the closet during his marriage. In a lighthearted way, Ventura exposes a very serious issue: In the safety of marriage, our demons may rear their ugly heads.

Any intimate relationship can serve as an excellent container for shadow-work, in which the fires of love can burn through the stuck places, open up the dark places, and introduce us to ourselves.

. . . .

12 · SISTERS AND BROTHERS CASTING SHADOWS

C H R I S T I N E   D O W N I N G

For a woman the sister is the other most like ourselves of any creature in the world. She is of the same gender and generation, of the same biological and social heritage. We have the same parents; we grew up in the same family, were exposed to the same values, assumptions, patterns of interaction.

The sibling relationship is among the most enduring of all human ties, beginning with birth and ending only with the death of one of the siblings. Although our culture seems to allow us the freedom to leave sibling relationships behind, to walk away from them, we tend to return to them in moments of celebration—marriages and births—as well as at times of crisis—divorces and deaths. At such moments we often discover to our surprise how quickly the patterns of childhood interaction and the intensity of childhood resentment and appreciation reappear.

Yet this other so like myself is, ineluctably, *other.* She, more than any other, serves as the one against whom I define myself. (Research suggests that children are aware of the distinct otherness of siblings well before they have fully separated from the mother.) Likeness and difference, intimacy and otherness—neither can be overcome. That paradox, that tension, lies at the very heart of the relationship.

Same-sex siblings seem to be for one another, paradoxically, both ideal self and what Jung calls "shadow." They are engaged in a uniquely reciprocal, mutual process of self-definition. Although daughters create mothers as much as mothers create daughters, the relationship is not symmetrical as the one between sisters is. Of course, even between sisters there is some asymmetry, some hierarchy; birth order, relative age, does make a difference. But unlike the overwhelming, somehow sacred difference that separates mother and infant child, the differences between sisters are subtle, relative, on a profane scale. The differences between siblings can be negotiated, worked on, redefined by the siblings themselves. The work of mutual self-definition seems typically to proceed by way of polarization that half-consciously exaggerates perceived differences and divides up attributes between the sisters ("I'm the bright one, and she's the pretty one"). Often, too, sisters seem to divide up their parents between them ("I'm Daddy's girl, and you're Mommy's"). I am who she is not. She is both what I would most aspire to be but feel I never can be *and* what I am most proud *not* to be but fearful of becoming.

The sister is different from even the closest peer friend (though such a friend may often serve as a sister surrogate), for sisterhood is an ascribed not chosen relationship. We are stuck with our particular sister as we never are with a friend. John Bowlby says that the most important thing about siblings is their *familiarity*—siblings easily become secondary attachment figures to whom we turn when tired, hungry, ill, alarmed, or insecure. Siblings may also serve as playmates, but the role is different: we seek out a playmate when in good spirits and confident and what we want is, precisely, play. The relationship to a sibling is permanent, lifelong, one from which it is almost impossible entirely to disengage. (One can divorce a mate much more finally than a sibling.) Because that permanence helps make it the safest relationship in which to express hostility and aggression (safer than with our parents because we are never so dependent on a sibling as we are in infancy—and in imagination always—on our mother and father), the bond between same-sex siblings is very likely the most stressful, volatile, ambivalent one we will ever know.

I have discovered that the longing for relationship with the sister is felt even by women without biological sisters, and that all of us search for "her" in many surrogates throughout our lives.

The Sister and the Brother are what Jung would call archetypes, as present in our psychic life irrespective of literal experience as are the Mother or the Father. Like all archetypes the Sister keeps reappearing in projected or "transference" form and has an inner aspect. Sorting through the meaning of sisterhood in our lives requires attending to all three modes: that of the literal sister(s), the surrogate sisters, and the sister within, the archetype.

I am who she is not. The inner sister—my ideal self and shadow self as strangely one—figures so significantly in the process of individuation that she is there whether I have a literal sister or not. Yet like all archetypes she demands actualization and particularization, demands to be brought into the outer world of distinct images. When there is no actual sister, there seem always to be imaginary sisters or surrogate sisters. Even when there is an actual sister, there are often fantasy figures or substitutes, as if the real sister were not quite adequate fully to carry the archetype, and yet the archetype needed nevertheless to be imagined, personified. The Sister appears with the particular face of a friend or a dream figure, of a character in a novel or a mythological heroine.

That the Sister is indeed one of those primal fantasies that Freud saw as active in our psychic life independent of historical experience has been confirmed for me by how frequently unsistered women have come to the workshops on sisters that I have led, knowing they, too, needed to work on the meaning of this relationship in their lives. The first time this happened, I wondered: "What do I have to say to them? What do I know of what it is like never to have had a biological sister?" Then I remembered: "Probably quite a bit." For I have a mother who was an only child and a daughter who has only brothers. My mother has told me how ardently she looked forward to my growing up, so that she might at last have a sister, and I know that as subtle counterpoint to the mother-daughter bond that relates me to my daughter there is a sister-sister one.

I realize also how my mother's understanding of sisterhood is colored by her not having had a sister as a child. She idealizes the relationship; she sees as sisterly only our intimacy, not our rivalry; nor could she see anything of value in the stressful moments of interaction between my sister and myself when we were young. For over fifty years the encounters between her and her sister-in-law have been contaminated by a mutually obsessive jealousy, yet it would not occur to her that theirs is a sisterly relationship. My daughter's lack of a biological sister shows differently: since she grew up with brothers, men carry little mystery for her; she turns to women as lovers—and as sisters.

To call the Sister an archetype helps express my sense that there is a transpersonal, extrarational, *religious* dimension to sisterhood that endows all the actual figures upon whom we "transfer" the archetype with a numinously daemonic or divine aura. Yet I do not mean that there exists some universal, ahistorical essence of sisterhood. The trigger for an archetype is always particular experience; the degree to which such experiences are shared, recurrent, evocative of similar responses, is always to be explored not assumed. I have also been deeply impressed by Freud's observation that though we have made something sacred of parent-child love we have left that between brothers and sisters profane. I, too, experience the Sister archetype as less overwhelmingly numinous than that of the Mother. The Sister's sanctity is somehow commensurate with that which characterizes my own soul; she is woman not goddess. The engagement with mortal Psyche occurs in a different dimension from the one with Persephone, the goddess with whom I began my search of Her.

The shadow is relevant to our interest in siblings because Jung says that in myth and literature and in our dreams the shadow is most often represented as a brother. Jung is especially fascinated by what he calls "the motif of the two hostile brothers," a motif that he sees as emblematic of all antitheses, especially of the two opposite approaches to grappling with the powerful influence of the unconcious: denial or acceptance, literalism or mysticism. Consideration of the motif almost always leads Jung to the two brothers in E. T. A. Hoffman's tale *The Devil's Elixir*. Jung's interpretation of the tale shows that the protagonist's denial and dread of his malicious and sinister brother leads to rigidity and narrow-mindedness, to a violent inflexibility, the one-dimensionality of a "man without a shadow."[1]

Jung believes that the primary task for males at mid-life is often learning how to reconnect with this brother figure. The apparent impossibility stimulates regression back to childhood, but because the means that worked then are of no avail, the regression continues beyond even early infancy into the legacy of ancestral life. Then mythological images, archetypes, are awakened, and an interior spiritual world whose existence was entirely unsuspected reveals itself. The confrontation with the archetypal shadow is like a primordial experience of the non-ego, and engagement with an interior opponent who throws down a challenge that initiates us into the labor of coming to terms with the unconscious.

Yet Jung's deepest reflections on the inner meaning of brotherhood are inspired not by antagonistic brothers but by the Greek Dioscuri, the twin brothers, one mortal, the other immortal, so devoted to one another they are unwilling to be separated even in death. In his essay on the rebirth archetype Jung writes:

> We are that pair of Dioscuri, one of whom is mortal and the other immortal, and who, though always together can never be made completely one. . . . We should prefer to be always "I" and nothing else. But we are confronted with that inner friend or foe, and whether he is our friend or foe depends on ourselves.

Jung sees in the mythological representations of friendship between two men an outer reflection of a relationship to that inner friend of the soul into whom Nature would like to change us—that other person who we are and yet can never completely become, that larger and greater personality maturing within us, the Self.[2]

As we reflect on this inner same-sex figure who may be either positive or negative, who is shadow or Self, it becomes evident that Jung's conception of the inner brother has much in common with the figure that Otto Rank calls the "Double." In his early work *The Myth of the Birth of the Hero,* as in his later voluminous study of the incest motif in myth and literature, Rank explored the importance of the hostile brother motif as a recurrent mythological and literary theme. Often the brothers are twins, and often one must die to assure the other's life. In his later writings Rank subsumes this motif under that of the Double. The brother is now seen as primarily an inner figure, an alter ego. The Double may represent either the mortal or the immortal self, may be feared as image of one's mortality or prized as signifying one's imperishability. The Double is Death or the Immortal Soul. It inspires fear and love, arouses the "eternal conflict" between our "need for likeness and desire for difference." The Double answers to the need for a mirror, a shadow, a reflection. It seems to take on an independent life but is so intimately bound to the hero's vital being that misfortune befalls him if he tries to detach himself too completely from it.

Rank reminds us that the primitive "considers the shadow his mysterious double, a spiritual yet real being" and that the Greek name for such a shadowlike double—for that aspect of the self which survives in death and which is active in dreams when the conscious ego has withdrawn—was *psyche.* Thus for Rank the relationship to an inner same-sex sibling, to a double, comes to signify relationship to one's unconscious self, one's psyche, and to both death and immortality. At its deepest it expresses our longing to let the ego die and to be united with a transcendent self. It signifies our longing for surrender to something larger than ego.

The image of sibling love represents our urge to move "beyond psychology." The first phase of psychic life proceeds by way of differentiation, often manifesting as hostility, but the second phase is accomplished through surrender and love. Yet Rank warns of the danger of taking this literally, externally. No human other, spouse or sibling, can bear the burden of playing the role of alter ego for another. "This reaching out for something bigger . . . originates in the individual's need for expansion beyond the realm of his self, . . . for some kind of 'beyond' . . . to which he can submit." But there is nothing in reality that "can carry the weight of this expansion." It is enormously difficult "to realize that there exists a difference between one's spiritual and one's purely human needs, and that the satisfaction or fulfillment for each has to be found in different spheres." The false personalizing of the need to be loved inevitably precipitates despair and the feeling of irredeemable inferiority. Rank hopes to help us recognize that the image of the complementing, completing double is a symbol that no human other can incarnate for us; we need to understand it religiously; to see it as embodying our dual need for differentiation and likeness, for individuality and connection, for natural life and immortality. His reflection on the sibling motif takes him "beyond psychology."[3]

At times Jung's conception of the shadow is equally profound; at other times he writes as though from the ego's perspective and sees the shadow as a negative figure, as embodiment simply of the devalued and denied aspects of our personal history that we must reintegrate before we are ready for the real work of individuation, which proceeds through engagement with the contrasexual archetypes. The last stage of the journey to psychological wholeness, as Jung describes it, again involves an archetype that appears as a same-sex figure, the Self. The model, when presented in this linear form, radically separates the engagements with the two inner same-sex figures, the shadow and the Self—one belongs to the beginning of the journey, the other to its end. The inner bond between shadow and Self is thus often obscured. The numinosity and ambivalence inherent in the same-sex figure are what we would expect if we simply spoke of him as our inner brother.

. . . .

13 · MY BROTHER/MYSELF

DARYL   SHARP

Being alone that night, my mind went back to the time with Arnold in Zurich. I learned almost as much about typology from living with him as I did from reading Jung.

Arnold was a raving intuitive. I met him at the station when he arrived. It was the third train I'd met. True to his type, his letter wasn't specific. True to mine, I was.

"I've rented a house in the country," I told him, hefting his bag. The lock was broken and the straps were gone. One wheel was missing. "Twelve and a half minutes on the train and it's never late. The house has green shutters and polka-dot wallpaper. The landlady is a sweetheart, we can furnish it the way we want."

"Great," said Arnold, holding a newspaper over his head. It was pouring out. He had no hat and he'd forgotten to bring his raincoat. He was wearing slippers, for god's sake. We couldn't find his trunk because he'd booked it through to Lucerne.

"Lucerne, Zurich, it's all Switzerland to me," he said philosophically.

It was quite amusing at first. At that time we didn't know each other very well. I didn't know what was in store. I'd never been close to anyone quite so . . . well, so *different*.

Time meant nothing to Arnold. He missed trains, he missed appointments. He was always late for class, and when he finally found the right room he didn't have anything to write with. He either had bags of money or none at all, because he didn't budget. He didn't know east from west, he got lost whenever he left the house. And sometimes in it.

"You need a seeing-eye dog," I joked.

"Not as long as you're around," he grinned.

He left the stove on overnight. He never turned out lights. Pots boiled over, meat turned black, while he sat on the porch watching the sky. The kitchen was forever filled with the smell of burnt toast. He lost his keys, his wallet, his lecture notes, his passport. He never had a clean shirt. In his old leather jacket, baggy jeans and two different socks he looked like a bum.

His room was always a mess, like a hurricane had hit.

"It drives me crazy just to look at you," I hummed, adjusting my tie in the mirror.

I liked to be neatly turned out, it made me feel good. I knew precisely where everything was. My desk was ordered, my room was always tidy. I turned out the lights when I left the house and I had an excellent sense of direction. I didn't lose anything and I was always on time. I could cook and I could sew. I knew exactly how much money was in my pocket. Nothing escaped me, I remembered all the details.

"You don't live in the real world," I observed, as Arnold set out to fry an egg. A real hero's journey. He couldn't find the frying pan and when he did he put it on the wrong burner.

"Reality as *you* know it," he said, quite hurt. "Damn!" he cursed. He'd burnt himself again.

I struggled to appreciate Arnold. I wanted to. His outgoing nature, his natural ebullience were charming. I admired his air of careless confidence. He was the life of every party. He easily adapted to new situations. He was a lot more adventurous than I was. Everywhere we went he made friends. And then brought them home.

He had an uncanny sense of perception. Whenever I got in a rut, bogged down in routine, he had something new to suggest. His mind was fertile; it seethed with plans and new ideas. His hunches were usually right. It was like he had a sixth sense, while I was restricted to the usual five. My vision was mundane—where I saw a "thing" or a "person," Arnold saw its soul.

But problems constantly arose between us. When he expressed an intention to do something I took him at his word. I believed he meant what he said, that he would do what he announced he was going to. This was particularly annoying whenever he failed to turn up at a certain time and place. It happened quite often.

"Look," I'd say, "I counted on you being there. I bought the tickets. Where were you?"

"I got waylaid," he'd counter defensively, "something else turned up, I couldn't resist."

"You're unstable, I can't depend on you. You're superficial and you're flighty. Why, you don't have a standpoint at all."

That isn't how Arnold saw it.

"I only express possibilities," he said, when for about the tenth time I accused him of being irresponsible, or at least misleading me. "They aren't real until I say them, and when I do they take on some shape. But that doesn't mean I'll follow up on them. Something better might occur to me. I'm not tied to what I say. I can't help it if you take everything so literally."

He went on: "Intuitions are like birds circling in my head. They come and they go. I may not go with them, I never know, but I need time to authenticate their flight."

One morning I got up to find yet another pot boiled empty on a hot burner. Arnold struggled out of bed, looking for his glasses.

"Have you seen my razor?" he called.

"God damn it!" I shouted, furious, grabbing an oven mitt, "one day you'll burn down the house. We'll both be cinders. 'Alas,' they'll say, scooping our remains into little jars to send back to our loved ones, 'they had such potential. Too bad one of them was such a a klutz!' "

Arnold shuffled into the kitchen as I threw the pot out the door.

"Oh yeah?" he said. "You made dinner last night for Cynthia. I wasn't even here."

It was true. My face got red. My balloon had been pricked. Reality as I knew it just got bigger.

"I'm sorry," I said meekly. "I forgot."

Arnold clapped his hands and danced around the room. "Join the human race!" he sang. As usual, he couldn't hold a note.

It was not until then that I realized Arnold was my shadow. This was a new revelation. It shouldn't have been—we had already established that our complexes were radically different—but it did, it struck me like a thunderbolt. I said as much to Arnold.

"Never mind," he said. "You're my shadow as well. That's why you drive me up the wall."

We embraced. I think that incident saved our relationship.

All that was a long time ago. In the intervening years I've become more like Arnold. And he, indeed, more like me. He can tell left from right now, and he actually learned to crochet. His attention to detail is often sharper than mine. He lives alone and has a magnificent garden. He knows the names of all the flowers, in Latin.

Meanwhile, I have dinner parties and sometimes I haunt the bars till dawn. I misplace precious papers. I forget names and telephone numbers. I can no longer find my way around a strange city. I pursue possibilities while things pile up around me. If I didn't have a cleaning lady I'd soon be overwhelmed by dirt.

Such developments are the unexpected consequences of getting to know your shadow and including it in your life. Once this process is underway it's difficult to stop. You can never go back to what you were, but what you lose on the roundabouts you make up on the swings. You lose something of what you've been, but you add a dimension that wasn't there before. Where you were one-sided, you find a balance. You learn to appreciate those who function differently and you develop a new attitude toward yourself.

I see Arnold from time to time. We are still shadow brothers, but now the tables are somewhat turned.

I tell him about my latest escapade. He shakes his head. "You damn gadabout," he says, punching my shoulder.

Arnold describes quiet evenings by the fire with a few intimate friends and says he never wants to travel again. This man, this great oaf, who as I used to know him would be off and running at the drop of a hat. "You're dull and predictable," I remark, cuffing him.

. . . .

14 · MEETING OUR OPPOSITES IN HUSBANDS AND WIVES

MAGGIE SCARF

It is a fact of marital reality, well known to experts in the field, that those qualities cited by intimate partners as having first attracted them to each other are usually *the same ones that are identified as sources of conflict* later on in the relationship. The "attractive" qualities have, in time, been relabeled; they have beome the bad, difficult things about the partner, the aspects of his or her personality and behavior that are viewed as problematical and negative.

The man who was, for example, attracted by the warmth, empathy and easy sociability of his spouse may at some future point redefine these same attributes as "loudness," "intrusiveness," and a way of relating to others that is "shallow." The woman who initially valued a man for his reliability, predictability and the sense of security he offered her, may—farther down the line—condemn these same qualities as dull, boring and constricting. Thus it is that the admirable, wonderful traits of the partner become the awful, terrible things that one wishes one had realized in time! Although they are, throughout, *identical* qualities, earlier and later on in the relationship they go under different names.

What is most attractive about the partner is often what is also most charged with feelings of ambivalence. That is why my conversations with couples always started out in the same way that my interview with the Bretts, seated side by side across from me, was beginning now. "Tell me," I asked the young couple, "what first attracted you two to one another?" My glance moved from the primly attentive Laura to the slightly wary face of her husband, Tom. "What was it that made you—and you—special to each other, do you think?"

Mundane though the questions sounded, in my own ears, they evoked the usual surprised, even startled response. Laura inhaled sharply, picked up a hank of her long brown-blond hair, flipped it over her shoulder. Tom looked as if he were about to spring from his seat, but instead of rising, he leaned backward against the plush maroon sofa. They turned to each other, with a smile; Laura blushed, and then they both laughed.

What became clear was that the Bretts saw themselves as very different sorts of individuals—as polar opposites in many respects.

Toward the close of our first conversation, for example, I asked them the following question: "If someone you both know—a friend, say, or a family member—were describing your relationship to a third person, what kinds of things do you think he'd say?"

"Improbable," Tom answered immediately, with a smile.

"Improbable—for what reason?" I asked. "Oh"—he shrugged— "newspaper and church; cynic and believer. . . . I'm pretty logical and reserved, and Laura's exactly the opposite."

He hesitated, looked at Laura, who was shaking her head in agreement, a rueful yet amused expression etched upon her features. "You're the calm and passive one," she acknowledged, "and I'm always freaking out all over the place, for better or for worse." He nodded at her, said to me, "We're different in every way that you can think of. . . ."

They, like many couples who appear to be in marriages of opposites, were actually dealing with that most pervasive of marital problems: distinguishing which feelings, wishes, thoughts, etc., are within the self and which are within the intimate partner.

The dilemma has to do with the drawing of personal boundaries. The prime cause of distress in close, committed relationships is, in fact, a basic confusion about exactly what is going on inside one's own head and what is going on inside the head of the mate.

Many couples, like the Bretts, appear to be polar opposites—*thoroughly different* sorts of people. They are like puppets in a Punch and Judy show: Each plays a vastly dissimilar role on that part of the stage which is open to the objective observer's view, but below stage their strings are entangled. They are deeply enmeshed and emotionally fused, beneath the level of each mate's conscious awareness. For each of them embodies, carries and expresses *for the other* disavowed aspects of that other's self—his or her own inner being.

If one looked, for instance, at what was happening in the Bretts' relationship, a division of emotional labors seemed to be occurring. It was as if the pair of them had taken certain human wishes, attitudes, emotions, ways of relating and behaving—a whole range of feelings and responses that might be integrated parts of *one person's* repertoire—and parceled them out in an "I'll take this, and you take that" fashion.

They had, as couples often do, accomplished this in an unarticulated but nevertheless powerfully operative kind of unconscious agreement. Laura, in their relationship, took the optimism, while Tom took the pessimism; she was all belief, and he was the skeptic; she wanted emotional openness and he wanted to keep himself to himself; she was the pursuer and he the distancer— the individual on the run from intimacy. Together, in fact, they made up one fully integrated, adaptive organism, except that Laura had to do all the breathing in and Tom had to do all the breathing out.

If, however, Laura appeared, onstage, to want total closeness, honesty, integrity and oneness, out of sight she and Tom actually had an arrangement. Whenever she tried to move nearer to him, his autonomy string would be activated, and he was impelled—in an almost reflexive fashion—to make some distance immediately. She depended upon him to preserve the necessary space between them.

For Laura, like other people, needed some autonomy of her own—some personal territory in which she could be an individual in her own right, pursue her own separate wishes and goals. But for Laura, meeting her own independent needs was perceived as something wrong, dangerous—something a good adult woman didn't do. Her rightful role, as a female, was to concentrate upon staying *close,* in the relationship; she could not acknowledge autonomous needs as anything that existed inside herself, anything that she actually wanted. She was aware only of the needs of the self (the separate, independent self) as they existed *in* and were expressed *by* her mate.

Similarly, Tom's natural desire for closeness to an intimate other was a need he saw *not* within himself but as something existing primarily *in Laura.* The need to be close to his partner, in the context of a trusting, mutually self-revelatory relationship, was seen as *her* need; Tom never experienced it as a wish or a need that originated from within his own being. He was, in his own view, self-sufficient; that is, sufficient unto himself.

But in the same way that Laura depended upon Tom to run when she chased, Tom depended on Laura to try to get closer so that he could feel necessary and wanted—intimate.

Rather than express directly any wish or need for intimacy (or even be aware of, and take responsibility for, such wishes and feelings), Tom had to dissociate them from consciousness. Such thoughts and wishes made him feel too exposed and too vulnerable! When he needed closeness, he had to experience that wish as coming from his wife; he had, without any conscious recognition of what he was doing, to make sure that her intimacy string was tugged. One way of doing this was, perhaps, looking soulful and abstracted, so that she would wonder if he was thinking about Karen. Then Laura would pursue him anxiously—for the intimate exchange that he himself desired.

What was going on, in this couple's relationship, is extremely common in marriages, in general. The conflict both partners were experiencing—a conflict between wanting to meet their own separate needs and wanting to meet the needs of the relationship—had been split evenly down the middle between them. Instead of being able to recognize that *both* of them wanted to be close, and *both* of them wanted to pursue their own independent goals—*that the autonomy/intimacy conflict was a conflict that existed inside each person's own head*—the Bretts had made an unconscious, collusive arrangement.

Laura would never have to take conscious ownership of her need for personal space, and Tom would never have to acknowledge to himself his own desire to be emotionally open, trusting, and close. She carried the intimacy needs (the needs of the relationship) for the pair of them, and he carried the autonomy needs (the needs of each person to pursue his or her separate goals) for them both. Laura, therefore, always seemed to want to get a little nearer and Tom always seemed to want to be more distant and unencumbered.

The upshot was that instead of an internal conflict—something which existed inside each person's subjective world—the dilemma had become an *interpersonal* conflict—one that could be fought out between them, over and over again.

This *shifting of an intrapsychic problem* (i.e., a problem within an individual's mind) *to an interpersonal conflict* (i.e., a difficulty that two people are having) occurs by means of projective identification.

This term refers to a very pervasive, tricky and often destructive mental mechanism which involves one person's projecting denied and disavowed aspects of his or her inner experience onto the intimate partner and then perceiving those dissociated feelings as *existing in the partner*. Not only are the unwanted thoughts and feelings seen as being inside the mate, but the mate is encouraged by means of cues and provocations—to behave as if they *were* there! The person can then identify vicariously with his or her partner's expression of the repudiated thoughts, feelings, and emotions.

One of the best and clearest examples of the way in which projective identification operates is seen in the totally nonaggressive and never angry individual. This person, who is uniquely devoid of anger, can become aware of angry feelings only as they exist in someone else—in the intimate partner, most predictably. When something disturbing *has* happened to the never angry individual, and he *is* experiencing angry emotions, he will be consciously out of contact with them. *He will not know that he is angry, but he will be wonderfully adept at triggering an explosion of hostility and anger in his spouse.*

The mate, who may not have been feeling angry at all before the interaction, may quickly find herself completely furious; her anger, which appears to be about some completely unrelated issue, is, in fact, anger that is being acted out for her spouse. She is thus, in some sense, "protecting" him from certain aspects of his inner being which he cannot consciously own and acknowledge.

The never angry person can then identify with the intimate partner's expression of the suppressed rage without ever having to take personal responsibility for it—even in terms of being conscious of the fact that he was the angry person in the first place! And, frequently, the feelings of anger which were so firmly repudiated within the self are just as sternly criticized in the mate. The never angry individual, in a projective identification situation, is often horrified by his spouse's hot-tempered, impulsive, uncontrolled expressions and behavior!

In a similar way, the never sad person may see his or her own depressed moods only as they exist in the partner (who can, in such a circumstance, be understood to be the person carrying the sadness and despair for them both).

Projections tend, generally speaking, to be *exchanges*—trades, so to speak, of denied parts of the self, which both members of the couple have agreed to make. Then each one sees, in the partner, what cannot be perceived in the self—and struggles, ceaselessly, to change it.

. . . .

15 · SHADOW DANCING IN THE MARRIAGE ZONE

MICHAEL VENTURA

Jan and I went straight from fling into marriage. We decided to marry within ten days of meeting each other. This saved us the relationship stint of getting to not-know each other, which usually and sadly consists of people trying out their various selves on one another, compulsively and/or intentionally, testing for commitment. That's necessary for one stage of life, but like many people our age we had each done that many times. We decided: This time no tests. Dance to the music.

Marry it.

Were we marrying each other or marrying the impulse? *Good question.* A question that can only be answered after it's too late. Fine. For love is nothing if it's not faith. Nothing.

When Brendan was born, almost nine years before Jan and I met, Jan had sent out announcements with the old blues refrain:

Baby I learned to love you
Honey 'fore I called
Baby 'fore I called your name

Love often occurs "in this wise," as the old phrase goes. As though love is *for* "calling the name." And certainly "to be loved" is to feel one's name called with an inflection that one has never heard before.

So we found ourselves sending out wedding invitations that went:

Come on over
We ain't fakin'
Whole lotta shakin' goin' on

Odd, now, to think how small a sense of foreboding we had at that Jerry Lee Lewis verse—though we've only "come to blows" (revealing old phrase, isn't it, with its odd sense of formality?) once, and she struck first, broke my glasses, and I hit her then, one time, and she slumped against the wall, both of us feeling so soiled and ugly and wrong. How many bitter, gone grandmothers and grandfathers stood in the room just then, cackling their satisfaction at our shame? Hers, Irish; mine, Sicilian. Both of them traditions that did not teach us to forgive. To learn to forgive is to break with an unforgiving past.

Pause at the word: "for-give." "For-to-give." Forgiveness is such a gift that "give" lives in the word. Christianist tradition has tried to make it a meek and passive word; turn the other cheek. But the word contains the active word "give," which reveals its truth: it involves the act of taking something of yours and handing it to another, so that from now on it is theirs. Nothing passive about it. It is an exchange. An exchange of faith: the faith that what has been done can be undone or can be transcended. When two people need to make this exchange with each other, it can be one of the most intimate acts of their lives.

One thing that forgiveness is, is a promise to *work* at the undoing, at the transcending. Marriage soon enough gives all concerned the opportunity to forgive. There have been enough broken chairs, broken plates—and one broken typewriter, my beloved old Olympia portable manual, that I'd had since high school and smashed myself—to testify to how desperate can be the joined desperations of all the Michaels, Jans, and Brendans. Whole *lotta* shakin' goin' on, and on and on, and sometimes when you are trying to break through the hardened crusts inside you and inside each other, some dishes and typewriters and furniture might go in the process.

The most odious aspect of goody-goody, I'm-okay-you're-okay dialogues is their failure to recognize that sometimes you have to scream, slam doors, break furniture, run red lights, and ride the wind even to *begin* to have the words to describe what is eating you. Sometimes meditation and dialogue just can't cut it. Sometimes "it" just plain needs "cutting"—or at least a whole lotta shakin'. Anyone afraid of breaking, within and without, is in the wrong marriage. Let it all go. Let the winds blow. Let's see what's left in the morning.

And *that* is "the solace of marriage"—a phrase I've heard in several contexts, but am otherwise unable to comprehend. The discovery of what is unbreakable among all that's been broken. The discovery that union can be as irreducible as solitude. The discovery that people must share not only what they *don't* know about each other, but what they *don't* know about themselves.

Sharing what we know is a puny exercise by comparison.

And did I say there were only myriads of Jans, Brendans, and Michaels encamped in the firelit cavern that appears to be an inexpensive old wood-frame duplex south of Santa Monica Boulevard in Los Angeles? Life is not so simple as even that. What about the raging mob we refer to, politely, as "the past"? Nothing abstract about "the past." What has marked you is still marking you. There is a place in us where wounds never heal, and where loves never end. Nobody knows much about this place except that it exists, feeding our dreams and reinforcing and/or haunting our days. In marriage, it can exist with a vengeance.

Bloody, half-flayed, partly dead, naked, tortured, my mother really does hang on a hook in my closet, because she hangs on a hook in me. Occasionally I have to take her out and we do a rending dance, tearing each other bloody as we go, and stuff splashes happily all over—all over Jan, several of the many Jans, and several of the many Brendans, and then run for the hills, my dears, for I am in my horror.

One of my several, my insistent, horrors.

We are all, every one of us, full of horror. If you are getting married to try to make yours go away, you will only succeed in marrying your horror to someone else's horror, your two horrors will have the marriage, you will bleed and call that love.

My closet is full of hooks, full of horrors, and I *also* love them, my horrors, and I know they love me, and they will always hang there for me, because they are also good for me, they are also on my side, they gave so much to *be* my horrors, they made me strong to survive. There is much in our new "enlightened" lexicon to suggest that one may move into a house that doesn't have such a closet. You move into a such a house and think everything is fine until after a while you start to hear a distant screaming, and start to smell something funny, and realize slowly that the closet is there, alright, but it's been walled over, and just when you need desperately to open it you find yourself faced with bricks instead of a door.

In our cavern on this hillside in this apartment, there is quite a closet, where my hooks hang next to Jan's, and to Brendan's—it's amazing how many you can accumulate at the mere age of eleven—which are also there for their good and harrowing reasons.

For a marriage to *be* a marriage, these encounters do not happen compulsively or accidentally, they happen by intention. I don't mean that the encounters with all the various selves and ghosts are planned (that's not possible, though they can sometimes be consciously evoked); I mean that this level of activity is recognized as part of the quest, part of the responsibility each person has for him/herself and for the other.

Which is the major difference between the expectations of a marriage and a relationship. My experience of a relationship is two people more or less compulsively playing musical chairs with each other's selected inner archetypes. My tough street kid is romancing your honky-tonk angel. I am your homeless waif and you are my loving mother. I am your lost father and you are my doting daughter. I am your worshiper and you are my goddess. I am your god and you are my priestess. I am your client and you are my analyst. I am your intensity and you are my ground. These are some of the more garish of the patterns. Animus, anima, bopping on a seesaw.

These hold up well enough while the archetypal pairings behave. But when the little boy inside him is looking for the mommy inside her and finds instead on this particular night a sharp-toothed analyst dissecting his guts. When the little girl inside her is looking for the daddy inside him, and finds instead a pagan worshiper who wants a goddess to lay with, which induces her to become a little girl playacting a goddess to please the daddy who's really a lecherous worshiper and . . . little girls can't come. Or if a woman is attracted to a macho-man who is secretly looking to be mothered: when a man's sexual self is in the service of an interior little boy it's not surprising that he can't get it up or comes too quick. Or they're really not *there* at all, they're masturbating, really, men in their little-boy psyches for whom the real woman is just a stand-in; while the woman who happens to be in the same bed, an extension of their masturbation, is wondering why even though the moves are pretty good she doesn't really feel slept with. And why he turns away so quickly when it's done.

On the other hand, teachers fuck pupils with excitement, analysts fuck clients with abandon, and people seeing each other, in bed, as gods and goddesses light up the sky—but the psyche is a multiple and a shifting entity, and none of these compatible pairings hold stable for long. The archetypal mismatches soon begin, and then it's a disaster of confrontations that can take years not even to sort out (it would be *worth* years to get it all sorted out) but simply to exhaust itself and fail. And then the cycle starts all over again with someone else.

My experience of a marriage is that all these same modes are present, but instinctively or consciously it becomes a case of two people running down each other's inner archetypes, tackling them, seducing them, cajoling them, waiting them out, making them talk, 'fessing up to them, running *from* them, raping them, falling in love with some, hating others, getting to know some, making friends with some, hanging some in the closet on each other's hooks—hooks on which hang fathers, mothers, sisters, brothers, other loves, idols, fantasies, maybe even past lives, and *true mythological consciousnesses* that sometimes come to life within one with such force that we feel a thread that goes back thousands of years, even to other realms of being.

All of this is what we "marry" in the other, a process that goes on while we manage to earn a living, go to the movies, watch television, go to the doctor, walk on the Palisades, drive to Texas, follow the election, try to stop drinking, eat too much Häagen-Dazs.

. . . .

The minute I heard my first love story
I started looking for you, not knowing
how blind that was.
Lovers don't finally meet somewhere.
They're in each other all along.

RUMI

. . . .

Perhaps all the dragons of our lives
are princesses who are only waiting to
see us once, beautiful and brave.
Perhaps everything terrible is in
its deepest being something
that needs our love.

RAINER MARIA RILKE

PART 4

. . . .

THE
DISOWNED
BODY: ILLNESS,
HEALTH, AND
SEXUALITY

To talk of the body as more than the shadow is to relinquish the pessimism of the twentieth century and take heart, once more affirming the living being of man.

JOHN P. CONGER

The human devil resides in the pit of the belly. . . . Carnal pleasure is the main temptation the devil uses to lure the ego into the abyss of hell. Against this catastrophe the terrified ego strives to maintain control of the body at all costs. Consciousness, associated with the ego, becomes opposed to the unconscious or the body as the respository of the dark forces.

ALEXANDER LOWEN

[A male shadow figure] the Wild Man encourages a trust in what is below: the lower half of our body, our genitals, our legs and ankles, our inadequacies, the soles of our feet, the animal ancestors, the Earth itself, the treasures in the Earth, the dead long buried there, the stubborn richness to which we descend. "Water prefers low places," says the *Tao Te Ching,* which is a true Wild Man book.

ROBERT BLY

INTRODUCTION

. . . .

The human body has lived for two thousand years in the shadow of Western culture. Its animal impulses, sexual passions, and decaying nature were banished to the darkness and filled with taboo by a priesthood that valued only the higher realms of spirit, mind, and rational thought. With the advent of the scientific age, the body was confirmed to be a mere sack of chemicals, a machine without a soul.

The result: The mind/body split became entrenched. Culture shines its light on left-brain logic and the striving of individual ego, while shading right-brain intuition and carnal matter. Like a river bed, the split runs deep in our cultural terrain, creating polarities anywhere it touches: flesh/spirit, sinful/innocent, animal/godlike, selfish/altruistic.

We feel the terrible results of this paradigm—body as shadow—in our own lives as guilt and shame about bodily functions, a lack of spontaneity in our movements and sensations, and a chronic struggle with psychosomatic disease. The disowned body also appears starkly in today's dreadful epidemics of child abuse, sex addiction, substance abuse, and eating disorders.

Our religious and spiritual traditions reinforce the mind/body split by proposing that a purpose of human evolution is to transcend the body. Christians and Hindus alike attempt to redirect bodily desires for "higher" purposes; our "lower" needs for pleasure and leisure are deemed base.

High-tech scientists in robotics and artificial intelligence fuel the debate by claiming that the body may become superfluous through electronic additions and corrections of parts, until we are less and less flesh of our flesh, and more and more hard-wired circuitry, a bit like the all-knowing humanoid Data, of TV's "Star Trek: The Next Generation."

This futuristic scenario of the body is, of course, only one possible path open to us. Rather than devalue it, advocates of somatic therapies view the body as the vehicle by which we gain transformation, the sacred temple in which to do spiritual work. As John P. Conger says: "The body is our school, our lesson, our protagonist, our beloved enemy . . . the jumping off place into the higher realms."

Women who are exploring emerging feminine spiritual values also espouse embodying the self, and a new generation of teachers and therapists are actively engaging the body in the symbolic process. By feeding it healing sounds, images, and rhythms, bypassing the lions guarding the gates of mind, they believe they can bring the body out of the shadow domain.

Most of us tend to think that the shadow is invisible, hidden away somewhere in the recesses of our minds. But people who work regularly with the human body and can read its mute language are able to see in it the dark shape of the shadow. It etches itself into our muscles and tissues, our blood and bones. Our full personal biography is recounted in our bodies, there to be read by those who know the language.

Of course, for people with natural predispositions toward kinesthetic awarenesses, such as dancers, athletes, or artisans, it is no news that the body holds a key to our awakening. But for those whose aptitudes lie in feeling or thinking, bringing the body out of the shadow can be exhilarating and can act as a primary tool of shadow-work.

The purpose of this section is to approach the shadow through the body, a road less traveled than the mind's symbolic route, which was chosen by Jung and others fascinated with the inner world. In Chapter 16, Berkeley bioenergetic analyst John P. Conger compares Carl Jung's and Wilhelm Reich's views of the unconscious and its relationship to the human body. Conger believes their differing definitions of psyche and soma are based in their differing personal styles and temperaments; however, he also uncovers some striking parallels.

Next, in "Anatomy of Evil," Reich's disciple John C. Pierrakos expands the discussion of body armoring as the root cause of evil human behavior. When emotional vitality is cut off, he says, and the body hardens against feeling, one's natural energies are damped, and brutality may result.

Physician/author Larry Dossey, in a reprint from *Beyond Illness,* explores a hidden role of disease in relation to health. They always go together, like black and white, he says, and each has a purpose and a gift.

In Chapter 19, from *Archetypal Medicine,* physician/Jungian analyst Alfred J. Ziegler eloquently explores the symptoms of disease as symptoms of the unlived life. He explains: "When our heroics mislead themselves, our inferiorities and recessive qualities revert to bodily manifestations. . . . Our shadows take on substance."

Because sexuality is a natural part of our bodily life, it, too, has a dark side and a light side. In a chapter from *Marriage Dead or Alive,* Swiss Jungian analyst Adolf Guggenbühl-Craig investigates the demonic side of sexuality: masochism, sadism, incest, and sex with forbidden partners. The demonic element in sexuality has a power and an allure all its own.

In sum, the body is a complete universe unto itself. As Heinrich Zimmer puts it, "All the gods are in our body." And all the devils, too, our contributors would add.

. . . .

16 · THE BODY AS SHADOW

JOHN P. CONGER

Strictly speaking, the shadow is the repressed part of the ego and represents what we are unable to acknowledge about ourselves. The body that hides beneath clothes often blatantly expresses what we consciously deny. In the image we present to others, we often do not want to show our anger, our anxiety, our sadness, our constrictedness, our depression, or our need. As early as 1912, Jung wrote: "It must be admitted that the Christian emphasis on spirit inevitably leads to an unbearable depreciation of man's physical side, and thus produces a sort of optimistic caricature of human nature."[1] In 1935, Jung lectured in England about his general theories and, in passing, indicated how the body might stand as the shadow:

> We do not like to look at the shadow-side of ourselves; therefore there are many people in our civilized society who have lost their shadow altogether, have lost the third dimension, and with it they have usually lost the body. The body is a most doubtful friend because it produces things we do not like: there are too many things about *the personification of this shadow of the ego.* Sometimes it forms the skeleton in the cupboard, and everybody naturally wants to get rid of such a thing.[2]

Indeed, the body *is* the shadow insofar as it contains the tragic history of how the spontaneous surging of life energy is murdered and rejected in a hundred ways until the body becomes a deadened object. The victory of an over-rationalized life is promoted at the expense of the more primitive and natural vitality. For those who can read the body, it holds the record of our rejected side, revealing what we dare not speak, expressing our current and past fears. The body as shadow is predominantly the body as "character," the body as bound energy that is unrecognized and untapped, unacknowledged and unavailable.

Although Jung was a vibrant, tall, physical man, he actually said little about the body. When he built his tower in Bollingen, he returned to a more primitive life, pumping his own water from the well and cutting his own wood. His physicality, spontaneity, and charm indicated a certain comfort and at-homeness in his body. A number of his incidental statements show an attitude toward the body that was in harmony with Wilhelm Reich's ideas but more detached, more metaphoric.

Reich, the one who taught us to observe and work with the body, was direct and concrete. He saw the mind and body as "functionally identical."[3] Reich worked with the psyche as a bodily expression and provided a brilliant alternative and antidote to the sophisticated analytic Vienna psychoanalysts, who at least in the early days were unaware of the power of bodily expression in psychoanalysis. Reich's nature was intense, somewhat rigid, without much tolerance for the play of the metaphysical, literary mind. He was a scientist grounded in what he could see, with an impatient predisposition to dismiss everything else as "mystical," a category he quite early adopted for Jung as he entered Freud's circle in the early 1920s. Later, in *Ether, God and Devil* (1949), Reich wrote:

> Functional identity as a research principle of orgonomic functionalism is nowhere as brilliantly expressed as in the unity of psyche and soma, of emotion

and excitation, of sensation and stimulus. This unity or identity as the base principle of life excludes once and for all any transcendentalism, or even autonomy of
the emotions.[4]

Jung, on the other hand, was influenced by Kant, whose theory of
knowledge kept Jung philosophically directed primarily to a study of the
psyche as a scientist, an empiricist, without concluding that he had hold of
Reality. In the essay "On the Nature of the Psyche," Jung wrote:

> Since psyche and matter are contained in one and the same world, and moreover
> are in continuous contact with one another and ultimately rest on irrepresent-
> able, transcendental factors, it is not only possible but fairly probable, even, that
> psyche and matter are two different aspects of one and the same thing.[5]

While there are startling and frequent agreements between them, Reich
and Jung approached their work in radically different ways. With such unset-
tling differences in style and disposition before us, the bringing together of
these two systems is an unexpected and awesome exercise. Ironically, it takes
place through the theoretical mediation of Freud. Reich and Jung neither
talked with each other nor wrote or communicated in any way. Only a few
random comments indicate that Reich knew of Jung's existence, and his
knowledge of Jung appears opinionated and based on superficial assessment.
On the other hand, there is no mention of Reich at all in Jung's writings. But
both Reich and Jung returned time and again to compare their concepts with
the tenets of Freud. In this unexpected way, a cross-relationship can be established between the concepts of Reich and Jung.

In a paper he wrote in 1939, Jung compared the shadow to Freud's concept of the unconscious. "The shadow," he said, "coincides with the 'personal' unconscious (which corresponds to Freud's conception of the unconscious)."[6] In the preface to the third edition of *The Mass Psychology of Fascism,*
which he wrote in August 1942, Reich said that his secondary layer corresponds to Freud's unconscious. Reich explained that fascism emerges out of
the second layer of biopsychic structure, which represents three layers of
character structure (or deposits of social development) that function autono-
mously. The surface layer of the average man, according to Reich, is "reserved, polite, compassionate, responsible, conscientious." But the surface
layer of "social cooperation is not in contact with the deep biologic core of
one's selfhood; it is borne by a second, and intermediate character layer, which
consists exclusively of cruel, sadistic, lascivious, rapacious, and envious impulses. It represents the Freudian 'unconscious' or 'what is repressed.'"[7]

Since Jung's "shadow" and Reich's "secondary layer" both correspond to
Freud's "unconscious," we can acknowledge at least a rough correspondence
between them. As reflected in the body, Reich saw the secondary layer as
rigid, chronic contractions of muscle and tissue, a defensive armoring against
assault from within and without, a way of shutting down so that the energy
flow in the afflicted body was severely reduced. Reich worked directly on the

armored layer in the body, in that way releasing the repressed material. The body as the shadow refers, then, to the armored aspect of the body.

In Hans Christian Andersen's fairy tale "The Shadow," a shadow manages to detach itself from its owner, a scholar.[8] The scholar gets along tolerably well, developing a new, somewhat more modest shadow. Some years later, he meets his old shadow, who has become wealthy and eminent. About to be married to a princess, the shadow has the audacity to attempt to hire his old master to be *his* shadow. The scholar attempts to expose his shadow, but the clever shadow has him imprisoned, convincing its betrothed that its shadow has gone mad, and so it is able to remove the man that endangers its love. The fairy tale tells us how the dark and discarded aspects of the ego can coalesce in a forceful unforeseen way and materialize so powerfully as to dominate and reverse the master-servant relationship, a story that demonstrates what Reich would have considered the development of the armored character.

In the strictest sense, then, the body as the shadow represents the body as armored, expressive of what is repressed by the ego. We might also guess that Jung's concept of the persona corresponds to Reich's first layer. "On the surface layer of his personality," wrote Reich (to quote the passage again), "the average man is reserved, polite, compassionate, responsible, conscientious."[9] "The persona," wrote Jung, "is a complicated system of relations between the individual consciousness and society, fittingly enough a kind of mask, designed on the one hand to make a definite impression upon others, and, on the other, to conceal the true nature of the individual."[10] Although Jung's "persona" functions in a more complex way than Reich's "first layer," there is a reasonable correspondence between the two systems. Jung saw the persona as part of a balance between the conscious and unconscious, a sequence of compensations. The more a man plays the strongman for the world, the more inwardly he is compensated by feminine weakness. The less aware he is of the feminine within him, the more likely a man is to project a primitive anima figure on the world, or to be subject to fits, moods, paranoias, hysterias. Reich tended to dismiss the surface layer as inconsequential, whereas Jung attended to the vital interaction between our mask and our inner life.

For Reich, the way to reach the core layer of man was to challenge the secondary shadow layer. The resistance for Reich became a kind of flag, marking the area of armoring, marking the way into the core of man. "In this core, under favorable social conditions, man is an essentially honest, industrious, cooperative, loving, and, if motivated, rationally hating animal."[11]

The equivalence between Jung's shadow concept and Reich's secondary layer is a rough but hardly exact fit. Jung saw the shadow as a part of the core of life within the nature of the God image in the human psyche. The dark side offers us a powerful entrance into the denied life of man. But for Reich, evil is a chronic mechanism that denies energetic life and is a hindrance to the spontaneous, biologic core of man. The devil never reaches the core level but is the personification of the restricted secondary layer.

After years of work, Reich came to share Freud's therapeutic despair. He had tried to dissolve armor on a mass scale through education and individually in therapy. His three-layer model does not acknowledge a value in the secondary layer, which appears virtually impossible to dissolve completely. These days, it is generally acknowledged among practitioners that everyone needs some armor as protection. Therapy seeks not only to dissolve armor but to introduce flexibility and conscious choice to what had been a rigid, unconscious, defense structure.

While the biological concept of armor has an appropriate specificity in its application to the energetic work with the body, the shadow as the functional equivalent on the psychic level enjoys a range of meaning appropriate to its psychological function. The shadow contains power that has been disowned. The shadow is not to be totally dissolved, nor can it be successfully disowned. The shadow must be related to and integrated even as we acknowledge that some deep core of shadow will never be tamed. The shadow and the double contain not only the dross of our conscious life but our primitive, undifferentiated life force, a promise of the future, whose presence enhances our awareness and strengthens us through the tension of opposites.

. . . .

17 · ANATOMY OF EVIL

JOHN C. PIERRAKOS

Let us explore the concept of evil by approaching it from its opposite—the good. In health, which is the good or the truth of life, the reality of the human being, energy and consciousness are very much unified. Man feels this unity. Recently a musician who came for consultation said that when he plays from his inner being, the movements of his organism just flow out spontaneously; it is they that are playing the instrument. They come free, they coordinate, they create beautiful sounds. When man is in a healthy state, his life is a constant creative process. He is inundated by feelings of love, of oneness with other human beings. The oneness is the awareness that he is not different from others. He wants to help them; he identifies with them; he senses that anything that is happening to them is happening to himself. A healthy person has a positive direction in his life. He wills his life in a positive direction, and he is successful—in business, in his thinking, in his feeling of contentment with himself. In that state there is little or no sickness and no evil.

In the diseased state, the first characteristic is that reality is distorted—the reality of the body, the reality of the emotions, and the reality of the true nature of other people and their actions. Evil, then, is a distortion of facts that in themselves are natural. Because the sick person does not perceive his own distortions, he feels that the ills in his life and functioning come from the outside. The sicker he is, the more he feels that his troubles are caused by outside forces. A person who is in a state of psychosis, for example, sees the world as hostile. He sits on a chair and he looks at the walls and he says, "They are doing it to me. They are going to kill me, they are going to poison me." He completely abdicates his personal responsibility for his life and his actions. He feels that everything happens to him from the outside. A healthy person is able to a great degree to do the exact opposite.

What happens in the sick person? His consciousness and his energies change in some way. His consciousness has changed its mind, as it were. It turns life into a distorted version of itself in him, and then his energy alters its manifestations. His thinking is limited. His feelings are expressed by hate and brutality and cruelty, fear and terror.

Wilhelm Reich, in describing the condition of armoring, sheds great light on how sickness operates. The armored person, he said, shuts himself off from nature, specifically by forming barriers against the impulses of life within his body. The armored body stiffens up and is inaccessible to feeling, and the organ sensations are diminished or subside. Then the person becomes lukewarm; he hates, but he doesn't even know it. He is ambivalent.

Reich thought that each entity, each human being, has a core, such as the heart, where the pulsatory movement of life starts. In the person who is relatively free, the pulsatory movement reaches the periphery undistorted, and he expresses, moves, feels, breathes, vibrates. But in the armored person, between the core and the periphery there is a Maginot line. When the impulses of life strike the fortifications of the armor, the person is in terror, and he thinks he must suppress them; for if they surface, he is certain he will be annihilated. To him, his feelings—especially his sexual feelings—are terrible, dirty, bad. When aggressive impulses held inside this nucleus hit the armor, they make it quake. And indeed if they break through the Maginot line, the person is absolutely brutal out of his terror. He is terrified because he cannot tolerate his feelings, the movement and possession of life in him, the sweet hum of emotion, the pulse of love, and he acts against himself and against other people, becoming antilife. He does not perceive that the armor is a deadness making the core of life inaccessible and that it is this armor which is ugly and hateful. In the armored state, then, man is divided—the mind from the body, the body from the emotions, the emotions from the spirit.

Armoring may make a person a mystic, because he can't embrace the fact that God is in him. He looks at God "out there," and he says, "If I pray, if I purify myself, I'll solve all my problems." But this is never possible, because a person who goes into spirituality without having worked out his negativities—his ego defenses, his resistances—flies high like Icarus, but when he reaches the burning sun, he falls into the sea, the sea of life, and drowns. It is only through transcending and working through the obstacles to life that the human being can rise into realms of creation and spirituality.

In contrast to the mystic, armoring may make a person brutal. When he expresses his feelings, he is a monster. Then he experiences terror, because he feels that if he perceives his genuine feelings, he will be extinguished.

How does an armored human being discard these barriers? Reich said that we must recognize not only the rational but the useful irrational. We must look upon our irrationality as very important. We must know it, admit it, expose it. For it holds the flow of the river of life. If we are cut off from the irrational, we become pedantic and dead. By that I do not mean that we should behave irrationally at all times; I mean that we must accept irrationality, take the energy that is invested in it, deactivate it, and understand the obstacles we have put in life that create irrationality. Reich said another basic thing: we must dismiss the concept of the antithesis of God and the devil. We must expand the boundaries of our thinking.

The manifestation of evil is thus not something that is intrinsically different from pure energy and consciousness; it is only creation that has changed its characteristic. In essence there is no evil, but in the realm of human manifestation there is.

What does evil mean in relation to energy and consciousness? In terms of energy, it means a slowing down, a diminution of frequency, a condensation. The person feels heavy, bound, immobilized. We know that when we feel hateful, dead, or in any other way negative, we feel very heavy. With power we feel the opposite: vibrancy. We take a walk in the woods and we say we fly. So the energy of the body slows down and condenses.

In terms of consciousness, the slower the frequency of the movement, the more the distortion of the consciousness, and vice versa. The heavier and more negative we are, the less creative we are, the less feeling, the less understanding. We can reach the point of blocking all movement and staying in the head; at this extreme, we become obstructed, and then nothing matters. Religion and every other organized ethic has presented all the negative attitudes like hate and deception and spite and cheating as evil, evil, evil. Religion sees these states and the actions that express them as the result of a distorted consciousness of what is good and bad according to its codification.

In the Bible Jesus said a sentence that in my interpretation makes a very important point. Speaking to his disciples he taught, "Do not resist evil" (Matthew 5:39). Let us examine this. The resistance itself is the evil. When there is no resistance, energy is unobstructed and flows. When there is resistance, movement stops, backs up, stagnates the organism. Resistance suffocates the emotions, deadens energy, and kills feelings. Resistance is bred of caution, a thinking mechanism—thinking not in the sense of abstract thinking but of organizational thinking.

The consciousness in some way is responsible for the energy flow in the organism, as consciousness in a cosmic dimension is responsible for the energy flow in the universe. When I say "responsible," I do not mean "guilty"; in psychiatry we avoid ever holding a person to blame for his negative actions or unconscious content. We try always to see them as the result of a dynamic state created in a way that the person is not aware of and is therefore not to be blamed for. When consciousness is negative, the person is resistive to the truth. There are resistances that are conscious, that a person uses intentionally and with awareness of what he chooses to do. A man whose wife has hurt him could choose to open up his love feelings and forgive or to keep up the negative and destructive feeling and get even with her. Not all of it is a result of unconscious behavior, though much of it is, and for the unconscious propulsion he is not accountable.

Evil, then, is a far deeper thing than the moral codes conceive of. It is antilife. Life is dynamic, pulsating force; it is energy and consciousness, manifested in many ways; and there is no evil as such unless there is resistance to life. The resistance is the manifestation of what is called evil. Energy and consciousness in distortion create evil.

· · · · · · · ·

18 · THE LIGHT OF HEALTH, THE SHADOW OF ILLNESS

LARRY DOSSEY

The poet Gary Snyder once remarked that only those persons who are capable of giving up the planet Earth are fit to work for its ecological survival. With this comment he illuminated a perspective that is frequently forgotten: There is an intrinsic relatedness between opposites, even the extremes of planetary death and survival.

The same unifying power undergirds the extremes of health and illness. There is a deep reciprocity at work, an unseverable linkage between the hideousness of illness and the splendor of health. It seems odd to even suggest that such a relationship exists in view of the common attitude that illness is to be exterminated, that it is the harbinger of death, a precursor of personal extinction. Yet these connections between "opposites" will not die. They remain in our bones and blood. They are part of our collective wisdom, and they still survive intact in many cultures on Earth. Even in our own society we have hardly driven them out in spite of the presidential "wars" on various diseases and a medical technology that promises eventual eradication of the major diseases of the day.

We have forgotten how to think about illness. Indeed, we try mightily to *not* think about it at all—putting it out of our minds until it is time for an annual exam or until we contract an illness of some sort. Part of being healthy, we are told, is to *think* healthy—which, we presume, does *not* include ruminating about illness. We eschew sickness, and we dread attending funerals of deceased friends or trips to the hospital to visit those who are ill, or even visits to the dentist, internist, family physician, pediatrician, or gynecologist.

Yet we cannot *not* think about illness. There are constant reminders of it in the form of common colds we experience, or the illness of friends. Death is a part of the collective social structure. Try as we might, no one can avoid confrontation with disease.

It would seem, then, that the sheer inability to hide from illness, to permanently trade its embrace for that of health, might tell us about the relationship of the two: that they are mysteriously united in some odd way; that to know one is to know the other; that one cannot have one without having the other. Just as one cannot know up without down, or black without white, it appears that we cannot partition our awareness in a way that would exclude illness and death in favor of health.

Indeed, we cannot engage in any kind of health care without asking ouselves the question, "What is it I am trying to prevent?" Even if we engage in something as routine as immunizations, we are confronted at some psychological level with the question, "What is it I am immunizing myself *against?*" If we attend the increasingly popular "health fairs" where, for example, blood pressure is checked for free, the subterranean fear always lurks: "What would happen if I ignore my blood pressure?" All acts of health carry this grayish, dark side to them, because they remind us what we most wish to avoid: Illness and death are inevitable, and, try as we might, we can never separate health from illness, nor death from birth. And our frenzy to be healthy only increases our sensitivity to the phenomena of illness and death, just as light, in a world of objects, always casts shadows. The two go together, they draw each other onward, they cannot be teased apart.

Most premodern cultures seem to have had a deeper understanding of the unseverable nature of health and illness, and their myths and rituals embody this wisdom. In many societies there was the attempt to *live with* illness rather than to *hide from* it. It can be argued, of course, that such cultures did not shrink from illness and death because they could not; and that if they had been as technologically advanced as our own society they would have abhorred disease and death just as we. While there may be merit to this argument, it is more likely that many premodern societies' attitudes toward death and disease were an expression of an organic way of being, a manner of living-in-the-world where acceptance was not a function of helplessness but an expression of a deep understanding of the world.

Illness [can be] regarded as if it were almost a thing in itself, with needs of its own—the need to be addressed and reasoned with, the need to be provided for and attended to. Disease [can be] seen as *reasonable*: bargains could be struck, deals could be made. [This] stands in stark contrast with our own way of seeing ourselves waylaid and struck down by cancer, heart attacks, or strokes.

Today, our sense of connectedness with illness has been all but lost, traded away for technological forms of intervention that have, in the bargaining, cost us much of our sense of connection to health as well. We do not know how to savor health because we have lost the vital connections between health and illness. One cannot replace an organic relatedness with the world with antibiotics, surgical procedures, and promissory immortality without destroying something that is vital, something that is health itself. It is not that modern interventions are "bad," but that they are no substitute for the wisdom of "the way things are," as philosopher of religion Huston Smith puts it. Technology is not wisdom of itself; it is no guarantor of the *experience* of health.

Are we in our own time rediscovering something of the organicity of the world that was known to the primitive peoples of the planet? Perhaps. It is clear that we do not have the answers we wish in understanding health and illness, and our society is aflame with resentment at unfulfilled promises and the perceived inhumaneness of modern medicine. I do not believe, however, that this rage, whose existence can hardly be doubted, is properly directed. It is anger that is overtly directed at the "system," but at a system which is really ourselves. We are disappointed in ourselves at being taken in, at selling out, of forgetting something we once knew, of severing our organic ties with the world we live in. We are learning, painfully and deeply, that longevity is not the equivalent of quality of life. We are seeing through the vacuity of concepts such as "the disease-free interval." We cannot ignore that something vital is missing from our health—something without which health is not health at all.

What is this "something," this missing element? It is, I feel, the shadow that is illness, the shadow that must always accompany the light of health. It is the felt organic connection to the world, the sure knowledge that the world cannot be forced into shapes that are not part of its nature. It is the willingness to take on illness as surely as we take on health, knowing in the process that either experience is meaningless without the other.

It is difficult to entertain such reciprocal necessities as the connectedness of health and illness, for we have come to believe in our culture that we *can* have it "one way or the other"—that we can have up without down, black without white. We *can* have health without illness, or perhaps even birth without death. It is only a matter of more research funding, manpower, and time. To ask that we go beyond this kind of "either-or" way of thinking seems an invitation to a primitive form of thought that does not square with the potential of the modern age.

Yet it is not just the primitive who has understood the unseverable nature of opposites. It is a vision that men of all ages have happened upon. It is an enduring wisdom, part of the lore of the mystics and poets of all ages.

· · · · · · ·

19 · ILLNESS AS DESCENT INTO THE BODY

ALFRED J. ZIEGLER

Man is a chimera, a monstrosity composed of an indeterminable number of contradictions. He is more of a monster than he is a rational being, a circumstance Nature has managed artfully to disguise to the extent that we feel more comfortable with him than we would with some bizarre creature from outer space. It is as if Oedipus himself were the very Sphinx he met on the way to Thebes who asked, "What is man?" It is as if the centaur whom the Greeks regarded as the ancestor of doctors already attested by means of his chimerical form to the truth that all essential knowledge about the nature of man has to be hybrid.

Or is it not true that in mankind love can be perverted to hate and the other way around, that efficiency carries slovenliness with it, or that behind all system and order the specter of disintegration shines through? Are we not confronted at every turn with the phenomena that paralyzing criticism glowers out of mother-love, that betrayal keeps the notion of fidelity alive and vice versa, that the fateful lot of the alcoholic stems from the insatiability of his sobriety, or that hypochondriacs expect the worst from themselves simply because they are so inconsiderate of their own needs?

Since psychology as a science, benumbed of spirit but rational in its approach, has grappled with existing conditions and phenomena, it has uncovered more and more such discrepancies. It seems, though, that psychology, upon discovering polarities—that extroversion and introversion intermingle in any individual, that a sadist lurks in every masochist, and that digital thinking must always be on the lookout for lapses into analogical superstition—rejoices unnecessarily. As enlightening as all knowledge of human opposites may be, our information to date is woefully meager. The entire wealth of human polarities seems only then to become visible when, in our brooding over the riddles of disease, we stumble upon the manifold human qualities which play such an important role in the genesis of malaise. Again and again a new polarity finds material reality, as when the conflict between submission and a stoic "No" comes to light in rheumatoid arthritis or when the discrepancy between a particularly dependent nature and a continually faltering intention to reject dependency manifests in multiple sclerosis.

Despite the fundamentally polar pattern, man's nature is not symmetrical; his characteristics are not arranged like the spokes on a wheel. Man is not a harmonic creation but has a definite profile and individual non-interchangeability. Poets have brought into being an immense abundance of these individual characteristics, while psychologists with their typologies cut very poor figures by comparison. There are the enlightened, the insidious, the fools; there are the upright who do right and shrink from no one, the direct, the roundabout, the crawlers, and many, many more. Yet, no matter what the contours, no matter what characterizes an individual as exemplary or revolting, we will discover that these characteristics are but the dominant, 'healthy' aspects within polarities, those traits which on a relatively consistent basis comprise the predominant personality and can more or less be relied upon. For the most part, the dominant traits assist us in making our way through life and in adapting to circumstances relative to our goals.

These same traits are also the overvalued, glorified sides of our personalities within which the dark and unadmitted traits lie hidden, completing us as dichotomous chimeras. The dark traits would be the recessive, deceptive qualities of which we generally remain unaware and which alternatingly make their unexpected appearance. Because of their sheer unpredictability we find them irritable, especially when they get us into uncomfortable situations. Frequently, they are the very thing which calls into question the image we present for public consumption and which acts as the source of doubt of our own identity. The recessive traits are also the least adapted sides of our personalities, having finally a curious tendency to 'descend' into the body where they stubbornly clamor for our attention as disease syndromes. While the dominant, overvalued traits would lead us to view ourselves as the crown of creation, our recessive inferiorities provide us every reason to doubt such a conclusion.

'The Fall,' the metamorphosis into physical suffering, is preceded by certain premonitions. Nature does not deal as underhandedly with us as it may sometimes seem. Long before the situation becomes serious from a medical point of view, our hearts are tortured with a hate which has only our best interests prophylactically 'at heart.' Long before any morphological changes are noticed in the spinal column of the hunchback-to-be, he is plagued by feelings of guilt. Long before the first asthmatic episode, nihilistic anxiety obtains, while actual diarrheic crises serve but as the culmination of psychic incontinence in the face of difficulties. In other words, infarcts occur without actual infarcts, hunchbacks are not necessarily misshapen, asthmatics do not have to manifest bronchial congestion, and diarrhea does not depend upon the presence of frequent and loose bowel movements.

Nature may even be said to nurse the rich variety of these premonitory adversities, lending them at the same time a special measure of reality. Put somewhat differently, pre-morbid premonitions intrude just enough to show us where we stand and to what extent we have exceeded the natural limits of health according to a *law of intensity,* to degrees of priority. The fact that the premonitions are always present, in one way or another, bears witness to Nature's intention of continual prevention. Pre-morbid premonitions support health, precede disease, and guide those of us who pay attention on the path of physical well-being.

As long as what we have called "premonitions" remain barely perceived in a pre-morbid state, they may enhance our abilities to an extent undreamed of. They serve as a kind of leaven, motivating or driving us to escape into the ostentation of health and concomitantly outstanding performances. In this manner the pre-morbid premonitions fatten us up, a process which, thanks to not inconsiderable possibilities of repression and suppression, allows us to develop an unusually exaggerated image of ourselves. Even though the process can easily lead us astray and, thereby, evoke illness, it also provides us with the understanding for the very reverse, namely, how genius thrives in the dung of pre-morbidity.

In the long run, however, health undermines itself for, as our daily experience teaches, human life meets increasingly with disease and ends finally in death. We would have to be terribly naive to regard Nature exclusively as having our well-being in mind: she does not work toward maintaining an eternally youthful state of health but toward our ultimate demise. It is as if Nature intended our greatest possible level of health to be our greatest possible level of tolerable disease. If our 'undoing' depends on the recessive portion of our inherent chimerical division (guiding habitual behavior so that we do not go too far astray) *and* if this same 'undoing' all-too-readily becomes perverted as physical disease, then obviously Nature has not planned the same sort of well-being for us that finds expression in contemporary notions of 'health.'

On the contrary, human beings seem less capable of *being* healthy the more they believe they *have* to be healthy. For this reason, sports are that much more dangerous to the extent that they incorporate an unreflective, unconsidered competitive thinking. The more we take for granted the necessity of a stiff-upper-lip attitude toward life and living, the more certainly will cowardice and timidity catch up with us and possess us in the form of trembling or through the reassuring voracity for food. The sort of health that Nature has planned for us behaves very much like weather conditions: there is no such thing as a permanent high-pressure area without the storms from encroaching frontal systems. There is no such thing as continuous health without the risk of death. In this regard, it seems, we are in no wise independent of Nature; rather we live as an integral part of the elemental landscape of our origin.

Human beings are healthier when they are sick. In its purest form, health is unbearable in the long run, for it carries too great a responsibility and too much freedom for us to take it upon ourselves unscathed for any length of time. The 'undoing' and its manifestation, illness, are in the final analysis necessary. Our daily afflictions are in no way solely an indictment of the *condition humaine* but an expression of satisfaction that our well-being and our human potential have boundaries at all. We are better grounded by the afflictions, protected and shielded, as if all our strivings assumed a touch of spontaneity. When we are short of breath due to obesity, we can take everything a little less seriously since we can, after a manner of speaking, hold fast to our own panting. Arthritic discomforts add a touch of pain to all our undertakings, legitimizing tendencies to indolence, while an acute or a chronic sinus condition enables us to hold the world at a distance with the excuse of "I have a cold."

As long as we know what to look for, we encounter examples of the law for the preservation of our 'undoing' and its corollary, the necessity of illness, on every corner of everyday life. When in the course of psychotherapeutic treatment the physical complaints or symptoms recede or disappear entirely, the circumstances and behavior which gave rise to the symptoms in the first place may well appear as banal dysphorias. Where previously a persistent abdominal discomfort—with or without an accompanying bladder infection—complicated a housewife's daily routine considerably, now 'gripes' or complaints of a different sort confront her and make her life difficult. When, on the other hand, *psychic* difficulties take a welcome turn for the better, there is no guarantee that they will not, if they have not already, manifest as bodily complaints, 'fall into body'! When the suffering, the 'undoing,' expressed heretofore in stubborn and futile social protest suddenly improves, for instance, it would not be surprising to see it reappear as a painful abdominal rheumatism.

· · · · · · ·

20 · THE DEMONIC SIDE OF SEXUALITY

A D O L F   G U G G E N B Ü H L – C R A I G

One of the great tasks of the individuation process is to experience the dark, destructive side. This can occur through the medium of sexuality, which can be one of many possible places for this experience. This certainly does not mean that one must be inundated by the fantasies of a Marquis de Sade or that one should enact such fantasies. It means rather that fantasies of such a kind can be understood as the symbolic expression of an individuation process which is unfolding in the territory of the sexual Gods.

I once treated a masochistic woman, a self-flagellator, whom I tried to help to normalize herself. I even had some success: her masochistic activities stopped, and she suppressed her masochistic fantasies. However she began to suffer from an inexplicable headache that caused her great problems in her professional life. In a sort of visionary experience—she was a black African woman and in her environment such things were not uncommon—Moses appeared to her and instructed her to continue with her flagellations; if she did not do so, the Egyptians would kill her. On the basis of this vision she developed a complicated theory, based in part on the flagellation rituals of the Mexican Christians, which held that only through her masochism could she confront and come to terms with the suffering of the world. She allowed herself once more to be overcome by masochistic fantasies; as she did so, her headaches disappeared and her psychological development proceeded very well. This example is meant to serve as an illustration, not as a recommendation.

The phenomenon of sado-masochism has often stimulated the wonder of psychologists. How can pleasure and pain coincide? Masochism seems to be something self-contradictory for many psychologists and psychoanalysts. Some of them go so far as to maintain that masochists may try now and then to act out their fantasies in great detail and with much theatricality, but when it actually comes down to suffering they immediately cease such behavior. However, this is not altogether correct, and moreover it relates in part to certain sexual variations. Actual sexual life is seldom fully in accord with sexual fantasies. We know that there exist many masochists who not only seek out degrading forms of pain but also experience them with pleasure.

Masochism played a large role in the Middle-Ages, when flagellators flooded through the cities and villages. Many of the saints devoted much time to beating themselves. Monks and nuns considered it routine practice to inflict pain and humiliation upon themselves. The attempt of modern psychiatry to understand this whole collective phenomenon as an expression of perverse and neurotic sexuality does not seem satisfying to me. We come closer to the phenomenon with the concept of individuation. Is not the suffering of our life, and of life in general, one of the most difficult things there is to accept? The world is so full of suffering, and all of us suffer so greatly in body and spirit, that even the saints have difficulty understanding this. It is one of the most difficult tasks of the individuation process to accept sorrow and joy, pain and pleasure, God's anger and God's grace. The opposites—suffering and joy, pain and pleasure—are symbolically united in masochism. Thus life can be actually accepted, and even pain can be joyfully experienced. The masochist, in a remarkable and fantastic way, confronts and comes to terms with the greatest opposites of our existence.

Sadism is in part to be understood as an expression of the destructive side of people: an expression of the core, of the shadow, of the murderer within us. It is a specifically human trait to find joy in destruction. This is not the place to consider whether destructiveness belongs to human nature or is the product of a faulty development, although I believe the former to be true. In any case, destructiveness is a psychological phenomenon with which every living human being must come to terms. The joy of destroying, of obliterating, of torturing, etc., is also experienced within the sexual medium.

The joy of destroying others is related to self-destructiveness. Thus it is not surprising that sadism and masochism appear together; the self-destructive killer is in the center of the archetypal shadow, the center of irreducible destructiveness in human beings.

Another component in sadism is the intoxication with power. It provides sexual pleasure to dominate the partner completely, to play with him like a cat with a mouse.

Still another aspect of sadism is to degrade the partner to the status of pure object. In sadistic fantasies, the binding of the partner and the "cool" watching of his reactions play a great role. The partner becomes purely a thing whose reactions are played with.

For a long time Christian theologians could recognize sexuality only in connection with reproduction. They experienced the erotic as something demonic and uncanny, as something that had to be fought against or neutralized. All of these medieval theologians were certainly intelligent and differentiated people, in honest search for truth and understanding. That they experienced sexuality as demonic, therefore, cannot be so easily discounted. They were expressing something quite true.

Sexuality is still demonized in our day. All attempts to render it completely harmless and to present it as something "completely natural" flounder and fail. To modern man, sexuality in certain forms continues to appear as something evil and sinfully sinister.

Certain women's liberation movements try to understand sexuality as a political weapon used by men to suppress women; thus they demonize sexuality, while at the same time implying that by an exchange of roles between man and woman sexuality can become harmless.

As another example of demonization I would like to cite the purported effect of the so-called primal scene. Students of Freud, and a large portion of educated official opinion under their influence, hold that one must expect serious psychological consequences in a child who has accidentally witnessed sexual contact between its parents. Many neurotic developments are attributed to such childhood experiences.

An unrestricted presentation of the sexual activities of parents overstimulates the incestuous wishes and related jealousy of children. Through this, the Oedipal situation gets uncomfortably intensified. On the other hand, it is fortunately impossible for very many parents to show their sexuality to their children openly and without inhibition. This too is related to the incest taboo. The parents as well defend themselves instinctively against overstimulation of their incest fantasies and tendencies. The repression of a taboo probably creates more psychological damage than does the respectful recognition of it. Some of the greatest taboos, like the incest taboo, protect us more than they restrict us.

Another contemporary example of how sexuality is still experienced as sinister is found in the regimentation and exclusion of sexuality from most of our hospitals. It is believed that a sexual life could in some puzzling, mysterious way harm these needy patients. But why is this believed? For what reason are the patients in a mental institution, for instance, not allowed to have sexual contact with one another within the institution?

The following is yet another example of how it is taken for granted that sexuality must be something sinister. Sexual intercourse with a mentally retarded person is considered a criminal act in Switzerland. The intent of this law was to protect the mentally retarded person from being misused. But the basic effect of this law was to make it impossible for the mentally retarded to have a sexual life. That such an inhumane law has not run into popular resistance demonstrates once again that an almost magical power is attributed to sexuality.

One last example. Athletes—the participants in the Olympics for instance—are often strictly forbidden by their coaches to engage in any sexual activities during the contests. It has happened that athletes in the Olympics have been sent home for engaging in surreptitious sexual adventures. Yet, at the same time, it is known to be beneficial for certain athletes to be sexually active before undertaking great athletic efforts.

Ancient prejudices are at work here. Among certain primitives the men dare not have sexual contact with women before going into battle.

The demonic element within sexuality shows itself also perhaps in the fact that it is very difficult to experience and to accept sexual activities purely as "enjoyment" or pleasurable experience. Few people can "simply enjoy" sexuality as they would a good meal. The "glass of water theory"—sexual experience as the quenching of thirst—is frequently advocated but seldom experienced by people over a long period of time.

What does it mean for psychology that sexuality always has something sinister about it, even today when we believe that we have liberated ourselves from this attitude? The sinister is always the unintelligible, the impressive, the numinous. Wherever something divine appears, we begin to experience fear. The individuation process, which has a strongly religious character, is experienced as numinous in many respects. Everything that has to do with salvation possesses, among other things, a sinister, unfamiliar character; it always includes the superhuman.

The demonization of sexuality is perhaps understandable given its individuational character. It is not simply a harmless biological activity, but rather a symbol for something that relates to the meaning of our lives, to our striving and longing for the divine.

Sexuality offers us symbols for all aspects of individuation. The encounter with the parental figures is experienced in the incest drama. The confrontation with the shadow leads to the destructive sado-masochistic components of the erotic. The encounter with one's own soul, with the anima and animus, with the feminine and the masculine, can have a sexual form. Self-love and love for others is experienced bodily in sexuality, whether via fantasies or activities. Nowhere is the union of all the opposites, the *unio mystica*, the *mysterium coniunctionis*, more impressively expressed than in the language of eroticism.

. . . .

All bibles or sacred codes have been the causes of the following errors:
1. *That man has two real existing principles: a body & a soul.*
2. *That energy, called evil, is alone from the body: & that reason, called good, is alone from the soul.*
3. *That God will torment man in eternity for following his energies.*

But the following contraries to these are true:
1. *Man has no body distinct from his soul; for that called body is a portion of soul discerned by the five senses, the chief inlets of soul in this age.*
2. *Energy is the only life, and is from the body; and reason is the bound or outward circumference of energy.*
3. *Energy is eternal delight.*

WILLIAM BLAKE

. . . .

PART 5

THE
SHADOW OF
ACHIEVEMENT:
THE DARK
SIDE OF
WORK AND
PROGRESS

The love of money is the root of all evil.

I TIMOTHY 6:10

I am not on this planet to get something done. . . . The things we accomplish are expressions of our purpose.

PAUL WILLIAMS

Progess is our most important product.

ADVERTISING SLOGAN

Our tendency is to exalt the bright side of industry over the dark side of nature or to exalt the bright side of nature over the dark side of industry. In reality we need to compare bright with bright and dark with dark.

THOMAS BERRY

INTRODUCTION

· · · · · · ·

The personal downside of America's work ethic has been explored at length in the ever-growing literature on stress and burn-out. The collective downside stares back at us with the face of ecological catastrophe.

Nearly everyone has seen someone they love, a father or grandfather perhaps, overvalue productivity to such an extent that the rest of life is sacrificed. Whatever the task, a workaholic pours lifeblood into a venture—sometimes with the dream of creating security for retirement or for future generations; sometimes with the dream of contributing to the greater welfare; sometimes without a dream, but simply unable to live for any other purpose, at any other pace. Possessed by the demonic self rather than enchanted by the creative process, a compulsive worker cannot let go of the reins on himself.

Workaholism is now seen as an addiction, a behavior of repetition compulsion, like gambling or overeating. And in some cases our organizations and their leaders expect and contribute to this shadow world of addictive work by the very ways in which they operate. Untenable workloads, unrealistic sales quotas, and martini lunches contribute to severely imbalanced lifestyles among all ranks of American workers.

The toll is high for everyone concerned: loved ones suffer from an absent spouse or parent; overworkers suffer physical and emotional deterioration from the demands of a one-sided life; and corporations suffer a typical seven-year turnover in executives.

Douglas LaBier, author of *Modern Madness,* calls them the working wounded, "healthy people adjusted at great emotional cost due to conditions that are good for the advancement of career but not of spirit." He points out that personal success for the working wounded often means merely successful adaptation, fitting into the collective persona of an organization by burying those qualities that don't fit the company image. For companies, too, have a persona that is created by a stated corporate mission—a pretty face to the world—and therefore they typically have an unseen, shady side that includes poor personnel benefits, low tolerance for internal feedback or conflict, external policies that have disastrous ecological consequences, or dishonesty with customers.

Everyone in the workplace has been faced with painful conflicts of values. We feel forced at times to violate principles, dominate others, disregard employees' personal needs, tell white lies, and sell out in other small ways. A lawyer joke that refers to making deals while turning the other way could just as well apply to any professional: A lawyer wants to be Number One. He meets the devil, who offers him all the money and power he could ever want in exchange for his soul. The lawyer says, "Okay—but what's the catch?"

The pressure of high-tension environments molds us into contorted shapes, leading us to make bargains at great cost to ourselves. Success leads to ego inflation, while failure leads to a biting shame. Like billionaire Donald Trump, we may be flying high one moment, diving low the next.

In every job, we develop certain skills and aptitudes while leaving others in the shadow. If we cultivate an extroverted ambition, a powerful, competitive personality like a salesman, politician, or entrepreneur, our introversion goes into the shadow. We forget how to thrive outside of the limelight, receive riches from solitude, find hidden resources within. If, on the other hand, we develop a more private persona, as an artist or writer, our ambition and greed may go into the shadow, never to emerge, or one day to emerge suddenly like a ghost from a closet. We have all read, for instance, about a moral, upstanding business person who gets caught red-handed in a shady deal, embezzling money or cheating on taxes. This possession by the shadow may be rooted in an inability to look at it more directly.

Just as the shadow occasionally takes hold of us in this way and turns us around 180 degrees, so it can take hold of a group or business. The conservative, materialistic values of the Depression generation led to the counterculture movement of the 1960s, which emphasized the renunciation of conformity and materialism, creating shadow heroes out of those who lived against the grain. This trend, in turn, led to another surge of materialism, whose symptoms we see around us today.

This swing of the pendulum now appears in yet another way. While the shadow of ambition can be seen in individual burn-out, the cultural shadow is being revealed in species-death. It has taken an ecological catastrophe of global import to wake us up to the dark side of unbounded economic growth and unlimited technological progress.

In *The End of Nature,* Bill McKibben points out that we are no longer the masters of our technologies: "As long as the desire for endless material advancement drives us, there is no way to set limits. We are unlikely to develop genetic engineering to eradicate disease and then not use it to manufacture perfectly efficient chickens."

Opening this section, Boston psychologist and organization consultant Bruce Shackleton describes meeting the shadow self in the workplace, both within individuals and within organizations. He explores how the interrelationships between individual and corporate shadows can help or hinder the bottom line.

In Chapter 22, John R. O'Neill, president of the California School of Professional Psychology, previews his work in a forthcoming book, *The Dark Side of Success.* O'Neill, an entrepreneur and consultant, offers us clues for how to sustain healthy achievement by staying aware of shadow issues.

In noncorporate domains, each profession also has its stated aim, its mission to help or to heal, as well as its hidden side. In Chapter 23, Jungian analyst Adolf Guggenbühl-Craig explores both sides of the helping professions: the heroic doctor and the scandalous quack, the godlike priest and the false prophet, the dedicated psychotherapist and the unknowing charlatan.

In an excerpt from *Do What You Love, The Money Will Follow,* Marsha Sinetar explores how our personal flaws and faults appear in the workplace, and how we can use them to our advantage in our creative lives.

In her book *When Technology Wounds,* writer Chellis Glendinning tells the stories of people with technology-induced illnesses, disclosing the previously invisible dangers of advances such as computers, fluorescent lights, birth control pills, asbestos, and pesticides. In this excerpt, she questions the idea of progress as unchecked technological development and urges us to look at its human costs.

Finally, Peter Bishop, an Australian teacher, closes this section with a vision of one earth and its shadow side—one death. His piece, originally published in the Jungian journal *Spring,* is an ode to the earth's wilderness as a victim of our unrelenting progress.

It seems that even our achievements, both personal and collective, have their dark sides. And progress, unchecked and unexamined, leaves chaos in its wake.

· · · · · · ·

21 · MEETING THE SHADOW AT WORK

BRUCE SHACKLETON

What stops us from achieving all that we consciously believe we seek to achieve? What is the nature of that side of us that sabotages our efforts, trips us up as we pursue our hopes and aspirations, and does not want to be exposed to the light of success? How do our workplace organizations contribute to undermining the achievement of our goals, rather than to helping us meet them?

Although it is less recognized as a key factor in shadow-making than the family, the school, or the church, the workplace influences us greatly to behave in certain ways in order to fit in, adapt, and succeed. All of us attempt to please our bosses, colleagues, and customers at work, often stuffing our unpleasing parts—our aggression, greed, competitiveness, or outspoken opinions—into the deeper recesses of our private selves. For many, psychological and spiritual compromise comes about when we throw so much of ourselves into the shadow that we find we have "sold our soul to the company store."

Of course, we need the shadow, in which we can hide our negative and destructive drives, even our weaknesses and inferior abilities. But the danger arises when we push too much of ourselves away too deeply. If an individual's work shadow becomes impermeable, inflexible, and dense, it can become destructive and take on a life of its own.

POWER AND COMPETENCE AS SHADOW

When I met Harold, a middle-aged man who had had aspirations ten years earlier of reaching "the top," he was vice-president of finance in a small high-technology company. During his career in larger organizations he had been moderately successful, but in his early forties he entered psychotherapy with me because he felt depressed, without motivation, and saw no point in pursuing greater success. He was resigned, settling into this smaller company in a position that did not test his ability, and spent a great deal of time thinking about retirement.

Harold had inherited a sense of inadequacy from his family, a classic case of low self-esteem. In his earlier work environments he had had difficulty dealing with authority because he did not really feel he was on equal footing with others.

Harold's current boss, a hard-driving man, was often arrogant and insensitive, running the company with a bottom-line management style. He did not allow open disagreement and was cruel with his employees occasionally. To the CEO's aggressiveness, Harold responded with an accommodating and often anxious willingness to be subordinate. He had found a boss onto whom he could project his shadowy feelings of power, arrogance, and competence, and around whom he felt ill at ease and insecure, reinforcing his family's image of him.

For a while it was a perfect fit. Harold put on a good front of getting the job done, but did nothing more. He was accepted for his abilities as well as for supporting the status quo. But beneath this facade of roles, Harold was withholding his creative energy and enthusiasm, thereby avoiding any confrontation that might bring risk—and also avoiding his own competence to move his career ahead. Harold was aware only of vague feelings of restlessness and dissatisfaction.

Soon the dam began to leak. Although he was generally an ethical and religious man, Harold began to resort to petty embezzlement and passive-aggressive behavior in an indirect effort to discharge his sense of anger, frustration, and belittlement. His behavior shocked him—it did not fit his good citizen self-image—and ultimately led him to look more deeply into the personal costs of his workstyle.

WORKAHOLISM AND THE SHADOW OF ORGANIZATIONS

We also witness the shadow in the workplace when people put aside their personal needs for leisure, intimacy, and family, becoming around-the-clock achievement machines. This addictive behavior inevitably leads to a highly imbalanced and compulsive lifestyle.

Like most addictions, workaholism may be rooted in family patterns. In some homes, boys and girls are given support only for their performance, and their self-worth becomes rooted entirely in winning. In other homes, a workaholic parent passes on the pattern to a child, who inherits it like eye color. In others, the failure of a nonachieving parent goads a child into the drive for success, into becoming, in effect, the parent's shadow self.

If the workaholic happens to belong to an addictive organization in which these patterns are supported and encouraged, the match will appear to be perfect for a while; the individual's shadow and the company's shadow are aligned. But generally, something somewhere will begin to give—the employee will reveal multiple addictions, such as alcohol or drugs, or will reach burn-out; the company will change directions or leadership—and the destructive side of the workaholism will wreak havoc.

Workaholism is not the only underside of organizations. While corporate culture—those rules, rituals, and values of a company that help people organize their activities—may be stated, corporations also have a less visible, unstated side, and their relationship to it can determine much about their financial and personnel achievements.

Organizations that deny the need for adequate human resource development and management of stress, for example, can become blaming and insensitive to employees. When there is too much focus on the bottom line and too little focus on individual needs, an atmosphere of distrust may develop. Some employees may become scapegoats, attacked or sacrificed in an effort to resolve unspoken dynamics within the organization.

On the other hand, corporate cultures that encourage open communication can set up checks and balances for individual and group shadow problems, with a very different type of outcome. A healthy organization can help to limit negative acting-out by building open feedback systems, setting agreements about values and purpose, and even helping employees develop their deeper capacities.

Employee motivation also is deeply tied to shadow material. For instance, people who are driven to the top may have to deny their more caring qualities, stepping on others' toes in order to achieve corporate images of climbing the ladder. When at the top, these individuals are likely to operate primarily out of their shadow sides, allowing their deeper humanity to reveal itself only at home with the family, in a modern Dr. Jekyll/Mr. Hyde split. In a more extreme form, possession by the shadow may lead to blatant disregard of others at home as well as at work.

These issues concerning individual and corporate shadow are too often neglected by human resource trainers and consultants. It would be of great benefit if we could more readily acknowledge the dark side and put it to work for us in individual, corporate, and social renewal.

· · · · · · ·

22 · THE DARK SIDE OF SUCCESS

JOHN R. O'NEILL

Everyone is supposed to seek success; the more, the better. But recently we have witnessed peculiar distortions in the definition of success, and we are now carrying the shadow results of this shift. People and organizations often enjoy a period of shining success that later tarnishes. The success seems to arrive with a built-in anxiety: Will it last? How can I get even more? Do I deserve it? What if I lost it? For this reason, it changes quickly from elation to worry, from joy to chronic fatigue, depression, or a crisis of personal meaning.

How does this change occur? During periods of success we become inflated and eventually suffer hubris, a great arrogance, thus failing to meet and eat the shadow. We stop listening and observing ourselves beyond the frantic antics of ego; we fail at our deep-learning tasks; and our true identities become distorted, twisted, even lost altogether.

Consider the case of James, a Wall Street darling in the 1980s, who has come to hate his highly successful business. He sells it and collects $130 million. Three months later he makes an appointment with me. He enters my office looking tanned and relaxed, his blond hair bleached and a little longer than usual. With some animation he tells me about his ocean yacht sailing, his ski trips, and his new ranch. I wonder why he has sought counseling.

Toward the end of our session he says quite casually, "I don't have a single person to talk to about my life, so you are it." Trying not to look startled about this revelation, I ask how this is possible. His response includes tales of betrayal, family fights, an impending divorce, fear of public reprisal if he talks to the wrong person, and dark nights of fitful sleep.

The substance of what James had stuffed away is similar to many people's shadows:

- Those parts of him that did not meet the ego ideal of his time. In a macho era, he had dropped his receptive, feminine aspects; in a material era, he had cast aside his spiritual feelings.

- Those parts of him that were considered unworthy by his parents or others whose approval he sought had been buried but were still very much alive.

- Those dreams or ambitions that were considered foolish or impractical were dumped with a small promise—"maybe someday."

More of him was hidden than visible. This vital denied material controls our life's direction, energy level, and biographical history. If we continue to stuff such pieces of ourselves into the darkness, we will inevitably pay with the coin of our soul.

On the other hand, people who know how to mine their shadow's rich potential and use it for future successes are success sustainers. They may be called deep learners. Winston Churchill, Eleanor Roosevelt, Florence Nightingale, Thomas Jefferson, and Abraham Lincoln are historical figures who learned from their disappointments, failure, and pain, and went on to another success. They knew how to fight hubris.

Frequently I am asked by leaders how they sustain learning and growing in their organizations. I suggest that the first problem is to avoid hubris by changing individual and organizational learning curves at the moment they reach the desired goal of success. The tall, sweet grass of success is the breeding ground of inflation and contains the hidden land mines of pride and greed.

Here is a quick checklist for spotting the signs of onrushing hubris:

- *Endowing ourselves with special gifts.* When we find that we have begun to take on certain airs of self-inflation, such as believing we can make unfailing assessments of others or avoid human errors, we are seeing the shadow's face.

- *Killing the messenger.* When we denounce contrary informants as cranky, slow-witted, jealous, or unable to grasp the big picture, we are on the way to suffering in the future. If as leaders we seal ourselves off, pulling our circle of trusted advisors tighter and tighter, we have begun to kill the messengers.

- *Needing to command the performance.* When hubris is present, the ego begins to assert itself in power-flexing demonstrations, such as fretting about social forms, seating arrangements, and meeting turf. Needing to see our importance constantly acknowledged by others is a sign of denied insecurity.

- *Living on higher moral ground.* When a person or group is on the path of righteousness, those who think differently may be labeled as wrong, evil, or an enemy. This may temporarily relieve the tension between good and bad, but it's actually hubris operating under the guise of goodness.

When hubris is operating, we stop learning. Our swollen ego screens the shadow, which threatens to pull us down by its dark and stealthful rage. But once we know it's there, it can be helpful to remember that new learning is contained within the very material that the shadow holds. The ego is only prancing because the shadow is really in control. If we can find a way to let go of the ego needs, roles, symbols, and righteous behavior, then we can enter the chaos of new learning and begin to discover once again new parts of ourselves.

In this way, every present success can be seen to contain a shadow that can become devastating. In order to discover and define future success, we must nibble away at the shadow each day. For this we will need to retreat for renewal, and we will need guides, mentors, and sometimes therapists.

Success sustainers know how to do this work. As author John Gardner said to me years ago, "Remember that while you are climbing your mountain, there are other mountains. Keep an eye on the next peak. Use the valley between to renew yourself."

. . . .

23 · QUACKS, CHARLATANS, AND FALSE PROPHETS

ADOLF GUGGENBÜHL-CRAIG

"I will exercise my art solely for the cure of my patients . . . in uprightness and honor. . . . Into whatsoever house I enter, it shall be for the good of the sick to the utmost of my power, holding myself far aloof from wrong, from corruption, from the tempting of others into vice . . . I count my life and art as holy."

These sentences are taken from the Hippocratic Oath. Down through the centuries and into our own day the model image of the physician has rested on this oath. The physician is the disinterested altruistic helper. He concerns himself with the sick and the suffering in order to serve them. This is the bright, light aspect of his work.

The dark side looks a little different. It is portrayed, for example, in Jules Romains' *Doctor Knock*. Dr. Knock has no altruistic desire to heal. He uses his medical knowledge for his own personal profit. He does not even hesitate to make healthy people sick. He is a quack. By quack I do not mean the medical or non-medical man who tries to help the sick by unorthodox, unapproved means, but rather the charlatan, the swindler, who at best deceives himself along with his patients—at worst, deceives only his patients. Quacks help themselves—through gains in prestige as well as financially—far more than they do any patient who comes to them. The actual medical activity of quacks in this sense may be useful or harmful or neither. But these medical practitioners are not interested in the medical aspect of their activity; they are false to the Oath and work only for themselves.

The quack is the shadow which forever accompanies the medical man. It is a shadow which may live in him or outside of him. His own patients exert great pressure on him to forego the Hippocratic model and imitate the caricature of Dr. Knock. The innumerable disabilities of unknown origin which he must treat in his daily practice, none with a recognized therapy—disabilities such as chronic fatigue, certain types of backaches and joint aches, vague heart or gastric pains, chronic headache, etc.—he treats them all with a pseudoscientific display of medical know-how. Instead of bringing the psychic components to the attention of those patients whose suffering is largely psychic, for example, he actually helps them turn their psychic problems into physical ones. If they get better he is the great healer; if they get worse it is because they did not follow his directions properly.

Let us leave the physician's shadow problem for a moment. In order to develop the main theme of this paper I must first take up the dark side of priest and pastor. The image of the "man of God" has undergone many transformations in the course of history, nor is it the same in all religions. What concerns us here is the priest or pastor of the Judeo-Christian tradition. He is expected, as member of the priest class, to have at least some intermittent relationship with the Lord. It is not necessary that each individual man of God have a direct mission from the Lord like an Old Testament prophet, but he is supposed to try, at least, to stand up honestly for God and His will, either by virtue of a genuine contact with the godhead or on the basis of his special conversance with Holy Writ and traditional holy wisdom.

The reverse of this noble image of the man of God is the hypocrite, the man who preaches not because he has faith but because he wants to influence others, to wield power over them. The congregation of any preacher exerts great pressure on him to act the hypocrite. Faith's inevitable companion is doubt. But no one wants doubt from his priest or pastor; everyone has enough doubts himself. What can a clergyman, do except pretend, now and again, to hide his doubts and seek to gloss over the momentary inner emptiness with highflown words. And if he is weak such occasions will form a habit. We expect the pastor or priest to know the soul's way to salvation. The shadow of this intimate of the deity is the little lord-almighty, the preacher who is never at a loss for words concerning the finalities of life and death. Ideally a man of God must bear witness to the Lord. He cannot prove what he preaches. We expect of him that his behavior, his testimony, will create the foundation that underlies the rightness of the way of salvation for which he stands. And immediately we see the shadow figure of the hypocritical man of God who wants to represent himself to the world—as well as to himself—as better than he really is.

The shadow of the false prophet accompanies the pastor or priest all his life. Sometimes it emerges into the outside world as a narrow sectarian or as a hated demagogue within the church's organization. Sometimes it resides within. The noble images of physician and clergyman are forever accompanied by the shadow figures of quack and false prophet.

Now the psychotherapist, the analyst, constitutes the meeting ground, in our day, of the images and the practices of physician and clergyman, of physical and psychic healer. It is thus that he carries a double shadow.

Let us look first at the shadow problems that beset the analyst externally, on his medical side. We analysts frequently deal with diseases (such as neuroses, psychosomatic illnesses and border-line psychoses) which make it impossible to employ methods that permit of generally acknowledged experimental controls. As everyone knows it is impossible for example to keep statistics relating to success or failure of treatment in the case of neuroses. What constitutes remission? Deterioration? Is social adjustment to be a proper criterion? Or the patient's ability to hold a job? Or the increase and acuity or the decrease and dulling of neurotic symptoms? Or the patient's subjective sense of well-being? Or progress made toward individuation? Improved contact with the unconscious? The criteria themselves are open to indefinite interpretation as compared, say, to the healing of a fracture where restored functioning provides an unequivocal criterion of the efficacy of treatment.

Whatever criteria one chooses, the statistical results in our profession are most unsatisfactory. It is impossible to ascertain whether a patient was treated by psychotherapy, by medication with tranquilizers or by nothing at all. And in this respect the psychosomatic illnesses are as bad as the neuroses.

Suppose we agree that the patient's distance from the Self, his worse or better contact with the unconscious, should be the proper criterion for ascertaining the efficacy of psychotherapy. How are we to measure this? How make a statistically valid investigation?

Anyone, in other words, who calls himself an analyst or a psychologist may claim success if he shows up at the right moment or endures long enough or is lucky enough to come up against a patient whose condition would have improved regardless of treatment, when measured by some criterion or other. The quack shadow or the medicine-oriented aspect of the analyst can thus be activated with relative lack of control.

But the analyst's shadow is further nourished by those features which the analyst has in common with the clergyman. Jungian analysts do not represent a specific faith, to be sure. We have no organized religion. Still we do, like the clergy, stand for a definite way of life. We represent no philosophy but we do adhere to a psychology about which we feel conviction, having, in our own lives and in our own analyses, lived through certain experiences which have convinced us and shaped us. Our confrontation with the irrational and the unconscious has moved us deeply. But whatever insights we have cannot be scientifically or statistically proved; they can only be affirmed by the honest and truthful account of other people. To the question that I have heard so often from American medical schools, "What studies have been done?" there is not much of an answer. The only proofs we can adduce are the personal experiences of ourselves and others, since the reality of the psyche cannot be proved statistically or causally in the usual scientific sense. Here we are in a position similar to that of the clergy.

The necessity of having recourse only to the personal experience of oneself and others makes for doubts. What if we and our trusted authorities have been deceived? After all, there are many people, including other psychotherapists of integrity, who hold a totally un-Jungian view of psychology. Are they all deceived? Are they all blind?

Are we capable of admitting such doubts to ourselves and to others? Or do we share the danger of the clergyman who pushes aside his ever-present doubts and never admits their existence?

Like the pastor and priest, furthermore, we work with our own psyche, our own person, without instruments, methods of technology. Our tools are ourselves, our honesty, our truthfulness, our own personal contact with the unconscious and the irrational. The pressure on us is great to represent these tools as better than they are and thus fall into our psychotherapist shadow. And there is one more parallel to pastor and priest. We are pushed into the role of omniscience. We work with the unconscious, with dreams, with the soul—all areas in which the transcendental makes itself felt. Hence we are expected to know more about first and last things than ordinary mortals. If we are weak we end up believing that we are better informed about matters of life and death than our fellow men.

Thus not only the bright model images of medicine and clergy meet in the person of the analyst but their shadows as well: quack and false prophet. Is it worthwhile wasting words on this situation? That there are quacks and false prophets among psychotherapists who consciously or unconsciously profit personally far more than do the human beings whom they supposedly serve is surely obvious and well understood.

The consciously cynical racketeers, we tend to say, are simply criminals who are usually soon recognized by their colleagues, although they do keep finding new victims among the ill and helpless. Through our professional associations we try to protect potential patients against these dark colleagues of ours. So far as the other sort is concerned, those who deceive not so much their patients as themselves with their unconscious identity with the shadow, we might say that it is simply a question of more consciousness and better professional education. The future analyst becomes conscious of his shadow during the course of a good training and control analysis and afterward is no longer threatened by it.

But there is an error here and because of it the problem of the psychotherapist's professional shadow is of the utmost importance. For here we come up against the tragedy inherent in being an analyst. The greater and broader the analyst's growing consciousness becomes, the greater in turn grows his unconsciousness. Unconsciousness, and along with it the problem of falling into the shadow, is *the* great problem of the analyst. Let us begin by considering the situation from the point of view of individuation. The more individuated a man becomes, *i.e.,* the wider the realm of the unconscious spreads out before him, the more powerful become the constellations of the unconscious. The process of becoming conscious, after all, is supposed to aid us in giving ourselves over to the unconscious time and again. We progress in individuation only in so far as we keep turning away from what has become conscious and submerge anew in the unconscious. This means, practically speaking, that a man who is becoming individuated acts, from time to time, straight from the unconscious—and this includes the psychotherapist engaging in his professional activity. But acting from unconsciousness means falling, ever and anew, into one's shadow.

There is another aspect of the process of individuation which concerns the analyst more specifically than the non-analyst. It is the analyst's special— one of his special—tasks to help patients and his fellow workers to come to consciousness, *i.e.,* to confront the collective and personal contents within the unconscious of others. Just as the knowledge of God plays an important role in the model image of the clergyman or the self-less healer in the archetypal image of the physician, so in the psychotherapist's model there is a figure which we might designate as guide to consciousness, light-bearer. It occupies, in fact, a central position. But such professional model images as are inherent in physician, clergyman, and psychotherapist always contain a dark brother who is the *opposite* of the bright and shining ideal. Thus the psychotherapist's professional shadow contains not only the quack and the false prophet but also the alter ego who dwells completely in unconsciousness—the opposite, in other words, of everything the analyst consciously strives for. We are faced thus with the paradox that unconsciousness is a greater threat to the analyst than to the non-analyst.

I have been told that the British Navy before the First World War did not teach its sailors to swim, assuming that non-swimmers are far less likely to drown than swimmers since they take great pains to keep away from the water. The analyst is a swimmer in this sense, equating water with the unconscious.

An honest analyst will realize with horror from time to time that in his daily work he has been acting exactly like an unconscious quack and false prophet.

The following is a brief description of the way the psychotherapist shadow operates. This shadow makes an effort to treat only wealthy people who pay well or else well-known personalities who will add to its prestige. It then diagnoses "highly dangerous tendencies toward psychosis." Jung's concept of latent psychosis is easily misused in this connection. The danger of imminent psychic collapse is exaggerated in order that the shadow might look like a savior. During the course of treatment the patient, rather than being confronted with his problems, is flattered and cajoled. His worst character faults are held to be interesting, in fact quite remarkable. Bossy women are indulged because they manifest the "queen archetype"; inability to love becomes fascinating introversion. Egotistic lack of piety for an aging mother is understood to be liberation from the mother's animus. Instead of attempting to relax the tension between a patient and his father, the shadow immediately talks of the "king who must die." There is no realization that a careful analysis can often render threatening parents into friendly and kindly old people whose threatening qualities disappear to the exact degree that the patient gets stronger.

Any sort of remission is understood to be one's own doing or, at the least, it is ascribed to powers awakened by oneself; any deterioration of the condition is due to the patient's inability or unwillingness to go the way the analyst shows him.

The analyst caught in the shadow lives more and more vicariously through his patients. Their gossip is his gossip; their friendships, love affairs and sexual adventures become his experiences. He stops living his own life altogether. His patients are everything and all to him. The patients live, love and suffer for him. Perhaps he lives only for his patients, as the saying goes; surely he lives only through them. Analysis and analyzing come to be life itself for the analyst. And the dictum that the patient's payment is part of his therapy? Is it not possible that this is an assertion of the shadow? Surely the payment is not primarily part of the therapy but exists in order for us to live decently, as we earn and deserve.

The shadow holds veritable orgies with the concepts of transference and countertransference. We are jealous, for example, of the patient's husband because his influence seems to be as great as ours. We will not stand for such abrogation of our power; over and over again we represent the husband as behaving outrageously, atrociously and the like. And we try to separate the patient from his friends and acquaintances. The analyst's shadow also drives him to devaluate his patient's former loves and by so doing to overvalue himself.

Whenever the suffering of a neurotic patient threatens to overwhelm the analyst, his shadow shows him a nice way out of this difficulty as well. Neurotic suffering is unreal suffering—so goes the dogma—enabling one to overlook the fact that the patient is actually suffering. In reality there is probably no such thing as unreal or improper suffering, only unreal or improper problems.

Even the Self is misused by the analyst when he is submerged in the shadow. How much immoral and unloving, aggressive behavior is frequently justified as being intrinsic to the Self! Adultery, for example, is not looked upon in the first place as a grave insult and aggression toward the marriage partner but as a liberation from collective norms in the name of the Self. Unfair and disloyal behavior toward friends, acquaintances, employees and employers, rejection of morality and mores: All these the shadow-submerged analyst aids and abets as being bold acts of liberation and redemption, of discovery of the Self.

The analyst caught in his shadow begins in small ways to play prophet. He satisfies the religious needs of his patients by pretending to transcendental wisdom. Just as the shadow-bound clergyman sees God's works everywhere and in everything, so the analyst sees the unconscious operating everywhere at all times. Every dream, every happening, event, illness, joy, grief, every accident and every lottery prize is understood to be the unconscious at work. We crawl out of the woodwork like little gods, we analysts, and know how to deduce everything from something. We fail to recognize the dark hand of Moira, of fate, to which even the gods, the unconscious, must bow. There is no tragedy for us, no blind cruel accident. People fall into misfortune, we believe, because they have lost contact with the unconscious. And ultimately we even believe, and let our patients believe, that we can peek behind the scenes of world events.

In order to continue to help the patient in a tragic life situation which remains tragic even though the contact with the unconscious may improve, we need to be able to face our own tragic life situation. What I take to be our special tragedy is that the more we try to be good therapists who aid our patients' consciousness, the more we must fall prey to the dark side of our bright professional image, to our—at the very least partial—blindness with respect to our shadow.

In a certain sense, the destiny of any man who strives for a goal of some kind—and our patients are usually such men—has a distinctly tragic side. Over and over again the opposite of what one wishes to achieve or wishes to avoid will be constellated.

The physician becomes a quack just because he wants to heal as many people as possible; the man of God becomes a hypocrite and a false prophet because he is so eager to increase the faith among his fellow men. Thus too the psychotherapist becomes an unconscious false prophet and quack although he works night and day at becoming ever more conscious.

. . . .

24 · USING OUR FLAWS AND FAULTS

MARSHA   SINETAR

People who function effectively in their work know their limits. They use them in the service of their lives, managing to integrate these limitations into the way they work best. Rightly, they have discovered that somehow they must attend to their own physical and psychological makeup, emotional tendencies and concentration patterns, and that these are good helpmates in getting a job done. In fact, a person's combined limitations form a complex of attributes that has meaning beyond anyone's current understanding—even the individual's. This complex is the essence of one's expressive life.

A client of mine is a hall wanderer. By nature restless, he thinks best when strolling around. Because he has come to accept this about himself, others have too. After many years of working with him, colleagues now expect him to walk the halls. Of course, his superior thinking has made millions of dollars for his company, and he has earned the "right" to stroll as much as he wishes.

Another person, a scientist, prefers to work in isolation in a company that values an open door policy. She regularly closes her door at work, even though at first she was soundly criticized for doing so. Stubbornly aware of how she needed to work in order to produce quality results, she stuck to her favored work-style. Others eventually came to accept it.

All of these people have adopted a way of working that harmonizes antagonistic tendencies: the desire to concentrate with the need to walk around, and the desire to fit into a corporation with the need to act out a personal working style.

"Use your faults" was the motto of French songstress Edith Piaf. Perhaps this matter of understanding and using our limitations revolves around just such a slogan. I'm not sure whether the traits I'm discussing here are "limitations," but certainly they can seem to be when measured against the behavior stereotype that others have for our way of being.

For instance, a writer friend of mine and I often discuss our "laziness." Each of us realized years ago that part of our creative process encompassed a period of complete torpor, a sort of resting or idea-incubation. This seems unattractive, even "bad," when looked at on the surface, when compared

with how we have been taught to work. The Puritan work ethic of my own upbringing strongly opposes resting during the day. Yet after some creative projects I find that this is what I must do in order to go on to the next project.

My friend laughingly tells of staying in bed all day, watching soap operas on television, while she unconsciously builds up a new storehouse of images and ideas for her next books. "I used to hate seeing myself lie there. It went against all my pictures of what I 'should' be doing and how I 'should' look. In my mind's eye, I felt that I was supposed to be a starched and immaculate vision in white all day, a Betty Crocker of the typewriter, constructively producing neat and clean copy twenty-four hours a day, like perfect cookies from the oven." She gradually realized that if she didn't give herself time out when she needed it, her next project was contrived, forced, never truly original.

I take long drives into the rural countryside where I live, listening to music as I drive. I have always loved barn and church architecture. A couple of days of looking at old, weather-beaten buildings of this type, traveling up and down dusty roads or along the Pacific Coast's rugged Highway One, is for me both a rest, and a symbolic visual journey. It mirrors the subjective, spiritual route that my creative side needs to take as I summon up energy to produce yet another chapter or article.

No other part of our personality reveals our basic temperament, our fundamental way of working, more than does our dark side—the part of ourselves which illogically unfolds at its own time and which has its own requirements. I'm referring to our uncontrollable impulses, the habits we simply can't break; the unacceptable, contradictory tendencies moving us in opposition to the way we intended to go. These are the opposing thrusts that give our life richness and mystery. These impulses, habits and contradictions even supply the dynamic energy that gives our lives distinction and drive. Jung described it this way:

> Conscious and unconscious do not make a whole when one of them is suppressed and injured by the other. If they must contend, let it at least be a fair fight with equal rights on both sides. Both are aspects of life . . . and the chaotic life of the unconscious should be given the chance of having its way too—as much of it as we can stand. This means open conflict and open collaboration at once. That, evidently, is the way human life should be. It is the old game of hammer and anvil: Between them the patient iron is forged into an indestructible whole, an "individual."

This attitude does not mean that we continue to harm ourselves, or that we ignore or escalate addictive, self-limiting behaviors. It means that we stop warring against ourselves. We try to take an objective, aerial view of what each behavior is saying about us, what it means in the big-picture of our self's journey unto itself. Here are some helpful questions to use in spotting the potential value of our "bad habits."

- Do you have work-habits which you may have rigidly suppressed in an attempt to conform and be more like others?

- Do you have personality traits which you, like my writer friend and myself, initially struggled against, thought were wrong and tried to change or hide?
- Have you stopped trying to achieve something in some "nonsignificant" areas of life because you were once told these weren't important enough to warrant attention?
- Is there a "time-out" activity (like sleeping, watching TV, fishing, listening to music, daydreaming, etc.) that gives your work efforts renewed vigor, but which you feel you shouldn't do?

If we can examine ourselves as constructed to express a total creative statement with our life, then our habits, daydreams, fantasy life, values, the dualities of our personality can all be understood and used in the service of this statement. It is not only our words, works and relationships which say something about us as individuals. It is what we are that makes a statement. As such, the controversial aspects of our personality may be adding a needed color, tone or impetus that energizes our movement toward selfhood and the life/creative statement of our very selves.

· · · · · · ·

25 · WHEN TECHNOLOGY WOUNDS

CHELLIS GLENDINNING

We live in a world of increasing numbers of health-threatening technologies—and increasing numbers of people made sick by technology. Today's development and use of technology pose danger not only to individual people, but to life itself: to the essence and survival of the earth's waters and soil and air, to your life and mine.

The historian Lewis Mumford calls these times the Age of Progress, in which "the myth of the machine . . . has so captured the modern mind that no human sacrifice seems too great."[1] With the invention of the telephone, television, missiles, nuclear weapons, supercomputers, fiber optics, and superconductivity, the social system we inhabit has repeatedly favored techologies that usher us further and further away from the communal, nature-bound roots that for millennia honored life and interrelationship in human culture. In their place, the values fueling our modern concept of "progress" as unchecked technological development have become the moral imperative of the modern age—and its curse.

At this tenuous moment in history, then, meeting and befriending the survivors of health-threatening technologies can serve to awaken us to a

pressing need: a comprehensive review of where modern technological society stands. In light of this need, the life experiences of those people who have become ill can no longer be confined to private reality. Revealed, they become a catalyst for opening our collective hearts to the passion and wisdom we need to make our world safe and livable. What the people who have endured the ordeal of technology-induced disease learn about technology, human relationships, and life's meaning are critical lessons for us all.

The crucial question that arises is one of knowledge. Who knows that a technology is dangerous? When do they know? How does a new technology get launched into public use? How complete are studies that research its potential impact? How influential? In some cases, as with the Dalkon Shield, the Pinto car, and leaking gasoline tanks, at the beginning no one really knows how safe or dangerous they are—not the inventors or the manufacturers, not the government or the consumers. No one has thought ahead to the possibility that they might have ill effects in the future, and sufficient testing and analysis have not been pursued. In cases like these, while neither purveyor nor user knows the dangers of the technology at first, eventually through unfortunate experience someone finds out. The discovery often pits defensive purveyor, who may not want to admit responsibility or invest in changing the technology, against wounded consumer, who may seek compensation for suffering or demand that the offending technology be banned.

In other cases, decision makers on the highest rungs of government, scientific, or corporate hierarchies do understand the dangers, but they determine that the "risk" to individual lives is worth the "benefit" to society, their own résumés, or their bank accounts. Seeing no advantage in confessing knowledge of the dangers, they often surround their technologies with secrecy. They tell neither workers nor public about potential problems, and as a result, people use dangerous technologies with no knowledge of risk.

The fact that asbestos could cause lung disease and death was known in the United States by 1918,[2] yet manufacturers persisted in employing workers in unsafe settings, avoiding responsibility through workers' compensation laws and legal corporate strategies. In the 1950s, Heather Maurer worked with her father cutting asbestos pipe for the family plumbing business. Her father died of multiple cancers, and her mother has pleural fibrosis today. "Believe me!" she asserts. "My father wouldn't have had his family work with the stuff if he knew it was killing us!"

Ultimately, we do not know the health effects of modern technologies because their developers and purveyors do not care to know. Our technologies are not created and chosen in an open, caring, or democratic manner, and we have not demanded that they be so. Rather their existence in the human community becomes, for both irresponsible developer and innocent consumer, *an unchosen fate.*

The discovery of the connection between a survivor's ill health and a technological event, then, occurs in an atmosphere of ignorance and innocence.

The problem is not just that many of us—from citizens to scientists—do not acknowledge the dangers. It is that we do not allow ourselves to admit that our neighbors, family members, and even we ourselves may be suffering from technology-induced illness. We have technology taboos to protect us from this perception, agreed-upon rules and unconcious restrictions we learn through socialization and that speak to our deep need to avoid certain experiences. There is a taboo against challenging our technology, there is a taboo against questioning the institutions that purvey our technology, and there is a taboo against confessing harm by technology.

The sociologist Jacques Ellul suggests how such a system of taboos functions. In his *Propaganda: The Formation of Men's Attitudes,* Ellul sees the determinant of public perception as more than indoctrination thrust upon the population by a cabal of self-serving officials and executives. He sees it as a system, a partnership, with all sectors of the population involved.

What we have in modern society is a set of technology taboos that directly benefits, at least in the short run, the creators and disseminators of technologies. What we have are taboos that indirectly satisfy the psychic needs of the general population with their promise of "the good life," glamour, and "progress."

· · · · · · · ·

26 · WILDERNESS AS A VICTIM OF PROGRESS

PETER BISHOP

The 1960s saw the first photographs of the Earth as a planet, and in 1968 it was revealed to its inhabitants by a direct television broadcast from an orbiting spacecraft. Concerning this, Metzner writes:

> The first photographs of the whole earth returned from space signaled the beginning of a new cycle of all-inclusiveness: there she hung like a blue-green jewel in the velvet black of deep-space, laced with sparkling atmospheric veils—our spaceship, our mother, our planet. The world is one. We are all together now.[1]

The abrupt creation of this idealized image of wholeness, the "Whole-Earth" fantasy, is an event unique to the industrial cultures. It is a complex holistic image of the Earth: physical, cultural, spiritual, its history and its future. "Space-ship Earth," "Earth Inc.," "Global Village," "the Earth as a cell," "Whole-Earth," "the Mandalic Earth"—all portray the Earth as a discrete evolutionary unit in an immense cosmic drama. But the confidence, exuberance and sense of rightness inspired by this imagistic event have obscured imaginative paradox. By what routes did the Whole-Earth image acquire its present massive coherence? At what moments within the emergence of this image have confidence and hope coincided with anxiety and despair?

The "Holistic Earth" relieves the burden of a formless immensity. This stable global image gives focus to the boundlessness of space. Futility, monotony and melancholy are the consistent results of such an extended imagining.

ECOLOGY AND THE DREAD OF INSECTS

Once the planet as a *system* rather than the evolutionary *process* becomes the prime focus, then we have shifted into the fantasy of ecology. Different hopes and fears arise, new coherences are mobilized. The word "ecology" first appeared in the English language in 1873.[2] Ecology lays emphasis on the whole rather than the parts, on the interaction between organism and environment. Harmony, balance, interdependence, unity, totality are used time and again to describe idealized systems. Life becomes coherence, the Earth a global cell. Humanity is imagined as merely one life form among many, a planetary-being inseparably enmeshed in a living web.[3]

Whilst the field of ecology was initially shaped by nineteenth-century biology and botany, in the twentieth century it has grown to encompass all disciplines from the arts to the social and physical sciences. "The only thinking worthy of the name must now be ecological," writes Mumford.[4] The organic and inspirational metaphors of those who proclaim a holy global unity—"Integrity is wholeness, the greatest beauty is organic wholeness . . ."—contrast with the systems language of the holistic pragmatists: "God . . . [is] an abstract love-momentumed gyro-compass. . . ."[5] Seemingly opposed to both are the images of an *unholy* unity. For Karl Marx the globe was indeed becoming united, but by capitalism and imperialism. Similarly, Margaret Mead writes that humanity has itself "woven the previously dispersed and unconnected population of the planet into a single, interconnected, mutually dependent and totally-at-hazard single group."[6] The global village euphoria of the 1960s seems naive alongside the contemporary shadow image of a "totally-at-hazard single group."

In *The Fate of the Earth,* Jonathan Schell comments gloomily that after an atomic holocaust all that may be left is "a republic of insects and grass."[7] This is a modern restatement of an ancient fear, that the insect kingdom will displace Homo sapiens as the dominant species and inherit the Earth. While the survival of birds or dolphins might offer slight consolation, the knowledge that planetary dominion would probably pass to the insects, especially ants and cockroaches, evokes disgust, despair and desolation. Insects have long been associated with the devil. In the Jungian tradition, a crowd of insects in a dream is often taken to symbolize a latent psychosis, a fragmentation of the basic personality. James Hillman suggests that they evoke the rejected autonomy of the Western psyche; insects in dreams present the natural mind or intelligence in the complexes.[8]

Holism fears fragmentation. It uses insects to evoke aggressive fantasies.

Homicide is a crime, insecticide a household product. Insects inspire a panicked shooting from the hip with toxic aerosols. Hillman comments: "Often, when the bug appears, so does fire." Insect fantasies touch upon a fear of disintegration, of pollution, of a loss of identity. They express fears of both an omnipotent, well-organized system and of the chaotic, faceless multitude. The dark images specific to alienation and the industrial age—the masses, bureaucracy, overpopulation, totalitarianism—have all at some point been expressed in entomological metaphors: hives of industry, ant-like city commuters. Even the information-systems language of modern biology and cybernetics has the feel of insects and their organization: units, bits, microchips, and of course "bugs." To imagine the Earth as a single cell, as a holistic unity, summons dreams of insects.

Yet insects are also mythologically associated with sorting out, sifting through, an attention to details. They are messengers of the underworld insisting that we move from our glorious abstractions of global unity into a fragmented imagining that is more Earth-bound. But to the onesided imagination of holism the insects are nibbling away everywhere, in the foundations of everything. Fantasies of global unity have been increasingly undermined by a pervasive sense of crisis. Everything is breaking down, everything seems to threaten us: the air we breathe, the water we drink, the food we eat. There is a profoundly diversified anxiety. The *reverse* side of global unity reveals the face of fragmentation, panic and crisis—not a single big one in the future but innumerable little ones, now, everywhere and every day. Crisis reporting, crisis intervention, crisis management, crisis care, crisis counseling are all peculiar to life in late twentieth-century Western society.[9]

Concern about ecology seems to promote ceaseless activity. The problems are always presented as *urgent,* the question always what to *do now!* Contemplation has been replaced by activism. As one ecological activist exclaimed: "We used to be studying guillemots: now we are trying to save the human species."[10]

An 1898 lecture, "Man's Dependence on the Earth," resignedly proclaims, "Man can never burst the bonds that subject him to nature."[11] Loren Eiseley wrote that "the discovery of the interlinked and evolving web of life" was pre-eminent among the causes of "an entirely new and less tangible terror."[12] And Jung warns, "It could easily be conjectured that the earth is growing too small for us, that humanity would like to escape from its prison. . . ."[13] Humanity seems trapped within its own dreams of unity. Insect fears of chaos, fragmentation, and loss of identity are complemented by those of being trapped, suffocated, and imprisoned. The *web* of life, the eco-*net*-work, summons up such fears.

The widespread celebration, even worship, of humanity's inescapable participation in the web of life belies the death and destruction threatened by the spider at the center. The web is an appropriate symbol for the shadow side of the much proclaimed "return to Mother Earth." The web is not only a holistic image to be contemplated in wonder but a labyrinth down which humanity stumbles after a sense of its own identity and security.

AN IMMENSE LOSS

Planetary holism does not simply present an exemplary image of order but also of immense loss. The sheer size and absoluteness of contemporary fantasies of loss are unprecedented:

> There is no survivor, there is no future, there is no life to be recreated in this form again. We are looking upon the uttermost finality which can be written, glimpsing the darkness which will not know another ray of light. We are in touch with the reality of extinction.[14]

Species have become extinct throughout the Earth's history, and the experience of extinction will have been consciously faced by many peoples. But no species has ever been forced to contemplate the distinct possibility of its own extinction. "Extinction," "annihilation" crush imagination. It is difficult to view as fantasy the prospect of the immediate extinction of the human species, to see it psychologically.

In 1848, just four years after the last two living Great Auks were clubbed to death and their solitary egg crushed by the boot of an Icelandic fisherman, Karl Marx wrote of humanity's "species-being." It was then a difficult concept to grasp. Three years later the Crystal Palace exhibition of 1851 was dedicated by Prince Albert with the words:

> Nobody who has paid attention to the peculiar features of the present era will doubt for a moment that we are living at a period of most wonderful transition, which tends rapidly to accomplish that great end, to which, indeed, all history points—the realization of the unity of mankind.[15]

One hundred and thirty years later we realize that global unity has its shadow side in global war and global pollution. Yet emerging from beneath this dark underside is the awareness of ourselves as a particular species. Today it is much easier to grasp Marx's image of a species-being. To imagine our identity in this way means facing death. To imagine species-existence necessitates the imagining of species-extinction; they are two sides of the same image. To the average Westerner of Marx's day, both the extinction of the peaceful Great Auk and Marx's image of species-being would have seemed alien, abstract and remote. To the contemporary ear they have a modern ring.

Not only human memory but the very ground of imagining is now threatened with extinction. Each of the imagined levels of loss—individuality, civilization, human species, the animal and plant world, the matrix which creates and supports life in the form we know it—expresses fears about the absence of psychological referencing, the death of *memoria*. Through these terrible images of loss, we are pulled down into the soul of things, the *Anima Mundi*.[16]

WILDERNESS AND THE LOSS OF BEAUTY

Wildernesses have been called "meccas for a pilgrimage into our species' past," "reservoirs of human freedom," "part of the geography of hope."[17]

Wilderness preservation has been urged for many reasons—as a rejection of industrial civilization and a return to primitivism, as repositories of invaluable scientific data, as training grounds for the development of self-reliance and survival skills, as places that enhance team spirit, as solitary retreats for contemplation and worship, as centers of healing where the stress and confusion of urban life can be released, as salutary correctives to anthropocentrism. Yet the basic property of wilderness is aesthetic.[18] A fundamental anxiety about beauty lies at the heart of wilderness imagining.

While advocates of wilderness consistently extol its beauties, contemporary appreciation scarcely matches the delight and awe it evoked in earlier days. Rousseau complained that the voluptuousness of nature overwhelmed him; Thoreau confided, "My senses get no rest"; Muir insisted that beauty was as important as bread. On his first walk among the Himalayas, Younghusband ecstatically exclaimed, "Oh Yes! Oh Yes! This really is splendid! How Splendid!" For us such places are now always touched with impermanence; they are reminders of loss.[19] But the imagination of wilderness still gives the image of a holistic Earth a sensual cohesion. It provides a preeminently *visual* experience of planetary life. Through the eros of beauty, both the ecological and evolutionary visions are restrained from excessive abstraction.

As seen from space, the image of the Earth elicits a scarcely veiled ache: "Wrapped in a mantle of cloud, she swam in loveliness through the sea of space. It is our choice to violate or to grace the beauty that is hers."[20] While ecology is concerned with the breakdown of connections and the destruction of an ancient and fundamental harmony, wilderness conservation consistently uses metaphors of violation, rape and despoliation.

But perhaps the great question of our time is less the alienation from "nature" than from "beauty." "Wilderness" originally had connotations of disorder and bewilderment. There is a madness about wilderness. The "savage and dreary" wilderness of Maine shocked Thoreau and forced him to temper his previously onesided enthusiasms. Few would share his reaction today. Are we more enlightened in proclaiming that such places no longer disturb us, or have we lost touch with some fundamental paradox? Wilderness activists frequently insist that their aim is to reeducate the West into an unequivocal appreciation of the beauty of "natural" wilderness. Such a goal is puzzling, for it is unlikely that any human culture has unparadoxically embraced *all* its known regions of landscape.[21] There is a concerted effort to clean up the imagination of wilderness and to remove any gloom associated with it. In the past this was achieved by literally clearing away the forests, swamps and jungles or by cultivating the deserts. Now it is being fantasized away by insisting that the oppressiveness and fear traditionally inspired by wilderness were biased and wrong.[22]

The very idea of wilderness had its origins in an oppositional fantasy: wild/tamed, savage/civilized, ungodly/godly, madness/sanity, chaos/order, confusion/harmony.[23] The image of wilderness has always been used as something to define and identify oneself by. It always invokes *another place* and can only exist by being set apart from somewhere else. Wildernesses mark the frontiers of an imagining of extremes. As unambiguous shrines of natural beauty, they are also contemporary entrances to the underworld, to landscapes where such beauty is imagined to be totally absent.

There is a danger that onesided fantasies will confine "natural beauty" to so-called wilderness areas and exclude it from everyday life in the city. Already wildernesses are being packaged for the quick high. They are quickly becoming a closed text: e.g., environmental psychology has already defined and proclaimed *the* "wilderness experience," which has become the focus of attention of educators, therapists, social workers and so on.[24] Ways have been devised to heighten its intensity and channel its direction. Presumably Thoreau would need reeducating in his attitude towards the wilderness landscape of Maine. The "wilderness experience" is taking shape as yet another programmed, instant consumer item. The wildernesses of the world are becoming either the adventure playgrounds of the wealthy nations or the cathedrals of a new dogma.

We bypass paradox either by chopping down ancient trees or uprooting "undesirable" Western fantasies. As the wilderness becomes a onesided place of salvation, fantasies of evil shift over to the city, the machine, the mining company. Already the variety of possible imaginative reactions to the wilderness is being constricted into the smug morality of holism and the packaged therapeutic milieu of the twentieth century.

VICTIM OF THE SHADOWS?

The routes by which the holistic planetary image arrived in Western consciousness were consequently not free from shadow. From evolutionary imagining comes images of humanity crushed beneath the burden of a remorseless continuity or negated into a state of despairing ennui by a limitless expanse of time and space. The ecological imagination embraces fears of fragmentation, chaos, of imprisonment within the web of life, with a loss of human identity. The imagination of wilderness is tinged with nostalgia and with the mood swings that always come with heavily literalized and unreflected fantasies about beauty. These are some of the deep pathologies specific to our time, though they commonly appear as dreams of insects or as irritating concerns about the minutiae of our everyday lives.

The well-known anthropologist Mary Douglas concludes her study of contemporary environmentalism by raising the question "why America is more passionately involved than any other Western nation in the debate about risks to nature."[25] Does a position at the center of global power allow a privileged insight into global issues, or does such an on-top position encourage and necessitate global imaginings? When power and manipulation are global, so are the images of hope and meaning. Global scenarios, global solutions, global problems are all part of the same specific fantasy.[26]

Eiseley insists that humanity "must in fact have walked the knife edge of extinction for untold years. As he defined his world he also fell victim to the shadows that lay behind it."[27] It seems the nightmare will be whispering at

our shoulders for quite a while. The important question is not one of accidental mechanical error, a technical fault, a malfunctioning microchip in an early-
warning installation. The basic issue is whether we can bear the unrelieved
intensity of our own nightmares. As these become less easily dismissed from
our daily life, they congeal into an image of darkness that is just as exemplary,
dense and coherent as that of the holistic Earth.

A FRAGMENTED ECOLOGY

Bachelard wryly remarks, "[Adults] demonstrate to the child that the earth is
round, that it revolves around the sun. And the poor dreaming child has to
listen to all that! What a release for your reverie when you . . . go back up the
side hill. . . ."[28] A specific, fragmented imagining in no way underestimates
the threat to the planet nor does it reveal any less concern about the environment. Certainly the image of a holistic Earth points to the urgent need for
imaginative vessels to hold, cook and digest the fantasies of our time. But
fragments also heal. The questions posed by a global imagining are in themselves *shattering*. They consistently fragment the comfort one might take in a
premature holism. As we have seen, there is an inherent shadow of destruction in idealistic holism. We need to descend into these shadows of the holistic Earth, for this image was born simultaneously with one of its own doom.
Eiseley writes of "the dark murmur that rises from the abyss beneath us and
that draws us with uncanny fascination." These murmurings are the world
calling attention to itself, reestablishing itself as a psychic reality.[29]

· · · · · · ·

*The story about the three masons illustrates how much difference our attitude
about our work makes:*

> *You know the story of the three brick masons. When the first man
> was asked what he was building, he answered gruffly, without
> even raising his eyes from his work, "I'm laying bricks." The
> second man replied, "I'm building a wall." But the third man
> said enthusiastically and with obvious pride, "I'm building a
> cathedral."*

. . . .

PART 6

MEETING DARKNESS ON THE PATH: THE HIDDEN SIDES OF RELIGION AND SPIRITUALITY

A disciple asked a learned Rabbi why it is that God used to speak directly to his people, yet he never does so today. The wise man, replied, "Man cannot bend low enough now to hear what God says."

JEWISH PROVERB

It belongs to the depth of the religious spirit to have felt forsaken, even by God.

ALFRED NORTH WHITEHEAD

Behind the repressed darkness and the personal shadow—that which has been and is rotting and that which is not yet and is germinating—is the archetypal darkness, the principle of not-being, which has been named and described as the Devil, as Evil, as Original Sin, as Death, as Nothingness.

JAMES HILLMAN

A spiritual life can't save you from shadow suffering.

SUZANNE WAGNER

INTRODUCTION

. . . .

One primary purpose of religion is, and always has been, to define the shadow, to set the world of darkness against the world of light, and to prescribe human moral behavior accordingly. Every religion has its way of slicing the great pie into good and evil; the more razor-sharp the slice, the more clear-cut the human ethics. Thus in the Old Testament Isaiah says: "Woe unto them that call evil good, and good evil; that put darkness for light, and light for darkness; that put bitter for sweet, and sweet for bitter. . . . Therefore is the anger of the Lord kindled against his people."

In such a black-and-white universe, right and wrong are two distinct paths, one leading to heaven, the other to hell. True believers of any tradition would say it is an either/or choice. As songmaker Bob Dylan so aptly puts it: "You got to serve somebody. It may be the Devil, or it may be the Lord. But you got to serve somebody."

Some religious proponents recognize the link between the dark side and the light, and the relativity of each in the human world. Twelfth-century Jewish philosopher Maimonides said: "Evils are evils only in relation to a certain thing."

The Jewish tradition also seems to recognize both the dark and light aspects of God—his wrathful and merciful nature—while the Christian God, who claims, "I am the Light," is forever sundered from his dark brother, the Devil, who contains only shadow.

The twin forces of good and evil, light and dark, appear in most traditions with variations on the theme. In Chinese Taoism, the well-known yin-yang symbol represents the alliance of opposites as they flow into one another; but in addition each pole *contains* the other in eternal embrace, inextricably linked by their very nature.

The mystical, esoteric teachers, such as Sufis, alchemists, and shamans, whose traditions have remained obscure until recently, suggest that shadow and evil have no objective, outer reality. Rather, they are misplaced, misunderstood energies within us. As Joseph Campbell said, "Anyone unable to understand a god sees it as a devil."

Mystics interpret the wisdom about good and evil on the inner planes. Instead of prescriptions of moral behavior, the teachings are seen as formulas for doing spiritual work. In this context, a meditative practice or shamanic ceremony aims to help an individual harmonize a malignant energy, such as rage or lust, and return it to its proper place in the inner world.

The Sufi poet Rumi points to this idea when he says: "If thou hast not seen the devil, look at thine own self." Rather than posit the devil as an outer independent actor, mystical teachings affirm the reality of the shadow within. Their introspective practices offer a way to gain the power to redeem it.

In Hinduism and Buddhism the shadings of evil and shadow are personified in gods and demons with whom we struggle and of whom we ask blessings. These inner forces or *rakshasas* are seen as parts of the meditator's mind, inner wrathful deities that represent jealousy, envy, or greed.

In occult traditions, which typically address the dark side with respect and caution, the shadow becomes a key figure with which to reckon. Black magic, for example, has turned the black/white polarity around. In Jungian terms, its practitioners are possessed by the shadow archetype. Certainly, Anton LeVey, head of the Satanist Church in the United States, and his devotion to the dark can be understood in this light (no pun intended).

Some spiritual seekers see their work with a mentor or guru as shadow-work. Author Joseph Chilton Pearce, for example, describes his relationship with his teacher psychologically:

> Every time I am around [the guru], some hidden child-part blurts out, some petty demon pops up to make an utter jackass of me in front of the one person I want to impress most. The guru exposes another of my fragments of self—not to make me look ridiculous, but to bring light to my darkness, my shadow-self—something I can't do for myself and resent anyone but her doing for me.

However, for most participants in the new age, the shadow has been conspicuous by its absence. Seekers often are led to believe that, with the right teacher or the right practice, they can transcend to higher levels of awareness without dealing with their more petty vices or ugly emotional attachments. As Colorado journalist Marc Barasch puts it: "Spirituality, as repackaged for the new age, is a confection of love and light, purified of pilgrimage and penance, of defeat and descent, of harrowing and humility."

Recently, the shadow of new age spirituality has begun to rear its ugly head. Many gurus are tumbling from their pedestals and revealing their all-too-human foibles; meditators, disillusioned with the ideal of enlightenment as personal perfection, have turned to psychotherapy to do the ego's homework or to a more earth-centered spirituality, in an effort to renew their humanity rather than transcend it.

Most spiritual teachers brought with them from the East their own unresolved personal issues—a need to control, a contempt for weakness, a naive sexuality, a hunger for money—and in many cases their groups were shaped by these forces. Psychiatrist James Gordon, author of *The Golden Guru: The Strange Journey of Bhagwan Shree Rajneesh,* has said he even suspects a correlation between those fears or desires that go unexamined in a spiritual leader—his or her shadow—and those that are enshrined in the group as making up the ideal character of a human being. For example, when Bhagwan Shree Rajneesh began to teach, he pointed a finger at the pompousness of priests and the power hunger of politicians; in the end, he fell into the very traps he said he despised.

As we begin to reclaim our projections of wisdom and heroism from others, and to build communities based on honesty and a recognition of human limits, we may yet discover an authentic spiritual life. To this end, Part 6 offers some surprising and insightful views on the dark side of contemporary spirituality. Rather than focus on historical issues or mainstream religions, we chose to emphasize some of today's pressing themes in an effort to take the next step on our journey.

In the opening chapter, Brother David Steindl-Rast, a Benedictine monk, criticizes his own Christian tradition for failing to provide a way to integrate the shadow. He contrasts the essential message of Jesus, which he thinks includes the tension between light and darkness, with the mainstream interpretation of Christianity.

William Carl Eichman, a teacher and student of esoteric teachings, explores the encounter with personal demons during meditation. He outlines several stages of practice and offers signposts for the practitioner along the way.

In an article published in *Common Boundary* magazine, California journalist Katy Butler describes the emotional fallout in several American Buddhist communities resulting from the sexual exploits, power struggles, and chronic lies of several spiritual teachers and their students. This unsentimental exposé already has touched the lives of many readers and is sure to disturb and arouse many more.

As a further explanaton of these recent events, yoga philosopher Georg Feuerstein wrote a piece for this volume to explain what happens to the guru's shadow in the development of consciousness along the Eastern path of enlightenment. Perhaps our understanding of enlightenment as the disappearance of shadow has been incorrect, he suggests; or perhaps a "phantom shadow" remains, much like the "phantom ego."

W. Brugh Joy, physician turned healer, writes extensively of the dark side of spiritual growth in *Avalanche*. In the piece we selected, he describes his personal experience at the new age community at Findhorn, Scotland, in which he became a scapegoat for people's anger and fear.

Liz Greene, a Jungian analyst and astrologer, describes the place and purpose of the shadow in an astrological chart. And Sallie Nichols tells the story of the Devil in the Tarot.

Finally, John Babbs gives a personal voice to the rising objection to new age fundamentalism and to a pervasive addiction to the light, which glorifies a worldview that robs us of the depths.

. . . .

27 · THE SHADOW IN CHRISTIANITY

BROTHER DAVID STEINDL-RAST

In contrast to some other traditions, Christians have not done particularly well in cultivating a practical method for integrating the shadow. This is part of the reason we have some of the problems that plague us today. In its enthusiasm for the divine light, Christian theology has not always done justice to the divine darkness. That has implications on the level of moral effort. If you are striving to be perfect and pure, everything depends on getting the right idea of what absolute purity and perfection mean. We tend to get trapped in the idea of a static perfection that leads to rigid perfectionism. Abstract speculation can create an image of God that is foreign to the human heart. On the level of religious doctrine, it's a God that is totally purged of anything that we call dark. Then we try to live up to the standards of a God that is purely light and we can't handle the darkness within us. And because we can't handle it, we suppress it. But the more we suppress it, the more it leads its own life, because it's not integrated. Before we know it, we are in serious trouble.

You can get out of that trap if you come back to the core of the Christian tradition, to the real message of Jesus. You find him, for instance, saying, "Be perfect as your heavenly Father is perfect." Yet he makes it clear that this is not the perfection of suppressing the darkness, but the perfection of integrated wholeness. That's the way Matthew puts it in the Sermon on the Mount. Jesus talks of our Father in heaven who lets the sun shine on the good and the bad, and lets the rain fall on the just and the unjust alike. It's both the rain and the sun, not only the sun. And it's both the just and the unjust. Jesus stresses the fact that God obviously allows the interplay of shadow and light. God approves of it. If God's perfection allows for tensions to work themselves out, who are we to insist on a perfection in which all tensions are suppressed?

In his own life, Jesus lives with tension and embraces darkness. And as Christians we see in Jesus what God is like. That's really what Christians believe about Jesus: in this man who is fully human—like us in all things except our alienation, our sinfulness—in this human we can see what God is like. And that human dies, crying out, "My God, why have you forsaken me?" At that moment darkness covers the whole earth, which is, of course, a poetic statement, not necessarily an historic account of what happened then. At that moment God reaches the greatest distance from God's own being and embraces the darkness of utmost alienation. If God's reality can embrace the one who cries out, "My God, why have you forsaken me?" and is, for all practical purposes, forsaken of God, and dies, then everything is embraced—death and life and every tension between them. And that moment is, according to the Gospel of John, not the prelude to the resurrection, not something that is then reversed by the resurrection, but *is* the resurrection. Jesus says earlier, "When I am lifted up from the earth, I shall draw all things to myself." According to the theology of the Gospel of John, the lifting up is the lifting up on the cross. His death on the cross is the moment of his glory. It's an upside-down glory. It's the ultimate shame for someone to be executed on the cross. But for the eyes of faith Jesus is "lifted up." That is the resurrection. That is the ascension. That is also the pouring out of the spirit: he dies with a loud cry—that means with power, not with a whimper—and he hands over his spirit. At that moment the whole world is filled with the divine spirit. The vessel is broken and the fragrance fills the whole house. It's all profoundly poetic. You cannot understand the Gospel of John without a sense of poetry.

It is a poem from beginning to end. Because we have often failed to read it in that way, we get into all sorts of traps.

The moral implications of all this are deeply anchored in the Christian tradition from its earliest statements on. We touch here the rock-bottom of the Christian tradition. Yet this integration of light and darkness hasn't been explored properly. This is the problem. Traditions do not always develop evenly. We have only had two thousand years. There are much older traditions. Give us another two thousand years and we may catch up.

Right now we are at an important stage of transition. We are beginning to look at certain areas that we haven't faced for a very long time. This area of integrating the shadow is one of them. Martin Luther saw it and the Reformation was a period in which this area was bravely faced. (It's too bad that there were so many diplomatic mistakes made on both sides, that the whole thing didn't lead to a renewal of the Church, but rather to a split of the Church.) Luther stressed a key conviction of the New Testament with which the Catholic Church is only now catching up; that is, "by grace you have been saved." That's one of the earliest insights in the Christian tradition: it's not by what you do that you earn God's love. Not because you are so bright and light and have purged out all the darkness does God accept you, but as you are. Not by doing something, not by your works, but gratis you have been saved. That means you belong. God has taken you in. God embraces you as you are—shadow and light, everything. God embraces it, by grace. And it has already happened.

But where does the moral struggle come in? We all know it has to come in somewhere. St. Paul, who says, "By grace you have been saved," encourages us in the next chapter, "Now live worthy of so great a gift." That's a totally different thing, however, from trying to earn it. Many Christians struggle to earn the great gift. How can you earn a gift? I'm simply telling you what Jesus taught, what Paul taught, what the Christian tradition at its core teaches.

Paul says, "Be angry, but do not sin." That has a contemporary ring for us. Sin is alienation. Do not let your anger separate you from others, but don't suppress your anger either. Be angry, all right. But "do not let the sun set over your anger." That is again a poetic statement. It may mean, literally, before evening, make up. That's one of the clearest meanings of it. But it may also mean never, not even at this moment when you are angry, let the sun set over this shadow. You see how beautifully it's expressed. Do not let the sun go down over your anger. Do not let your anger lead to alienation.

I can only touch upon these things, but I hope that it at least gives you a taste and makes you realize that when you go deeply into the Christian tradition, whether it is your own or not, you will find all these things. They are there. But then you ask, "Why don't we ever hear of it? Why hasn't it been developed?" Well, it hasn't been sufficiently developed yet. But you are there. You have your share to contribute. When you are through with your tradition, it must be different from what you found or else you have failed. It is your responsibility to make your religious tradition, whatever it may be, Christian or otherwise, more truly religious by the time you are through with it. That's the great challenge we face.

. . . .

28 · MEETING THE DARK SIDE
IN SPIRITUAL PRACTICE

WILLIAM   CARL   EICHMAN

If you undertake spiritual practice you will be confronted by your dark side. This is an axiom. The spiritual quest is dangerous, just as the books say. Seeking truth means experiencing pain and darkness, as well as the clear white light. Practioners must prepare themselves to deal with the dark underside of life.

This dark side can take many forms. Religious stories personify it in images of devils and dark, angry gods. Buddha, Christ, Mohammed, and virtually every other lesser figure report dealing with the temptations of the "Evil One," prince of the world—Mara, Satan, Iblis. The teaching story of temptation, which occurs before illumination, is more than just another "Hero vanquished Monster" myth—it is a description of a specific peril of the spiritual path. The Christian and Sufi mystics experienced it more personally, as the obstinate pride and trickery of the ego and the "dark night of the soul." For the modern practitioner the dark nature is even more multi-faceted; our complicated world has many evil faces, and dealing with the dark side has never been more difficult.

Today the dark side is everywhere. We are completely saturated in it. It declares itself in every news broadcast, television show, and tabloid. No one growing up in a society like ours escapes being conditioned by this violence. Every one of us, from the most perfectly civilized to the imprisoned criminal, harbors an inner, festering, neurotic sore, a private shadow of anger, terror, lust, and pain. This shadow, this "dark side," is a miniature copy of the greater darkness of society which manifests in war, oppression, and starvation. We are surrounded, inside and out, by evil and suffering of all description.

When we practice meditation and contemplation the dark side within us is washed to the surface of consciousness by the purifying and energizing effect of these exercises. The ability to deal with these emerging dark impulses is a basic skill which must be mastered by every practitioner. Moral, ethical, and spiritual integrity is required, but accurate practical knowledge is just as important. Without study, our conception of the dark side tends to be a primitive relic of childhood creepie-crawlies and bogeymen. If we attempt to confront our dark side with this programming we are quickly paralyzed. Instead, we must gather reliable information, read books, observe and analyze our personal psychologies, and in time develop a more complete picture of the nature of the dark side. An educated and mature attitude toward evil is a necessity for the practitioner.

With study, certain characteristics of the so-called "dark side" become obvious. This darkness is not really a "side," or a shadow, or a persona—it is a tangled web of complex forces, programs, and effects which we repress from ordinary consciousness so that we rarely see its true nature.

The personal dark side rises up in meditation to torment and tempt the practitioner. It is the personal "Devil," the private hell, which must be confronted and transformed when it blocks the path of the esoteric student. The biological, cosmological, and cultural dark sides are the foundation of the personal experience of evil; in the end, however, individual practitioners struggling with the Work must face, by themselves, their *own* darkness.

When studied, all of these dark sides seem to operate as impersonal tendencies, programs, or neurotic complexes. There is no good evidence (unless religious myths or texts are counted) for the existence of a "Devil." If inherent evil exists, it is an aspect of natural predation, disease, and accident, all of which work to prevent overpopulation and to strengthen the species. The Buddhist doctrine that good and evil, god and devil alike, are all illusory and temporary aspects of a constantly changing pure mind and universe may be the picture of evil closest to the truth. By studying the dark side we see that "evil" is not an all-powerful, consciously spiteful agency determined to do us in—rather, evil is imbalance, ignorance, and accident. Armed with this knowledge the practitioner can break free of the yoke of superstition. This is vital—as a source of true knowledge of the world, nothing is more unreliable than a superstitious mystic.

Today, the biological dark side poses far fewer problems than it did in past centuries. Modern culture provides tremendous security, and the miraculous products of our technology and medicine have helped us overcome many terrors. This does not mean that we are really safe from the biological dark side. Anyone can get hit by a car, or develop a cancer. Aging and death are still part of every life. Moreover, biological and cosmological terrors must be accepted as the backdrop of life. Meditation on death, corpses, and birth can be useful for dealing with the biological dark side, for they flush out morbid fantasy, awaken us to our own mortality, and remind us that change— death as well as life—is the universal constant.

Death, aging, and accident must be accepted, but the incessant conditioning of the cultural dark side must be resisted. The first stage of any practice is Yama and Niyama, the duties and proscriptions that keep the practitioner free of (further) cultural contamination. Classic eastern yogis, for example, are pictured as spending most of their time insulating themselves from the spiritual impurities of their society. Hermitage, fasting, and rituals created a microclimate around the yogi that was thought necessary for success in meditation. This has become difficult for the modern practitioner. Monasteries and hermitages are hard to come by. New strategies are needed to establish and maintain the necessary "refuge of sanity" in a high-pressure world.

An earmark of authentic esoteric teaching is that it is alive, and adapts itself to changing situations. Lacking monasteries, we must adopt the method of "being in the world but not of it." Resisting the hypnotizing background drone of society must become our new Zhikr, a "remembrance" that we must sweep our minds clear of excess cultural programing. A new prayer is needed: "Lord have Mercy on me a poor sinner. Let me not be controlled by the images on the screen." New types of personal temples, sanctifying rituals, and purifying practices are evolving. Biofeedback devices, flotation tanks, and alternative healing regimes speed up relaxation and the shedding of the stresses and suggestions of daily life. There are many possibilities for the modern esoteric practitioner, and the test of time will shape the new methods for dealing with the cultural dark side.

In the second stage of practice, in which meditation and exercises are performed, a whole new struggle with darkness arises. Personal repressed "evil" is released by meditation, and it must be examined and integrated by the practitioner as a necessary part of the meditation process.

As the repressed dark material rises, the practitioner is likely to experience frightening visions, feelings of terror, rage, uncontrollable ego reactions, and countless other usually minor but annoying and embarrassing manifestations. These reactions must be expected and properly dealt with: they should neither be blown out of proportion nor minimized and avoided. Instead, it should be recognized that these eruptions of the dark side can be of great benefit for one's self-development. Ultimately, transforming these frightening visions into usable psychic energy is the only way to deal with them, and the nuances of this process of "turning lead into gold" will require every bit of skillful means that the practitioner possesses.

The usual first reaction upon seeing one's personal evil is to feel tremendous guilt and shame, and to identify with the shadow, feeling as though one had just been exposed as evil incarnate. This is a false idea, as useless as medieval beliefs about demons causing disease. Personal darkness is a type of illness or injury, caused primarily by accidentally cruel programming during childhood, and it should be treated as such. Everyone has a dark nature; it's a condition of life in our world, not a "sin." The goal of the practitioner must be to heal the illness and bring the injured area back into full operation. The modern esoteric student must apply treatment to his dark nature; self-recrimination and wallowing in guilt simply does no good.

By healing the dark nature, vast amounts of personal power and ability can be reclaimed, for much of our ordinary powers as human beings are now hideously crippled by the personal dark side. These crippled areas, in effect, represent vast resources of contaminated and stagnant psychic energy. As one progresses on the path each confrontation with "evil" is an opportunity to grow stronger. This is desirable, for the repressed personal devils also grow stronger until one breaks through to the God in the Center.

The actual process of healing and transforming the eruptions of the dark side can be very complicated. Because these dark complexes were written into the psyche during our childhood, reasoning with the "dark side" has almost no effect. On the other hand, rituals, purifactory regimes, healings, protective power objects, and special meditative and grounding exercises can all be of benefit when used in the right time and right place. The energy of the dark nature must be frequently released and expressed, and this should be done *consciously*, using art or ritual, to prevent an excess flow of psychic energy from harming family and friends.

In the final stages of practice, the biological, cultural, and personal dark sides have become integrated into the psyche where they function smoothly, fulfilling their dark side purposes. At this stage the cosmological dark side rises up like a black mountain to bar the way. Death returns, the ugliness of society returns, and the personal devil returns, all dancing like puppets on the strings of nihilism, meaninglessness, suffering, and heedless despair at the impersonal nature of the cosmos. In the face of visions of Billion-of-Years, nothing that we mystics do matters. There is no answer that we can comprehend, no purpose of life that we can understand. Faced with this helplessness, the practitioner is left with no option but surrender—"Giving up the Ghost." At this point, we're each on our own—and it's not very comforting to know that the books say we'll live through it.

Light is infinite; dark is infinite. There may never be an end to the struggle with darkness. This does not depress the true practitioner. To struggle with darkness is the same as to strive for light. Both darkness and light are illusions; what lies underneath them both is nothing but Being, Bliss, and Consciousness. This should never be forgotten.

* * * * * * *

29 · ENCOUNTERING THE SHADOW IN BUDDHIST AMERICA

KATY BUTLER

One summer afternoon in 1982, a friend of mine stood on a street in Boulder, Colorado—under a bright blue Rocky Mountain sky—holding a bottle of sake. The wine, a gesture of gratitude, was a gift for Vajra Regent Osel Tendzin, "Radiant Holder of the Teachings," second-in-command of Vajradhatu, the largest branch of Tibetan Buddhism in the United States.

Moments later, my friend entered an elegant, minimally furnished office nearby. Tendzin—the former Thomas Rich of Passaic, New Jersey, round-eyed, mustachioed and wearing a well-cut business suit—rose from his chair and smiled. My friend shook his hand, grateful for the rare private audience. He had recently emerged from an emotionally repressive religious community in Los Angeles, and a meditation retreat led by the Regent had introduced him to a more colorful, less guilt-inducing, spiritual path. As the afternoon wore on, the men talked about Buddhism, love and theology.

Gradually, the sake level dropped inside the bottle. Then my friend, a little drunk, grew bold and raised the subject he feared most: homosexuality. There was a moment of silence.

"Stand up," Tendzin said. "Kiss me." My friend complied.

When the Regent requested oral sex, my friend, slightly dismayed, declined. "I think you can do it," the Regent said cheerfully. The two men moved to a couch, where my friend's taboo against homosexuality was broken.

When it was over, Tendzin mentioned in passing that he had similar sexual encounters several times a day. He offered my friend a ride, opened the office door and led the way through clusters of waiting assistants to a sleek car purring in the twilight below, a driver waiting at the wheel.

My friend later felt confused and embarrassed about that afternoon, but not bitter. "He pushed me into a homosexual experience, and yet at the same time, he was generous. I asked to see him, and he made time for me," he told me. "I felt a mixture of embarrassment and honor. I don't feel Tendzin abused me, and I don't want my sexual experience judged by anybody."

After my friend told me his story, I often replayed it in my mind, like a videotape, searching for hidden clues to later events. I noted my friend's fascination with the trappings of spiritual power and his discomfort with moral judgments. I observed Tendzin's apparently routine transformation of a religious audience into an afternoon of drinking and sexual relations, and how casually he admitted to addictively frequent sex. I had to acknowledge that my friend had not been harmed; yet I saw in the incident the seeds of the disaster that followed.

CRISIS OF LEADERSHIP

In April 1987, Vajra Regent Osel Tendzin assumed leadership of the Vajradhatu community, following the death of the well-known and widely respected Tibetan Buddhist teacher, Chogyam Trungpa Rinpoche.

Less than two years later, in December 1988, the most harmful crisis ever to strike an American Buddhist community unfolded when Vajradhatu administrators told their members that the Regent had been infected with the AIDS virus for nearly three years. Members of the Vajradhatu board of directors conceded that, except for some months of celibacy, he had neither protected his sexual partners nor told them the truth. One of the Regent's sexual partners, the son of long-term students, was infected, as was a young woman who had later made love to the young man.

Two members of the Vajradhatu board of directors had known of his infection for more than two years, and chose to do nothing. Trungpa Rinpoche had also known about it before his death. Board members had reluctantly informed the *sangha* (community) only after trying for three months to persuade the Regent to act on his own.

"Thinking I had some extraordinary means of protection, I went ahead with my business as if something would take care of it for me," Tendzin reportedly told a stunned community meeting organized in Berkeley in mid-December.

This crisis of leadership was hardly the only disaster to befall an American Buddhist sangha. In 13 years of practicing Buddhist meditation, I have seen venerated, black-robed Japanese roshis and their American dharma heirs (including my own former teacher) exposed for having secret affairs. Other Buddhist teachers—Tibetan, Japanese and American—have misused money, become alcoholic or indulged in eccentric behavior.

As an American Buddhist, I found the scandals heartbreaking and puzzling. I thought of Buddhism not as a cult but as a 2,500-year-old religion devoted to ending suffering, not causing it. I also knew that the teachers involved were not charlatans, but sincere, thoroughly trained spiritual mentors, dedicated to transmitting the Buddhist dharma to the West.

As a journalist, I noticed that media coverage of the scandals seemed to reinforce secular America's deeply held suspicion of all religious impulses. The teachers came across as cynical exploiters; their followers as gullible fools.

But having watched and participated in Buddhist communities for more than a decade, I know that these misfortunes are more than a tragic dance between exploitation and naivete. Their roots lie not in individual villainy, but in cultural misunderstandings and hidden emotional wounds. And all community members, however unconsciously, play a part in them.

When Buddhism moved West, an ancient and profound Eastern tradition encountered a younger, more fragmented American society. The new American Buddhists enthusiastically built Japanese meditation halls lined with sweet-smelling tatami mats, and Tibetan-style shrine rooms with altars laden with ceremonial bowls of water and rice. Trying to build new communities, they cobbled together structures that combined elements of Eastern hierarchy and devotion and Western individualism. This blending of widely divergent cultural values was complicated by the fact that many students hoped to find a sanctuary from the wounds of painful childhoods and from the loneliness of their own culture. When the scandals erupted, however, many found themselves, like Dorothy at the end of the *Wizard of Oz*, "back in their own back yards," having unconsciously replicated patterns they hoped to leave behind.

Now, as the shadow side has come to light, certain common elements within the communities are apparent:

- Patterns of denial, shame, secrecy and invasiveness reminiscent of alcoholic and incestuous families;
- Soft-pedaling of basic Buddhist precepts against the harmful use of alcohol and sex;
- An unhealthy marriage of Asian hierarchy and American license that distorts the teacher-disciple relationship; and
- A tendency, once scandals are uncovered, to either scapegoat the disgraced teachers or blindly deny that anything has changed.

A LINEAGE OF DENIAL

As a member of San Francisco Zen Center in the 1980s, I was mystified by my own failure—and the failure of my friends—to challenge the behavior of our teacher, Richard Baker-roshi, when it seemed to defy common sense. Since then, friends from alcoholic families have told me that our community reproduced patterns of denial and enablement similar to those in their families. When our teacher kept us waiting, failed to meditate and was extravagant with money, we ignored it or explained it away as a teaching. A cadre of well-organized subordinates picked up the pieces behind him, just as the wife of an alcoholic might cover her husband's bounced check or bail him out of jail. This "enabling," as alcoholism counselors call it, allowed damaging behavior to continue to grow. It insulated our teacher from the consequences of his actions and deprived him of the chance to learn from his mistakes. The process damaged us as well: We habitually denied what was in front of our faces, felt powerless and lost touch with our inner experience.

Similar patterns were acknowledged at Zen Center of Los Angeles in 1983, when their teacher, the respected Hakuyu Taizan Maezumi-roshi, entered a treatment program and acknowledged his alcoholism. "We were all co-alcoholics," one of Maezumi's students told Buddhist historian Sandy Boucher. "We in subtle ways encouraged his alcoholism [because when he was drunk] he would become piercingly honest."

A similar process may have taken place at Vajradhatu in the 1970s, as students attempted to come to terms with their teacher, Chogyam Trungpa, Rinpoche, a maverick, Oxford-educated Tibetan exile who was brilliant, compassionate and alcoholic.

Trungpa Rinpoche, the 11th incarnation of the Trungpa Tulku, was the teenage head of several large Tibetan monasteries when the 1959 Chinese invasion tore him from his native culture. Eager to meet the West on its own terms, he gave up his robes for a business suit, fell in love with Shakespeare and Mozart, and married an English woman. He sometimes lectured with a glass of sake in his hand.

Trungpa Rinpoche taught that every aspect of human existence—neurosis, passion, desire, alcohol, the dark and the light—was to be embraced and transmuted. He called his wild approach "crazy wisdom," referring to a small but genuine tradition of revered, eccentric Tibetan yogis—most of whom worked intimately with one or two students.

Buddhist teachers—even those uneasy with his behavior—admired Trungpa Rinpoche for his brilliant translation of Buddhism into Western terms. Wary of importing Tibetan cultural forms, he first taught his American students a simple, Zen-based sitting meditation. He then gradually introduced the elaborate Tantric disciplines that distinguish Tibetan Vajrayana Buddhism from almost all other Buddhist schools. Students completed foundational practices, including 100,000 prostrations, and attended a three-month seminary in the mountains. Advanced students were ceremonially initiated into confidential Tibetan practices of meditative visualization. Teacher and student entered into a relationship, traditionally more devotional than anything in other Buddhist schools.

Trungpa attracted thousands of well-educated people who soon created the largest, most creative and least conventional of America's non-Asian Buddhist communities. He counted among his students poets Allen Ginsberg and Anne Waldman, playwright Jean-Claude van Italie, Shambhala Publications publisher Sam Bercholz, and Rick Fields, author of a respected history of American Buddhism. Based primarily in Boulder, students ran businesses; founded Naropa Institute, an accredited Buddhist university; edited a journal on contemplative psychotherapy; and published a widely-read bimonthly Buddhist newspaper, the *Vajradhatu Sun*.

Yet woven into the discipline and creativity was a strand of hedonism. Vajradhatu students had a reputation for the wildest parties in Buddhist America. Although most Tibetan Tantric schools clearly discourage "acting out" passions and impulses, Trungpa Rinpoche did not. In fact, drunk and speeding, he once crashed a sports car into the side of a joke shop and was left partly paralyzed. He openly slept with students. In Boulder, he lectured brilliantly, yet sometimes so drunk that he had to be carried off-stage or held upright in his chair.

To student Jules Levinson, a Tibetan scholar and Ph.D. candidate at the University of Virginia, the stories "were very upsetting—that he drank a lot, that he slept around." Yet at the same time, Levinson was grateful to Trungpa. "I found him gentle, delicate, provocative and nurturing—the most compassionate person I have ever known. I just couldn't put it together," he said.

Some students, replaying dynamics from their alcoholic families, responded to Trungpa Rinpoche by denying and enabling his addictive drinking and sexual activity. "I served Rinpoche big glasses of gin first thing in the morning, if you want to talk about enabling," said one woman, who had watched her own father die of alcoholism.

Others resolved their cognitive dissonance by believing that their teacher had transcended the limitations of a human body. "Trungpa Rinpoche said that because he had *Vajra nature* [a yogically transformed and stabilized psychophysiology], he was immune to the normal physiological effects of alcohol," said one student. "We bought the story that it was a way of putting 'earth' into his system, so that he could . . . relate to us. It never occurred to anyone I knew that he was possibly an alcoholic, since that was a disease that could only happen to an ordinary mortal. And many of us were ignorant—we thought of an alcoholic only as the classic bum in the street."

An atmosphere of denial permeated the community in the 1970s and early 1980s, and other Vajradhatu students became heavy drinkers. "I found myself a nice little nest where I could keep on drinking," said one long-time Vajradhatu Buddhist, who was among a handful of Vajradhatu members who joined Alcoholics Anonymous (AA) in the early 1980s. Their recovery seemed to threaten others. The first woman to get sober was asked to quit the board of a home care organization found by Vajradhatu members. "I felt such contempt for someone who had to quit drinking, and I treated her like a mental case," said the woman who got rid of her—a woman who has since joined AA herself.

When Trungpa Rinpoche lay dying in 1986 at the age of 47, only an inner circle knew the symptoms of this final illness. Few could bear to acknowledge that their beloved and brilliant teacher was dying of terminal alcoholism, even when he lay incontinent in his bedroom, belly distended and skin discolored, hallucinating and suffering from varicose veins, gastritis and esophageal varices, a swelling of veins in the esophagus caused almost exclusively by cirrhosis of the liver.

"Rinpoche was certainly not an ordinary Joe, but he sure died like every alcoholic I've ever seen who drank uninterruptedly," said Victoria Fitch, a member of his household staff with years of experience as a nursing attendant. "The denial was bone-deep," she continued. "I watched his alcoholic dementia explained as his being in the realm of the *daikinis* [guardians of the teachings, visualized in female form]. When he requested alcohol, no one could bring themselves not to bring it to him, although they tried to water his beer or bring him a little less. In that final time of his life . . . he could no longer walk independently. At the same time there was a power about him and an equanimity to his presence that was phenomenal, that I don't know how to explain."

Some students now feel that the Regent Osel Tendzin suffered from a similar denial of human limitation, as well as ignorance of addictive behavior.

"Many students who are outraged by the Regent's behavior seem to think he arose out of nowhere," one student said. " They're not using their Buddhist training about cause and effect. I think the Regent has emulated in more extreme and deadly fashion a pattern of denial and ignorance exemplified by Trungpa Rinpoche's own attitude to alcohol."

FAMILY SECRETS

By the time the crisis broke, a small but significant minority of Vajradhatu students had begun to deal with wounds left by family alcoholism and incest. By the mid-1980s, about 250 Vajradhatu members around the country— mostly wives of alcoholic husbands—had joined Al-Anon, an organization modeled after AA for the families of alcoholics, and more than a score of sangha members had joined AA. Soft drinks were also served at Vajradhatu ceremonies, and the atmosphere of excessive drinking diminished.

Those in the 12-Step movement were a minority, however, and certain stubborn patterns persisted. For example, the Regent himself sought to suppress any public discussion of the crisis, creating an atmosphere reminiscent of an alcoholic family's defensive secrecy.

When editor Rick Fields prepared a short article for the *Vajradhatu Sun* describing the bare bones of the crisis, he was forbidden to print it. "There have been ongoing discussions, both within community meetings and among many individuals, about the underlying issues that permitted the current situation to occur," read the banned article. "These issues include the abuse of power and the betrayal of trust, the proper relationship between teachers with spiritual authority and students, particularly in the West, and the relationship between devotion and critical intelligence on the spiritual path."

In the article's place, Fields printed a mute drawing of the Vajradhatu logo—a knot of eternity—stretched to the breaking point over a broken heart. In March, Fields again attempted to run his article and was fired by the Regent. When the board of directors refused to support him, he formally resigned, saying the Buddhist teaching in the West "would be best served in the long run by openness and honesty, painful as that may be."

The suppression of public discussion echoed both the Asian tradition of face-saving as well as the dynamics of alcoholic families. "There's a sense of family secrets, things you don't talk about, especially with outsiders," said Levinson. "Shortly after the news came out I wrote to the Regent and said, 'If the rumors are true, then [those actions] don't seem to be in accord with the dharma, but it doesn't make you a devil. The most important thing is what we do now. I would really like you to come talk to us openly, in small groups, at least in Boulder and Halifax, as your health permits. If you can do that we . . . may be able to re-establish some trust.' My biggest heartbreak is that he hasn't done that."

CROSS-CULTURAL CLASHES

For more than a year, the stalemate stretched Vajradhatu to the breaking point. Tendzin publicly but obliquely acknowledged violating Buddhist vows, but he declined to accept responsibility for infecting others. He remained on retreat in California with a small group of devoted students, defying a request by the board of directors that he withdraw from teaching. In Boulder, some anti-Regent students virulently and unrealistically blamed him for the entire disaster, while pro-Regent students practiced what might be called "devotional or transcendental denial." They urged the preservation of the Buddhist teaching lineage at the expense of facing what had happened. Many others fell into what one senior student called "the heartbroken middle." In a letter widely distributed in Boulder, one student wrote, "If the Board and the Regent cannot work out their differences with compassion and intelligence, the sangha will be shattered."

The community consulted Tibetan lamas to resolve the impasse, but their responses reflected an Asian emphasis on face-saving, hierarchy and avoidance of open conflict. Although it is unclear how much he understood the situation, one venerated lama, the late Kalu Rinpoche, forbade his American students to comment on the Vajradhatu disaster. Another, the Venerable Dilgo Khyentse, Rinpoche, first asked the Regent to go into retreat but urged Vajradhatu students to respect the Regent's authority.

It was too much for many students to stomach. "This is a living nightmare for us," said Robin Kornman, a long-time Vajradhatu meditation teacher and a graduate student at Princeton University. "We are being told to follow a person we are certain is deeply confused."

Buddhist students at other centers have experienced similar cross-cultural problems. In the late 1970s, Zen student Andrew Cooper became disturbed when he realized that his Japanese roshi "discouraged the expression of personal disagreement, doubt or problems within the community, even when those problems were undeniably real and potentially disruptive."

Cooper, now a graduate student in psychology, thought his teacher was hypocritical until a friend who had lived in Japan told him that the Japanese have no notion of hypocrisy, at least not in the sense we in the West do. "For the Japanese, withholding one's personal feelings in order to maintain the appearance of harmony within the group is seen as virtuous and noble," Cooper wrote in an unpublished paper. "This attitude is part of the structuring of Japanese social relations—it has a place there. But when it is imported under the banner of enlightenment and overlaid on an American community, the results are cultish and bizarre."

ASIAN DEFERENCE AND WESTERN LICENSE

The results are particularly troublesome when communities import Asian devotional traditions without importing corresponding Asian social controls. Chogyam Trungpa, for instance, came from a society where the sense of "self" and the social controls on that self were very different from those in the West. Raised from infancy in Eastern Tibet as an incarnate lama, he headed a huge institutional monastery at 19. He was granted tremendous devotion and power, but his freedom was rigidly circumscribed by monastic vows of chastity and abstinence, and by obligations to his monastery and the surrounding community.

Community standards were based on an intricate system of reciprocal obligation. They were clear and often unspoken. Almost everyone's behavior—serf, lama or landowner—was closely but subtly controlled by a strong and often unspoken desire to save face.

But these social controls did not exist in the society to which Trungpa Rinpoche came in the freewheeling 1970s. His American students' behavior was loosely governed by contractual relationships; by frank, open discussions; and by individual choices rather than by shared social ethics and mutual obligation. His ancestors had lived in the same valley for generations; when he first arrived in America, he flew from city to city like a rock star. While America removed all social limits from Trungpa Rinpoche's behavior, his students became his household servants, chauffeured his car and showed him a deference appropriate to a Tibetan lama or feudal lord.

The same deference was shown to his dharma heir, Osel Tendzin. "His meals were occasions for frenzies of linen-pressing, silver-polishing, hair-breadth calibrations in table settings, and exact choreographies of servers," said television producer Deborah Mendelsohn, who helped host Tendzin when he gave two meditation retreats in Los Angeles, but has since left the community. "When he traveled, a handbook went with him to guide his hosts through the particulars of caring for him, including instructions on how and in what order to offer his towel, underpants and robe after he stepped from the shower."

This parody of Asian deference, combined with American license, ultimately proved disastrous, and not only at Vajradhatu. At Zen centers as well, students took on Asian gestures of subservience while their teachers sometimes acted "freely": drinking, spending money, making sexual advances to women or men, all with precious little negative feedback. The deference often went far beyond what would have been granted a teacher in Japan or Tibet.

"Pressure from the community is very important in controlling behavior in Tibetan communities," said Dr. Barbara Aziz, an internationally known social anthropologist at the City University of New York who has spent 20 years doing fieldwork among Tibetans in Nepal and Tibet. "In Tibetan society, they expect more of the guy they put on the pedestal . . . If such a scandal had happened in Tibet, the whole community might have felt polluted. Osel Tendzin might have been driven from the valley. Depending on the degree of community outrage, his family might have made substantial offerings to the monastery for purification rites and prayers to infuse society with compassion."

Furthermore, Aziz pointed out, Tibetans may "demonstrate all kinds of reverence to a rinpoche, but they won't necessarily do what he says. I see far more discernment among my Tibetan and Nepali friends," she concluded, "than among Westerners."

THE NEED FOR DISCERNMENT

In this confusing cross-cultural context, the teacher-student bond can be easily misunderstood. In the early days of my Zen training, I would make a formal prostration before my teacher when visiting him for practice instruction. I tried to see him as "enlightened," and I hoped that over time I would internalize the qualities of awareness, self-containment and energy that I admired in him.

Idealizing one's teacher is part of a long and healthy tradition in Tibet, Japan and India, according to Alan Roland, a psychoanalyst and author of *In Search of Self in India and Japan.* "The need to have a figure to respect, idealize and imitate is a crucial part of every person's self-development. But Eastern cultures are far more articulate about that need and culturally support it," he explained.

Roland believes that Asian students approach the teacher-student relationships more subtly than Americans—who often commit rapidly and completely, or not at all. Asian students may display deference, but withhold veneration, until they have studied with a teacher for years. They seem to have a "private self" unknown to many Americans, which is capable of reserving judgment even while scrupulously following the forms. When a teacher fails,

Asians may continue to defer to his superior rank but silently withdraw affection and respect.

In America, it's often the reverse. Some Vajradhatu students could forgive Osel Tendzin as a human being, but could not treat him as a leader. Few Americans can show deference to someone they don't venerate without feeling hypocritical. Faced with this cognitive dissonance, they either abandon deference and leave, or they deny inner feelings.

If they deny their perceptions, reality becomes distorted and a mutual dance of delusion begins. "Part of the blame lies with the student, because too much obedience, devotion and blind acceptance spoils a teacher," explained His Holiness the Dalai Lama last year at a conference in Newport Beach, California. "Part also lies with the spiritual master because he lacks the integrity to be immune to that kind of vulnerability. . . . I recommend never adopting the attitude toward one's spiritual teacher of seeing his or her every action as divine or noble. This may seem a little bit bold, but if one has a teacher who is not qualified, who is engaging in unsuitable or wrong behavior, then it is appropriate for the student to criticize that behavior."

TURNING POINT

Last autumn, it looked as though the Vajradhatu sangha would be torn in two. After the long retreat advised by Dilgo Khyentse Rinpoche, Tendzin boldly reasserted authority. Those who refused to accept his spiritual leadership were fired from key committees, denied permission to teach meditation and barred from taking part in advanced practices with the rest of their community. The conflict became so intense that the two opposing factions sent delegations to Nepal and India to implore senior lamas to support their positions.

In response, Khyentse Rinpoche advised Tendzin to enter into a "strict retreat" for a year. Tendzin complied, retaining nominal authority but effectively abdicating his teaching and leadership role. Senior Tibetan lamas were invited to Boulder to teach, and Vajradhatu began to connect again to a wider Tibetan religious tradition.

"This is a real turning point," said a relieved David Rome, a member of the board of directors. "This is a way to come together and feel basic unity, and to look at the issues that this crisis brought to the surface. This is not the end; really, it's the beginning," he said.

AFTER THE FALL

As Vajradhatu struggles to pick up the pieces, other Buddhist sanghas, which have undergone similar crises, are likewise dealing with ways to heal their communities. In one of the most promising side effects, American teachers of Insight (*vipassana*) meditation have recently created a clear set of ethical standards for teachers and a community board to oversee them.

In other Buddhist communities, however, where teachers have stone-walled accusations of misconduct, successive waves of dissenting students have departed. At San Francisco Zen Center, my own practice home, our teacher resigned under pressure. We brought in psychological consultants and learned to talk more honestly to each other, and adopted more democratic forms of decision-making. Even so, many students left. The meditation hall emptied. Friendships were broken, and some people lost the energy for spiritual practice. Our former teacher moved to Santa Fe and continued teaching; my husband and I moved to the suburbs.

My black meditation robe still hangs in the back of my closet. I never lost faith in Buddhist teachings, but for some years I didn't know how to reconnect with them. Instead, I did what a friend called "remedial work," examining my personal history and the anger and self-righteousness I expressed when the scandal broke. I was among those who hoped to find a sanctuary within Buddhism for my personal wounds. But my culture and family history trailed me into my Buddhist community like a can tied to the tail of a dog.

I study with another Buddhist teacher now, and I constantly remind myself to allow him—and me—to have imperfections. Once a month or so, I gather with others in a friend's living room to recite the lay Buddhist precepts.

Yet something of the past remains unfinished. My old teacher simply left when he could not bear his students' anger any more. I remember a senior priest saying at the time, "Students are expecting him to transform himself without safety. You can't learn a whole new way when you are under attack."

The bitterness from that unresolved schism still hurts, like a splinter working its way deeper into one's palm. A friend of mine, Yvonne Rand—an ordained Buddhist teacher who still participates closely in the community—said to me recently, "We're still struggling with the fallout of his departure. I don't think the shoe will fully drop until we find a way to be in the same room together. As long as there's a fear of having him around, there's a way people don't understand their part in the situation."

We lack rituals that would allow communities to acknowledge these crises and to heal them. I remember reading about the Full Moon Ceremony used by monks in the first few centuries after Buddha's death. On the eve of every full and new moon during the rainy season, monks would gather in the forest for a ritual called "confession before the community." There, they publicly recited the precepts, admitted their shortcomings, their violations and any damage they had done to their community.

If we reinstated such a quiet ritual, perhaps a brave, disgraced teacher might safely acknowledge his misconduct and the wounds that brought him to it. Perhaps the sangha could confess its deep disappointment and feelings of betrayal, and its participation in what had gone wrong. Perhaps the whole sangha could publicly apologize to the men or women who had been misused sexually or in other ways, and compensate them in some way.

After full acknowledgment and restitution, forgiveness might be possible and healing begin.

· · · · · · ·

30 · THE SHADOW OF
THE ENLIGHTENED GURU

GEORG FEUERSTEIN

In his book *The Lotus and the Robot,* Arthur Koestler tells of an incident that happened while he was sitting at the feet of the female Indian guru Anandamayi Ma, who is venerated by tens of thousands of Hindus as an incarnation of the Divine. An old woman approached the dais and begged Anandamayi Ma to intercede for her son, who had been missing in action after a recent border incident. The saint ignored her completely. When the woman became hysterical, Anandamayi Ma dismissed her rather harshly, which was a signal to the attendants to swiftly conduct the woman out of the room.

Koestler was taken aback by Anandamayi Ma's indifference to the woman's suffering. He concluded that the saint was, at least in that moment, lacking compassion. He found it perplexing that an allegedly enlightened being, acting spontaneously out of the fullness of the Divine, should display such abruptness and seeming callousness. This story highlights the fact that even supposedly "perfect" beings can and do engage in actions that seem to contradict their followers' idealized image of them.

Some "perfect" masters are notorious for their angry outbursts, others for their authoritarianism. Of late a number of allegedly celibate super-gurus have made headlines for their clandestine sexual relationships with women followers. Spiritual geniuses—saints, sages, and mystics—are not immune to neurotic traits or to having experiences much like psychotic states. Indeed, even apparently enlightened adepts can be subject to personality characteristics that consensus opinion finds undesirable.

That the personality of enlightened beings and advanced mystics remains largely intact is obvious when one examines biographies and autobiographies of adepts, past and present. Each one manifests specific psychological qualities, as determined by his or her genetics and life history. Some are inclined toward passivity, others are spectacularly dynamic. Some are gentle, others fierce. Some have no interest in learning, others are great scholars. What these fully awakened beings have in common is that they no longer identify with the personality complex, however it may be configured, but live out of the identity of the Self. Enlightenment, then, consists in the transcendence of the ego-habit, but enlightment does *not* obliterate the personality. If it did, we would be justified in equating it with psychosis.

The fact that the basic personality structure is essentially the same after enlightenment as it was before raises the crucial question of whether enlightenment also leaves untouched traits that in the unenlightened individual might be called neurotic. I believe that this is so. If they are true teachers, their overriding purpose can be expected to be the communication of the transcendental Reality. Yet, their behavior is, in the outside world, always a matter of personal style.

Devotees, of course, like to think that their ideal guru is free from whims and that apparent idiosyncracies must be for the sake of teaching others. But a moment's reflection would show this to be based in fantasy and projection.

Some teachers have claimed that their conduct reflects the psychic state of those with whom they come in contact, that their sometimes curious exploits are, in other words, triggered by disciples. This may be, because enlightened adepts are like chameleons. But such mirroring still proceeds along personal lines. For instance, some gurus will not sit on garbage heaps, consume human flesh (as did the modern Tantric master Vimalananda), or meditate on corpses to instruct others, while few of those who engage in such practices would consider training their intellects or acquiring musical skills in order to serve a disciple better.

The personality of the adept is, to be sure, oriented toward self-transcendence rather than self-fulfillment. However, it is characteristically not on a self-actualizing trajectory. I use *self-actualization* here in a more restricted sense than it was intended by Abraham Maslow: as the intention toward realizing psychic wholeness based on the integration of the shadow. The shadow, in Jungian terms, is the dark aspect of the personality, the aggregate of repressed materials. The individual shadow is ineluctably tied up with the collective shadow. This integration is not a once-and-for-all event but a lifelong process. It can occur either prior to enlightenment or afterward. If integration is not a conscious program of the pre-enlightened personality, it is also unlikely to form part of the personality after enlightenment, because of the relative stability of the personality structures.

The claim has been made by some contemporary adepts that in the breakthrough of enlightenment, the shadow is entirely flooded with the light of supraconsciousness. The implication is that the enlightened being is without shadow. This is difficult to accept as a statement about the conditional personality. The shadow is the product of the near-infinite permutations of unconscious processes that are essential to human life as we know it. While the personality is experiencing life, unconscious content is formed simply because no one can be continuously aware of everything.

The uprooting of the ego-identity in enlightenment does not terminate the processes of attention: it merely ends the anchorage of attention to the ego. Moreover, the enlightened being continues to think and emote, which inevitably leaves an unconscious residue even when there is no inner attachment to these processes. The important difference is that this residue is not experienced as a hindrance to ego-transcendence simply because this is an ongoing process in the enlightened condition.

A few adepts have resolved this issue by admitting that there is a phantom ego, a vestigial personality center, even after awakening as the universal Reality. If we accept this proposition, then we could perhaps also speak of the existence of a phantom shadow or a vestigial shadow, which permits the enlightened being to function in the dimensions of conditional reality. In the unenlightened individual, ego and shadow go together; we can postulate an analogous polarization between phantom ego and phantom shadow after enlightenment.

Even if we were to assume that enlightenment illumines and evaporates the shadow, we must still seriously question whether this illumination corresponds to integration—the basis for higher self-transformation. This means that it involves intentional change in the direction of psychic wholeness that can be observed by others. When I examine the lives of contemporary adepts claiming to be enlightened, I do not see evidence that such integration work is being done. One of the first indications would be a visible willingness not only to reflect disciples back to themselves but also to have disciples be a mirror for the adept's further growth. However, this kind of willingness calls for an openness that is precluded by the authoritarian style adopted by most gurus.

The traditional spiritual paths are by and large grounded in the vertical ideal of liberation *from* the conditioning of the body-mind. Therefore, they focus on what is conceived to be the ultimate good—transcendental Being. This spiritual single-mindedness jars the human psyche out of focus: its personal concerns become insignificant and its structures are viewed as something to be transcended as quickly as possible rather than transformed. Of course, all self-transcending methods involve a degree of self-transformation. But, as a rule, this does not entail a concerted effort to work with the shadow and accomplish psychic integration. This may explain why so many mystics and adepts are highly eccentric and authoritarian and appear socially to have weakly integrated personalities.

Unlike transcendence, integration occurs in the horizontal plane. It extends the ideal of wholeness to the conditional personality and its social nexus. Yet, integration makes sense only when the conditional personality and the conditional world are not treated as irrevocable opponents of the ultimate Reality but are valued as manifestations of it.

Having discovered the Divine in the depths of his or her own soul, the adept must then find the Divine in all life. This is, in fact, the adept's principal obligation and responsibility. To put it differently, having drunk at the fountain of life, the adept must complete the spiritual opus and practice compassion on the basis of the recognition that everything participates in the universal field of the Divine.

. . . .

31 · A HERETIC IN A NEW AGE COMMUNITY

W .   B R U G H   J O Y

When I first visited the Findhorn community in 1975, I was just beginning to explore the possibility of training individuals to feel the energies that radiate from the body and to be able, themselves, to transfer energy into another person's body for purposes of physical healing and psychological balance.

The Findhorn community at that time was youthful and very much under the influence of the Divine Parent/Divine Child energetics. When I was asked to give an impression of what I felt was to transpire in the immediate future for the community as a whole, I said I sensed that a forthcoming vast influx of people would bring with them the danger that the innate "soul" of the community might be diluted, by their numbers and by the business concerns to which they would have to attend. I was a welcome guest. The community generally loved my talk!

Five years later, I was again asked to talk to them about what I sensed was ahead for the community as a whole. This talk followed the two-week Conference, subsequent to which each participant was to enter the communal life of Findhorn, and with heightened awareness. The participants were not tourists or just visitors. They had been prepared to experience the full range of the community's life, including what is not ordinarily seen upon the first approach: its dark side.

When I shared my then current impressions at one of the community's evening gatherings, I presented a different picture from before . . . and a difficult one. I said that the forthcoming period was to be a time for contraction and for the release of physical assets. The community had enjoyed a phase of increase and abundance, but the counterphase of that cycle was approaching. Best to prepare for it ahead of time, I said.

I talked about the consequences of feeling "special" and how doing battle against the "evils of the world" not only creates the "enemy," but is actually a projection of the darker aspects of the community onto the world screen. Needless to say, the talk was not popular and I was fast falling into the "unwelcome guest" category. I would soon be seen as whatever was unresolved in the community at the unconscious level. In other words, I would be viewed as carrying the shadow side of the community, and I knew it!

When we attempt to deny what is, to deny such things as the natural cycles of time and space, enormous energy is required. That energy is then not available as a resource for other activities. In this case, the denial by the vast majority of the members of the community of anything that threatened their external values and beliefs was evident. The wisdom of recognizing both expansion and contraction was not part of the general belief system of the Findhorn community, as it is not part of the New Age thought process in general. Despite assertions by most partisans of the New Age that they are promoting such virtues as selfless service to the world, New Age beliefs in the specialness and innocence of the New Age are, in my opinion, regressive . . . toward the infantile, if not the fetal. Such ideation tends to be self-centered . . . concentrating, for example, on images that ignore the contribution of the destructive.

Near the end of this communal post-Conference living experience with the Findhorn community, an evening of sharing and entertainment was at hand. As I was on my way into the meeting hall, the community poet aggressively approached me. I had already had one brief encounter with him a few days earlier when he asked if I would talk to his students, and I declined. Now he was filled with rage and anger. I thought he was going to hit me, but instead he hissed something about what he was going to present in the hall that evening. I began to center myself.

The first part of the evening's entertainment consisted of amusing skits and some singing. Then the community poet came on. He caught my eye . . . and I knew I was to be his sacrifice. In venomous poetry, powerful and afire with wrathful righteousness, he unleashed the dark feelings and destructive forces of the community. The objects of his rage were the Americans in general and myself in particular. We were portrayed in terms that would make fecal material seem sunny by comparison. His attack centered around money and power . . . the dark side of any endeavor that wears the mask of great good and service. The only thing explicitly missing was sex, except he covered that by using the words "fuck" and "fucking" with an extraordinary frequency.

The function of poets is to give voice to the collective. When the content is infantile rage and resentment that has been disowned—and how natural for such to exist in a community that perceives itself only as manifesting love and light—an object must be found to carry the unconscious forces. Through the mechanism of projection, destructive energies were unleashed that night without the participants' having to accept that the forces of contempt and jealousy were not only within the poet but also within the community itself! By his projecting this material onto me and the other Americans, he was actually promoting a healing or balancing of the unconscious forces of the community. However, it would have been better for all concerned had the community been further along in the process of owning the dark side of its nature . . . but that isn't how things transpired that evening. For me, as long as I recognized that his accusations did, in fact, have their counterpart in me and I owned them consciously, I would be able to remain centered and could also appreciate that an eruption of long-held unconscious shadow content of the community was at hand.

While the poet continued his volcanic outpouring of dark emotions, the community as a whole was displaying a wide range of reactivity. Some people called for him to stop. Some began to cry and leave the room. Others were elated that someone had the courage to state what many were feeling. Some began to defend the Americans and the American way of life. Some were humiliated and embarrassed, looking to me to defend myself or the others, or to do something about what was occurring. I encouraged the poet to continue, thinking he couldn't have too much more to ventilate . . . but he did!

He continued for another fifteen to twenty minutes before Eileen Caddy, one of the founders of the community, asked him to stop. He did, and moved out of the room almost gleefully. The community gathered around those who organized the evening's events to console them and to share an embrace of love and nourishment through touch.

I had never been involved in a public attack of that magnitude. My resources for centering and becoming transparent to the assailing forces—for being able to find that place in consciousness where there is no need to defend from the content of the attack—were nearly depleted.

Becoming transparent to accusations does not mean parts of oneself do not feel hurt, humiliated, angry, and defensive. It means realizing what is actually transpiring and not going unconscious or falling victim to one's own disowned material! I knew the shadow of the community was erupting and I was the mirror. I also recognized that those forces and qualities which were being attacked were parts of myself as well. For me, this was a huge leap in maturation. I was being initiated into those collective arenas of consciousness where one handles the unconscious projections not just of one individual or a few individuals but of a large collective, in this case an entire community.

. . . .

32 · THE SHADOW IN ASTROLOGY

LIZ GREENE

One of the most interesting things you can do with a horoscope is to look at it from the point of view of what is in the dark and what is in the light. I would like to work with the shadow figure in particular because the shadow usually wears the mask of one's own sex. I don't think this is a hard-and-fast rule, but in general the problem of the shadow isn't one of sexual attraction or repulsion. More often it deals with the dilemma of accepting one's own sexuality, one's masculinity or one's feminity. It would seem that anything in a horoscope can drop into the shadow. Any point in the chart can be appropriated by that figure. These missing elements not only have to do with the kind of people we fall in love with. They are also bound up with the dark side of the soul. Planetary aspects also can have as much to do with the shadow as with the sort of people that fascinate you among the opposite sex. Points in the chart such as the descendant and the IC [the nadir or bottom point] also have a great deal to do with what falls into shadow in the personality.

I will mention something about the IC first because it's a point that is often overlooked in the horoscope. The midheaven or MC seems most of the time to be connected with how we wish to appear in the eyes of the collective. The opposite point, the IC, seems relevant in terms of what we don't want the collective to see. The sign which is at the very base of the chart is the area of darkness, the place of the sun's lowest ebb, and it is one of the points of greatest vulnerability through which the shadow enters.

If you bear in mind the kind of people and groups which irritate or *antagonize* you, and the kind of people and groups which you idealize, consider what sign is placed at the IC in the birth horoscope and what its particular qualities are. Likewise you might consider what sign falls at the descendant. There is something very queer about the relationship of what we love and what we hate. They are often the same thing in slightly different form. If you take those two images of what you idealize and what you despise and stand those images side by side, you may find that the same root exists beneath them both. It's the same figure, but it wears a different garb.

For example, if you have Taurus on the ascendant and are typical of the sign, you may despise people who are not overt and out in the open. Taurus often dislikes those who seem to be secretive or manipulative, who aren't straightforward, or who complicate things and create crises when there could be peace and quiet. But at the same time, Taurus is fascinated with people who have a mystery about them, who are not easy to read and who seem to have insights into human nature in a magical way. It's the same figure. But if you don't like it, then it's evil or slippery or vicious, and if you do like it, then it's deep and profound and strong. Both sides are wrapped up in the Scorpio descendant.

If you have an Aquarian midheaven, then you are likely to present to the world the tolerant, humanitarian face of Aquarius with its wonderful reasonableness and fairness and concern with other people's rights. You may loathe and despise those self-centered people who aggrandize themselves at the expense of the group, and who draw too much attention to themselves in social situations. You might be profoundly annoyed at the exhibitionist who puts himself before others, because you believe that everyone is special and entitled to the same rights and benefits. Yet you might have a tremendous admiration for the creative person, the artist who can ignore everybody and lock himself in his room for five years and produce a great painting or a magnificent novel. To create like that one must, of course, be megomaniacal enough to believe that his vision is important enough to be seen or read by everybody. But Aquarius frequently idealizes the artist, while failing to recognize that every artist must of necessity be egotistical and ruthless about other people's demands and rights. Once again it is the same figure, but seen in opposite ways.

Another example might be a Gemini ascendant, which is cool and rational and clever and never takes anything all that seriously. Gemini loves to play with words and ideas, which are like the balls which the juggler juggles. Information interests Gemini, who is the reporter and observer of life. Gemini will always remember the little anecdote or notice the little idiosyncrasy about another person which everyone else misses. But if you have a Gemini ascendant then it's all likely to be terribly interesting but none of it will passionately concern you. Passion and intensity may be annoying and even frightening. You may really dislike the fanatic, the proselytizer who believes in something with fervent emotion but who can't be bothered with facts. Or you may despise people who wear their hearts on their sleeves, who throw themselves about, showing wild emotion, whether it's emotion about a person or a philosophy. Someone who is very committed to a religion or a philosophy can really anger Gemini—the one who comes up to you on the street and says, "You should join Scientology" or "Are you saved?" or whatever. Gemini recoils from this because he's much too intellectually sophisticated to believe there's only one truth. Yet you may secretly admire the person who is able to have real spiritual vision and real commitment, who can throw himself into life with passion. You may idealize the person who has imagination and intuition, and never realize that the same fire inspires both these figures.

If you identify very strongly with a particular set of qualities in your own nature, then when the opposite surfaces or appears in someone else, then the result is often repugnance. It's frequently a deep moral repugnance, a real distaste of what that other person stands for. It isn't just a casual disinterest or dislike. The shadow arouses anger far out of proportion to the situation. You don't just ignore the fanatic with the leaflets on the street corner. You want to beat in his head. Why should there be this kind of anger and repulsion? If you penetrate at all deeply into the feelings around a confrontation with the shadow, you will see that the shadow is experienced as a terrible threat. It is a kind of death to allow the shadow any recognition or acceptance. If you are prepared to permit even an inch of tolerance or compassion or value, then the whole edifice of the ego is threatened. Of course the more rigid and entrenched you are in particular attitudes and a particular self-image, the more threatening the shadow becomes. And it's particularly painful because sometimes you must recognize it yet still make the moral choice of not acting it out.

Some time ago I did a chart for an Aquarian woman with Capricorn on the ascendant. She had a number of very strong Saturn contacts in her horoscope, most of them trines and sextiles, and it was terribly important to her to be self-sufficient. She was proud of her capability and her strength. She had raised two children to adulthood in a loveless marriage with a very weak and unsupportive husband, and had carved a successful career for herself in banking. The one thing she could never admit to anyone was a feeling of helplessness or neediness or dependency. She preferred to suffer in stern silence rather than demonstrate any kind of need that might make her vulnerable to another person. She needed an unsupportive husband because a supportive one would have forced her to confront her own shadow. When we began to talk about these issues she told me a dream that had recurred two or three times which disturbed her. There was a particular woman who worked in her office that she disliked terribly. She dreamed that she was in her home and this woman knocked at the door and asked to be let in. She became very angry and slammed the door in the other woman's face.

I asked her to tell me about the other woman. My client said, "Oh, I can't bear her. I find her absolutely hateful." I said, "Well, what is it about her that you hate?" She went on to tell me that this woman, who was about twenty years younger than my client, was "one of those silly little receptionists." It seemed that the younger woman was easily hurt and cried a lot, and played very helpless around all the men in the office. She was always asking for assistance and pretended that she didn't know how to do things even when she did know, so that other people had to help her. My client kept using the most charged adjectives—the young woman was slimy, deceitful, horrible, disgusting. One of the ways in which you can easily see this dynamic of shadow projection is in the adjectives, which go right over the top. My client couldn't just say, "I disapprove of this woman." She went on and on for some time.

Then I said, "Do you suppose this woman's behavior might have something to do with you?" and she snapped, "Certainly not!" At that point in the chart reading she did precisely what she had done in the dream. She slammed the door to keep the shadow out. After a while I changed the subject. That is a shadow figure, and my client reacted to it in a very typical way.

You see that the issue of the shadow isn't a question of admitting faults. It's a question of being shaken right down to your foundations by realizing that you are not as you appear—not only to others, but also to yourself. The shadow reminds you that what you value the most may be badly shaken if you let it in. My client with her strongly Saturnian personality had built up her whole life and self-image around proud self-sufficiency. The shadow kept knocking at the door, and she kept refusing to allow it entry. The repugnance usually hides a very deep fear, a fear of being annihilated as the person you know yourself to be.

I think that the older you get, the harder it is to face this threat of having everything you have built in your life destroyed. Of course it doesn't have to mean destruction, but that is the fear. The more crystallized the personality becomes, the stronger the ego gets, the harder you have fought to get things you want, then the more difficult the whole issue becomes. If you have exercized self-restraint and self-denial in order to achieve some value or ideal, then the more painful the confrontation is, because letting the shadow in may mean that the whole house of cards comes tumbling down.

So you can see why there is fear and repulsion. It isn't just an idle dislike. It's a threat to established values. The more lopsided we are, the harder we fight to keep that figure out. Even if my client had acknowledged that her horrible colleague was actually an image of something in herself, she would not have thanked me for pointing it out to her.

· · · · · · ·

33 · THE DEVIL IN THE TAROT

SALLIE NICHOLS

The time has come to face the Devil. As a major archetypal figure he properly belongs in heaven, the top row of our Tarot chart. But he fell . . . remember? To hear him tell it, he quit his job and resigned from heaven. He said he deserved a better break; he felt he should have been given a raise and more authority.

But that isn't the way others report the story. According to most accounts, Satan was fired. His sin, they say, was arrogance and pride. He had an overbearing nature, too much ambition, and an inflated sense of his own worth. Nevertheless, he had lots of charm and considerable influence. His ways were subtle: he organized the angels to rebellion behind the Boss's back, at the same time currying the Master's favor.

He was jealous of everyone—especially mankind. He likes to think of himself as the favored son. He hated Adam and resented his rulership of that tidy Garden of Eden. Complacent security was (and still is) anathema to him. Perfection made him reach for his firebrand. Innocence made him squirm. How he did enjoy tempting Eve and busting up Paradise! Temptation was— and continues to be—his specialty. Some even say it was he who tempted the Lord to harass Job. Since God is good, they tell us, He could never have played such devilish tricks had He not been conned into it by Satan. Others argue that, since the Lord is omniscient and all-powerful, He must bear the sole responsibility for putting Job through the third degree.

The argument as to who was responsible for Job's suffering has been going on for centuries. It hasn't been settled yet and it may never be. The reason is plain: the Devil is confusing because he himself is confused. If you look at his Tarot portrait, you will see why. He presents himself as an absurd conglomeration of parts. He wears the antlers of a stag, yet he has the talons of a predatory bird and the wings of a bat. He refers to himself as a man, but he possesses the breasts of a woman—or perhaps more accurately, *wears* them, for they have the appearance of something stuck or painted on him. This odd breastplate can be little protection. It is perhaps worn as an insignia intended to camouflage the wearer's cruelty; but symbolically it might indicate that Satan uses feminine naiveté and innocence as a front in order to charm his way into our garden. And, as the Eden story makes clear, it is through this same innocent naiveté in us (as personified by Eve) that he operates.

That his breastplate is rigid and superimposed might also indicate that the Devil's feminine side is mechanical and uncoordinated, so that it is not always under his control. Significantly, his golden helmet belongs to Wotan, a god who also was subject to womanish temper tantrums and sought vengeance whenever his authority was threatened.

The Devil carries a sword, but he holds his weapon carelessly by the blade, and in his left hand. It is obvious that his relationship to his weapon is so unconscious that he would be unable to use it in a purposeful manner, meaning symbolically that his relationship to the masculine Logos is similarly ineffectual. In this version of the Tarot, Satan's sword seems only to wound himself. But its blade is all the more dangerous because it is not under his control. Organized crime operates by logic. It can be ferreted out and dealt with in a systematic way. Even crimes of passion have a certain emotional logic that makes them humanly understandable and sometimes even preventable. But indiscriminate destruction, wanton murder in the streets, the berserker who takes random potshots on the freeways—against these we have no defense. Such forces, we feel, operate in a darkness beyond human comprehension.

The Devil is an archetypal figure whose lineage, direct and indirect, reaches back into antiquity. There he usually appeared as a beastly demon more powerful and less human than the figure pictured in the Tarot. As Set, Egyptian god of evil, he often took the form of a snake or crocodile. In ancient Mesopotamia, Pazazu (a malaria-bearing demon of the southwest wind, king of the evil spirits of the air) embodied some of the qualities now attributed to Satan. Our Devil may also have inherited certain attributes from Tiamat, Babylonian goddess of chaos, who took the form of a horned and clawed fowl. It was not until Satan appeared in our Judeo-Christian culture that he began to assume more human characteristics and conduct his nefarious activities in ways we humans could more readily understand.

That the Devil's image has become more humanized in the course of centuries means, symbolically, that we are more ready now to view him as a shadow aspect of ourselves rather than as a supernatural god or an infernal demon. Perhaps it may mean that we are ready at last to wrestle with our own satanic underside. But human—and even handsome—he has not shed his enormous bat wings. If anything, they have grown darker and larger than those worn by the Marseilles Devil. This indicates that Satan's relationship to the bat is particularly important and requires our special attention.

The bat is a night flyer. Avoiding daylight, he retreats each morning to a dark cave where he hangs upside down, gathering energy for his nighttime escapades. He is a blood sucker whose bite spreads pestilence and whose droppings defile the environment. He swoops around in the dark and according to folk belief, has a penchant for entangling himself in one's hair, causing hysteric confusion.

The Devil, too, flies at night—a time when the lights of civilization are extinguished and the rational mind is asleep. It is at this time that human beings lie unconscious, unprotected, and open to suggestion. In the daylight hours, when human consciousness is awake and man's ability to differentiate is keen, the Devil retreats to the dark recesses of the psyche where he too hangs upside down, hiding his contrariness, recharging his energies, and biding his time. The Devil metaphorically sucks our blood, sapping our substance. The effects of his bite are contagious, infecting whole communities or even states. Just as a bat could cause unreasoned panic in a crowded auditorium were he to swoop down among the spectators, so the Devil can fly blind into a crowd, literally threatening to entangle himself in everyone's hair, messing up logical thought and producing mass hysteria.

Our loathing of the bat goes beyond all logic. So, too, our fear of the Devil—and for similar reasons. The bat seems to us a monstrous aberration of nature—a squeaking mouse with wings. As with the Devil, his disparate parts defy natural laws. We tend to view all such malformations—the dwarf, the hunchback, the calf with two heads—as the work of some sinister, irrational power, and the creature itself as an instrument of this power. One uncanny talent shared by bat and Devil is the ability to navigate blind in the dark. We intuitively fear such black magic.

Scientists have found ways to protect themselves against the bat's dangerous, filthy habits so that they can re-enter the beasts' cave and examine the inhabitant in a more rational way. As a result, the bat's peculiar form and repulsive behaviour seem less frightening than formerly. Even his mysterious radar system is now discovered to operate according to understandable laws. Modern technology has decoded its black magic to create a similar device whereby man, too, can fly blind.

Perhaps, by a similar kind of objective examination of the Devil, we can learn to protect ourselves against him; and, by discovering within ourselves a proclivity toward satanic black magic, we may learn to conquer those irrational fears that paralyze the will and make it impossible to face and deal with the Devil. Perhaps in the ghastly illumination of Hiroshima, with its aftermath of twisted and warped humanity, we can at long last see the monstrous shape of our own devilish shadow.

With each succeeding war, it becomes increasingly apparent that we and the Devil share many characteristics in common. Some say that it is precisely the function of war to reveal to mankind his enormous capacity for evil in such an unforgettable way that each of us will ultimately acknowledge his own dark shadow and come to grips with the unconscious forces of his inner nature. Alan McGlashan views war specifically as "the punishment of man's disbelief in those forces within himself."[1]

Paradoxically, as man's conscious life becomes more "civilized" his pagan, animal nature, as revealed in war, becomes increasingly ruthless. Commenting on this, Jung says:

> The dammed-up instinct-forces in civilized man are immensely more destructive, and hence more dangerous, than the instincts of the primitive, who in a modest degree is constantly living negative instincts. Consequently no war of the historical past can rival a war between civilized nations in its colossal scale of horror.[2]

Jung goes on to say that the classic picture of the Devil as half man, half beast "exactly describes the grotesque and sinister side of the unconscious, for we have never really come to grips with it and consequently it has remained in its original savage state."[3]

If we examine this "beastly man" as he appears in the Tarot, we can see that no one individual component in itself is overpowering. What makes this figure so obnoxious is the senseless conglomeration of its various parts. Such an irrational assemblage threatens the very order of things, undermining the cosmic scheme upon which all life rests. To face such a shadow would mean facing the fear that not only we humans but Nature herself may have gone berserk.

But this strange beast within, which we project onto the Devil is, after all, Lucifer the Light Bringer. He is an angel—albeit a fallen one—and as such he is a messenger of God. It behooves us to get acquainted with him.

· · · · · · ·

34 · NEW AGE FUNDAMENTALISM

JOHN BABBS

I went last night, as I have so many other nights, to one of these wondrous New Age gatherings. And I don't think I can take it any more. I get sick. I must escape the torture of being blessed to death during evenings such as this. There is something frighteningly unreal about them that I can't quite put my finger on. All I know is that afterwards I want to scream profanities, drink whiskey out of a bottle, go to sleazy blues joints, and chase wild, wild women.

At this event a beautiful young man told of his travels throughout the globe visiting sacred ceremonial sites—four hundred all told. He has been around the world 14 times in his 34 years, living in many of these places for months, sometimes years on end.

He has a vision, too. A vision of a more peaceful world. A world that's healthy and clean, that supports each of us in a meaningful work, as we in turn support her and one another.

He described how these sites have been used since four or five thousand years before Christ by ancient pagans and goddess worshippers; how they have been used as interstellar landing sites by visitors from far distant galaxies, and as settlements for ancient civilizations far more advanced than our own.

He also prophesized doom, describing a future full of horror, because we have allowed our right brain lobes to atrophy, resulting in lost connections with these ancient power points. He described how the patriarchal religions of the world have appropriated these sites for their own uses and in the process have destroyed the ancient wisdoms and truths that these places once contained.

I guess I have been to over a hundred of these wonderful evenings. Beautiful people. Soft. Gentle. Spiritual. Visionary. Fascinating. But underlying all of this beauty lurks a darkness, only thinly veiled by beatific platitudes of sweetness. I call this beast New Age Fundamentalism, a belief that I am right and everyone else is wrong, stupid or evil; a belief that I represent the forces of light and goodness, while everyone else is duped by the forces of evil.

It is not ever actually stated. It is veiled, but, still, it is there. I never thought I would ever speak favorably about Jerry Falwell, but at least with Jerry you know where he stands, you know what his judgments are. I can deal with that. He at least has the courage to state them. What is so maddening about New Age Fundamentalists is that their judgments and moralizing are hidden behind facades of New Age doctrine, behind smoke screens of "we love everyone" and "we are one."

This young man felt that the pagan, Greek and Roman stories and goddess myths which described this grand mystery of life were "truth" and that the Christian, Muslim and Judaic stories were fabrications and distortions of the "real" truth. Further, since he has developed his right-brain functions, he now can "verify" that these sites were used as extraterrestrial landing strips and as settlements for the lost tribes of Atlantis, Lemuria and Mu. How can he? Why, he knows it is true because he channeled it, that's why. End of discussion.

Give me a break. . . . Please (I never thought I would be hearing myself say this) *Give me some facts!* Is there any material plane verification for the phantasmagorical assertions that we make?

And why is it that we are so obsessively preoccupied with the past and the future? What difference does it really make what happened 5,000 years ago? And what does it matter just when the Space Brothers are going to arrive to save us from our madness? Are not these preoccupations simply another way of avoiding what is before us right now, avoiding what we are called upon to do to clean up our own lives and alleviate the suffering we see before us?

If the New Age is to begin to offer anything substantial to the reordering of life on earth, we Peter Pans have to land on *terra firma* and begin the hard work of transformation—first in our own lives, then in the world in front of us here and now, not in some distant past or uncertain future. To paraphrase the Buddhist sage: "Do you want to change the world? Then park your mountain bike, get a job and start sweeping the street in front of your door."

. . . .

THE SHADOW IN THE ZEN TRADITION

At the ritual meal, one takes a few grains of the Buddha's rice and puts them on the end of a spatula to offer to all evil spirits for their satisfaction. The servers come by and take the few grains off the spatula, offering them to a plant or animal and thus returning them to the life cycle. This is a way to consciously acknowledge evil spirits or the shadow, to feed them the best food, yet not to feed them too much.

Later in the day, if one comes across the evil spirits, one can say, "I already fed you. I don't need to feed you again."

In the Buddhist tradition, it's believed that there is a realm of hungry ghosts with huge appetites and throats the size of a needle. So, they're never satisfied, like the shadow with its ravenous appetite. By feeding it in small, regular amounts, the shadow doesn't need to take on a devouring attitude.

We know we can't eliminate the realm of hungry ghosts; they exist, so we have to take care of them. Then the effect of their grumbling will be less. So it is with the shadow.

AS TOLD BY PETER LEAVITT

. . . .

DEVILS, DEMONS, AND SCAPEGOATS: A PSYCHOLOGY OF EVIL

The web of our life is of a mingled yarn, good and ill together: our virtues would be proud, if our faults whipped them not; and our crimes would despair, if they were not cherished by our virtues.

WILLIAM SHAKESPEARE

There is no doubt that healthy-mindedness is inadequate as a philosophical doctrine, because the evil facts which it positively refuses to account for are a genuine portion of reality; and they may after all be the best key to life's significance, and possibly the only openers of our eyes to the deepest levels of truth.

WILLIAM JAMES

The sad truth is that man's real life consists of a complex of inexorable opposites—day and night, birth and death, happiness and misery, good and evil. We are not even sure that one will prevail against the other, that good will overcome evil, or joy defeat pain. Life is a battleground. It always has been, and always will be; and if it were not so, existence would come to an end.

C. G. JUNG

INTRODUCTION

. . . .

While the personal shadow is an entirely subjective development, the experience of the collective shadow is an objective reality, which we commonly call evil. Unlike the personal shadow, which gives hopeful signs when engaged by moral effort, the collective shadow is not touched by rational efforts and therefore can leave one with a feeling of utter and complete powerlessness. For some people, refuge from this despair can be found in faith and obedience to the absolute value systems of religions and ideologies, which historically have provided psychological protection from the evil threats abounding in the world. To the extent that these institutionalized values support our own, we may feel inoculated against the negative effects of evil.

Evil and its consequent problems have remained spiritual and intellectual concerns in human affairs from the earliest times. Each generation's *Zeitgeist*—the spirit of its era—colors the perceptions of what is good and what is evil. Among aboriginal peoples, whose lives remain virtually unchanged since the Stone Age, evil always has been associated with darkness and the night. During the daylight hours evil is nonexistent, but when the sun disappears, evil lurks menacingly in the shadows. The daily lives of native peoples are permeated by superstitious beliefs associated with the literal and symbolic idea of the shadow.

In his classic study *The Double,* Otto Rank reviewed some of the ways in which the literal shadow we cast is internalized symbolically as a living expression of the soul's involvement with good and evil. He explored how native peoples ritualize and regulate their relationships to shadow through custom and taboo.

In ancient Egypt, evil was deified as the god Set, dark brother of Osiris. Set gave personification to the arid Egyptian desert, the source of drought and scourges to the human culture that flourished in the fertile Nile plain. In Persian mythology, life was symbolized as a battle waged between opposing forces: Ahura-Mazda was the life-force, bringer of light and truth, while Ahriman represented the force of collective evil, the lord of darkness, deceit, sickness, and death.

Throughout the Indian subcontinent, traditional Hindu culture views transpersonal evil as a part of the changing expression of the one divine substance or energy of life. According to Indian scholar Heinrich Zimmer, evil is an integral part of the karmic cycle of cause and effect. Indians believe that it is by individual deeds, and by the intention behind those deeds, that we merit happiness or anguish. "In unending cycles the good and evil alternate," goes one Hindu tale. "Hence, the wise are attached to neither the evil nor the good. The wise are not attached to anything at all."

Western thinking about evil can be seen clearly in the moral stories of the Jewish and Christian bibles and in Greek mythology. Our culture is imbued with the images of Old Testament drama, stories of a people guided by conscience and a privileged dialogue with a Creator. The parables of Jesus and the folklore of the dark angel Satan provide our most basic symbols for understanding human evil.

Greek myth attributes collective evil to the gods of the pantheon. The greater and lesser gods of Olympus show a striking psychological correspondence to our own world of hubris and shadow. All Greek gods are fallible beings, capable of both good and evil. They are archetypal forces—real and palpable phenomena that exist invisibly among people, though beyond human cause and effect. In these great stories, objective evil is a preexisting force to be reckoned with by mortals.

According to the Greek mythology, evil came to us through the curiosity of Pandora. The story of its origins is worth retelling:

> Great Zeus, mighty lord of the skies and ruler of all the gods, in his wrath over the theft of fire from the gods, spoke thus to Prometheus: "Thou art wiser than all of us, thou rejoicest that thou hast stolen fire and hast deceived me. This shall work harm unto thyself and unto men yet to be. For they shall receive from me, in retaliation for the theft of fire, an evil thing in which they will all rejoice, surrounding with love their own pain."
>
> At Zeus's bidding, the master-craftsman god Hephaistos modeled an innocent maiden from the earth in the image of beautiful Aphrodite, goddess of love. This female figure, who is the ancestress of all mortal women, was called Pandora ("the rich in gifts"). She was radiant with charm, adorned by Athene, and given goddesslike qualities. All of the gods and goddesses participated in her preparation, such was the wrath of the Olympians at Prometheus' trickery. Zeus himself endowed Pandora with an insatiable curiosity, then gave her a sealed earthenware jar with the warning never to open it.
>
> Prometheus, defier of the accepted gods, knew not to accept gifts from the gods. He had cautioned his brother Epimetheus of the dangers of gods bearing gifts. But when the messenger-god Hermes arrived with the offering of Pandora, Epimetheus could not resist the beautiful woman. Thus Pandora came to live among mortals.
>
> It was not long before Pandora was overcome by curiosity. She opened the jar and out swarmed all the evils that had been shut up in it. Until then, such evils had been unknown to humankind. She clapped the lid shut, just in time to keep Hope inside, but by then the earth was swarming with numberless sorrow-bringing evils. With these came sickness and death. Thus was completed the separation between humans and the immortal gods.

We sometimes see these evils in the world with frightening clarity, though sometimes we do not see them at all. As classicist Carl Kerenyi has noted about Epimetheus in the Pandora story, it is human nature to take the gift and only later perceive the evil. Our perception of evil is imposed on us by the conflict between what we hope life would be and what it actually is. We want to be optimistic about our world and see the beauty; however, the historical memory of evil is ignored at great cost. The discrepancy can easily obscure the reality of evil. Naiveté can account for the abominations enacted among us in the name of a good cause.

The collective shadow can take form as mass phenomena in which entire nations can become possessed by the archetypal force of evil. This can be explained by the unconscious process known as *participation mystique,* whereby individuals and groups make a feeling-toned identification with an object, person, or idea, failing to make moral distinctions within themselves or in their perception of the object. In the case of collective shadow, this can mean that people identify with an ideology or leader that gives expression to the fears and inferiorities of the entire society. Often this takes form collectively as fanatical fascinations such as religious persecution, racial bigotry, caste systems, scapegoating, witch-hunting, or genocidal hatred. When a minority carries the projection of that which a society rejects, the potential for great evil is activated. Examples of this mass phenomenon in our time include the Czarist pogroms in Russia at the turn of the century, Nazi persecution of Jews, gypsies, and homosexuals in the World War II holocaust, U.S. anticommunism and McCarthyism in the 1950s, and South Africa's constitutional apartheid system. Our century bears witness to these mass psychoses, acted out in cruelties that have reached previously unimagined proportions.

Collective evil often defies understanding. These forces arise from the unconscious minds of great numbers of people. When such mental epidemics occur, we are often helpless in combating the scourge that ensues. The few who are not caught up in a *participation mystique* can easily become victims themselves. Consider the German people's denial of Nazi death camps, the entire world's blindness to the genocidal regime of the Khmer Rouge in Cambodia, or the global neglect of the Tibetans' plight at the hands of the ruthless Chinese communists.

These collective effects often are personified in the form of a political leader—Napoleon, Stalin, Hitler, Pol Pot, or Saddam Hussein, for example—who then carries the collective projections that have been repressed in an entire culture. "Not only is the collective shadow alive in such leaders," says Liliane Frey-Rohn, but "they themselves are representatives of the collective shadow, of the adversary, and of evil."

In recent decades there have been courageous examples of human attempts to neutralize evil: the modern Indian saint Mohandas Gandhi successfully restored Indian dignity and independence through nonviolence, which spawned a movement that has virtually freed Third World nations from overt imperialistic colonization. Martin Luther King and the American civil rights movement advanced the cause of racial equality and continue to inspire people and nations alike to confront the repressive forces of evil. Today's unified world sanctions against South African apartheid are a direct result of this achievement. The movements for the rights of women, children, the handicapped, and the aged all openly defy the forces of unconscious evil in American life. In the Soviet Union today, we see a stunning effort by an entire nation to throw off the grip of a destructive ideology. It has been hopeful and heartening to witness the Soviets try to recant the dark forces that have ruled their political system for half a century.

In order to avoid being duped unwittingly into naive unconsciousness, we constantly need new ways to think about evil. For most of us, evil remains a sleeping tiger, off in a darkened corner of life. From time to time it awakens, roars menacingly, and—if nothing terrible occurs—is lulled back to sleep by our need to deny its dangerous presence.

The denial of evil is learned behavior. We can bear just so much reality. Since early life, each of us has experienced evil, directly and vicariously, through the inexplicable behavior of others and through impersonal images from television, news media, cinema, story, and fairy tale. This exposure requires our young minds to develop some explanation for the objective reality of evil and its threat of impending annihilation.

Some of us have been left to sort out such frightening experiences on our own, without the benefit or comfort of help. Childhood formulations about shadow and evil, such as the bogeyman, remove the immediacy of such foreboding danger but become poor adaptations later in life, producing symptoms ranging from fear of the dark to debilitating phobic reactions. There are those among us—victims of child abuse, war, and other crimes—who were prematurely and tragically exposed to the yawning abyss of meaningless evil and have never quite recovered from the experiences. Others have had extremely dogmatic religious indoctrination to the appearance of evil in the world; they survive with stereotypes of fire and brimstone, hell and damnation, or superstitious ways of thinking about good and evil.

For the rest of us, the idea of evil is always subject to avoidance and denial, our greatest coping mechanisms. To deny that evil is a permanent affliction of humankind is perhaps the most dangerous kind of thinking. In *Escape from Evil,* Ernest Becker suggests that it is our impossible hopes and desires to deny the greatest of evils, death, that have heaped evil on the world: "In seeking to avoid evil, man is responsible for bringing more evil into the world than organisms could ever do merely by exercising their digestive tracts. It is man's ingenuity, rather than his animal nature, that has given his fellow creatures such a bitter earthly fate."

Not everyone agrees with the idea that evil is a permanent part of the human condition. Since St. Augustine, there has existed the idea that evil is nothing but the absence of good, which is known as the doctrine of *privatio boni.* This idea suggests that evil can be eradicated by good works. In *Aion,* Jung criticized such thinking, saying:

> There is a tendency, existing right from the start, to give priority to "good," and to do so with all the means in our power, whether suitable or unsuitable . . . the tendency always to increase the good and diminish the bad. The *privatio boni* may therefore be a metaphysical truth. I presume to no judgment on this matter. I must only insist that in our field of experience white and black, light and dark, good and bad, are equivalent opposites which always predicate one another.

In a recent book, *Banished Knowledge,* prolific author and psychoanalyst Alice Miller takes up this controversial notion of *privatio boni* when she boldly asserts that the collective shadow does not exist, that such ideas in themselves are a denial of evil:

> The Jungian doctrine of the shadow, and the notion that evil is the reverse of good, are aimed at denying the reality of evil. But evil is real. It is not innate but acquired, and it is never the reverse of good but rather its destroyer. . . . It is not true that evil, destructiveness, and perversion inevitably form part of human existence, no matter how often this is maintained. But it is true that evil is always engaged in producing more evil and, with it, an ocean of suffering for millions that is similarly avoidable. When one day the ignorance arising from childhood repression is eliminated and humanity has awakened, an end can be put to this production of evil.

The working hypothesis of *Meeting the Shadow,* however, is that evil is a permanent fixture in life, inextricably intertwined with the best of humanity. To reject the legacy of Pandora would require us to vacuum the evil swarm back into the jar. This seems both proverbially and realistically impossible. Historically, great misfortune has resulted when humans have become unintentionally blinded to the full realities of evil and have dispensed miseries much worse than the evil they sought to eradicate. One only has to think of the Crusades against the infidels during the Middle Ages or of the Vietnam War in our time.

If we are to have any real power in meeting the challenge of the world's evil, each of us must take responsibility at an individual level. "We have to recognize and accept as part of ourselves that evil and dirt which belong to each of us by virtue of the fact that we are human and have developed an ego," says Jungian analyst Edward C. Whitmont. "We have to acknowledge the archetypal objectivity of evil as a terrible aspect of sacred force, which includes destructiveness and decay no less than growing and maturing. Then we can relate to our fellow beings as fellow victims rather than as scapegoats."

There are no infallible doctrines; the most honest attempts to get at the truth about evil in our lives can yield only a promise of greater awareness. Each generation has its own encounter with the increasingly frightening specter of evil. Our children, born in an age of unprecedented potential for human destructiveness and of simplistic dogmas, require and deserve the benefits of a balanced and enlightened knowledge of evil.

Part 7 attempts to organize and compare some outstanding ideas about the subject of evil from the psychological view. There are many psychologies of evil; these essays are reprinted with the intention of provoking the reader's own incomplete ideas about evil.

Chapter 35, from C. G. Jung's autobiography, *Memories, Dreams, Reflections,* was written at the end of his life. It contains Jung's late thoughts about the challenge of evil and the need for psychology and for greater individual self-knowledge.

The second essay comes from *Power and Innocence* by psychologist Rollo May, who believes that innocence (which he terms "pseudo-innocence") can act as a childlike defense against the crucial awareness of evil.

In Chapter 37, from *People of the Lie,* psychiatrist and best-selling author M. Scott Peck delineates a psychology of evil that includes a Christian-influenced definition of the characteristics of evil people. "Strangely enough," says Peck, "evil people are often destructive because they are attempting to destroy evil. The problem is that they misplace the locus of evil. Instead of destroying others, they should be destroying the sickness within themselves."

Stephen A. Diamond reviews several psychologies of evil, including a critical comparison of the ideas presented by May and Peck in the two preceding chapters. His discussion of demons and the daimonic adds depth to our simplistic understanding of evil and makes a step toward a progressive psychology of evil.

Chapter 39, "The Basic Dynamic of Human Evil," represents the final work of the late Ernest Becker. An excerpt from *Escape from Evil,* it compares the psychological ideas of Otto Rank, Freud, and Jung, with a special emphasis on the work of Wilhelm Reich. Becker says that the enduring benefit of psychoanalysis is its contribution to the understanding of the dynamics of human misery.

In his piece, "Acknowledging Our Inner Split," Andrew Bard Schmookler suggests that only when we engage in the inner struggle with evil does it becomes possible to make peace with the shadow. His remarks about Erik Erikson's study of Mahatma Gandhi's shadow problem add an important dimension to the dialogue developed in this section. Schmookler's article comes from his book *Out of Weakness.*

These essays, though not an exhaustive study of the subject of evil, comprise a provocative roundtable of ideas that leaves room for our own thoughts to enter. Pull up a chair. The dialogue continues.

．　．　．　．　．　．　．

35 · THE PROBLEM OF EVIL TODAY

C . G .   J U N G

The Christian myth remained unassailably vital for a millennium—until the first signs of a further transformation of consciousness began appearing in the eleventh century.[1] From then on, the symptoms of unrest and doubt increased, until at the end of the second millennium the outlines of a universal catastrophe became apparent, at first in the form of a threat to consciousness. This threat consists in giantism—in other words, a hubris of consciousness—in the assertion: "Nothing is greater than man and his deeds." The other-worldliness, the transcendence of the Christian myth was lost, and with it the view that wholeness is achieved in the other world.

Light is followed by shadow, the other side of the Creator. This development reached its peak in the twentieth century. The Christian world is now truly confronted by the principle of evil, by naked injustice, tyranny, lies, slavery, and coercion of conscience. Its first violent eruption came in Germany. That outpouring of evil revealed to what extent Christianity has been undermined in the twentieth century. In the face of that, evil can no longer be minimized by the euphemism of the *privatio boni*. Evil has become a determinant reality. It can no longer be dismissed from the world by a circumlocution. We must learn how to handle it, since it is here to stay. How we can live with it without terrible consequences cannot for the present be conceived.

In any case, we stand in need of a reorientation, a *metanoia*. Touching evil brings with it the grave peril of succumbing to it. We must, therefore, no longer succumb to anything at all, not even to good. A so-called good to which we succumb loses its ethical character. Not that there is anything bad in it on that score, but to have succumbed to it may breed trouble. Every form of addiction is bad, no matter whether the narcotic be alcohol or morphine or idealism. We must beware of thinking of good and evil as absolute opposites. The criterion of ethical action can no longer consist in the simple view that good has the force of a categorical imperative, while so-called evil can resolutely be shunned. Recognition of the reality of evil necessarily relativizes the good, and the evil likewise, converting both into halves of a paradoxical whole.

In practical terms, this means that good and evil are no longer so self-evident. We have to realize that each represents a *judgment*. In view of the fallibility of all human judgment, we cannot believe that we will always judge rightly. We might so easily be the victims of misjudgment. The ethical problem is affected by this principle only to the extent that we become somewhat uncertain about moral evaluations. Nevertheless we have to make ethical decisions. The relativity of "good" and "evil" by no means signifies that these categories are invalid, or do not exist. Moral judgment is always present and carries with it characteristic psychological consequences. I have pointed out many times that as in the past, so in the future the wrong we have done, thought, or intended will wreak its vengeance on our souls. Only the contents of judgment are subject to the differing conditions of time and place and, therefore, take correspondingly different forms. For moral evaluation is always founded upon the apparent certitudes of a moral code which pretends to know precisely what is good and what evil. But once we know how uncertain the foundation is, ethical decision becomes a subjective, creative act.

Nothing can spare us the torment of ethical decision. Nevertheless, harsh as it may sound, we must have the freedom in some circumstances to avoid the known moral good and do what is considered to be evil, if our ethical decision so requires. In other words, again: *we must not succumb to either of the opposites.* A useful pattern is provided by the *neti-neti* of Indian philosophy. In given cases, the moral code is undeniably abrogated and ethical choice is left to the individual. In itself there is nothing new about this idea; in pre-psychology days such difficult choices were also known and came under the heading of "conflict of duties."

As a rule, however, the individual is so unconscious that he altogether fails to see his own potentialities for decision. Instead he is constantly and anxiously looking around for external rules and regulations which can guide him in his perplexity. Aside from general human inadequacy, a good deal of the blame for this rests with education, which promulgates the old generalizations and says nothing about the secrets of private experience. Thus, every effort is made to teach idealistic beliefs or conduct which people know in their hearts they can never live up to, and such ideals are preached by officials who know that they themselves have never lived up to these high standards and never will. What is more, nobody ever questions the value of this kind of teaching.

Therefore the individual who wishes to have an answer to the problem of evil, as it is posed today, has need, first and foremost, of *self-knowledge*, that is, the utmost possible knowledge of his own wholeness. He must know relentlessly how much good he can do, and what crimes he is capable of, and must beware of regarding the one as real and the other as illusion. Both are elements within his nature, and both are bound to come to light in him, should he wish—as he ought—to live without self-deception or self-delusion.

In general, however, most people are hopelessly ill equipped for living on this level, although there are also many persons today who have the capacity for profounder insight into themselves. Such self-knowledge is of prime importance, because through it we approach that fundamental stratum or core of human nature where the instincts dwell. Here are those preexistent dynamic factors which ultimately govern the ethical decisions of our consciousness. This core is the unconscious and its contents, concerning which we cannot pass any final judgment. Our ideas about it are bound to be inadequate, for we are unable to comprehend its essence cognitively and set rational limits to it. We achieve knowledge of nature only through science, which enlarges consciousness; hence deepened self-knowledge also requires science, that is, psychology. No one builds a telescope or microscope with one turn of the wrist, out of good will alone, without a knowledge of optics.

Today we need psychology for reasons that involve our very existence. We stand perplexed and stupefied before the phenomenon of Nazism and Bolshevism because we know nothing about man, or at any rate have only a lopsided and distorted picture of him. If we had self-knowledge, that would not be the case. We stand face to face with the terrible question of evil and do not even know what is before us, let alone what to pit against it. And even if we did know, we still could not understand "how it could happen here." With glorious naïveté a statesman comes out with the proud declaration that he has no "imagination for evil." Quite right: *we* have no imagination for evil, but evil *has us in its grip.* Some do not want to know this, and others are identified with evil. That is the psychological situation in the world today: some call themselves Christian and imagine that they can trample so-called evil underfoot by merely willing to; others have succumbed to it and no longer see the good. Evil today has become a visible Great Power. One half of humanity battens and grows strong on a doctrine fabricated by human ratiocination; the other half sickens from the lack of a myth commensurate with the situation.

The Christian nations have come to a sorry pass; their Christianity slumbers and has neglected to develop its myth further in the course of the centuries.

Our myth has become mute, and gives no answers. The fault lies not in it as it is set down in the Scriptures, but solely in us, who have not developed it further, who, rather, have suppressed any such attempts. The original version of the myth offers ample points of departure and possibilities of development. For example, the words are put into Christ's mouth: "Be ye therefore wise as serpents, and harmless as doves." For what purpose do men need the cunning of serpents? And what is the link between this cunning and the innocence of the dove?

The old question posed by the Gnostics, "Whence comes evil?" has been given no answer by the Christian world, and Origen's cautious suggestion of a possible redemption of the devil was termed a heresy. Today we are compelled to meet that question; but we stand empty-handed, bewildered, and perplexed, and cannot even get it into our heads that no myth will come to our aid although we have such urgent need of one. As the result of the political situation and the frightful, not to say diabolic, triumphs of science, we are shaken by secret shudders and dark forebodings; but we know no way out, and very few persons indeed draw the conclusion that this time the issue is the long-since-forgotten *soul of man.*

Just as the Creator is whole, so His creature, His son, ought to be whole. Nothing can take away from the concept of divine wholeness. But unbeknownst to all, a splitting of that wholeness ensued; there emerged a realm of light and a realm of darkness. This outcome, even before Christ appeared, was clearly prefigured, as we may observe *inter alia* in the experience of Job, or in the widely disseminated Book of Enoch, which belongs to immediate pre-Christian times. In Christianity, too, this metaphysical split was plainly perpetuated: Satan, who in the Old Testament still belonged to the intimate entourage of Yahweh, now formed the diametrical and eternal opposite of the divine world. He could not be uprooted. It is therefore not surprising that as early as the beginning of the eleventh century the belief arose that the devil, not God, had created the world. Thus the keynote was struck for the second half of the Christian aeon, after the myth of the fall of the angels had already explained that these fallen angels had taught men a dangerous knowledge of science and the arts. What would these old storytellers have to say about Hiroshima?

· · · · · · ·

36 · THE DANGERS OF INNOCENCE

ROLLO MAY

The awareness that human existence is both joy and woe is prerequisite to accepting responsibility for the effect of one's intentions. My intentions will sometimes be evil—the dragon or the Sphinx in me will often be clamoring and will sometimes be expressed—but I ought to do my best to accept it as part of myself rather than to project it on you.

Growth cannot be a basis for ethics, for growth is evil as well as good. Each day we grow toward infirmity and death. Many a neurotic sees this better than the rest of us: he fears growing into greater maturity because he recognizes, in a neurotic way of course, that each step upward brings him nearer to death. Cancer is a growth. It is a disproportionate growth where some cells run wild growing. The sun is generally good for the body, but when one has tuberculosis, it is disproportionately better for the t.b. bacilli, and therefore the affected parts have to be shielded. Whenever we find we have to balance one element against another, we find that we need other, more profound criteria than the one-dimensional ethic of growth.

The question will arise: What is the relation of the ethic suggested here to our present ethical system in Christianity? Christianity has to be taken realistically, in terms of what it has become rather than what was ideally meant by Jesus. The Christian ethic evolved from the "an eye for an eye and a tooth for a tooth" system of justice present at the beginning of the Old Testament—i.e., the concept of justice attained by the balance of evils. The Christian and Hebrew ethic then shifted its focus to the inner attitudes: "As a man thinketh in his heart, so is he." The ethic of love ultimately became the criterion, even to the extent of the ideal commandment: "Love your enemies."

But in the course of this development it was forgotten that love for one's enemies is a matter of grace. It is, in Reinhold Neibuhr's phrase, "a possible impossibility," never to be realized in a real sense except by an act of grace. It would require grace for me to love Hitler—a grace for which I have no inclination to apply at the present moment. When the element of grace is omitted the commandment of loving one's enemies becomes moralistic: it is advocated as a state an individual can achieve by working on his own character, a result of moral effort. Then we have something very different: an oversimplified, hypocritical form of ethical pretense. This leads to those moral calisthenics that are based on a blocking-off of one's awareness of reality and that prevent the actually valuable actions one could make for social betterment. The innocent person in religion, the one who lacks the "wisdom of serpents," can do considerable harm without knowing it.

Another thing that occurred in cultural evolution is that the ethic of Christianity in our time became allied, especially in the last five centuries, with the individualism which emerged in the Renaissance. This increasingly became the ethics of the isolated individual, standing bravely in his lonely situation of self-enclosed integrity. The emphasis was on being true to one's own convictions. This was true especially in American sectarian Protestantism, strongly aided by the individualism cultivated by our life on the frontier. Hence the great emphasis in America on *sincerity* as one lived by one's own convictions. We idealized men such as Thoreau, who supposedly did that. Hence also the emphasis on one's own character development, which in America seems always to have a moral connotation. Woodrow Wilson called this "the character that makes one intolerable to other men." Ethics and religion became largely a matter of Sunday, the weekdays being relegated to making money—which one always did by ways that kept one's own character impeccable. We had then the curious situation of the man of impeccable character directing a factory that unconscionably exploited its thousands of employees. It is interesting that fundamentalism, that form of Protestantism which puts most emphasis on the individualistic habits of character, tends to be also the most nationalistic and war-minded of the sects, and the most rabid against any form of international understanding with China or Russia.

We need not—indeed, we must not—surrender our concern with integrity and our valuing of the individual. I am proposing that our individualistic gains since the Renaissance be set in balance with our new solidarity, our willingly assumed responsibility for our fellow men and women. In these days of mass communication, we can no longer be oblivious to their needs; and to ignore them is to express our hatred. Understanding, in contrast to ideal love, is a human possibility—understanding for our enemies as well as our friends. There is in understanding the beginnings of compassion, of pity, and of charity.

Granted that human potentialities are not fulfilled by a movement upward but by an increase in scope downward as well. As Daniel Berrigan says: "Every step forward also digs the depths to which one can likewise go." No longer shall we feel that virtues are to be gained merely by leaving behind vices; the distance up the ladder ethically is not to be defined in terms of what we have left behind. Otherwise goodness is no longer good but self-righteous pride in one's own character. Evil also, if it is not balanced by capacities for good, becomes insipid, banal, gutless, and apathetic. Actually we become more *sensitive* to both good and evil each day; and this dialectic is essential for our creativity.

To admit frankly, our capacity for evil hinges on our breaking through our pseudoinnocence. So long as we preserve our one-dimensional thinking, we can cover up our deeds by pleading innocent. This antediluvian escape from conscience is no longer possible. We are responsible for the effect of our actions, and we are also responsible for becoming as aware as we can of these effects.

It is especially hard for the person in psychotherapy to accept his or her increased potentiality for evil which goes along with the capacity for good. Patients have been so used to assuming their own powerlessness. Any direct awareness of power throws their orientation to life off balance, and they don't know what they would do *if* they were to admit their own evil.

It is a considerable boon for a person to realize that he has his negative side like everyone else, that the daimonic works in potentiality for both good and evil, and that he can neither disown it nor live without it. It is similarly beneficial when he also comes to see that much of his achievement is bound up with the very conflicts this daimonic impulse engenders. This is the seat of the experience that life is a mixture of good and evil; that there is no such thing as *pure* good; and that if the evil weren't there as a potentiality, the good would not be either. Life consists of achieving good not apart from evil but *in spite of it*.

. . . .

37 · HEALING HUMAN EVIL

M .   S C O T T   P E C K

The problem of evil is a very big mystery indeed. It does not submit itself easily to reductionism. We shall, however, find that some questions about human evil can be reduced to a size manageable for proper scientific investigation. Nonetheless, the pieces of the puzzle are so interlocking, it is both difficult and distorting to pry them apart. Moreover, the size of the puzzle is so grand, we cannot truly hope to obtain more than glimmerings of the big picture. In common with any early attempt at scientific exploration, we shall end up with more questions than answers.

The problem of evil, for instance, can hardly be separated from the problem of goodness. Were there no goodness in the world, we would not even be considering the problem of evil.

It is a strange thing. Dozens of times I have been asked by patients or acquaintances: "Dr. Peck, why is there evil in the world?" Yet no one has ever asked me in all these years: "Why is there good in the world?" It is as if we automatically assume this is a naturally good world that has somehow been contaminated by evil. In terms of what we know of science, however, it is actually easier to explain evil. That things decay is quite explainable in accord with the natural law of physics. That life should evolve into more and more complex forms is not so easily understandable. That children generally lie and steal and cheat is routinely observable. The fact that sometimes they grow up to become truly honest adults is what seems the more remarkable. Laziness is more the rule than diligence. If we seriously think about it, it probably makes more sense to assume this is a naturally evil world that has somehow been mysteriously "contaminated" by goodness, rather than the other way around. The mystery of goodness is even greater than the mystery of evil.

To name something correctly gives us a certain amount of power over it. Knowing its name, I know something of the dimensions of that force. Because I have that much of safe ground on which to stand, I can afford to be curious as to its nature. I can afford to move toward it.

It is necessary that we first draw the distinction between evil and ordinary sin. It is not their sins per se that characterize evil people, rather it is the subtlety and persistence and consistency of their sins. This is because the central defect of the evil is not the sin but the refusal to acknowledge it.

[Evil people] may be rich or poor, educated or uneducated. There is little that is dramatic about them. They are not designated criminals. More often than not they will be "solid citizens"—Sunday school teachers, policemen, or bankers, and active in the PTA.

How can this be? How can they be evil and not designated as criminals?

The key lies in the world "designated." They are criminals in that they commit "crimes" against life and liveliness. But except in rare instances—such as the case of a Hitler—when they might achieve extraordinary degrees of political power that remove them from ordinary restraints, their "crimes" are so subtle and covert that they cannot clearly be designated as crimes.

I have spent a good deal of time working in prisons with designated criminals. Almost never have I experienced them as evil people. Obviously they are destructive, and usually repetitively so. But there is a kind of randomness to their destructiveness. Moreover, although to the authorities they generally deny responsibility for their evil deeds, there is still a quality of openness to their wickedness. They themselves are quick to point this out, claiming that they have been caught precisely because they are the "honest criminals." The truly evil, they will tell you, always reside outside of jail. Clearly these proclamations are self-justifying. They are also, I believe, generally accurate.

People in jail can almost always be assigned a standard psychiatric diagnosis of one kind or another. The diagnoses range all over the map and correspond, in layman's terms, to such qualities as craziness or impulsiveness or aggressiveness or lack of conscience. The men and women I shall be talking about such as Bobby's parents have no such obvious defects and do not fall clearly into our routine psychiatric pigeonholes. This is not because the evil are healthy. It is simply because we have not yet developed a definition for their disease.

Since I distinguish between evil people and ordinary criminals, I also obviously make the distinction between evil as a personality characteristic and evil deeds. In other words, evil deeds do not an evil person make. Otherwise we should all be evil, because we all do evil things.

Sinning is most broadly defined as "missing the mark." This means that we sin every time we fail to hit the bull's-eye. Sin is nothing more and nothing less than a failure to be continually perfect. Because it is impossible for us to be continually perfect, we are all sinners. We routinely fail to do the very best of which we are capable, and with each failure we commit a crime of sorts—against God, our neighbors, or ourselves, if not frankly against the law.

Of course there are crimes of greater and lesser magnitude. It is a mistake, however, to think of sin or evil as a matter of degree. It may seem less odious to cheat the rich than the poor, but it is still cheating. There are differences before the law between defrauding a business, claiming a false deduction on your income tax, using a crib sheet in an examination, telling your wife that you have to work late when you are unfaithful, or telling your husband (or yourself) that you didn't have time to pick up his clothes at the cleaner, when you spent an hour on the phone with your neighbor. Surely one is more excusable than the other—and perhaps all the more so under certain circumstances—but the fact remains that they are all lies and betrayals. If you are sufficiently scrupulous not to have done any such thing recently, then ask whether there is any way in which you have lied to yourself. Or have kidded yourself. Or have been less than you could be—which is a self-betrayal. Be perfectly honest with yourself, and you will realize that you sin. If you do not realize it, then you are not perfectly honest with yourself, which is itself a sin. It is inescapable: we are all sinners.[1]

If evil people cannot be defined by the illegality of their deeds or the magnitude of their sins, then how are we to define them? The answer is by the consistency of their sins. While usually subtle, their destructiveness is remarkably consistent. This is because those who have "crossed over the line" are characterized by their *absolute* refusal to tolerate the sense of their own sinfulness. More than anything else, it is the sense of our own sinfulness that prevents any of us from undergoing a similar deterioration.

The varieties of people's wickedness are manifold. As a result of their refusal to tolerate the sense of their own sinfulness, the evil ones become uncorrectable grab bags of sin. They are, for instance, in my experience, remarkably greedy people. Thus they are cheap—so cheap that their "gifts" may be murderous. In *The Road Less Traveled,* I suggested the most basic sin is laziness. In the next subsection I suggest it may be pride—because all sins are reparable except the sin of believing one is without sin. But perhaps the question of which sin is the greatest is, on a certain level, a moot issue. All sins betray—and isolate us from—both the divine and our fellow creatures. As one deep religious thinker put it, any sin "can harden into hell."[2]

A predominant characteristic, however, of the behavior of those I call evil is scapegoating. Because in their hearts they consider themselves above reproach, they must lash out at anyone who does reproach them. They sacrifice others to preserve their self-image of perfection. Take a simple example of a six-year-old boy who asks his father, "Daddy, why did you call Grandmommy a bitch?" "I told you to stop bothering me," the father roars. "Now you're going to get it. I'm going to teach you not to use such filthy language, I'm going to wash your mouth out with soap. Maybe that will teach you to clean up what you say and keep your mouth shut when you're told." Dragging the boy upstairs to the soap dish, the father inflicts this punishment on him. In the name of "proper discipline" evil has been committed.

Scapegoating works through a mechanism psychiatrists call projection. Since the evil, deep down, feel themselves to be faultless, it is inevitable that when they are in conflict with the world they will invariably perceive the conflict as the world's fault. Since they must deny their own badness, they must perceive others as bad. They *project* their own evil onto the world. They never think of themselves as evil; on the other hand, they consequently see much evil in others. The father perceived the profanity and uncleanliness as existing in his son and took action to cleanse his son's "filthiness." Yet we know it was the father who was profane and unclean. The father projected his own filth onto his son and then assaulted his son in the name of good parenting.

Evil, then, is most often committed in order to scapegoat, and the people I label as evil are chronic scapegoaters. In *The Road Less Traveled* I defined evil "as the exercise of political power—that is, the imposition of one's will upon others by overt or covert coercion—in order to avoid . . . spiritual growth." In other words, the evil attack others instead of facing their own failures. Spiritual growth requires the acknowledgment of one's need to grow. If we cannot make that acknowledgment, we have no option except to attempt to eradicate the evidence of our imperfection.[3]

Strangely enough, evil people are often destructive because they are attempting to destroy evil. The problem is that they misplace the locus of the evil. Instead of destroying others they should be destroying the sickness within themselves. As life often threatens their self-image of perfection, they are often busily engaged in hating and destroying that life—usually in the name of righteousness. The fault, however, may not be so much that they hate life as that they do *not* hate the sinful part of themselves.

What is the cause of this failure of self-hatred, this failure to be displeasing to oneself, which seems to be the central sin at the root of the scapegoating behavior of those I call evil? The cause is not, I believe, an absent conscience. There are people, both in and out of jail, who seem utterly lacking in conscience or superego. Pyschiatrists call them psychopaths or sociopaths. Guiltless, they not only commit crimes but may often do so with a kind of reckless abandon. There is little pattern or meaning to their criminality; it is not particularly characterized by scapegoating. Conscienceless, psychopaths appear to be bothered or worried by very little—including their own criminality. They seem to be about as happy inside a jail as out. They do attempt to hide their crimes, but their efforts to do so are often feeble and careless and poorly planned. They have sometimes been referred to as "moral imbeciles," and there is almost a quality of innocence to their lack of worry and concern.

This is hardly the case with those I call evil. Utterly dedicated to preserving their self-image of perfection, they are unceasingly engaged in the effort to maintain the appearance of moral purity. They worry about this a great deal. They are acutely sensitive to social norms and what others might think of them. They dress well, go to work on time, pay their taxes, and outwardly seem to live lives that are above reproach.

The words "image," "appearance," and "outwardly" are crucial to understanding the morality of the evil. While they seem to lack any motivation to *be* good, they intensely desire to appear good. Their "goodness" is on a level of pretense. It is, in effect, a lie. This is why they are the "people of the lie."

Actually, the lie is designed not so much to deceive others as to deceive themselves. They cannot or will not tolerate the pain of self-reproach. The decorum with which they lead their lives is maintained as a mirror in which they can see themselves reflected righteously. Yet the self-deceit would be unnecessary if the evil had no sense of right and wrong. We lie only when we are attempting to cover up something we know to be illicit. Some rudimentary form of conscience must precede the act of lying. There is no need to hide unless we first feel that something needs to be hidden.

We come now to a sort of paradox. I have said that evil people feel themselves to be perfect. At the same time, however, I think they have an unacknowledged sense of their own evil nature. Indeed, it is this very sense from which they are frantically trying to flee. The essential component of evil is not the absence of a sense of sin or imperfection but the unwillingness to tolerate that sense. At one and the same time, the evil are aware of their evil and desperately trying to avoid the awareness. Rather than blissfully lacking a sense of morality, like the psychopath, they are continually engaged in sweeping the evidence of their evil under the rug of their own consciousness. The problem is not a defect of conscience but the effort to deny the conscience its due. We become evil by attempting to hide from ourselves. The wickedness of the evil is not committed directly, but indirectly as a part of this cover-up process. Evil originates not in the absence of guilt but in the effort to escape it.

If often happens, then, that the evil may be recognized by its very disguise. The lie can be perceived before the misdeed it is designed to hide—the cover-up before the fact. We see the smile that hides the hatred, the smooth and oily manner that masks the fury, the velvet glove that covers the fist. Because they are such experts at disguise, it is seldom possible to pinpoint the maliciousness of the evil. The diguise is usually impenetrable. But what we can catch are glimpses of "The uncanny game of hide-and-seek in the obscurity of the soul, in which it, the single human soul, evades itself, avoids itself, hides from itself."[4]

In *The Road Less Traveled* I suggested that laziness or the desire to escape "legitimate suffering" lies at the root of all mental illness. Here we are also talking about avoidance and evasion of pain. What distinguishes the evil, however, from the rest of us mentally ill sinners is the specific type of pain they are running away from. They are not pain avoiders or lazy people in general. To the contrary, they are likely to exert themselves more than most in their continuing effort to obtain and maintain an image of high respectability. They may willingly, even eagerly, undergo great hardships in their search for status. It is only one particular kind of pain they cannot tolerate: the pain of their own conscience, the pain of the realization of their own sinfulness and imperfection.

Since they will do almost anything to avoid the particular pain that comes from self-examination, under ordinary circumstances the evil are the last people who would ever come to psychotherapy. The evil hate the light—the light of goodness that shows them up, the light of scrutiny that exposes them, the light of truth that penetrates their deception. Psychotherapy is a light-shedding process par excellence. Except for the most twisted motives, an evil person would be more likely to choose any other conceivable route than the psychiatrist's couch. The submission to the discipline of self-observation required by psychoanalysis does, in fact, seem to them like suicide. The most significant reason we know so little scientifically about human evil is simply that the evil are so extremely reluctant to be studied.

· · · · · · ·

38 · REDEEMING OUR DEVILS
AND DEMONS

STEPHEN A. DIAMOND

A preoccupation with the perplexing problem of evil is not new to psychology—though it is certainly timely. Freud wrestled with this thorny issue, as have many other psychologists and psychiatrists in this century, including Jung, Fromm, May, Menninger, Lifton, and recently, M. Scott Peck.

Freud's solution took the form of an evil "death instinct" (Thanatos) doing eternal battle with a good "life instinct" (Eros), with evil everdominating this tragic duel. Jung, drawing on Nietzsche's philosophy, preferred "the term 'shadow' to that of 'evil' in order to differentiate between individual evil and evil in collective morality."[1] His position, rooted in a Swiss-Protestant tradition of individual conscience, was that social morality cannot be considered the causal source of evil, but only "becomes negative [i.e., evil] whenever the individual takes its commandments and prohibitions as absolutes, and ignores his other impulses. It is not the cultural canon itself, therefore, but the moral attitude of the individual which we must hold responsible for what is pathological, negative and evil."[2]

Prefiguring Peck, Rollo May steadfastly has held that in America we still comprehend little of evil's true nature, and thus are pitifully ill-prepared to deal with it. May echoes Jung's warning to Europe: "Evil has become a determinant reality. It can no longer be dismissed from the world by a circumlocution. We must learn to handle it, since it is here to stay. How we can live with it without terrible consequences cannot for the present be conceived."[3]

Following the lead of his long-time teacher and friend, theologian Paul Tillich, May introduced the *daimonic* as a concept designed to rival the "devil," the traditional Judeo-Christian symbol of cosmic evil. It is May's contention that the term, the devil, "is unsatisfactory because it projects the power outside the self and opens the way for all kinds of psychological projection."[4]

Peck, whose writing has been compared to May's by some, focuses mainly on the spiritual/theological domain; his current belief system is conventionally Christian. Peck draws a distinction between *human* evil and *demonic* evil. He sees human evil as a "specific form of mental illness," a chronic, insidious kind of "malignant narcissism." Peck believes demonic evil, however, to be supernatural in origin, a direct product of "possession by minor demons" or by Satan, for which exorcism is the necessary treatment.[5]

In my estimation, Jung's concept of the shadow and, in particular, May's less familiar model of the daimonic, have paved the way toward a more progressive psychology of evil. Because the daimonic stands in contrast to Peck's premise of the demonic, it is worthwhile to examine May's model in more detail.

DEVILS, DEMONS, AND THE DAIMONIC

Devils and demons have long been seen as the source and personification of evil. Freud suggests that native peoples projected their hostility onto imaginary demons. Moreover, he considered it "quite possible that the whole conception of demons was derived from the extremely important relation to the dead," adding that "nothing testifies so much to the influence of mourning on the origin of belief in demons as the fact that demons were always taken to be the spirits of persons not long dead."[6]

Historically, demons have served as scapegoats and repositories for all sorts of unacceptable, threatening human impulses and emotions, especially surrounding the inescapable fact of death. But the popular, one-sidedly negative view of demons is simplistic and psychologically unsophisticated. For Freud informs us that demons, though feared at first by our forebears, were also instrumental in the mourning process. Once confronted and integrated by the mourners, these same evil demons were "revered as ancestors and appealed to for help in times of distress."[7]

Referring to the medieval idea of the "daemonic," Jung writes that "demons are nothing other than intruders from the unconscious, spontaneous irruptions of the unconscious complexes into the continuity of the conscious process. Complexes are comparable to demons which fitfully harass our thought and actions; hence in antiquity and the Middle Ages acute neurotic disturbances were conceived as possession."[8]

Indeed, prior to the seventeenth-century philosophical revelations of René Descartes, which later gave rise to scientific objectivism, it was commonly believed that an emotional disorder or insanity was literally the work of demons, who in their winged travels would inhabit the unwitting body (or brain) of the unfortunate sufferer. This imagery of invasive flying entities with supernatural powers can still be seen in such euphemisms for insanity as "having bats in the belfry," and in the paranoid patient's certainty of being influenced by aliens in flying saucers.

Descartes' approach, which separated mind and body, subject and object, deemed "real" only that aspect of human experience which is objectively measurable or quantifiable. This advance led, notoriously, to the abject neglect of "irrational," subjective phenomena. His breakthrough was a dubious development in human thought: It enabled late Renaissance people to rid the world of superstition, witchcraft, magic, and the gamut of mythical creatures—both evil and good—in one clean, scientific sweep. But as May laments, "what we did in getting rid of fairies and the elves and their ilk was to impoverish our lives; and impoverishment is not the lasting way to clear men's minds of superstition. . . . Our world became disenchanted; and it leaves us not only out of tune with nature, but with ourselves as well."[9]

Jung's life-long exploration of the powerful, archetypal forces of the unconscious led him to conclude that they "possess a specific energy which causes or compels definite modes of behavior or impulses; that is, they may under certain circumstances have a possessive or obsessive force (numinosity!). The conception of them as daimonia is therefore quite in accord with their nature."[10]

Along similar lines, May reminds us that our modern word *demon* derives from the classical Greek idea of the *daimon,* which provides the basis for his mythological model of the daimonic: "The daimonic is any natural function which has the power to take over the whole person. Sex and eros, anger and rage, and the craving for power are examples. The daimonic can be either creative or destructive and is normally both. When this power goes awry, and one element usurps control over the total personality, we have 'daimon possession,' the traditional name through history for psychosis. The daimonic is obviously not an entity but refers to a fundamental, archetypal function of human experience—an existential reality."[11]

According to Jung's disciple Marie-Louise von Franz, "in pre-Hellenic Greece the demons, as in Egypt, were part of a nameless collectivity."[12] This is the way that May, too, conceives of the daimonic: as an essentially undifferentiated, impersonal, primal force of nature. For the early Greeks, the daimon was both evil and creative, it was the source of destruction as well as spiritual guidance, much like those primitive demons described by Freud. The word *daimon* was sometimes used by Plato as a synonym for *theos* or god; and mighty Eros was also a daimon.

Daimons were potentially both good and evil, constructive and destructive, depending upon how the person would relate to them. But later on in history, reports May, during "the Hellenistic and Christian eras, the dualistic split between the good and evil side of the daimon became more pronounced. We now have a celestial population separated into two camps—devils and angels, the former on the side of their leader, Satan, and the latter allied to God. Though such developments are never fully rationalized, there must have existed in those days the expectation that with this split it would be easier for man to face and conquer the devil."[13]

Contemporary perpetuators of this artificial dichotomy fail to see that we can never hope to conquer our so-called devils and demons by destroying them; we must learn instead to acknowledge and assimilate what they symbolize into our selves and our daily lives. Native peoples managed to achieve this, but it has now become a task for which we modern post-Christians—with our "gods" of science and technology, and even our newly found religions—are poorly equipped.

THE DAIMONIC VS. THE DEVIL

Today, the devil has largely been reduced to a lifeless concept lacking the kind of authority it once enjoyed. Indeed, for many of us, Satan has become a sign—not a true symbol—of a rejected, unscientific, and superstitious religious system.

Nevertheless, we live in an era when the problem of personal and collective evil appears with alarming regularity in our daily newspaper headlines and nightly televison news. Evil, it seems, is everywhere—most visibly in the form of pathological anger and rage, hostility, vicious interpersonal savagery, and so-called senseless violence.

"Violence," writes May, "is the daimonic gone awry. It is 'demon possession' in its starkest from. Our age is one of transition, in which the normal channels for utilizing the daimonic are denied; and such ages tend to be times when the daimonic is expressed in its most destructive form."[14]

These turbulent times force us to come face-to-face with the ugly reality of evil. For lack of a more psychologically accurate, integrating, and meaningful myth, some people seize upon the timeworn symbol of the devil to express their disturbing encounter with the destructive side of the daimonic. The sudden resurgence of such an ancient symbol can be accompanied by a morbid fascination with the devil and demonology, as evidenced by the rapid proliferation of Satanic cults. In my view, the current trend toward Satanism is a tragically misdirected, desperate effort to find some sense of personal significance, belonging, and relationship with the transpersonal realm. Pursuit of these legitimate goals through such perverse—sometimes deadly—behavior bespeaks the dilemma that plagues us. The problem appears to lie in the split between good and evil promulgated by Western religious tradition, a rigid dualism that condemns the daimonic as being evil, and evil only. This is precisely the same misconception we find in Peck's thought.

What we need is a new or re-newed conception of that realm of reality represented by the devil, which can include the creative side of this elemental power. For the devil holds truly what Jung might call a *coincidentia oppositorum*. In fact, the word devil according to May,

> comes from the Greek word *diabolos;* "diabolic" is the term in contemporary English. *Diabolos,* interestingly enough, literally means "to tear apart" (*dia-bollein*). Now it is fascinating to note that this diabolic is the antonym of "symbolic." The latter comes from *sym-bollein,* which means "to throw together," to unite. There lie in these words tremendous implications with respect to an ontology of good and evil. The symbolic is that which draws together, ties, integrates the individual in himself and with his group; the diabolic, in contrast, is that which disintegrates and tears apart. Both of these are present in the daimonic.[15]

THE SHADOW AND THE DAIMONIC

While similar, the concepts of the shadow and the daimonic also contain noteworthy differences. May's resurrection of the daimonic model is in part an effort to counteract and correct any movement in modern depth psychology toward dogmatizing, dehumanizing, mechanizing, or otherwise abusing Jung's original conception of the shadow, with its tremendous psychological significance—especially regarding the nature of human evil.

A potential pitfall with the Jungian doctrine of the shadow is the temptation to project evil, not onto some external entity such as the devil, but rather onto "a relatively autonomous 'splinter personality'"[16] residing deep within us—namely, the compensatory "shadow," "stranger," or "other." Thus, instead of saying "The devil made me do it," one could conveniently claim "The shadow (or the daimonic) made me do it." May seeks to minimize this fragmenting loss of integrity, freedom, and responsibility by retaining in his model of the daimonic "a decisive element, that is, the choice the self asserts to work for or against the integration of the self."[17] The daimonic becomes evil (i.e., demonic) when we begin to deem it so, and subsequently suppress, deny, drug, or otherwise try to exclude it from consciousness. In so doing, we participate in the *process of evil,* potentiating the violent eruptions of anger, rage, social destructiveness, and assorted psychopathologies that result from the daimonic reasserting itself—with a vengeance—in its most negative forms. When we choose instead to constructively integrate the daimonic into our personality, we participate in the metamorphic *process of creativity.*

James Hillman reminds us that Jung's personal encounter with the daimonic convinced him of the "great responsibility" placed upon us by its various manifestations. Like Jung, May sees an implicit ethical and moral obligation to carefully choose our response to the often blind, obliging, psychobiological urgings of the daimonic, and to courageously carry out the constructive choices we then make. It is well known that Jung's salvation during his nearly overwhelming inundation by the unconscious was to religiously engage in "active imagination," and the faithful observing and recording—rather than suppressing or acting-out—of his subjective experience. This conscious, existential decision, consistently reaffirmed over time, eventually led to Jung becoming, as Hillman says, a "daimonic man."[18]

As envisioned by May, the daimonic includes and incorporates Jung's concepts of the shadow and Self, as well as the archetypes of anima and animus. While Jung differentiates the shadow from the Self, and the personal shadow from the collective and archetypal shadow, May makes no such distinctions. This recalls a recent caution by Marie-Louise von Franz:

> We should be skeptical about attempts to relate some of these "souls" or "daimons" to the Jungian concepts of shadow, anima, animus, and Self. It would be a great mistake, as Jung himself often emphasized, to suppose that the shadow, the anima (or animus), and the Self appear separately in a person's unconscious, neatly timed and in definable order. . . . If we look for personifications of the Self among the daimons of antiquity, we see that certain daimons are more like a mixture of shadow and Self, or of animus-anima and Self, and that is, in fact, what they are. In other words, they represent the still undifferentiated "other" unconscious personality of the individual.[19]

Despite these differences, Jung's unifying notion of the shadow serves also to reconcile the sundering imposed upon us by the conflict of opposites. Facing and assimilating our shadows forces the recognition of a totality of being consisting of good and evil, rational and irrational, masculine and feminine, as well as conscious and unconscious polarities. When we consider the psychological concepts of the shadow and the daimonic side-by-side, we are left with the strong impression that both Jung and May are trying to convey the same basic truths about human existence. For Peck, on the other hand, the "demonic" is purely negative, a power so vile it can only be exorcised, expelled, and excluded from consciousness; it has no redeeming qualities and is unworthy of redemption. Clearly, this is not true of the Jungian shadow or of the daimonic.

Psychotherapy is one way of coming to terms with the daimonic. By bravely voicing our inner "demons"—symbolizing those tendencies in us that we most fear, flee from, and hence, are obsessed or haunted by—we transmute them into helpful allies, in the form of newly liberated, life-giving psychic energy, for use in constructive activity. During this process, we come to discover the paradox that many artists perceive: That which we had previously run from and rejected turns out to be the redemptive source of vitality, creativity, and authentic spirituality.

. . . .

39 · THE BASIC DYNAMIC
OF HUMAN EVIL

ERNEST BECKER

Take three disparate thinkers like Otto Rank, Wilhelm Reich, and Carl Jung. There is nothing to identify them with one another except that they dissented from Freud; each had his own work and distinctive style, sometimes at a polar opposite from the other dissenters. What two people are more dissimilar than Reich and Jung? Yet at the bottom of all this unlikeness there is the fact of a fundamental agreement on what exactly causes evil in human affairs. This is not a remarkable coincidence: it is a solid scientific achievement that argues for the basic truth of what the dissenters found.

We have already had a preview of this truth in our overview of history with Rank: that man wants above all to endure and prosper, to achieve immortality in some way. Because he knows he is mortal, the thing he wants most to deny is this mortality. Mortality is connected to the natural, animal side of his existence; and so man reaches beyond and away from that side, so much so that he tries to deny it completely. As soon as man reached new historical forms of power, he turned against the animals with whom he had previously identified—with a vengeance, we now see, because the animals embodied what man feared most, a nameless and faceless death.

I have shown elsewhere that the whole edifice of Rank's superb thought is built on a single foundation stone: man's fear of life and death. There is no point repeating this here except to remind us why these fundamental motives are so well hidden from ourselves. After all, it took the genius of Freud and the whole psychoanalytic movement to uncover and document the twin fears of life and death. The answer is that men do not actually live stretched openly on a rack of cowardice and terror; if they did, they couldn't continue on with such apparent equanimity and thoughtlessness. Men's fears are buried deeply by repression, which gives to everyday life its tranquil façade; only occasionally does the desperation show through, and only for some people. It is repression, then, that great discovery of psychoanalysis, that explains how well men can hide their basic motivations even from themselves. But men also live in a dimension of carefreeness, trust, hope, and joy which gives them a buoyancy beyond that which repression alone could give. This, as we saw with Rank, is achieved by the symbolic engineering of culture, which everywhere serves men as an antidote to terror by giving them a new and durable life beyond that of the body.

At about the same time that Rank wrote, Wilhelm Reich also based his entire work on the same few basic propositions. In a few wonderful pages in *The Mass Psychology of Fascism* Reich lays bare the dynamic of human misery on this planet: it all stems from man trying to be other than he is, trying to deny his animal nature. This, say Reich, is the cause of all psychic illness, sadism, and war. The guiding principles of the formation of all human ideology "harp on the same monotonous tune: 'We are not animals. . . .' "[1]

In his book Reich is out to explain fascism, why men so willingly give over their destiny to the state and the great leader. And he explains it in the most direct way: it is the politician who promises to engineer the world, to raise man above his natural destiny, and so men put their whole trust in him. We saw how easily men passed from egalitarian into kingship society, and for that very reason: because the central power promised to give them unlimited immunities and prosperities.

This new arrangement unleashed on mankind regular and massive miseries that primitive societies encountered only occasionally and usually on a small scale. Men tried to avoid the natural plagues of existence by giving themselves over to structures which embodied immunity power, but they only succeeded in laying waste to themselves with the new plagues unleashed by their obedience to the politicians. Reich coined the apt term "political plague-mongers" to describe all politicians. They are the ones who lied to people about the real and the possible and launched mankind on impossible dreams which took impossible tolls of real life. Once you base your whole life-striving on a desperate lie and try to implement that lie, try to make the world just the opposite of what it is, then you instrument your own undoing. The theory of the German superman—or any other theory of group or racial superiority—"has its origin in man's effort to disassociate himself from the animal." All you have to do is to say that your group is pure and good, eligible for a full life and for some kind of eternal meaning. But others like Jews or Gypsies are the real animals, are spoiling everything for you, contaminating your purity and bringing disease and weakness into your vitality. Then you have a mandate to launch a political plague, a campaign to make the world pure. It is all in Hitler's *Mein Kampf,* in those frightening pages about how the Jews lie in wait in the dark alleys ready to infect young German virgins with syphilis. Nothing more theoretically basic needs to be said about the general theory of scapegoating in society.

Reich asks why hardly anyone knows the names of the real benefactors of mankind, whereas "every child knows the name of the generals of the political plague?" The answer is that:

Natural science is constantly drilling into man's consciousness that fundamentally he is a worm in the universe. The political plague-monger is constantly harping upon the fact that man is not an animal, but a "zoon politikon," i.e., a non-animal, an upholder of values, a "moral being." How much mischief has been perpetuated by the Platonic philosophy of the state! It is quite clear why man knows the politicos better than the natural scientists: He does not want to be reminded of the fact that he is fundamentally a sexual animal. *He does not want to be an animal.*[2]

I give Reich's view of the dynamic of evil without any technical adornment because I don't think that it needs any. But there is plenty of adornment in the psychoanalytic literature, for anyone who wants to follow out the intricate theoretical workings of the psyche. The marvelous thing about psychoanalytic theory is that it took simple statements about the human condition, such as man's denial of his own animality, and showed how this denial was grounded in the psyche from earliest childhood. Thus psychoanalysts talk about "good" objects and "bad" ones, about "paranoid" stages of development, "denials," "split-off" segments of the psyche which includes a "death enclave," etc.

In my view no one has summed up these complex psychic workings better than Jung did in his own poetic scientific way by talking about the "shadow" in each human psyche. To speak of the shadow is another way of referring to the individual's sense of creature inferiority, the thing he wants most to deny. As Erich Neumann so succinctly summed up the Jungian view:

> The shadow is the other side. It is the expression of our own imperfection and earthliness, the negative which is incompatible with the absolute values [i.e., the horror of passing life and the knowledge of death].[3]

As Jung put it, the shadow becomes a dark thing in one's own psyche, "an inferiority which nonetheless really exists even though only dimly suspected."[4] The person wants to get away from this inferiority, naturally; he wants to "jump over his own shadow." The most direct way of doing this is by "looking for everything dark, inferior, and culpable in *others*."[5]

Men are not comfortable with guilt, it chokes them; literally it is the shadow that falls over their existence. Neumann sums it up again very nicely:

> The guilt-feeling is attributable . . . to the apperception of the shadow. . . . This guilt-feeling based on the existence of the shadow is discharged from the system in the same way both by the individual and the collective—that is to say, by the phenomenon of the *projection of the shadow.* The shadow, which is in conflict with the acknowledged values [i.e., the cultural façade over animality] cannot be accepted as a negative part of one's own psyche and is therefore projected—that is, it is transferred to the outside world and experienced as an outside object. It is combated, punished, and exterminated as "the alien out there" instead of being dealt with as one's own inner problem.[6]

And so, as Neumann concludes, we have the dynamics for the classic and age-old expedient for discharging the negative forces of the psyche and the guilt: scapegoating. It is precisely the split-off sense of inferiority and animality which is projected onto the scapegoat and then destroyed symbolically with him. When all explanations are compared on the slaughter of the Jews, Gypsies, Poles, and so many others by the Nazis, and all the many reasons are adduced, there is one reason that goes right into the heart and mind of each person, and that is the projection of the shadow. No wonder Jung could observe—even more damningly than Rank or Reich—that "the principal and indeed the only thing that is wrong with the world is man."[7]

· · · · · · ·

40 · ACKNOWLEDGING OUR INNER SPLIT

ANDREW BARD SCHMOOKLER

The "central defect of evil," says Scott Peck, "is not the sin but the refusal to acknowledge it."[1] What we cannot face will catch us from behind. When we gain the true strength to acknowledge our imperfect moral condition, we are no longer possessed by demons.

Another contrast with Moby Dick. As Ahab's quest of the white whale is an emblem of the way of war, Joseph Conrad's tale of "The Secret Sharer" provides an emblem of the way of peace. This too is a story about a ship's captain, and how he deals with his own dark side.

Esther Harding, another Jungian psychologist, interprets Conrad's tale as a discourse on the shadow. The "secret sharer" in the story is a naked stranger who climbs aboard the ship while the captain is on watch. The stranger is an officer from another ship who has killed one of his men for shirking his duty. While the captain hides the stranger away, an aura of unease and danger lurks over the becalmed ship. At a crucial point, the captain himself comes close to committing a violent act like that of his secret companion. When he recognizes that he, too, could commit murder, Harding says, the tension is relieved. "Then and only then the shadow man slipped back into the ocean from which he had so mysteriously come, and we are given to understand that the strange tension that had hung over the whole ship and her untried captain dissolved, and they sailed home with a fair breeze."[2]

As long as we maintain that all the evil is out there, our ship, like Ahab's, is on the course of destruction. When we acknowledge that the capacity for evil lives within us as well, we can make peace with our shadow, and our ship can sail safely.

Of course, there *is* evil out there. We do have enemies, and they do threaten us. But just as war is cycled between levels of the human system, so can peace begin anywhere in the cycle. Change the chicken or the egg, and the bird can begin to evolve into a new species. Just as inescapable trauma in a fragmented world system has made us crazy, so can any movement in us to-ward sanity help us create a more whole world order. Overcoming the cleav-age in the human spirit is one important step toward the transcendence of the boundaries that divide our endangered planet.

There is a Hasidic story.

> The son of a Rabbi went to worship on the Sabbath in a nearby town. On his return, his family asked, "Well, did they do anything different from what we do here?" "Yes, of course," said the son. "Then what was the lesson?" "Love thy enemy as thyself." "So, it's the same as we say. And how is it you learned some-thing else?" "They taught me to love the enemy within myself."[3]

Loving the enemy within ourselves does not eliminate the enemy out there, but it can change our relationship with him. When evil ceases to be de-monized, we are forced to deal with it in human terms. This is at once a poten-tially painful spiritual task and an opportunity for spiritual peace. This is the way it always is with humility.

The heart of darkness is our own heart. There is a comfort in demoniz-ing the most monstrous and destructive among us, as if their being a different *kind* of creature made their example irrelevant to ourselves. Thus a German has written that all efforts to understand the character of the Nazi, Himmler, must fail "because they entail the understanding of a madman in terms of human experience."[4] A wiser voice is that of a German journalist, who re-minds his countrymen, "We knew that [Hitler was one of us] from the begin-ning. We should not forget it now."[5] He was also one of *us,* a human being. In the dance before the mirror, we find a false inner peace by demonizing the enemy. But recognizing even a truly demonic enemy as made of the same stuff as we is part of the true path toward peace.

Our inner split makes us attached to the war of good against evil. But if we hold that the warring mode is itself the evil, then we are challenged to find a new moral dynamic that embodies the peace for which we strive. To the ex-tent that morality takes the form of war, we will be compelled to choose sides, identifying with one part of ourselves and repudiating another. By this warlike path, we raise ourselves above ourselves, perched precariously above a void.

In our world, the "peacemakers" too often share with the war-makers this fundamental paradigm of morality. In the peace movement, the warriors are demonized into lovers of the bomb, while "we" are the good people who want peace: as if the warriors were not *also* protecting us against very real dangers, and as if we "peace lovers" did not *also* have our own need to assert our superiority over the "enemies" we have chosen. The mode of war con-tinues to hold sway even under the banner of peace.

In *Gandhi's Truth,* Erik Erikson helps illuminate some of the moral pit-falls that lie on the path toward the making of peace. Gandhi is, of course, a hero of the ideological movement in our century to transcend the system of violence—and appropriately so. Gandhi clearly deserves the admiration he receives, and Erikson's book is itself a tribute: Gandhi in his loincloth embodying a simplicity of spirit; Gandhi teaching us not to demonize our adversaries but to appeal to their better selves; Gandhi showing how to stop the escalating cycle of violence by a courageous willingness to absorb the blow without returning it.

But there is a problematic side to Gandhi, one that Erikson addresses in an open letter to the Mahatma. This dark dimension stems from Gandhi's overzealous striving for moral perfection. Erikson sees in Gandhi's relationship with himself a kind of violence. Also, from the dynamic of that effort to triumph over himself in the mode of war, there grew tyrannical and exploitive relations between Gandhi and the people who were closest and most vulnerable to him.[6] In Gandhi's very striving for sainthood, Erikson discerns the toils that bind us to the cycle of violence.

The way of nonviolence (*Satyagraha*), says Erikson to Gandhi in his open letter, "will have little chance to find its universal relevance unless we learn to apply it also to whatever feels 'evil' in ourselves and makes us afraid of instinctual satisfactions without which man would not only wither as a sensual being but would also become a doubly destructive creature."[7] Figuring prominently in Erikson's argument here is Gandhi's war with his own sexuality, a war in which projection played a role and in which, partly in consequence, other people were injured. One is reminded here of George Orwell's reservations about the example of Gandhi: "No doubt alcohol, tobacco and so forth are things that a saint must avoid, but sainthood is also a thing that human beings must avoid."[8] Sainthood involves that overidentification with the "good" part, as irreconcilably opposed to the bad part. It connects with the warring mode: "Much of that excess of violence which distinguishes man from animals," Erikson goes on to say of Gandhi, "is created in him by those child-training methods which set one part of him against another."[9]

Perhaps there is another mode. Goodness can be conceived as health. The linguistic root of "health" connects with "whole." Evil is then sickness—to be cured, made whole, rather than destroyed in the way of the war-maker. Through making ourselves whole we find the way toward the goodness of peace, the fitting together of shalom. And at the core of that is coming to peace with our being the imperfect, sinful creatures that we are. Erich Neumann speaks of the "moral courage not to want to be either worse *or better* than [one] actually is."[10] This, he says, is a major part of the therapeutic aim of depth psychology. And similarly, Erikson writes to Gandhi that to the Mahatma's path of *Satyagraha* should be added the therapeutic encounter with oneself, as taught by the psychoanalytic method. The two are kindred, Erikson says, because the latter teaches how to "confront the inner enemy nonviolently . . ."[11] The mode of war, which divides, is here supplanted by the mode of reconciliation, which makes whole.

Goodness will reign in the world not when it triumphs over evil, but when our love of goodness ceases to express itself in terms of the triumph over evil. Peace, if it comes, will not be made by people who have rendered themselves into saints, but by people who have humbly accepted their condition as sinners. It was in fact a saint—Saint Theresa of Lisieux—who expressed what it takes to allow the spirit of peace to reside in our hearts. "If you are willing to serenely bear the trial of being displeasing to yourself, then you will be for Jesus a pleasant place of shelter."[12]

* * * * * *

Is there a difference between yes and no?
Is there a difference between good and evil?
Must I fear what others fear? What nonsense!
Having and not having arise together
Difficult and easy complement each other
Long and short contrast each other
High and low rest upon each other
Front and back follow one another.

LAO TZU

. . . .

PART 8

ENEMY-MAKING: US AND THEM IN THE BODY POLITIC

We live in a time when there dawns upon us a realization that the people living on the other side of the mountain are not made up exclusively of red-headed devils responsible for all the evil on this side of the mountain.

C. G. JUNG

Our friends show us what we can do,
our enemies teach us what we must do.

GOETHE

An enemy is like a treasure found in my house, won without labor of mine; I must cherish him, for he is a helper in the way to Enlightenment.

SANTI-DEVA

If we could read the secret history of our enemies, we should find in each man's life sorrow and suffering enough to disarm all hostility.

HENRY WADSWORTH LONGFELLOW

INTRODUCTION

. . . .

As repugnant as the idea may seem, we need enemies. Human life seems to thrive and depend upon them. Part 8 explores the creation and function of enemies, personally and collectively, with essays that emphasize the moral, practical, and philosophical challenges of the enemy.

Enemy-making seems to serve a vital purpose: those qualities that we cannot tolerate in ourselves we can unconsciously and painlessly attribute to our enemies. When observed through psychological lenses, enemy-making is a transposition of shadow onto others who, for often complicated reasons, fit our images of the inferior. We need only to think of the people whom we judge or dislike or against whom we hold secret prejudices to find ourselves in the grip of our darker nature.

At the level of nation, race, religion, or other collective identity, we can witness enemy-making being enacted in mythic, dramatic, and often tragic proportions. Wars, crusades, and persecutions are the terrible estate of this form of the human shadow, which is, to some degree, a legacy of our instinctual tribal heritage. The greatest cruelties in human history have been carried out in the name of righteous causes, when the shadows of entire nations have been projected onto the face of an enemy, and thus an alien group can be made into a foe, a scapegoat, or an infidel.

The ultimate function of warring with an enemy is redemption. According to social critic Ernest Becker: "If there is one thing that the tragic wars of our time have taught us it is that the enemy has a ritual role to play by means of which evil is redeemed. All wars are conducted as 'holy' wars in the double sense then—as a revelation of fate, a testing of divine favor, and as a means of purging evil from the world."

Our time has seen an incredible waste of human and material resources, squandered to keep the enemy-making game of the cold war in place. We have already mortgaged the future for our children in armaments and war technologies. Hopefully, we can apply these lessons of futility as we dismantle the weapons of this obsolete machinery.

The world seems to be waiting for a new age of constructive cooperation, a millennial era when we will use the energy of enemy-making for problem solving. The new enemy to engage requires no projection; it may be accessed by simply owning our own collective shadows and taking responsibility, for it is now made manifest in the form of ecological disaster, global warming, the death of countless other species, and the economic deprivation and malnutrition of many people.

However, as we go to press, a new war and a new enemy are upon us. The projection of the shadow, lifted off of the U.S.S.R., has moved to a new target, Iraq and its brazen leader Saddam Hussein. Once again, our nations have locked horns in a dance of death, once again we are in the grip of the archetype of the shadow.

The essays of Part 8 continue the elaboration of evil in the collective mentality, specifically developing the theme of shadow in the social and political fabric of humanity. Writer and philosopher Sam Keen sets the tone for this section with his essay "The Enemy Maker," excerpted from *Faces of the Enemy.* Keen describes the process of creating enemies and explores the mind of what he terms *homo hostilis,* "hostile human," while observing that the real hope for human survival lies in changing the way we think about enemies and warfare.

Fran Peavey, a teacher, activist, and comedian, (with Myrna Levy and Charles Varon) continue the theme with a first-person narrative, "Us and Them," in which she reflects on the nature of hate and fear, the difficulties of working for social change while abandoning the adversarial approach, and the ultimate task: how not to hate your enemy.

Feminist author Susan Griffin gives us a new language with which to think about shadow in her article, "The Chauvinist Mind," excerpted from *Pornography and Silence.* She calls pornography the mythology of chauvinism and shows that the objects of the racist, the misogynist, and the anti-Semite are in actuality lost parts of the soul. No one in our culture, says Griffin, escapes participation in the chauvinist mind.

Poet and essayist Audre Lorde, who is both black and lesbian, exposes the American cultural shadow as a form of institutionalized oppression, beginning with the distortions by which we mislead our children. She writes of a mythical norm in culture, in which the power of society resides, and describes how those who deviate from this homogenized stereotype become outsiders. This article is from *Sister Outsider.*

In Chapter 45, Jungian analyst Jerome Bernstein examines the nature of shadow projections that Americans and Soviets and their governments have placed on each other and how these are changing in the era of Glasnost. "The U.S.-Soviet Mirror," reprinted from Bernstein's *Power and Politics: The Psychology of the Soviet-American Partnership,* shows what good enemies the two superpowers made during the cold war era: They each carried political ideals that were denied in the other's system of government.

Distinguished author and psychologist Robert Jay Lifton gives us a portrait of mass murder and genocide in his analysis of the dark side at work in the Nazi war machine. In "Doubling and the Nazi Doctors," drawn from *The Nazi Doctors: Medical Killing and the Psychology of Genocide,* Lifton uses the concepts of the double and psychological splitting to explain how supposedly ethical professionals were able to commit unimaginable medical atrocities on the "enemies" at Auschwitz and other death camps, and yet remain functional and apparently unaffected.

Making the connection between insanity and the shadow, Swiss Jungian analyst Adolf Guggenbühl-Craig says that one of the major problems in any society is preventing unscrupulous people from gaining power. Chapter 47, "Why Psychopaths Do Not Rule the World," is excerpted from *Eros on Crutches.*

Chapter 48, "Who Are the Criminals?" uses the elaborate metaphor of alchemy to critique the way culture makes its criminals carry its dark, unworthy parts. Rather than look seriously at the rehabilitation of the criminal elements in society, says writer Jerry Fjerkenstad, we make the criminal class
into our sacrificial scapegoats. "We need crooks in order to have someone get
caught other than ourselves," he jests. This article first appeared in the journal
Inroads.

We end this section with the humorous parable "Devils on the Freeway,"
in which Jungian analyst James Yandell turns freeway driving into a moral
struggle with the adversary in the other lane.

With this broad sweep, we can see that we are all at once friends and enemies, allies and foes. The choice is ours.

. . . .

41 · THE ENEMY MAKER

SAM   KEEN

TO CREATE AN ENEMY

Start with an empty canvas
Sketch in broad outline the forms of
men, women, and children.

Dip into the unconscious well of your own
disowned darkness
with a wide brush and
stain the strangers with the sinister hue
of the shadow.

Trace onto the face of the enemy the greed,
hatred, carelessness you dare not claim as
your own.

Obscure the sweet individuality of each face.

Erase all hints of the myraid loves, hopes,
fears that play through the kaleidoscope of
every finite heart.

Twist the smile until it forms the downward
arc of cruelty.

Strip flesh from bone until only the
abstract skeleton of death remains.

Exaggerate each feature until man is
metamorphosized into beast, vermin, insect.

Fill in the background with malignant
figures from ancient nightmares—devils,
demons, myrmidons of evil.

When your icon of the enemy is complete
you will be able to kill without guilt,
slaughter without shame.

The thing you destroy will have become
merely an enemy of God, an impediment
to the sacred dialectic of history.

In the beginning we create the enemy. Before the weapon comes the image. We *think* others to death and then invent the battle-axe or the ballistic missiles with which to actually kill them. Propaganda precedes technology.

Politicians of both the left and right keep getting things backward. They assume the enemy will vanish if only we manage our weapons differently. Conservatives believe the enemy will be frightened into civility if we have bigger and better weapons. Liberals believe the enemy will become our friend if we have smaller and fewer weapons. Both proceed from rationalistic, optimistic assumptions: we human beings are reasonable, pragmatic, tool-making animals. We have progressed thus far in history by becoming *Homo sapiens* ("rational human") and *Homo faber* ("tool-making human"). Therefore, we can make peace by rational negotiation and arms control.

But it isn't working. The problem seems to lie not in our reason or our technology, but in the hardness of our hearts. Generation after generation, we find excuses to hate and dehumanize each other, and we always justify ourselves with the most mature-sounding political rhetoric. And we refuse to admit the obvious. We human beings are *Homo hostilis,* the hostile species, the enemy-making animal. We are driven to fabricate an enemy as a scapegoat to bear the burden of our denied enmity. From the unconscious residue of our hostility, we create a target; from our private demons, we conjure a public enemy. And, perhaps, more than anything else, the wars we engage in are compulsive rituals, shadow dramas in which we continually try to kill those parts of ourselves we deny and despise.

Our best hope for survival is to change the way we think about enemies and warfare. Instead of being hypnotized by the enemy we need to begin looking at the eyes with which we see the enemy. Now it is time to explore the mind of *Homo hostilis* ("hostile human"), we need to examine in detail how we manufacture the image of the enemy, how we create surplus evil, how we turn the world into a killing ground. It seems unlikely that we will have any considerable success in controlling warfare unless we come to understand the logic of political paranoia, and the process of creating propaganda that justifies our hostility. We need to become conscious of what Carl Jung called "the shadow." The heroes and leaders toward peace in our time will be those men and women who have the courage to plunge into the darkness at the bottom of the personal and the corporate psyche and face the enemy within. Depth psychology has presented us with the undeniable wisdom that the enemy is constructed from denied aspects of the self. Therefore, the radical commandment "Love your enemy as yourself" points the way toward both self-knowledge and peace. We do, in fact, love or hate our enemies to the same degree that we love or hate ourselves. In the image of the enemy, we will find the mirror in which we may see our own face most clearly.

But wait a minute. Not so fast! A chorus of objections arises from the practitioners of realistic power politics: "What do you mean, 'create' enemies? We don't make enemies. There are aggressors, evil empires, bad men, and wicked women in the real world. And they will destory us if we don't destroy them first. There are real villains—Hitler, Stalin, Pol Pot (leader of the Cambodian Khmer Rouge, responsible for the murder of two million of his own people). You can't psychologize political events, or solve the problem of war by studying perceptions of the enemy."

Objections sustained. In part. Half-truths of a psychological or political nature are not apt to advance the cause of peace. We should be as wary of psychologizing political events as we should be of politicizing psychological events. War is a complex problem that is not likely to be solved by any single approach or discipline. To deal with it we need, at the very minimum, a *quantum* theory of warfare rather than a single-cause theory. As we understand light only by considering it as both particle and wave, we will get leverage on the problem of war only by seeing it as a system that is sustained by both:

The warrior psyche	and	The violent polis
Paranoia	and	Propaganda
The hostile imagination	and	Value and geopolitical conflicts between nations

Creative thinking about war will always involve considering both the individual psyche and social institutions. Society shapes the psyche and vice versa. Therefore, we have to work at the tasks of creating psychological and political alternatives to war, changing the psyche of *Homo hostilis* and the structure of international relations. Both a heroic journey into the self and a new form of compassionate politics. We have no chance of lessening warfare unless we look at the psychological roots of paranoia, projection, and propaganda, nor if we ignore the harsh child-rearing practices, the injustice, the special interests of the power elites, the historic racial, economical, and religious conflicts and population pressures that sustain the war system.

The problem in military psychology is how to convert the act of murder into patriotism. For the most part, this process of dehumanizing the enemy has not been closely examined. When we project our shadows, we systematically blind ourselves to what we are doing. To mass produce hatred, the body politic must remain unconscious of its own paranoia, projection, and propaganda. "The enemy" is thus considered as real and objective as a rock or a mad dog. Our first task is to break this taboo, make conscious the unconscious of the body politic, and examine the ways in which we create an enemy.

Consensual paranoia—the pathology of the normal person who is a member of a war-justifying society—forms the template from which all the images of the enemy are created. By studying the logic of paranoia, we can see why certain archetypes of the enemy must necessarily recur, no matter what the historical circumstances.

Paranoia involves a complex of mental, emotional, and social mechanisms by which a person or a people claim righteousness and purity, and attribute hostility and evil to the enemy. The process begins with a splitting of the "good" self, with which we consciously identify and which is celebrated by myth and media, from the "bad" self, which remains unconscious so long as it may be projected onto an enemy. By this sleight of hand, the unacceptable parts of the self—its greed, cruelty, sadism, hostility, what Jung called "the shadow"—are made to disappear and are recognized only as qualities of the enemy. Paranoia reduces anxiety and guilt by transferring to the other all the characteristics one does not want to recognize in oneself. It is maintained by selective perception and recall. We only see and acknowledge those negative aspects of the enemy that support the stereotype we have already created. Thus, American television mainly reports bad news about the Russians, and vice versa. We remember only the evidence that confirms our prejudice.

Nowhere is the paranoid mode better illustrated than in anti-Semitic propaganda. For the anti-Semite, the Jew is the fountainhead of evil. In back of the accidental, historical enemies of Germany—England, America, Russia—lurked the conspiratorial Jew. The threat was single and hidden to the casual eye, but obvious to the true believer in Aryan supremacy. Within this twisted logic, it made perfect sense for the Nazis to divert trains badly needed to transport troops to the front lines to take Jews to concentration camps for the "final solution."

Shades of the same paranoid vision color right-wing American anticommunists and obsessional Soviet anticapitalists, both of whom attribute to their adversaries more power, cohesion, and conspiratorial success than either has. True believers in both camps consider the world a battleground in which all countries will eventually have to be included within the sphere of influence of either capitalism or communism.

A major function of the paranoid mind is to escape from guilt and responsibility and affix blame elsewhere. This inversion can go to terrible extremes.

Blame produces blame. Hence the paranoid person or nation will create a shared delusional system, a *paranoia à deux*. The enemy system involves a process of two or more enemies dumping their (unconscious) psychological wastes in each others' back yards. All we despise in ourselves we attribute to them. And vice versa. Since this process of unconscious projection of the shadow is universal, enemies "need" each other to dispose of their accumulated, disowned, psychological toxins. We form a hate bond, an "adversarial symbiosis," an integrated system that guarantees that neither of us will be faced with our own shadow.

In the current U.S.S.R.–U.S. conflict, we require each other as group-transference targets. Clearly, Soviet propaganda picturing the United States as an abuser of civil rights is the pot calling the kettle black. And just as clearly, our tirades against Soviet state control and lack of individual property reflect an unconscious anger at the real loss of individual freedom under corporate capitalism, and our dependence on the government to care for us from womb to tomb, neither of which fits our frontier image of ourselves as rugged individualists. We officially see their dependence on the state as slavery, and yet we have embraced big government and galloping socialism, and obviously have deep dependency needs that do not fit in with our conscious image of ourselves as "Marlboro man." And when the Soviets see our freedom to produce profit and consume as a form of license, it is clear that they long for greater personal freedom. We see the Soviets as making the individual a mere means to the goals of the state. They see us as sanctifying the greed of powerful individuals at the cost of community, and allowing the profit of the few at the expense of the many. And so long as we trade insults, we are both saved from the embarrassing task of looking at the serious faults and cruelties of our own systems.

Inevitably the paranoid, infantile psyche sees the enemy as having some of the paradoxical qualities of the bad parent. The formula necessary to destroy the enemy with moral impunity always attributes near-omnipotent power and a degraded moral character to the enemy. The U.S. Defense Department, in characteristic paranoid style, regularly discovers some gap—bomber gap, tank gap, missile gap, spending gap—that shows the Soviets are more powerful than the United States and it simultaneously paints a portrait of the ruthless advance of atheistic communism. The Kremlin plays the same game.

What is impossible for the paranoid mind is the very notion of equality. A paranoid must be either sadistically superior and dominate others, or masochistically inferior and feel threatened by them. Adults may be equal to one another, may share responsibility for good and evil, but in the infantile world, the giant—the parent, the enemy—has the power and therefore is morally despicable for not eliminating the pain and evil for which he alone is responsible.

Homo hostilis is incurably dualistic, a moralistic Manichean:

We are innocent,	They are guilty.
We tell the truth—inform.	They lie—use propaganda.
We only defend ourselves.	They are aggressors.
We have a defense department.	They have a war department.
Our missiles and weapons are designed to deter.	Their weapons are designed for a first strike.

The most terrible of all the moral paradoxes, the Gordian knot that must be unraveled if history is to continue, is that we create evil out of our highest ideals and most noble aspirations. We so need to be heroic, to be on the side of God, to eliminate evil, to clean up the world, to be victorious over death, that we visit destruction and death on all who stand in the way of our heroic historical destiny. We scapegoat and create absolute enemies, not because we are intrinsically cruel, but because focusing our anger on an outside target, striking at strangers, brings our tribe or nation together and allows us to be a part of a close and loving in-group. We create surplus evil because we need to belong.

How do we create psychonauts, explorers of the heights and depths of the psyche? How do we dramatize the warrior of the inner battle who struggles against paranoia, illusions, self-indulgence, infantile guilt and shame, sloth, cruelty, hostility, fear, blame, meaninglessness? How does a society recognize and celebrate the courage of those who struggle against the demonic temptations of the self, who undertake a holy war against all that is evil, distorted, perverse, injurious within the self?

If we desire peace, each of us must begin to demythologize the enemy; cease politicizing psychological events; re-own our shadows; make an intricate study of the myriad ways in which we disown, deny, and project our selfishness, cruelty, greed, and so on onto others; be conscious of how we have unconsciously created a warrior psyche and have perpetuated warfare in its many modes.

. . . .

42 · US AND THEM

FRAN PEAVEY (WITH MYRNA LEVY
AND CHARLES VARON)

Time was when I knew that the racists were the lunch-counter owners who refused to serve blacks, the warmongers were the generals who planned wars and ordered the killing of innocent people, and the polluters were the industrialists whose factories fouled the air, water and land. I could be a good guy by boycotting, marching, and sitting in to protest the actions of the bad guys.

But no matter how much I protest, an honest look at myself and my relationship with the rest of the world reveals ways that I too am part of the problem. I notice that on initial contact I am more suspicious of Mexicans than of whites. I see that I'm addicted to a standard of living maintained at the expense of poorer people around the world—a situation that can only be perpetuated through military force. And the problem of pollution seems to include my consumption of resources and creation of waste. The line that separates me from the bad guys is blurred.

When I was working to stop the Vietnam War, I'd feel uneasy seeing people in military uniform. I remember thinking, "How could that guy be so dumb as to have gotten into that uniform? How could he be so acquiescent, so credulous as to have fallen for the government's story on Vietnam?" I'd get furious inside when I imagined the horrible things he'd probably done in the war.

Several years after the end of the war, a small group of Vietnam veterans wanted to hold a retreat at our farm in Watsonville. I consented, although I felt ambivalent about hosting them. That weekend, I listened to a dozen men and women who had served in Vietnam. Having returned home only to face ostracism for their involvement in the war, they were struggling to come to terms with their experiences.

They spoke of some of the awful things they'd done and seen, as well as some things they were proud of. They told why they had enlisted in the army or cooperated with the draft: their love of the United States, their eagerness to serve, their wish to be brave and heroic. They felt their noble motives had been betrayed, leaving them with little confidence in their own judgment. Some questioned their own manhood or womanhood and even their basic humanity. They wondered whether they had been a positive force or a negative one overall, and what their buddies' sacrifices meant. Their anguish disarmed me, and I could no longer view them simply as perpetrators of evil.

How had I come to view military people as my enemies? Did vilifying soldiers serve to get me off the hook and allow me to divorce myself from responsibility for what my country was doing in Vietnam? Did my own anger and righteousness keep me from seeing the situation in its full complexity? How had this limited view affected my work against the war?

When my youngest sister and her husband, a young career military man, visited me several years ago, I was again challenged to see the human being within the soldier. I learned that as a farm boy in Utah, he'd been recruited to be a sniper.

One night toward the end of their visit, we got to talking about his work. Though he had also been trained as a medical corpsman, he could still be called on at any time to work as a sniper. He couldn't tell me much about this part of his career—he'd been sworn to secrecy. I'm not sure he would have wanted to tell me even if he could. But he did say that a sniper's work involved going abroad, "bumping off" a leader, and disappearing into a crowd.

When you're given an order, he said, you're not supposed to think about it. You feel alone and helpless. Rather than take on the Army and maybe the whole country himself, he chose not to consider the possibility that certain orders shouldn't be carried out.

I could see that feeling isolated can make it seem impossible to follow one's own moral standards and disobey an order. I leaned toward him and said, "If you're ever ordered to do something that you know you shouldn't do, call me immediately and I'll find a way to help. I know a lot of people would support your stand. You're not alone." He and my sister looked at each other and their eyes filled with tears.

How do we learn whom to hate and fear? During my short lifetime, the national enemies of the United States have changed several times. Our World War II foes, the Japanese and the Germans, have become our allies. The Russians have been in vogue as our enemy for some time, although during a few periods relations improved somewhat. The North Vietnamese, Cubans, and

Chinese have done stints as our enemy. So many countries seem capable of incurring our national wrath—how do we choose among them?

As individuals, do we choose our enemies based on cues from national leaders? From our schoolteachers and religious leaders? From newspapers and TV? Do we hate and fear our parents' enemies as part of our family identity? Or those of our culture, subculture, or peer group?

Whose economic and political interests does our enemy mentality serve?

At a conference on holocaust and genocide I met someone who showed me that it is not necessary to hate our opponents, even under the most extreme circumstances. While sitting in the hotel lobby after a session on the German holocaust, I struck up a conversation with a woman named Helen Waterford. When I learned she was a Jewish survivor of Auschwitz, I told her how angry I was at the Nazis. (I guess I was trying to prove to her that I was one of the good guys.)

"You know," she said, "I don't hate the Nazis." This took me aback. How could anyone who had lived through a concentration camp not hate the Nazis?

Then I learned that Helen does public speaking engagements with a former leader of the Hitler Youth movement: they talk about how terrible facism is as viewed from both sides. Fascinated, I arranged to spend more time with Helen and learn as much as I could from her.

In 1980, Helen read an intriguing newspaper article in which a man named Alfons Heck described his experiences growing up in Nazi Germany. When he was a young boy in Catholic school, the priest would come in every morning and say, "Heil Hitler," and then "Good Morning," and finally, "In the name of the Father and the Son and the Holy Spirit . . ." In Heck's mind, Hitler came before God. At ten, he volunteered for the Hitler Youth, and he loved it. It was in 1944, when he was sixteen, that Heck first learned that the Nazis were systematically killing the Jews. He thought, "This can't be true." But gradually he came to believe that he had served a mass murderer.

Heck's frankness impressed Helen, and she thought, "I want to meet that man." She found him soft-spoken, intelligent and pleasant. Helen had already been speaking publicly about her own experiences of the holocaust, and she asked Heck to share a podium with her at an upcoming engagement with a group of 400 schoolteachers. They spoke in chronological format, taking turns telling their own stories of the Nazi period. Helen told of leaving Frankfurt in 1934 at age twenty-five.

She and her husband, an accountant who had lost his job when the Nazis came to power, escaped to Holland. There they worked with the underground Resistance, and Helen gave birth to a daughter. In 1940 the Nazis invaded Holland. Helen and her husband went into hiding in 1942. Two years later, they were discovered and sent to Auschwitz. Their daughter was hidden by friends in the Resistance. Helen's husband died in the concentration camp.

Heck and Waterford's first joint presentation went well, and they decided to continue working as a team. Once, at an assembly of 800 high school students, Heck was asked, "If you had been ordered to shoot some Jews, maybe Mrs. Waterford, would you have shot them?" The audience gasped. Heck swallowed and said, "Yes. I obeyed orders. I would have." Afterward he apologized to Helen, saying he hadn't wanted to upset her. She told him, "I'm glad you answered the way you did. Otherwise, I would never again believe a word you said."

Heck is often faced with the "once a Nazi, always a Nazi" attitude. "You may give a good speech," people will say, "but I don't believe any of it. Once you have believed something, you don't throw it away." Again and again, he patiently explains that it took years before he could accept the fact that he'd been brought up believing falsehoods. Heck is also harassed by neo-Nazis, who call him in the middle of the night and threaten: "We haven't gotten you yet, but we'll kill you, you traitor."

How did Helen feel about the Nazis in Auschwitz? "I disliked them. I cannot say that I wished I could kick them to death—I never did. I guess that I am just not a vengeful person." She is often denounced by Jews for having no hate, for not wanting revenge. "It is impossible that you don't hate," people tell her.

At the conference on the holocaust and genocide and in subsequent conversations with Helen, I have tried to understand what has enabled her to remain so objective and to avoid blaming individual Germans for the holocaust, for her suffering and for her husband's death. I have found a clue in her passionate study of history.

For many people, the only explanation of the holocaust is that it was the creation of a madman. But Helen believes that such an analysis only serves to shield people from believing that a holocaust could happen to them. An appraisal of Hitler's mental health, she says, is less important than an examination of the historical forces at play and the ways Hitler was able to manipulate them.

"As soon as the war was over," Helen told me, "I began to read about what had happened since 1933, when my world closed. I read and read. How did the 'S.S. State' develop? What was the role of Britain, Hungary, Yugoslavia, the United States, France? How can it be possible that the holocaust really happened? What is the first step, the second step? What are people searching for when they join fanatical movements? I guess I will be asking these questions until my last days."

Those of us working for social change tend to view our adversaries as enemies, to consider them unreliable, suspect, and generally of lower moral character. Saul Alinsky, a brilliant community organizer, explained the rationale for polarization this way:

> One acts decisively only in the conviction that all the angels are on one side and all the devils are on the other. A leader may struggle toward a decision and weigh the merits and demerits of a situation which is 52 percent positive and 48 percent negative, but once the decision is reached he must assume that his cause is 100 percent positive and the opposition 100 percent negative. . . . Many liberals, during our attack on the then-school superintendent [in Chicago], were pointing out that after all he wasn't a 100-percent devil, he was a regular churchgoer, he

was a good family man, and he was generous in his contributions to charity. Can you imagine in the arena of conflict charging that so-and-so is a racist bastard and then diluting the impact of the attack with qualifying remarks? This becomes political idiocy.

But demonizing one's adversaries has great costs. It is a strategy that tacitly accepts and helps perpetuate our dangerous enemy mentality.

Instead of focusing on the 52-percent "devil" in my adversary, I choose to look at the other 48 percent, to start from the premise that within each adversary I have an ally. That ally may be silent, faltering, or hidden from my view. It may be only the person's sense of ambivalence about morally questionable parts of his or her job. Such doubts rarely have a chance to flower because of the overwhelming power of the social context to which the person is accountable. *My* ability to be *their* ally also suffers from such pressures. In 1970, while the Vietnam War was still going on, a group of us spent the summer in Long Beach, California, organizing against a napalm factory there. It was a small factory that mixed the chemicals and put the napalm in canisters. An accidental explosion a few months before had spewed hunks of napalm gel onto nearby homes and lawns. The incident had, in a real sense, brought the war home. It spurred local residents who opposed the war to recognize their community's connection with one of its most despicable elements. At their request, we worked with and strengthened their local group. Together we presented a slide show and tour of the local military-industrial complex for community leaders, and we picketed the napalm factory. We also met with the president of the conglomerate that owned the factory.

We spent three weeks preparing for this meeting, studying the company's holdings and financial picture and investigating whether there were any lawsuits filed against the president or his corporation. And we found out as much as we could about his personal life: his family, his church, his country club, his hobbies. We studied his photograph, thinking of the people who loved him and the people he loved, trying to get a sense of his worldview and the context to which he was accountable.

We also talked a lot about how angry we were at him for the part he played in killing and maiming children in Vietnam. But though our anger fueled our determination, we decided that venting it at him would make him defensive and reduce our effectiveness.

When three of us met with him, he was not a stranger to us. Without blaming him personally or attacking his corporation, we asked him to close the plant, not to bid for the contract when it came up for renewal that year, and to think about the consequences of his company's operations. We told him we knew where his corporation was vulnerable (it owned a chain of motels that could be boycotted), and said we intended to continue working strategically to force his company out of the business of burning people. We also discussed the company's other war-related contracts, because changing just a small part of his corporation's function was not enough; we wanted to raise the issue of economic dependence on munitions and war.

Above all, we wanted him to see us as real people, not so different from himself. If we had seemed like flaming radicals, he would have been likely to dismiss our concerns. We assumed he was already carrying doubts inside himself, and we saw our role as giving voice to those doubts. Our goal was to introduce ourselves and our perspective into his context, so he would remember us and consider our position when making decisions.

When the contract came up for renewal two months later, his company did not bid for it.

Working for social change without relying on the concept of enemies raises some practical difficulties. For example, what do we do with all the anger that we're accustomed to unleashing against an enemy? Is it possible to hate actions and policies without hating the people who are implementing them? Does empathizing with those whose actions we oppose create a dissonance that undermines our determination?

I don't delude myself into believing that everything will work out for the best if we make friends with our adversaries. I recognize that certain military strategists are making decisions that raise the risks for us all. I know that some police officers will rough up demonstrators when arresting them. Treating our adversaries as potential allies need not entail unthinking acceptance of their actions. Our challenge is to call forth the humanity within each adversary, while preparing for the full range of possible responses. Our challenge is to find a path between cynicism and naivete.

· · · · · · ·

43 · THE CHAUVINIST MIND

SUSAN GRIFFIN

We must look into the mind that I will call "the chauvinist mind," which has defined this second use of the word "human" to exclude women, and decipher what the image of woman, or "the black," or "the Jew," means in that mind. But this is why I write of pornography. For pornography is the mythology of this mind; it is, to use a phrase of the poet Judy Grahn, "the poetry of oppression." Through its images we can draw a geography of this mind, and predict, even, where the paths of this mind will lead us.

This is of the greatest importance to us now, for we have imagined, under the spell of this mind, in which we all to some degree participate, that the paths this mind gives us are given us by destiny. And thus we have looked at certain behaviors and events in our civilization, such as rape or the Holocaust, as fateful. We suspect there is something dark and sinister in the human soul which causes violence to ourselves and others. We have blamed a decision made by human culture on our own natures, and thus on nature. But instead, what we find when we look closely at the meanings of pornography is that culture has opposed itself in violence to the natural, and takes revenge on nature.

As we explore the images from the pornographer's mind we will begin to decipher his iconography. We will see that the bodies of women in pornography, mastered, bound, silenced, beaten, and even murdered, are symbols for natural feeling and the power of nature, which the pornographic mind hates and fears. And above all, we will come to see that "the woman" in pornography, like "the Jew" in anti-Semitism and "the black" in racism, is simply a lost part of the soul, that region of being the pornographic or the racist mind would forget and deny. And finally, we shall see that to have knowledge of this forbidden part of the soul is to have eros.

Both the church and pornography have chosen the same victim on which to push this denied knowledge. In these twin cultures, a woman is a blank screen. The nature of her real being is erased, as if her cultural image had been carefully prepared for a clear projection of an image, and she comes to stand for all that man would deny in himself. But she herself, as we shall later see, is no accidental victim. A woman's body evokes the self-knowledge a man tries to forget. And thus he dreads this body. But he does not understand this dread as belonging to himself, and a fear of what the female body calls up in him. Rather, he pretends to himself that she *is* evil. His conscious mind believes she is evil. As Karen Horney says, "Everywhere, the man strives to rid himself of his dread of women by objectifying it." Pornography offers us a clear example of this "objectification" in the words of de Sade, who tells us that woman is "a miserable creature, always inferior, less handsome than he is, less ingenious, less wise, disgustingly shaped, the opposite of what should please a man or delight him . . . a tyrant . . . always nasty, always dangerous. . . ."

The pornographer, like the church father, hates and denies a part of himself. He rejects his knowledge of the physical world and of his own materiality. He rejects knowledge of his own body. This is a part of his mind he would forget. But he cannot reject this knowledge entirely. It comes back to him through his own body: through desire. Just as he pushes away a part of himself, he desires it. What he hates and fears, what he would loathe, he desires. He is in a terrible conflict with himself. And instead he comes to imagine that he struggles with a woman. Onto her body he projects his fear and his desire. So the female body, like the whore of Babylon in church iconography, simultaneously lures the pornographer and incites his rage.

On the leaflet are two familiar figures. A monstrous black man menaces a voluptuous white woman. Her dress is cut low, her skirt torn so that a thigh shows through; the sleeves of her dress fall off her shoulders. She looks over her shoulder in fear and runs. The man's body is huge and apelike. The expression on his face is the personification of bestiality, greed, and lust. Under the words "Conquer and Breed," and above a text which warns the reader against intermarriage, these two figures act out an age-old drama.

At the heart of the racist imagination we discover a pornographic fantasy: the specter of miscegenation. This image of a dark man raping a fair woman embodies all that the racist fears. This fantasy preoccupies his mind. A rational argument exists which argues that the racist simply uses pornographic images to manipulate the mind. But these images seem to belong to the racist. They are predictable in a way that suggests a more intrinsic part in the genesis of this ideology.

We know that the sufferings women experience in a pornographic culture are different in kind and quality from the sufferings of black people in a racist society, or of Jewish people under anti-Semitism. (And we know that the hatred of homosexuality has again another effect on the lives of women and men outside of the traditional sexual roles.) But if we look closely at the portrait which the racist draws of a man or a woman of color, or that the anti-Semite draws of the Jew, or that the pornographer draws of a woman, we begin to see that these fantasized figures resemble one another. For they are the creations of one mind. This is the chauvinist mind, a mind which projects all it fears in itself onto another: a mind which defines itself by what it hates.

The black man as stupid, as passive, as bestial; the woman as highly emotional, unthinking, a being closer to the earth. The Jews as a dark, avaricious race. The whore. The nymphomaniac. Carnal lust in a woman insatiable. The virgin. The docile slave. The effeminate Jew. The usurious Jew. The African, a "greedy eater," lecherous, addicted to uncleanness. The black woman as lust: "These sooty dames, well vers'd in Venus' school/Make love an art, and boast they kiss by rule." As easy. The Jew who practices sexual orgies, who practices cannibalism. The Jewish and the black man with enormous sexual endowment.

The famous materialism of the Jew, the black, the woman. The woman who spends her husband's paychecks on hats. The black who drives a Cadillac while his children starve. The Jewish moneylender who sells his daughter. "There is nothing more intolerable than a wealthy woman," we read in Juvenal. (And in an eighteenth-century pornographic work, the pornographer writes that his heroine had "a natty little bourgeois brain." And in a contemporary pornographic novel, the hero murders a woman because she prefers "guys who drive Cadillacs.") The appetite which swallows. The black man who takes away the white man's job or the woman who takes a man's job.

Over and over again the chauvinist draws a portrait of the other which reminds us of that part of his own mind he would deny and which he has made dark to himself. The other has appetite and instinct. The other has a body. The other has an emotional life which is uncontrolled. And in the wake of this denied self, the chauvinist constructs a false self with which he himself identifies.

Wherever we find the racist idea of another being as evil and inferior, we also discover a racial *ideal*, a portrait of the self as superior, good, and righteous. Such was certainly the case with the white Southern slave owner. The Southern white man imagined himself as the heir to all the best traditions of civilization. He thought of himself as the final repository of culture. In his own mind, he was an aristocrat. Thus Southern life was filled with his pretensions, his decorum, his manners, and his ceremonies of social ascension.

Just as he conferred the black men and women he enslaved with inferior qualities, so also he blessed himself with superiorities. He was "knightly" and "magnanimous," filled with "honesty" which emanated from the "flame of his strong and steady eye." He was honorable, responsible and above all, noble.

And the anti-Semite frames himself in the same polarity. Against his portrait of the Jew, he poses himself as the ideal, the Aryan: fair, courageous, honest, physically and morally stronger.

But this is a polarity deeply familiar to us. We learn it almost at birth from our mothers and fathers. Early in our lives, the ideal of masculinity is opposed to the idea of femininity. We learn that a man is more intelligent, that he is stronger than a woman. And in pornography, the male hero possesses an intrinsic moral rightness which, like Hitler's Aryan, allows him to behave toward women in ways outside morality. For according to this ideology, he is the more valuable member of the species. As the Marquis de Sade tells us, "the flesh of women," like the "flesh of all female animals," is inferior.

It is because the chauvinist has used the idea that he is superior as a justification to enslave and exploit the other, whom he describes as inferior, that certain historians of culture have imagined the ideology of chauvinism exists only to justify exploitation. But this ideology has a raison d'être intrinsic to the mind itself. Exploring this mind, one discovers that the chauvinist values his delusion for its own sake, that above all, the chauvinist mind needs to believe in the delusion it has created. For this delusion has another purpose than social exploitation. Indeed, the delusions of the chauvinist mind are born from the same condition which gives birth to all delusion, and this condition is the mind's desire to escape truth. The chauvinist cannot face the truth that the other he despises is himself.

This is why one so often discovers in chauvinist thinking a kind of hysterical denial that the other could possibly be like the self. The chauvinist insists upon an ultimate and defining difference between himself and the other. This insistence is both the starting point and the essence of all his thinking. Thus, Hitler writes on the beginnings of his own anti-Semitism:

> One day, when passing through the Inner City, I suddenly came across an apparition in a long caftan and wearing black sidelocks. My first thought was: is this a Jew? . . . but the longer I gazed at this strange countenance and examined it section by section, the more the first question took another shape in my brain: is this a German? . . . For the first time in my life I bought myself some anti-Semitic pamphlets for a few coins.

In this way, by inventing a figure different from itself, the chauvinist mind constructs an allegory of self. Within this allegory, the chauvinist himself represents the soul, and the knowledge of culture. Whoever is the object of his hatred represents the denied self, the natural self, the self which contains the knowledge of the body. Therefore this other must have no soul.

· · · · · · · ·

44 · AMERICA'S OUTSIDERS

A U D R E   L O R D E

Much of Western European history conditions us to see human differences in simplistic opposition to each other: dominant/subordinate, good/bad, up/down, superior/inferior. In a society where the good is defined in terms of profit rather than in terms of human need, there must always be some group of people who, through systematized oppression, can be made to feel surplus, to occupy the place of the dehumanized inferior. Within this society, that group is made up of Black and Third World people, working-class people, older people, and women.

As a forty-nine-year-old Black lesbian feminist socialist mother of two, including one boy, and a member of an inter-racial couple, I usually find myself a part of some group defined as other, deviant, inferior, or just plain wrong. Traditionally, in American society, it is the members of oppressed, objectified groups who are expected to stretch out and bridge the gap between the actualities of our lives and the consciousness of our oppressor. For in order to survive, those of us for whom oppression is as American as apple pie have always had to be watchers, to become familiar with the language and manners of the oppressor, even sometimes adopting them for some illusion of protection. Whenever the need for some pretense of communication arises, those who profit from our oppression call upon us to share our knowledge with them. In other words, it is the responsibility of the oppressed to teach the oppressors their mistakes. I am responsible for educating teachers who dismiss my children's culture in school. Black and Third World people are expected to educate white people as to our humanity. Women are expected to educate men. Lesbians and gay men are expected to educate the heterosexual world. The oppressors maintain their position and evade responsibility for their own actions. There is a constant drain of energy which might be better used in redefining ourselves and devising realistic scenarios for altering the present and constructing the future.

Institutionalized rejection of difference is an absolute necessity in a profit economy which needs outsiders as surplus people. As members of such an economy, we have *all* been programmed to respond to the human differences between us with fear and loathing and to handle that difference in one of three ways: ignore it, and if that is not possible, copy it if we think it is dominant, or destroy it if we think it is subordinate. But we have no patterns for relating across our human differences as equals. As a result, those differences have been misnamed and misused in the service of separation and confusion.

Certainly there are very real differences between us of race, age, and sex. But it is not those differences between us that are separating us. It is rather our refusal to recognize those differences, and to examine the distortions which result from our misnaming them and their effects upon human behavior and expectation.

Racism, the belief in the inherent superiority of one race over all others and thereby the right to dominance. Sexism, the belief in the inherent superiority of one sex over the other and thereby the right to dominance. Ageism. Heterosexism. Elitism. Classism.

It is a lifetime pursuit for each one of us to extract these distortions from our living at the same time as we recognize, reclaim, and define those differences upon which they are imposed. For we have all been raised in a society where those distortions were endemic within our living. Too often, we pour the energy needed for recognizing and exploring difference into pretending those differences are insurmountable barriers, or that they do not exist at all. This results in a voluntary isolation, or false and treacherous connections. Either way, we do not develop tools for using human difference as a springboard for creative change within our lives. We speak not of human difference, but of human deviance.

Somewhere, on the edge of consciousness, there is what I call a *mythical norm*, which each one of us within our hearts knows "that is not me." In America, this norm is usually defined as white, thin, male, young, heterosexual, Christian, and financially secure. It is with this mythical norm that the trappings of power reside within this society. Those of us who stand outside that power often identify one way in which we are different, and we assume that to be the primary cause of all oppression, forgetting other distortions around difference, some of which we ourselves may be practising. By and large within the women's movement today, white women focus upon their oppression as women and ignore differences of race, sexual preference, class, and age. There is a pretense to a homogeneity of experience covered by the word *sisterhood* that does not in fact exist.

As we move toward creating a society within which we can each flourish, ageism is another distortion of relationship which interferes without vision. By ignoring the past, we are encouraged to repeat its mistakes. The "generation gap" is an important social tool for any repressive society. If the younger members of a community view the older members as contemptible or suspect or excess, they will never be able to join hands and examine the living memories of the community, nor ask the all important question, "Why?" This gives rise to a historical amnesia that keeps us working to invent the wheel every time we have to go to the store for bread.

We find ourselves having to repeat and relearn the same old lessons over and over that our mothers did because we do not pass on what we have learned, or because we are unable to listen. For instance, how many times has this all been said before? For another, who would have believed that once again our daughters are allowing their bodies to be hampered and purgatoried by girdles and high heels and hobble skirts?

Ignoring the differences of race between women and the implications of those differences presents the most serious threat to the mobilization of women's joint power.

As white women ignore their built-in privilege of whiteness and define *woman* in terms of their own experience alone, then women of Color become "other," the outsider whose experience and tradition is too "alien" to comprehend. An example of this is the signal absence of the experience of women of Color as a resource for women's studies courses. The literature of women of Color is seldom included in women's literature courses and almost never in other literature courses, nor in women's studies as a whole. All too often, the excuse given is that the literatures of women of Color can only be taught by Colored women, or that they are too difficult to understand, or that classes cannot "get into" them because they come out of experiences that are "too different." I have heard this argument presented by white women of otherwise quite clear intelligence, women who seem to have no trouble at all teaching and reviewing work that comes out of the vastly different experiences of Shakespeare, Moliere, Dostoyevsky, and Aristophanes. Surely there must be some other explanation.

This is a very complex question, but I believe one of the reasons white women have such difficulty reading Black women's work is because of their reluctance to see Black women as women and different from themselves. To examine Black women's literature effectively requires that we be seen as whole people in our actual complexities—as individuals, as women, as human—rather than as one of those problematic but familiar stereotypes provided in this society in place of genuine images of Black women. And I believe this holds true for the literatures of other women of Color who are not Black.

The literatures of all women of Color recreate the textures of our lives, and many white women are heavily invested in ignoring the real differences. For as long as any difference between us means one of us must be inferior, then the recognition of any difference must be fraught with guilt. To allow women of Color to step out of stereotypes is too guilt provoking, for it threatens the complacency of those women who view oppression only in terms of sex.

Refusing to recognize difference makes it impossible to see the different problems and pitfalls facing us as women. Thus, in a patriarchal power system where white skin privilege is a major prop, the entrapments used to neutralize Black women and white women are not the same. For example, it is easy for Black women to be used by the power structure against Black men, not because they are men, but because they are Black. Therefore, for Black women, it is necessary at all times to separate the needs of the oppressor from our own legitimate conflicts within our communities. This same problem does not exist for white women. Black women and men have shared racist oppression and still share it, although in different ways. Out of that shared oppression we have developed joint defenses and joint vulnerabilities to each other that are not duplicated in the white community, with the exception of the relationship between Jewish women and Jewish men.

On the other hand, white women face the pitfall of being seduced into joining the oppressor under the pretense of sharing power. This possibility does not exist in the same way for women of Color. The tokenism that is sometimes extended to us is not an invitation to join power; our racial "otherness" is a visible reality that makes that quite clear. For white women there is a wider range of pretended choices and rewards for identifying with patriarchal power and its tools.

Today, with the defeat of ERA, the tightening economy, and increased conservatism, it is easier once again for white women to believe the dangerous fantasy that if you are good enough, pretty enough, sweet enough, quiet enough, teach the children to behave, hate the right people, and marry the right men, then you will be allowed to co-exist with patriarchy in relative peace, at least until a man needs your job or the neighborhood rapist happens along. And true, unless one lives and loves in the trenches it is difficult to remember that the war against dehumanization is ceaseless.

· · · · · · ·

45 · THE U.S.-SOVIET MIRROR

JEROME S. BERNSTEIN

In conjunction with the archetype of the scapegoat and the archetype of power, the shadow probably has been the most active, disruptive, and dangerous psychic energy operative between the United States and the Soviet Union. During the present period of unprecedented relaxation of tension between the Soviet Union and the United States, it is tempting to ignore altogether the shadow dynamics between the two superpowers. (Literally, "Why look for trouble?") However, since shadow dynamics are archetypal in origin, they may wax and wane, but they do not go away. Indeed, from this *psychological* perspective, these are dangerous times, for if we ignore the shadow dynamics between the two countries, they can arise again—much to our surprise—in another form. Just as likely, those shadow dynamics can be projected onto a new target by either side or both.

A brief historical look at the respective shadows of the United States and the Soviet Union is revealing in terms of the psychodynamics that governed Soviet-American relations from 1917 to 1985. Because neither side considered its own power ambitions fully consistent with its stated ideology, each denied them and in doing so projected them onto the other. "*We* do not wish to dominate anyone; we *must* enter into alliances, build missiles, use spies, plan for war, because *they* want to dominate others." Although there have been and remain profound differences in ideology between the two countries and systems, a primary source of the negative power projections onto each other has been the incompatibility of the respective power drives of each with *its own* ideology.

Each side has believed that the political system of the other is the source of all social injustice and evil in the world. As a result, each has been ideologically committed to the elimination of the sociopolitical system of the other. This standpoint has put each in instant conflict with its own self-image of supporting world peace and freedom, since, short of going to war, each side has used tactics of subversion and violence to bring about the demise of the other's system—wherever it exists. (The Soviet military invasion of Czechoslovakia in 1968 to abort that country's popular political liberalization and the United States-engineered overthrow of the democratically elected Allende regime in Chile in 1973 are but two examples.)

The degree to which each side denies and lies about its complicity and the actual reasons for its actions represents prima facie evidence of its feeling that the action taken is inconsistent with its ideological self-image. Perhaps the archetypal example of this phenomenon in contemporary terms was the 1986-1987 Iran-Contra affair, wherein the United States covertly sold arms to Iran in exchange for the release of American hostages and illegally used the funds obtained to support the Contras in Nicaragua—all of this in the face of a vociferous official policy of opposing negotiations with terrorists and terrorist nations as well as the shipment of any arms to Iran. Not only did government officials lie to the American public—even after the basic facts were known—but the president himself apparently lied on several occasions.

It is important to recognize that, psychodynamically, shadow projection has more to do with domestic self-image than it does with the nature of the perceived enemy, although there may be many truths in the content of the projection. When the United States government denies CIA involvement, and otherwise lies about the U.S. role in mining Nicaragua's harbors in 1984 and the sinking of a Russian freighter by one of those mines, for example, the lie is not told for the consumption of the Nicaraguans or the Russians, both of whom, in the age of satellite surveillance and supersensitive electronic eavesdropping, surely know the nature and source of the act. The lie is told to protect *domestic* self-image in the United States. Most dangerously, particularly in a democracy, it is also told to manipulate the Congress and the public into supporting a policy that it would otherwise oppose. The Gulf of Tonkin Resolution of August 7, 1964, is a case in point.

When the Soviets lie about the nature of the facts that led up to its 1979 invasion of Afghanistan, for example, it is doing so for its domestic self-image, not because it believes that the United States and the rest of the world will believe its lie.

In this regard, the Grenada incident of 1983 represents a lost opportunity because of the unanimity of bipartisan and public support for military intervention by the United States and the low risk of adverse consequences, politically or militarily. If the United States could have been more forthright concerning what appeared to be the predominant reasons for that invasion and had not claimed that the *primary* reason for intervention was the ostensible threat by a left-wing government to American medical students on the island, a piece of our shadow could have been owned and thereby removed from the dynamic that perpetuates conflict with the Soviet Union. (In official Washington circles it is openly acknowledged that military intervention would have occurred with or without the presence of the medical students. Notwithstanding, the official governmental position as of December 1984 was that military intervention was dictated primarily by the imminent threat to life of American citizens [that is, the medical students].)

However, if the United States government were willing to take a more open and honest stance with respect to its actual power needs and ambitions, *and if it had been willing to face the arguments that some aspects of that power stance might be inconsistent with its own professed ideology and traditions,* a significant portion of the unconscious power shadow could have been redeemed, with the result that the United States could be measurably less prone to projecting it onto the Soviet Union (and vice versa).

One of the dangerous consequences of shadow projection between the superpowers is that both the Soviet Union and the United States have been seen as being more negative, dangerous, and aggressive than either really is. Shadow projection also distorts each country's view of itself and prevents insight into destructive tendencies that, in some instances, can be as destructive as, if not more so than, those perceived in the adversary. Nuclear annihilation looms in our age, and gross distortions in perception, such as exaggerated perception of threat, are extremely dangerous because they increase the possibility of miscalculation and misunderstanding. Until the advent of the Gorbachev administration in the Soviet Union, we have lived in a time when shadow projection on both sides was at its height.

Moreover the dynamics of mutual shadow projection are self-reinforcing. The more one side projects negative contents onto the other, the more it will tend to become self-righteously inflated by the "positive" content of its own distorted self-image. In addition, each side needs the other as the "bad guy" to receive its negative projection, and thus each has an unconscious investment in the other side's remaining at least as negative as perceived. Therefore, movement away from the status quo creates an unconscious psychic imbalance, which moves one side or the other to take aggressive action that will reestablish the equilibrium.

The shadow of one side always suspects the motives of the other side—it must, for its own needs as well as for the "facts."

Deadly Gambits, by Strobe Talbott, has provided a more detailed view from the American perspective of how the two superpowers unconsciously manipulated themselves and each other into maintaining the status quo with respect to their shadow projections onto each other. In it, Talbott asserts that a significant and dominating element in the Reagan administration believed that ". . . the United States would do best with gambits at the negotiating table that would lead to diplomatic stalemate; that way the United States might more freely acquire and deploy new pieces on its side of the board and position itself, if necessary, to make winning military moves against the Soviet Union."

An almost humorous example of this phenomenon concerns the issue of civil defense programs in both countries. Since American intelligence sources reported early in the Reagan administration that the Soviet Union was building a massive civil defense system that would be capable of evacuating large numbers of its citizens, some highly placed American officials became convinced that the Soviets were planning for a "first strike capability" against the United States and urged commensurate planning within the United States defense establishment. Why else would the Soviets need such an elaborate civil defense system unless they were planning a "first strike" against the United States and were preparing for a retaliatory strike by the United States?

At the same time, since the United States had virtually no civil defense program to speak of and was planning none, some highly placed Soviet officials became convinced that the United States was planning a "first strike" against the Soviet Union and urged appropriate action on the part of the Soviet defense establishment. What other reason could the United States have for not developing a civil defense program to protect its population unless it were planning a "first strike" and therefore would not need one? As of the fall of 1988, this issue still had currency in the Gorbachev and Reagan administrations.

Here, totally opposite and contradictory "logic" was used by each side to justify its own shadow projection onto the other. Indeed, there has been a twenty-year history of "flip-flopping" between the two superpowers in arms reduction negotiations.

From a psychological point of view, it does not matter who is right and who is wrong. In most cases, both are right and both are wrong. Shadow projections produce profound distortions of perceived reality and thus augment war-inducing tensions between the antagonists. Unless these shadow projections are worked through and withdrawn, rational negotiations between the two will be of only marginal and short-term value because the most powerful issues lie unseen in the unconscious and remain undealt with. Shadow projection is an unconscious phenomenon and therefore is almost never affected by negotiations over "objective" issues (for example, arms control), but can negatively impact on such negotiations between the superpowers. Therefore a psychological resolution of shadow issues must take place before long-term transformative political resolution is possible. The superpowers, after years of arduous work, may indeed finally negotiate an arms reduction treaty (for example, the two Strategic Arms Limitation agreements—SALT I and II—and the INF Treaty of 1988). However, without psychological resolution of shadow issues, new weapons systems (for example, the MX missile, SS-20 missiles, "Midgetman," and SDI technology) will come into being, thus vitiating past agreements and requiring that the process be started all over again.

One other important observation is crucial to understanding the nature of shadow projection and how that dynamic might be dealt with: until the advent of the Gorbachev administration, the Soviet Union has made an ideal "hook" (receptor) for the projection of the American national shadow and, vice versa, the United States for the Soviet shadow, for the very reason that both do hold opposite ideologies and values. Americans value individual rights above the collective; Soviets value collective rights above those of the individual; Americans insist on the free exercise of religious convictions; Soviets are officially atheistic, et cetera. A closed collective society is antithetical to American self-image and therefore is repressed into the American shadow. On the other hand, an open society that places its highest value on the rights of the individual is incompatible with the Soviet self-image and is therefore part of the Soviet shadow. The American shadow is, in part, fascistic, repressive, and collective—witness Watergate and the Iran-Contra scandal. The Soviet shadow is, in part, capitalistic and democratic. Poland's Solidarity, and its press for democratization, has been an active aspect of the Soviet shadow.

· · · · · · ·

46 · DOUBLING AND THE NAZI DOCTORS

ROBERT JAY LIFTON

The behavior of Nazi doctors suggests the beginnings of a psychology of genocide. To clarify the principles involved, I will first focus systematically on the psychological pattern of doubling, which was the doctors' overall mechanism for participating in evil. Then it is also necessary to identify certain tendencies in their behavior, promulgated and even demanded by the Auschwitz environment, which greatly facilitated the doubling. This exploration is meant to serve two purposes: First, it can provide new insight into the motivations and actions of Nazi doctors and of Nazis in general. Second, it can raise broader questions about human behavior, about ways in which people, individually and collectively, can embrace various forms of destructiveness and evil, with or without the awareness of doing so. The two purposes, in a very real sense, are one. If there is any truth to the psychological and moral judgments we make about the specific and unique characteristics of Nazi mass murder, we are bound to derive from them *principles* that apply more widely—principles that speak to the extraordinary threat and potential for self-annihilation that now haunt humankind.

The key to understanding how Nazi doctors came to do the work of Auschwitz is the psychological principle I call "doubling": the division of the self into two functioning wholes, so that a part-self acts as an entire self. An Auschwitz doctor could, through doubling, not only kill and contribute to killing but organize silently, on behalf of that evil project, an entire self-structure (or self-process) encompassing virtually all aspects of his behavior.

Doubling, then, was the psychological vehicle for the Nazi doctor's Faustian bargain with the diabolical environment in exchange for his contribution to the killing; he was offered various psychological and material benefits on behalf of privileged adaptation. Beyond Auschwitz was the larger Faustian temptation offered to German doctors in general: that of becoming the theorists and implementers of a cosmic scheme of racial cure by means of victimization and mass murder.

One is always ethically responsible for Faustian bargains—a responsibility in no way abrogated by the fact that much doubling takes place outside of awareness. In exploring doubling, I engage in psychological probing on behalf of illuminating evil. For the individual Nazi doctor in Auschwitz, doubling was likely to mean a choice for evil.

Generally speaking, doubling involves five characteristics. There is, first, a dialectic between two selves in terms of autonomy and connection. The individual Nazi doctor needed his Auschwitz self to function psychologically in an environment so antithetical to his previous ethical standards. At the same time, he needed his prior self in order to continue to see himself as humane physician, husband, father. The Auschwitz self had to be both autonomous and connected to the prior self that gave rise to it. Second, doubling follows a holistic principle. The Auschwitz self "succeeded" because it was inclusive and could connect with the entire Auschwitz environment; it rendered coherent, and gave form to, various themes and mechanisms, which I shall discuss shortly. Third, doubling has a life-death dimension; the Auschwitz self was perceived by the perpetrator as a form of psychological survival in a death-dominated environment; in other words, we have the paradox of a "killing self" being created on behalf of what one perceives as one's own healing or survival. Fourth, a major function of doubling, as in Auschwitz, is likely to be the avoidance of guilt: the second self tends to be the one performing the "dirty work." And, finally, doubling involves both an unconscious dimension—taking place, as stated, largely outside of awareness—and a significant change in moral consciousness. These five characteristics frame and pervade all else that goes on psychologically in doubling.

For instance, the holistic principle differentiates doubling from the traditional psychoanalytic concept of "splitting." This latter term has had several meanings but tends to suggest a sequestering off of a portion of the self so that the "split off" element ceases to respond to the environment (as in what I have been calling "psychic numbing") or else is in some way at odds with the remainder of the self. Splitting in this sense resembles what Pierre Janet, Freud's nineteenth-century contemporary, originally called "dissociation," and Freud himself tended to equate the two terms. But in regard to sustained forms of adaptation, there has been confusion about how to explain the autonomy of that separated "piece" of the self—confusion over (as one, thoughtful commentator has put it) "What splits in splitting?"[1-2]

"Splitting" or "dissociation" can thus denote something about Nazi doctors' suppression of feeling, or psychic numbing, in relation to their participation in murder.[3] But to chart their involvement in a continuous routine of killing, over a year or two or more, one needs an explanatory principle that draws upon the entire, functioning self. (The same principle applies in sustained psychiatric disturbance, and my stress on doubling is consistent with the increasing contemporary focus upon the holistic function of the self.)[4]

Doubling is part of the universal potential for what William James called the "divided self": that is, for opposing tendencies in the self. James quoted the nineteenth-century French writer Alphonse Daudet's despairing cry "*Homo duplex, homo duplex!*" in noting his "horrible duality"—as, in the face of his brother Henri's death, Daudet's "first self wept" while his "second self" sat back and somewhat mockingly staged the scene for an imagined theatrical performance.[5] To James and Daudet, the potential for doubling is part of being human, and the process is likely to take place in extremity, in relation to death.

But that "opposing self" can become dangerously unrestrained, as it did in the Nazi doctors. And when it becomes so, as Otto Rank discovered in his extensive studies of the "double" in literature and folklore, that opposing self can become the usurper from within and replace the original self until it "speaks" for the entire person.[6] Rank's work also suggests that the potential for an opposing self, in effect the potential for evil, is *necessary* to the human psyche: the loss of one's shadow or soul or "double" means death.

In general psychological terms, the adaptive potential for doubling is integral to the human psyche and can, at times, be life saving: for a soldier in combat, for instance; or for a victim of brutality such as an Auschwitz inmate, who must also undergo a form of doubling in order to survive. Clearly, the "opposing self" can be life enhancing. But under certain conditions it can embrace evil with an extreme lack of restraint.

The Nazi doctor's situation resembles that of one of Rank's examples (taken from a 1913 German film, *The Student of Prague*): a student fencing champion accepts an evil magician's offer of great wealth and the chance for marriage with his beloved in return for anything the old magician wishes to take from the room; what he takes is the student's mirror image, a frequent representation of the double. That double eventually becomes a killer by making use of the student's fencing skills in a duel with his beloved's suitor, despite the fact that the student (his original self) has promised the woman's father that he will not engage in such a duel. This variation on the Faust legend parallels the Nazi doctor's "bargain" with Auschwitz and the regime: to do the killing, he offered an opposing self (the evolving Auschwitz self)—a self that, in violating his own prior moral standards, met with no effective resistance and in fact made use of his original skills (in this case, medical-scientific).[7]

Rank stressed the death symbolism of the double as "symptomatic of the disintegration of the modern personality type." That disintegration leads to a need for "self-perpetuation in one's own image"[8]—what I would call a literalized form of immortality—as compared with "the perpetuation of the self in work reflecting one's personality" or a creative symbolic form of immortality. Rank saw the Narcissus legend as depicting both the danger of the literalized mode and the necessity of the shift to the creative mode (as embodied by the "artist-hero")[9]. But the Nazi movement encouraged its would-be artist-hero, the physician, to remain like Narcissus, in thralldom to his own image. Here Mengele comes immediately to mind, his extreme narcissism in the service of his quest for omnipotence, and his exemplification to the point of caricature of the general situation of Nazi doctors in Auschwitz.[10]

The way in which doubling allowed Nazi doctors to avoid guilt was not by the elimination of conscience but by what can be called the *transfer of conscience*. The requirements of conscience were transferred to the Auschwitz self, which placed it within its own criteria for good (duty, loyalty to group, "improving" Auschwitz conditions, etc.), thereby freeing the original self from responsibility for actions there. Rank spoke similarly of guilt "which forces the hero no longer to accept the responsibility for certain actions of his ego, but to place it upon another ego, a double, who is either personified by the devil himself or is created by making a diabolical pact"; that is, the Faustian bargain of Nazi doctors mentioned earlier, Rank spoke of a "powerful consciousness of guilt" as initiating the transfer;[11] but for most Nazi doctors, the doubling maneuver seemed to fend off that sense of guilt prior to its developing, or to its reaching conscious dimensions.

There is an inevitable connection between death and guilt. Rank equates the opposing self with a "form of evil which represents the perishable and mortal part of the personality."[12] The double is evil in that it represents one's own death. The Auschwitz self of the Nazi doctor similarly assumed the death issue for him but at the same time used its evil project as a way of staving off awareness of his own "perishable and mortal part." It does the "dirty work" for the entire self by rendering that work "proper" and in that way protects the entire self from awareness of its own guilt and its own death.

In doubling, one part of the self "disavows" another part. What is repudiated is not reality itself—the individual Nazi doctor was aware of what he was doing via the Auschwitz self—but the meaning of that reality. The Nazi doctor knew that he selected, but did not interpret selections as murder. One level of disavowal, then, was the Auschwitz self's altering of the meaning of murder; and on another, the repudiation by the original self of *anything* done by the Auschwitz self. From the moment of its formation, the Auschwitz self so violated the Nazi doctor's previous self-concept as to require more or less permanent disavowal. Indeed, disavowal was the life blood of the Auschwitz self.[13]

DOUBLING, SPLITTING, AND EVIL

Doubling is an active psychological process, a means of *adaptation to extremity*. That is why I use the very form, as opposed to the more usual noun form, "the double." The adaptation requires a dissolving of "psychic glue"[14] as an alternative to a radical breakdown of the self. In Auschwitz, the pattern was established under the duress of the individual doctor's transition period. At that time the Nazi doctor experienced his own death anxiety as well as such death equivalents as fear of disintegration, separation, and stasis. He needed a functional Auschwitz self to still his anxiety. And that Auschwitz self had to assume hegemony on an everyday basis, reducing expressions of the prior self to odd moments and to contacts with family and friends outside the camp. Nor did most Nazi doctors resist that usurpation as long as they remained in the camp. Rather they welcomed it as the only means of psychological function. If an environment is sufficiently extreme, and one chooses to remain in it, one may be able to do so *only* by means of doubling.

Yet doubling does not include the radical dissociation and sustained separateness characteristic of multiple or "dual personality." In the latter condition, the two selves are more profoundly distinct and autonomous, and tend either not to know about each other or else to see each other as alien. The pattern for dual or multiple personality, moreover, is thought to begin early in childhood, and to solidify and maintain itself more or less indefinitely. Yet in the development of multiple personality, there are likely to be such influences as intense psychic or physical trauma, an atmosphere of extreme ambivalence, and severe conflict and confusion over identifications[15]—all of which can also be instrumental in doubling. Also relevant to both conditions is Janet's principle that "once baptized"—that is, named or confirmed by someone in authority—a particular self is likely to become more clear and definite. Though never as stable as a self in multiple personality, the Auschwitz self nonetheless underwent a similar baptism when the Nazi doctor conducted his first selections.

A recent writer has employed the metaphor of a tree to delineate the depth of "splitting" in schizophrenia and multiple personality—a metaphor that could be expanded to include doubling. In schizophrenia, the rent in the self is "like the crumbling and breaking of a tree that has deteriorated generally, at least in some imporant course of the trunk, down toward or to the roots." In multiple personality, that rent is specific and limited, "as in an essentially sound tree that does not split very far down."[16] Doubling takes place still higher on a tree whose roots, trunk, and larger branches have previously experienced no impairment; of the two branches artifically separated, one grows fetid bark and leaves in a way that enables the other to maintain ordinary growth, and the two intertwine sufficiently to merge again should external conditions favor that merging.

Was the doubling of Nazi doctors an antisocial "character disorder"? Not in the classical sense, in that the process tended to be more a form of adaptation than a lifelong pattern. But doubling can include elements considered characteristic of "sociopathic" character impairment: these include a disorder of feeling (swings between numbing and rage), pathological avoidance of a sense of guilt, and resort to violence to overcome "masked depression" (related to repressed guilt and numbing) and maintain a sense of vitality.[17] Similarly, in both situations, destructive or even murderous behavior may cover over feared disintegration of the self.

The disorder in the type of doubling I have described is more focused and temporary and occurs as part of a larger institutional structure which encourages or even demands it. In that sense, Nazi doctors' behavior resembles that of certain terrorists—and members of the Mafia, of "death squads" organized by dictators, or even of delinquent gangs. In all these situations, profound ideological, family, ethnic, and sometimes age-specific ties help shape criminal behavior. Doubling may well be an important psychological mechanism for individuals living with any criminal subculture: the Mafia or "death squad" chief who coldly orders (or himself carries out) the murder of a rival while remaining a loving husband, father, and churchgoer. The doubling is adaptive to the extreme conditions created by the subculture, but additional influences, some of which can begin early in life, always contribute to the process.[18] That, too, was the case with the Nazi doctors.

In sum, doubling is the psychological means by which one invokes the evil potential of the self. That evil is neither inherent in the self nor foreign to it. To live out the doubling and call forth the evil is a moral choice for which one is responsible, whatever the level of consciousness involved.[19] By means of doubling, Nazi doctors made a Faustian choice for evil: in the process of doubling, in fact, lies an overall key to human evil.

. . . .

47 · WHY PSYCHOPATHS DO NOT RULE THE WORLD

ADOLF GUGGENBÜHL-CRAIG

Let us make the distinction between aggression and the core or essence of the element we call the shadow, a distinction Jungians make, but which in most psychological texts is anything but clear. Aggression is the ability to dispose of one's adversary without being troubled by too many scruples. Aggression is not so much the desire to defeat one's opponent, but rather to advance oneself. A lawyer, for example, tries to win his case, not to harm the other party, but so that he and his client may achieve what they want.

As it is defined in Jungian psychology, the shadow consists of several different levels. We define the shadow as those elements, feelings, emotions, ideas, and beliefs with which we cannot identify, which are repressed due to education, culture, or value system. The shadow can be primarily individual or primarily collective—the former when we are the ones, personally, repressing particular psychic contents, the latter when an entire culture or subculture effects this repression. Certain conceptions of sexuality and instinct, for instance, can be relegated to the shadow. In a particular family, anger may be viewed as something so reprehensible that, as children grow older, they will not show anger openly, and it can only exist in the realm of the shadow. Another example is a split between official tolerance of other nationalities or races and racism that privately thrives as a part of our collective shadow.

The shadow, is as one might note, a complex matter, comprised of many different elements. Because it is a complex, it has as its basis an archetypal core, a potential for behavior with which we have probably been born, which might be designated the murderer or suicidal element, that which is in and of itself destructive. A point which is widely debated is whether or not there is such a thing in human beings. Jungian psychologists assume that human nature includes an archetype which is primarily destructive, Freud's Thanatos instinct, the instinct to destroy and be destroyed. It would be easy to conclude that the shadow with its destructive core and aggressive component is of central importance in the understanding of psychopathy, especially when we regard psychopaths as individuals who commit shocking and aggressive acts.

As I stated before, we can consider aggression as a quantum, something of which some individuals possess more from the time of earliest childhood. We all know aggressive persons who compensate, when Eros is absent, with a highly differentiated moral code. Put somewhat simplistically, aggression serves these individuals to move from desiring good to living and asserting what *is* good. Psychopaths or compensated psychopaths, on the other hand, employ aggression to achieve their own, egoistic goals. A compensated psychopath with a great deal of aggression dominates his classmates, family, or business associates with his harsh and unyielding morality. When, however, there is little aggression present, the story is quite different. Both the individual with some experience of Eros and the compensated psychopath have difficulty asserting themselves and in reaching their goals, regardless of what those goals are.

Even that archetypal core of the shadow, what we have called the ultimately destructive elements of murder and suicide, does not really have that much to do with the actual problem of psychopathy, that core we all have and worry about. It shocks us when we see it at work in ourselves and in others, something we can observe on the highways of any country in a suicidal manner of driving, especially evident in youthful motorcycle riders, their reckless disregard for the life and limb of themselves and others, flirting with death, tempting the grim reaper. Although the murderous elements are usually deeper than the suicidal ones, we observe them occasionally when a motorist brushes past a pedestrian in a cross-walk or passes a stopped school bus. Usually it takes a war to bring out our "murderer," and then it is dumbfounding how so-called normal men, neither psychopaths nor compensated psychopaths, succeed in simultaneously killing their fellow man and revolting and disgusting themselves. Even the vicarious pleasure we all derive from a murder mystery or from the brutality of some films seems to remind us of our own murderous characteristics.

While the murderous and suicidal aspects may seem uncanny or even inhuman to us, they are crucial for our lives because they are linked to the psyche's creative potential. In his book *Moses*, Leopold Szondi demonstrates how the truly creative individuals also posses pronouncedly destructive sides. Szondi introduces his argument with the case of Moses, whose "case history" begins with the murder of an Egyptian overseer and ends with his becoming the father of his nation, leader and law-giver in one. One is tempted to conclude that a strong archetypal shadow, what we called the murderous and suicidal elements, results in a high degree of creativity when combined with an equally powerful sense of Eros. This same conflict, the conflict between love—for one's fellow-man, for one's environment, for one's psyche—and a murderous passion for destruction drives the individual to the borders of his existential framework. The murderer would fain destroy, Eros would renew, and out of the admixture of the two, destruction and renewal, comes something creative, comes *the* Creative.

Though a pronounced archetypal shadow is not characteristic of or determining for psychopaths, a shadow without Eros, which can wreak considerable havoc, is. Just as certain psychopaths willingly surrender themselves to sexuality in any form, so those who are unequivocally psychopathic sometimes have little hesitation about living out the core of the shadow, the murder/suicide. The results are often shocking and monstrous, acts which, in truth, occur much less frequently than we are led to believe but which are then pointed out as being typical for psychopaths. In the first place, there are very few "pure" psychopaths, and these seldom have particularly strong shadows or archetypal shadows. Furthermore, the desire to adapt and prevail in the world, even if it is an alien one, usually holds the psychopath in check when it comes to living out his shadow.

Because psychopaths provide particularly fertile ground for the cultivation of our own shadow projections, when we do not pity them, we hate them, seeing in them our own destructive potential. Actually, we make into demons those psychopaths who have called attention to themselves through criminal or pseudo-criminal activity. We demonize those who have committed murder and are astounded to discover how harmless they seem when we actually see them. To us, infamous swindlers and cheats appear to be the devil incarnate. We enjoy reading about people who achieve notoriety from their by-hook-or-crook approach to life, who do not even stop short of murder. We see them as instruments of evil and destruction, and all the while they are merely invalids, human beings lacking something essentially human.

Contrary to popular belief, there are certain advantages to being a psychopath or compensated psychopath. Many of them have a relatively easy time adapting to society, unencumbered as they are by moral or neurotic scruples. They replace the lack of love or of true relationship with a love of power, something they can achieve without too much difficulty owing to the absence of moral or Eros-related restraints. Even a compensated psychopath can find room for a justification of unrestrained power-seeking within his rigid morality. It is little wonder that psychopaths occupy so many of the top positions in society and rather astonishing that there are not more in such positions. Let me put it somewhat differently. One of the major problems of any society, of any political or large organization in general is that of preventing unscrupulous, socially adapted psychopaths from gradually taking over the helm. There are many countries in which the problem is a long way from being solved. There are certain countries whose political organization encourages psychopaths to rise to positions of power, even where *only* psychopaths can achieve such positions. It is not difficult to imagine in what spirit such nations are ruled. Nazi Germany is a good example. All dictatorial forms of government, be they left-wing or right-wing regimes, are certainly to some extent dominated by psychopaths. Stalin was probably a psychopath with a pronounced shadow and a decided power drive. Trotsky, originally his friend, was more of an idealist, but observe: Stalin died of natural causes at a ripe old age; Trotsky was murdered. There seems to be some truth to the expression, "the good die young."

One is inclined to ask how, in a democratic country, we may prevent psychopaths from inveigling their way to the top. The power of the highest administrative positions is so strictly curtailed in Switzerland, for example, that it hardly tempts psychopaths. It seems to me more important that the people be able to see through a psychopath, to see through their own psychopathic side. In most democracies, this ability is well enough developed so that a dangerous psychopath is usually detected when he appears on the scene.

I am convinced that a democracy whose citizens are incapable of discerning a psychopath will be destroyed by power-hungry demagogues. In Switzerland the resistance towards "great men" and the preference for mediocre political figures would seem to result from an instinctual desire to prevent psychopaths from coming to power. Although there is certainly such a thing as a "great man," many such figures are probably nothing more than unrecognized psychopaths. Think of personages such as Alexander the Great, Genghis Khan, Napoleon, William II of Germany and many, many other more or less esteemed leaders of the past and present. These "great" criminals—and one must include Hitler and Stalin among them—destroyed the lives of millions. Themselves "erotically" stunted, they succeeded in obtaining recognition and power over societies in which they, themselves, felt shut out, power which was necessary to maintain the illusion that they actually belonged. Happy the nation which gives such "great" men (and women) short shrift.

. . . .

48 · WHO ARE THE CRIMINALS?

JERRY FJERKENSTAD

Slime, sleaze, rejects. Crooked, bent, needing to straighten out. Rascals, hooligans, thieves, scoundrels. Corrupt, rotten, stinking. Shitheads, assholes. People with no respect for the law, the straight and narrow, the right way, the one way. People who don't fear God or man. Animals, perverts, dogs, mongrels, coyotes. Mixed up, confused, crazy, insane, psychopathic. Wayward souls, lost souls, ingrates. Butchers, skull-bashers, cold-blooded murderers. Cold as ice—they'd rob their own mothers.

We think that criminals are everything we're not and don't want to be, everything we reject and seek to eliminate from society. "How wonderful life would be if we could permanently get rid of all of them. These worthless people, beyond hope, in need of execution: lock 'em up and throw away the key. They're all on the wrong road." But the wrong road is the Via Negativa, the negative way, the wrong-seeming road—all alchemical terms for the soul's journey.

ALCHEMY IN A NUTSHELL

Alchemy is quite simple. You begin with the massa confusa—the base substance, the crude ingredients, the lead. They are placed in a Vas Hermeticus, a sealed container. Heat is applied to that container and a series of operations are conducted upon the substance to change its nature and transform it into "gold." The operations can include condensation, distillation, "repetitio," "mortificatio" and "the marriage of the king and queen." It is a very metaphorical process that is not considered esoteric by Jung and Hillman—rather, it is a process that reveals the true nature of the original substance. The massa confusa is equated with the rejected cornerstone of biblical tradition. The god, or golden child, created in the end is equated with the birth of the soul.

The whole process is said to be guided by Hermes Mercurius, who is present throughout. Alchemy is a Hermetic Art and Hermes is its God. Hermes is also the God of thieves and criminals and other underworldly denizens.

Criminals are the massa confusa, a mass of confusion. They are, in the mind of this culture, the rejected cornerstone, worthless: Nothing solid or safe can be built on them. Rilke describes these kind of people as "those in need," the people who are flawed, the ones whom people wouldn't notice at all if they "didn't sing," didn't act out. Rilke says "this is where you hear good singing" as opposed to good-boy "castratos in boy choirs" who bore even God. This is where it all begins. Grace can only descend on what is imperfect and willing to claim its own destitution, ugliness and inferiority.

We distance ourselves from all this, choosing the common criminal to embody all these ugly and unwanted traits while we remain "straight," good, law-abiding. Is this because we are by nature good people? Or is this because we are afraid of being "caught"?

The criminal flounders into the unknown, outside the world of law and order, over the border, into the world of Hermes and the unconscious. The crook is crude, violent, indifferent, but he crosses the border. It is a border we all need to cross, somehow. Sebastian Moore, an alchemical theologian, puts it this way:

"This is the ultimate mystery of us: that even our evil, even our tendency against wholeness, exposes us to the love of God. And it exposes us to that love in a way and at a depth to which even our desire for wholeness does not expose us."

Our criminals are those who cannot or will not make gold in the ways we have decided are okay. They are the ones who sell us things we pretend we don't want—like cocaine and sex and "discounted" stereos, bikes and cars.

They are the ones who are made desperate by their failure to make their way in accordance with the "gold standard." They make their living exploiting the hidden realms of human nature we deny through splitting and hypocrisy. Cleaning out all the criminals won't eliminate these vices—the vices express something essential about human nature, something that needs to be worked alchemically, caught, participated with, not just imprisoned, abandoned and scapegoated.

THE HOLY IN THE UNHOLY

Jung believed that God, the living God, could be found only where we least want to look, the place we have the most resistance to exploring. This living God is entwined with our own darkness and shadow, woven in our wounds and complexes, laced with pathologies. On the other hand, the God of Belief, the God removed from creation and from everyday life, frees us from our imperfections, ultimately cleanses us of all worldly contamination and gets us off the hook as far as dealing with the most difficult aspects of the human dilemma.

Alchemy is a process for extracting the living God from the most venal aspects of life. But that process cannot begin until the venality is acknowledged. It's not that we need to create venality. It already exists—explicitly and complicitly. It's more a matter of acknowledging it, admitting its existence in ourselves: in little actions, in fantasies, in secret deals, in hidden moments.

We're really talking about the difference between spirit and soul here. The path of the spirit is straight and upward. The path of the soul is crooked, downward and disturbing. The soul's road is the road of initiation into manhood as well. Our purpose is not to be "good" but to be real, to know our darkness, the via negativa, not to be naive and innocent. Initiation means knowing what we're capable of, our limits, our hungers, our desires. That is often painful knowledge to acquire. But we are only capable of responsibility and wise choice when we are aware of those factors.

Consider the Prince and the Wurm story (Wurm = dragon). An old couple wants a child and consults a midwife. She tells them to go home and throw their dirty dishwater under the bed before sleeping. In the morning there is a flower with a black and white blossom. The couple are supposed to pick only the white blossom, but they pick both.

The months go by and soon the midwife is brought in for the woman's delivery. The first thing to pop out is a slimy lizard which the midwife, with the mother's semi-conscious blessing, tosses out the window to fend for itself, forgotten and abandoned. Moments later a healthy, beautiful boy is born who grows up perfect, successful and loved by all. So admired is he that he is to marry the King's daughter.

The Wurm's life is spent sneaking about, spying on the life of his brother and family, stealing to eat and keep himself warm, and longing for what he doesn't have. The Wurm is bitter, angry and vengeful.

On the day of the wedding the Prince leaves for the castle. His coach is stopped suddenly by the huge Wurm blocking the road. The Wurm declares itself to be the Prince's long-lost brother and demands the Prince find him a bride as well or the Prince will never see his. Then begins the difficult process of finding a woman who can spend the night with the Wurm in a special room and still be there the next morning, which is finally acheived after many long years.

The turning point of the story is when the Wurm declares himself, comes out of hiding, demands a bride who is capable of "loving" him as he is. The Wurm has to quit living as a criminal and outcast. But he is not offering to change his Wurm nature. Rather, he is himself the prima materia, placing himself in the special room, a Vas Hermeticus, to see if any alchemy takes place, any soul is made. Only by revealing himself, by demanding what he needed, could he ever be loved and have a place of honor in the world. This is what both the criminal and we as scapegoaters refuse to do—to reveal ourselves, come out, acknowledge the "strange feeling" come over us, the "insane desire." As long as we "haven't experienced this," we are undeclared, hidden: "only a troubled guest on the dark earth," as Goethe says.

We are afraid of getting caught, of getting burned (by the oil), of our Wurm-self coming out of hiding, of asking for what the ugliest part of ourselves needs. So most of us pretend to be wholly good. But being good just isn't good enough.

Most of us believe in transformation, death and rebirth, being emulsified by Hermes/Mercurius, but we still don't want to undergo the death. We want to change without being changed—sort of remodeled for that "new look" but without the muss and fuss and ego-dystonic decompensation that a complete change brings.

Developmental psychology, especially as described by Robert Kegan, lays out stages we need to progress through in order to mature as human beings. Most of us get stuck in the early stages because we've never been trained on how to make the sacrifices necessary for the series of deaths and rebirths that are the alchemical process as represented by developmental psychology. As a result, the lesson represented by each stage or operation remains unlearned.

INCARCERATION: ENTERING THE VAS HERMETICUS

Incarceration, imprisonment, the death penalty, longer sentences—all these terms are really quite alchemical. The vas hermeticus is the container the prima materia, the massa confusa, is placed in. It must be kept sealed until the process is complete. This sounds a lot like penology: we seal up the criminal in the prison until (we hope) he undergoes a transformation. Punishment and therapy could be said to represent various alchemical operations such as distillation and putrefaction.

Fine, let's send criminals through an alchemical process and change their nature, keep them contained until it's over. But let's not reserve this painful and difficult process for criminals only. We all need it. In fact, many of us non-criminals need it worse than they do. But since we'll never get *caught,* our process will never begin. If only something would catch us! God knows we won't *turn ourselves in,* turn inwards towards the hermetic process being neglected. In order to get caught, you need someone to rat on you. If you don't get caught, there is no placement in the vas hermeticus, the sacred enclosure, and the alchemical process cannot begin.

As in The Prince and The Wurm and Eros and Psyche, nothing happens until the Wurm, the monster in the darkened bed, is "caught," comes out in the open, is seen, is known. Then the real work begins. Until then, everything is unconscious, unknown, blind.

But in relation to criminality, we normals are voyeurs, fascinated but removed. Few of us can confess as Mick Jagger does in the song, "Sympathy for the Devil," that we unwittingly participate in dark forces. We are unwilling to enter the zone where true humanness begins. We prefer a God we can worship and adore to a co-creator who expects us to do our part of the work. We're unwilling to celebrate "the sacrament of murder" and recognize that our heart of darkness, our tendency toward evil and away from wholeness, is as essential to attaining grace and soul and "gold" as are our beliefs in and efforts toward wholeness, goodness and perfection.

Crime is considered unnatural, inhuman, an act against nature and culture. How is crime then a metaphor for something necessary and essential? Breaking in, stealing away, raping the innocent, violating the sacred, beating and maiming, harassing and intimidating: all these resemble what dreams try to do to our habitual egos of everyday consciousness. Dreams try to introduce us to our own massa confusa, to "relativize" the ego. Dreams are the main way our souls attempt to speak to us (aside from disease). Our culture's refusal to engage in this alchemical opus of dreamwork increases the likelihood of crime. Our increased defenses, our personal defense budgets, our concerns about safety and security systems, only increase the likelihood of crime. All these measures widen the gap, increase the split, and insure the inevitability of invasion. If we let them in and let them affect us, and don't just interpret them into meanings that fit our pre-existing notions, dreams provide a way for us to access our dark, criminal side and make it into "gold."

The convicted criminal has a different route. Part of his "cure" (another alchemical operation—curing leather, getting your hide tanned, a metaphor for punishment as well) is learning the role of the victim, feeling into that place, becoming aware of the whole story, not just playing *only* his role, the role of the criminal. This is what seems unnatural to the criminal, his opus contra naturam. This is what closes the gap and split for him.

TURNING UP THE HEAT

The flame and its heat play an essential role in a multitude of alchemical operations, such as distillation or calcinatio (drying). The police are also called "the heat." A criminal who hasn't been caught yet is always concerned about avoiding the heat. A criminal who has been detected wants to escape or outwit the heat.

Being "in heat" is also an impassioned and driven state in which one has got to have it, and have it now, and if you don't get it, you'll go fuckin' crazy. Someone in heat is unreasonable, unpredictable, singleminded. Being in heat is also about arousal, getting hard, being unbendable until one's desire is satisfied. If the criminal is "in heat," what is his motivation, what drives him or her? What is a criminal willing to sacrifice anything for? What is this pearl of great price he seems to know about that none of us will sacrifice hardly anything for? Is it power, control, wealth, beautiful things, busty women, drugs? Gregory Bateson suggests that the criminal seeks something essential in his crime. What is it? What is he "imagining" he will attain? What does he want to mate with, lay with, fuck with? Whatever it is, just hope you don't find yourself between him and his object of desire!

PUTREFACTION AND REPETITION AND OTHER OPERATIONS

Repetitio: if we see the earth itself as vas hermeticus then the things we use one time and throw away contain no sense of repetitio. All the garbage and refuse becomes the rejected massa confusa we need to learn to honor and transform rather than continue to pile up. We can also question our need to always have the "new look," never repeating.

Distillation: the paring down of what we are to an essence, boiling off all the unnecessary. Most of us tend to accumulate objects, ideals, and projects, never getting them done, much less sorting them out, never deciding what is essential and then acting on it.

Putrefactio: learning what is rotten about us, discovering that our own shit stinks. For a convicted criminal this means reaching the point where he or she honestly realizes how his or her actions harm others. Most criminals are oblivious about that, as are many corporate people, politicians, and religious leaders. Our myopic defenses need to decay so that empathy for the world beyond our own ego and its imperative needs can be experienced. For non-criminals, putrefactio, noticing our own smell, can mean getting out of the everlasting improvement and perfection trip.

Containment: the alchemical process is ruined and must be started over if anything leaks from the vas hermeticus. Although based on these ancient chemical principles, modern science, industry and technology have immense amounts of leakage—toxic waste, emissions of radon gas from nuclear plants, ground water pollution. The leakage signifies a lack of integrity and a soulless process incapable of any useful transformation.

THE IMPORTANCE OF SALT

Salt was a necessary material to the alchemists. Salt is strongly associated with memory because it preserves things, keeps them in edible and useable condition. Memory is a quality the criminal is usually quite short on. Treatment of criminals seems to work best when they are required to retrace their steps, their planning, their decision to offend—putting salt into the container that is their psyche or soul. Salt is also important in catching these jailbirds—after all, we've all been taught about putting salt on a bird's tail to catch it.

But seeing how the criminal has been put on the hook for us doesn't mean the criminal gets off the hook. That is performing a different operation, finding a new angle from which to see the whole process. This would hold true on a dream perspective as well—if we see the criminal as another part of our own story, needing to get into our private space, needing to carry off things we can live without, needing to create pain and loss in us. All this as a way to get us to care about the larger vessel, beyond our personal, private opus—the Vas Hermeticus that is the Earth. The criminal does two things at once: acts out his personal drama and its petty needs and simultaneously enacts the drama of the soul in our lives, serving as an agent provocateur.

CRIMINALS AS SPIRITUAL SLAVES LABORING IN THE MINES OF OUR IGNORANCE

The desire to eliminate crime is really a desire to eliminate soul, imperfection, and the need for grace. It is an effort to create a world taken over by consultants, behaviorists, management consultants, and public relations people. Then we'd have a well-managed fascism that is gentler and kinder with no dead bodies (as Noam Chomsky points out over and over in his writings about subtle American fascism that is non-violent in a literal sense).

We need crooks in order to have someone to get caught other than ourselves. We prefer someone out there in the mine fields, someone desperate, to be our scapegoats, guinea pigs, volunteers, and sacrifices. It is little wonder our culture embraces the Christian religion so fundamentally, it espousing a theology which sanctifies having someone else (Christ) doing the most crucial task for us, dying for our sins. This creates yet another avoided crucifixion, aborting the alchemical work before its completion, preventing the deepest transformation.

If we can begin to view the world of crime imaginally as well as literally, we could begin to realize we need "criminals" to assault, rape and murder our habitual egos, our typical patterns of thought and emotion that destroy our souls and allow us to make decisions and take actions that destroy the fabric of community and the objects and creatures of the world. This crime must be committed. In addition, the criminal must be caught so we can face our attacker and have it out. We need to hear the criminal's reasons for attacking us. If we lock him away and throw away the key, execute or banish him, then nothing will be gained.

We would have only sacrificed more of humanity. Along with the humans we killed we would be killing our chance to become more human ourselves, giving up our chance to comprise more of the full spectrum of humanness, both the dark and the light. Worst of all, we would have sacrificed the earth around us and the common human soul. We consider the Aztecs primitive for sacrificing a human being now and again to please their gods. We sooth our consciences by closing our eyes to the people we throw from the cliffs, the criminals we destroy, the third worlds we sacrifice to our prosperity, the future generations we sacrifice in order to have all the consumer goods we lust after now.

. . . .

49 · DEVILS ON THE FREEWAY

JAMES YANDELL

Two mornings a week I have a rush-hour commute in the course of which, approaching a tunnel, four lanes converge to two. The change is announced by a sequence of signs—"2 LEFT LANES CLOSED ½ MILE," "LEFT LANES CLOSED ¼ MILE," and "2 LEFT LANES CLOSED. MERGE RIGHT." The final merger is enforced by barriers eliminating the left two lanes, and by the reality of the impending two-lane tunnel.

When I began making this trip, I would use one of the two right lanes since these survived into the tunnel. The extreme right lane was made unattractive by the entrance of outside traffic into it, and usually I would find myself in the second lane. If I were in either of the two left lanes, as soon as I saw the first warning sign I would move right to be in a surviving lane, again the second from the right.

At that time, even if I had thought about it, I would not have seen anything remarkable in my prompt compliance with the warning signs. I did not experience a choice; I simply took if for granted that one obeys the signs. With later reflection, I see my compliance in psychological context. I was a younger sibling, the son of a schoolteacher, a good child who caused no trouble, oriented toward doing right and achieving. I grew up to be a responsible, law-abiding citizen. Breaking the rules, at any level, would not be my way.

The trouble was, on the freeway, that as I sat in the second lane, waiting patiently or impatiently to get into the tunnel, I would notice that a few less conscientious citizens stayed in the left lanes as long as possible, until they were physically forced to merge right, at which point they would crowd into *my* lane, *ahead of me*. Even worse, sometimes I would see in my rear-view mirror that some psychopathic scofflaw, approaching the bottleneck, would putt out of my lane into the clearing left lanes, speed past me, and gain some advantage before he had to pull back in.

I was surprised at what this situation brought out in me. Initially I was merely annoyed at the spectacle of other people, unhampered by proper super-egos, profiting from doing wrong while I did right. But I grew increasingly resentful about it. My younger-sibling sensitivity to unfairness was activated. They were getting away with something forbidden to me.

I was angry not only at the interlopers, but also at the Highway Patrol motorcyclists, who I felt should be in there preventing this sort of thing rather than on the shoulder ticketing speeders they had targeted back on the freeway. I found myself surprisingly competitive. Often the aggressors were driving Porsches or BMWs, or they were cowboys in little pickup trucks, which when unloaded are very nimble. While my sedan is roomy and gets over thirty miles to the gallon, a rocket ship it isn't. Inferior and envious, I entertained fantasies of big engines and turbos. Unable to compete directly, I expressed my anger passively by trying to keep the bad guys from horning in ahead. I became proficient at the art of bumper-to-bumper driving that left no room for the intruder to enter. I knew this was at the expense of my clutch, but the satisfaction of frustrating the ambitious was worth it.

I had not yet questioned my assumptions about the morality of the situation. Those people in the left lanes passing me and barging in ahead clearly were bad guys. I was in the morally correct position, and if the world were just, other people would behave as I did. The trouble was, it wasn't and they didn't. Or rather, most people did—I was in the law-abiding majority—but that fact didn't take care of my feelings about the rest. My indignation was righteous, and if my counter-aggression got a bit nasty, they deserved worse than that for their transgressions.

I could have spared myself the whole problem by starting ten minutes earlier, before the bottleneck had formed, but usually I had left home at the last possible moment and was guiltily worried that I might be late to my first appointment. I wanted to get through the tunnel, and saw no reason why others should get through it ahead of me by cheating. Perhaps I thought of cheating too, but I felt a certain gratifying moral superiority, a self-satisfied pride in my persistence in virtue against temptation. In the immediate situation, though, virtue was expensive; I was losing. I was a virtuous victim.

I think what finally happened came out of a simultaneous combination of unusual tardiness, accumulated anger and envy, moral collapse, and curiosity about life in the fast lane. One morning I deliberately got into the far left lane and stayed there as long as I could. Then I merged right into the next and stayed there as long as I could. Finally, I entered my usual lane and passed into the tunnel.

I can't say that it felt just great, or anything equally simple. I had gone over to the enemy, but the enemy was still the enemy. I was uncomfortably aware that I was violating my own principles for immediate gain, that I had sold out. My sympathies really were with the well-behaved people into whose lane I was now squeezing, some of whom were viewing me with the same righteous hostility in which I myself had only recently been indulging. So I was conflicted about my outlaw status. On the other hand, the guilt wasn't really that bad. And I did get through the tunnel faster.

Since then, interesting things have happened. I have deliberately experimented with all four lanes, trying them out psychologically and seeing how they feel, how the world looks from each of them. When I am not being consciously experimental I approach the bottleneck from the far left lane, because it works better, it's faster. When I do this I am a member of a relatively small minority. Most drivers don't even wait for the signs to tell them to move right, but have already put themselves in the tunnel lanes some distance back. Knowing the route, perhaps they don't get into the left lanes at all, so that they won't have to get out of them approaching the tunnel. That's what I used to do. From my new vantage-point this seems like remarkable self-restraint. How is it that there are so many unnecessarily good citizens when it is clearly advantageous not to be good?

Actually, it is the virtuous behavior of this moral majority that clears the left lanes for the rest of us to be sociopathic in; if all four lanes were equally used there would be no point in maneuvering. Those who merge right early create the opportunity and temptation for the rest of us to go as far as possible before complying. We are two sides of a coin, those angels and us devils, complementary and interdependent. We need them to be good to provide our opportunity; they need us to be bad to disapprove of, feel superior to, and punish by exclusion.

When I play the devil and look over to the right at the people I am passing by, I do become aware of a sense of loss, of something sacrificed in breaking out into the freedom of naked self-interest. No doubt that's why it took me so long to lose my virtue. With some nostalgia I remember the comfortable feeling of community, rectitude, and self-esteem that I enjoyed when I was still a sheep and not yet a coyote, and how scornful I felt then toward the depraved anarchists rolling by on my left. But when I try to recover my moral purity back in the sheep lanes I am reminded of the bumper sticker, NOSTALGIA AIN'T WHAT IT USED TO BE. The satisfactions of virtue don't quite make up for the price of being passed up.

But the most interesting development is that for me the situation finally has got de-moralized, unloaded of virtue and vice. My perception is that this is just a place where four lanes narrow to two, and there is nothing right or wrong, good or bad, about the resulting merger. My former experience of it as an ethical issue was my interpretation and contribution, my projection onto it. I defined myself as the virtuous victim and those others as bad guys— aggressive, selfish, lacking in community feeling, successful, and enviable. When people now glare at me as I invite myself into *their* lane, I can appreciate their anger from the memory of my own experience, and so I don't feel angry back when they try to shut me out. I feel rather calm and matter-of-fact about it all. But *they* seem a bit strange, turning a simple take-turns merger into a morality play. And amusing. I try not to smile as they prove their virtue, manhood, and patriotism by making me drop back behind them, because some of them might be packing guns.

Apparently I can no longer project that war movie onto this particular screen. I'll have to find a new arena in which to distinguish the good guys from the bad; I feel like none of the above. I need a new bumper sticker: MERGE EASY.

. . . .

I was angry with my friend;
I told my wrath, my wrath did end.
I was angry with my foe;
I told it not, my wrath did grow.
And I watered it in fears,
Night and morning with my tears.
And I sunned it with smiles,
And with soft deceitful wiles.
And it grew both day and night,
Till it bore an apple bright.
And my foe beheld it shine,
And he knew that it was mine.
And into my garden stole,
When the night had veil'd the pole;
In the morning glad I see;
My foe outstretched beneath the tree.

WILLIAM BLAKE

PART 9

. . . .

SHADOW-WORK: BRINGING LIGHT TO THE DARKNESS THROUGH THERAPY, STORY, AND DREAMS

The great epochs of our lives are at the points when we gain courage to rebaptize our badness as the best in us.

FRIEDRICH NIETZSCHE

Midway upon the journey of our life
I found myself within a forest dark,
For the straightforward pathway had been lost . . .
So bitter is it, death is little more.

DANTE

One thing that comes out in myths is that at the bottom of the abyss comes the voice of salvation. The black moment is the moment when the real message of transformation is going to come. At the darkest moment comes the light.

JOSEPH CAMPBELL

Evil in the human psyche comes from a failure to bring together, to reconcile, the pieces of our experience. When we embrace all that we are, even the evil, the evil in us is transformed. When the diverse living energies of the human system are harmonized, the present bloody face of the world will be transformed into an image of the face of God.

ANDREW BARD SCHMOOKLER

INTRODUCTION

. . . .

Owning the shadow involves confronting it and assimilating its contents into an enlarged self-concept. Such healing encounters typically occur in midlife, but meetings with the shadow can happen whenever we feel life stagnate and lose its color and meaning. Especially when we recognize and feel the constricting effects of denial, or when we doubt the values we live by and watch our illusions about ourselves and the world shatter, or when we are overcome by envy, jealousy, sexual drives, or ambition, or feel the hollowness of our convictions—then shadow-work can begin.

Shakespeare understood the necessity to meet the shadow, and he frequently describes in his plays the tragic consequences of ignoring the call to this work. To the villainous character Macbeth he gave poignant words, describing the emptiness and misery wreaked by unredeemed darkness:

Life's but a walking shadow. . . .
it is a tale
told by an idiot, full of sound and fury,
signifying nothing.

A truly tragic figure, Macbeth's life has lost all meaning. It is too late to do anything about his dark side, for he has acted out his shadow homicidally; his fate is sealed irrevocably. In less poetic language, tragedy could be defined as becoming aware of the shadow when it is too late to do anything about our predicament.

But for most of us, the realization of the shadow is what Jung called "an eminently practical problem." What we have termed in this collection *shadow-work* is the conscious and intentional process of admitting to that which we have chosen to ignore or repress. Therapy requires us to take up what we have rejected previously in the service of our ego–ideal, and to establish a new personal order that accounts for our destructive side.

Establishing that new order, however, may require a process of facing and releasing the illusions we have lived by. Sociologist Philip Slater describes it this way in his book *Earthwalk:*

A patient in psychotherapy does not literally return to childhood to unlearn the self-destructive pattern he evolved in growing up, although he may engage in much regressive experimentation in order to undo that negative learning. What is essential is that he be able to relinquish his attachment to his pathway—be able to say to himself, "I have wasted X years of my life in a painful and useless pursuit; this is sad, but I now have an opportunity to try another approach." This is hard for people to do. There is a strong temptation either to rationalize our wrong turnings as a necessary part of our development ("it taught me discipline"), or to deny that we participated fully in them ("that was before I became enlightened"). Giving up these two evasions leads initially to despair, but as Alexander Lowen points out, despair is the only cure for illusion. Without despair we cannot transfer our allegiance to reality—it is a kind of mourning period for our fantasies. Some people do not survive this despair, but no major change within a person can occur without it.

Individuation—the process of a person becoming whole and unique—aims at embracing the light and dark simultaneously to create a constructive relationship between the ego and the self (our personal symbol of individual wholeness). In the therapeutic encounter, through honest dialogue and dream interpretation, we have the means to face our elaborate charade of appearances and to accept who we are.

This task of owning our inferior personality often requires and is accelerated by the presence of a witness in the form of a therapist or guide. This process is a gradual awakening to the shadow, as described in the following passage from Marie-Louise von Franz's *Shadow and Evil in Fairy Tales:*

> If someone who knows nothing about psychology comes to an analytical hour and you try to explain that there are certain processes at the back of the mind of which people are not aware, that is the shadow to them. So in the first stage of approach to the unconscious the shadow is simply a "mythological" name for all that within me of which I cannot directly know. Only when we start to dig into the shadow sphere of the personality and to investigate the different aspects, does there, after a time, appear in the dreams a personification of the unconscious, of the same sex as the dreamer.

As the awareness of shadow grows, the dream figures become more apparent and important to integrate. Ultimately, relating the personal shadow to the collective shadow of one's culture is a natural outgrowth. The Israeli psychoanalyst Erich Neumann described the next stage of shadow-work as the individuation process proceeds:

> The differentiation of "my" evil from the general evil is an essential item of self-knowledge from which no one who undertakes the journey of individuation is allowed to escape. But as the process of individuation unfolds, the ego's former drive toward perfection simultaneously disintegrates. The inflationary exaltation of the ego has to be sacrificed, and it becomes necessary for the ego to enter into some kind of gentleman's agreement with the shadow—a development which is diametrically opposed to the old ethic's ideal of absolutism and perfection.

For the person ready to meet his or her enemies—inside and outside—the path is always available. Shadow-work is predicated on a confessional (and sometimes cathartic) act. For Jung this is the quintessential activity. "Modern man," he maintained, "must rediscover a deeper source of his own spiritual life. To do this, he is obliged to struggle with evil, to confront his shadow, to integrate the devil. There is no other choice."

The contributors in Part 9 show enthusiasm for the enterprise of shadow-work. As a composite handbook for confronting the shadow, these essays bring to bear the skills of the analyst, the insights of literature and myth, the wisdom of dreams, and the experience of midlife change.

In Chapter 50, "Curing the Shadow," Jungian analyst and archetypal pyschologist James Hillman reminds us that love is the important ingredient; however, love may not be enough, Hillman suggests. This piece is excerpted from the author's 1967 book, *Insearch: Psychology and Religion.*

Sheldon B. Kopp's "Tale of a Descent into Hell" takes us on a guided tour through Dante's vision of Hell on a tour bus driven by a therapist. Our turnaround point is the very center of Hell, in the presence of King Satan. "Once having come to the very center of Evil, having faced every sin and seen its consequences, only now can Dante hope to purify his soul." In therapy, the devil is in our neurotic suffering. The road to joy passes through the gates of Hell. This essay is from *If You Meet the Buddha on the Road, Kill Him.*

When we cross a threshold into the unknown, which involves a symbolic self-annihilation and renewal, we enter "the belly of the whale," the theme of Chapter 52 by Joseph Campbell. He calls this shadow-passage a "life-centering, life-renewing act," and he traces the motif through culture and across time. This essay is from the late mythologist's classic *The Hero with a Thousand Faces.*

Chapter 53, Gary Toub's "The Usefulness of the Useless," originally appeared in the journal *Psychological Perspectives.* Using Taoist parable and Jungian psychology to illustrate his thesis, Toub suggests that embracing those qualities we have not valued forces us to confront the lost shadow qualities within. He gently exhorts us to live our own unique lives, to understand the nature of opposites in life and the tension and balance they require, and perhaps subtlest of all, to find meaning where we would least expect it.

Jungian-trained psychologist Karen Signell approaches shadow-work via the royal road of dreams. Her essay "Working with Women's Dreams," from *Wisdom of the Heart,* demonstrates the application of dream interpretation skills to indentifying and integrating the shadow personality. Though the focus is on women's lives, Signell does not limit herself to gender barriers. Her insight into dreams is intended to "help you soften your heart toward yourself and others."

Midlife crisis is the notorious dark night of the soul, when the shadow comes to finds *you.* Midlife counselors Janice Brewi and Anne Brennan have written a thorough study of shadow-work at ths time, excerpted here from *Celebrate Mid-Life.* Relying on Jung's guiding ideas, the authors distinguish the shadow issues of the first half of life from the themes that begin to emerge as one enters the second half of life.

Noted author and psychologist Daniel J. Levinson, in his essay "For the Man at Midlife," covers the sea changes for a man as he traverses these white waters. An awareness of mortality and our potential for destructiveness is part of the transition, and if a man turns away from the responsibility to face these challenges to his ego, he may sacrifice his future generativity. Chapter 56 is excerpted from Levinson's best-seller, *The Seasons of a Man's Life.*

Finally, in "How to Deal with Evil," Jungian analyst Liliane Frey-Rohn tells us that the challenge of transforming evil is a moral problem demanding the highest effort of consciousness. To do the work of personal shadow integration, she says, is essential for the stability of culture as well. This excerpt was first published in the Jungian journal *Spring* in 1965.

Today, these essays point the way through this dark passage, offering a helping hand and a guiding light.

. . . .

50 · THE CURE OF THE SHADOW

JAMES HILLMAN

The cure of the shadow is on the one hand a moral problem, that is, recognition of what we have repressed, how we perform our repressions, how we rationalize and deceive ourselves, what sort of goals we have and what we have hurt, even maimed, in the name of these goals. On the other hand, the cure of the shadow is a problem of love. How far can our love extend to the broken and ruined parts of ourselves, the disgusting and perverse? How much charity and compassion have we for our own weakness and sickness? How far can we build an inner society on the principle of love, allowing a place for everyone? And I use the term "cure of the shadow" to emphasize the importance of love. If we approach ourselves to cure ourselves, putting "*me*" in the center, it too often degenerates into the aim of curing the ego—getting stronger, better, growing in accord with the ego's goals, which are often mechanical copies of society's goals. But if we approach ourselves to cure those fixed intractable congenital weaknesses of stubbornness and blindness, of meanness and cruelty, of sham and pomp, we come up against the need for a new way of being altogether, in which the ego must serve and listen to and cooperate with a host of shadowy unpleasant figures and discover an ability to love even the least of these traits.

Loving oneself is no easy matter just because it means loving all of oneself, including the shadow where one is inferior and socially so unacceptable. The care one gives this humiliating part is also the cure. More: as the cure depends on care, so does caring sometimes mean nothing more than carrying. The first essential in redemption of the shadow is the ability to carry it along with you, as did the old Puritans, or the Jews in endless exile, daily aware of their sins, watching for the Devil, on guard lest they slip, a long existential trek with a pack of rocks on the back, with no one on whom to unload it and no sure goal at the end. Yet this carrying and caring cannot be programmatic, in order to develop, in order that the inferiority comply with the ego's goals, for this is hardly love.

Loving the shadow may begin with carrying it, but even that is not enough. At one moment something else must break through, that laughing insight at the paradox of one's own folly which is also everyman's. Then may come the joyful acceptance of the rejected and inferior, a going with it and even a partial living of it. This love may even lead to an identification with and acting-out of the shadow, falling into its fascination. Therefore the moral dimension can never be abandoned. Thus is cure a paradox requiring two incommensurables: the moral recognition that these parts of me are burdensome and intolerable and must change, and the loving laughing acceptance which takes them just as they are, joyfully, forever. One both tries hard and lets go, both judges harshly and joins gladly. Western moralism and Eastern abandon: each holds only one side of the truth.

I believe this paradoxical attitude of consciousness toward the shadow finds an archetypal example in Jewish religious mysticism, where God has two sides: one of moral righteousness and justice and the other of mercy, forgiveness, love. The Chassidim held the paradox, and the tales of them show their deep moral piety coupled with astounding delight in life.

The description Freud gave of the dark world which he found did not do justice to the psyche. The description was too rational. He did not grasp enough the paradoxical symbolic language in which the psyche speaks. He did not see fully that each image and each experience has a prospective aspect as well as a reductive aspect, a positive as well as a negative side. He did not see clearly enough the paradox that rotten garbage is also fertilizer, that childishness is also childlikeness, that polymorphous perversity is also joy and physical liberty, that the ugliest man is at the same time the redeemer in disguise.

In other words, Freud's description and Jung's description of the shadow are not two distinct and conflicting positions. Rather, Jung's position is to be superimposed upon Freud's, amplifying it, adding a dimension to it; and this dimension takes the same facts, the same discoveries, but shows them to be paradoxical symbols.

. . . .

51 · TALE OF A DESCENT INTO HELL

SHELDON B. KOPP

At Easter time, in the Year of Our Lord 1300, the Florentine poet Dante Alighieri descended into the Inferno of Hell.[1]

Some say that his tale is mainly a medium for exposing the social and political evils of his time. Others insist that Dante represents Mankind, that human life itself is the journey, and that "Hell is the death which must precede rebirth."[2] It is also possible to view his trip as taking place in inner space, as a descent into the pit of his own soul, showing that the sinful soul itself is Hell.

I agree with Eliot, that "the aim of the poet is to state a vision . . . [and that] Dante, more than any other poet, has succeeded in dealing with his philosophy, not as a theory . . . or as his comment or reflection, but in terms of something *perceived*."[3] Open yourself to listening to his tale, if you dare, and surely you will see what he saw.

Midway through his life, Dante, on the eve of Good Friday, 1300, discovers that he has strayed from the True Way of the religious life, and has wandered into the Dark Wood of Error, where he must spend a miserable night. At sunrise, hopeful once more, he turns to climb the Mount of Joy, only to find that he is distracted and blocked by the Three Beasts of Worldliness: the leopard of malice and fraud, the lion of violence and ambition, and the she-wolf of incontinence.

Terrified, he is driven back down into the Wood, and begins to despair. It is then that the Shade of Virgil comes to his aid, explaining that he represents Human Reason, and has been sent to lead Dante out of Error by another path. He will take Dante as far as reason can, and then will turn him over to another guide, Beatrice, the revelation of Divine Love. Virgil leads and Dante follows.

They begin their descent into the pit, for it is only through the recognition of sin that purification may take place. Arriving at the Gates of Hell, Dante reads an inscription cut deeply into stone:

ABANDON ALL HOPE YE WHO ENTER HERE[4]

Passing through the Gates, they enter an anteroom filled with noise and confusion. Here are the first of the souls in torment whom Dante will meet. Here are the Opportunists, those who, in life, pursued neither good nor evil, "who were neither for God nor Satan, but only for themselves."[5]

Here in Hell, they must pursue for Eternity a banner they cannot catch, neither quite in Hell, nor quite out of it.

> *These wretches never born and never dead ran naked in a swarm of wasps*
>   *and hornets that goaded them the more and the more they fled.*
> *And made their faces stream with bloody gouts of pus and tears that dribbled to*
>   *their feet,*
> *To be swallowed there by loathsome worms and maggots.*[6]

Because of the darkness of their sin, they run through darkness. As they pursued every passing opportunity in life, so they must now chase an elusive banner forever. Stung by swarms of conscience, feeding the maggots in death, as they produced moral filth in life, they are punished in accordance with their sins. This is the Law of Symbolic Retribution, the Immutable Law of Hell. The punishment is already implied in each sin. Turned back upon the sinner, it causes him to suffer in a way he really has brought upon himself.

This descent into the pit of his own soul is the journey of every pilgrim. No patient in psychotherapy can recover his own beauty and innocence without first facing the ugliness and evil in himself. Jung tells us we have "dealt the devil . . . [no] serious blow by calling him neurosis."[7] The ways in which we live, the experience of our own sinful souls, still is itself our only Hell.

A clear example of the built-in self-torment of neurotic behavior is apparent in the ways of the manipulative patient. Such a man strives for the power to control other people, so that he will not have to experience his own helplessness, and so that he can escape from the fear that others will manipulate him. Trusting in others in the past, as he had to do as a child, resulted in the experience of being used by others, turned this way and that, without regard for his welfare or for how it made him feel. No one seemed to care enough about him for it to be safe to count on them to be considerate, unless he himself could take over and be in control.

Now he is out to make people treat him differently. But he finds, as we all do, that you can't *make* anyone love you. You just have to reveal who you are and take your chances. Oh, sure, you can give a pleasing impression to others, flatter and appease them. Or, you can intimidate other people, threaten and menace them. But whether by cajoling or by coercing, you cannot elicit a gift of love. Instead, you may call forth a reward for good behavior. But then you are stuck with living with the aching feeling in your chest that, if people really knew what you were like, no one would really care about you. Or, if you succeed in getting your own way by bullying other people, then you must live with the dread of retaliation, if ever you should drop your menacing guard.

But perhaps the most poetic, symbolic retribution for being manipulative is that it leaves you completely open to the manipulations of others. He who seems to be taken in by your flattery is merely another manipulator rewarding your offerings as a way of controlling your behavior. And he who gives in to your threats is surely just waiting to get to his feet once more. His surrender is temporary and political, without any quality of loving trust and yielding.

By way of example, Bertolt Brecht somewhere tells the story of a European peasant caught in the holocaust of the Nazi invasion. A Storm Trooper comes to his cottage, drags him out and tells him: "From now on I am in charge. I will live in your house. You will feed me and polish my boots every day. I will be the master and you the servant. If you disagree, I will kill you. Will you submit to me?" Without answering, the peasant gives over his cottage, feeds the invader each day, and polishes his boots. Months later the Allied armies of liberation come through the village. They drag the Storm Trooper out of the cottage. Just as the Allied soldiers are taking the oppressor off to a prison camp, the peasant goes to him, stands proudly before him, and into his face, answers: "No."

The victims of confidence men are always those secret thieves who hope to get something for nothing. That great psychologist, W. C. Fields, used to say: "You can't cheat an honest man." Only the devious manipulator cannot resist the opportunity to believe the illusion that he is in control, that he can get away with it.

I remember early in my practice treating men who "used" prostitutes. All they had to do to control these women was to give them some money and they could manipulate them into doing whatever they wanted. They could make a whore not only do any sexual trick they commanded, but could get her to be nice to them as well. If such men couldn't buy love, at least they could rent it. The women needed the money. The men had it. The women had to give in. The men were contemptuous, superior, in control.

Later in my practice, I began to treat some hookers and strippers. They made it clear to me that the Johns with whom they dealt were suckers. Give them a little sexual excitement, and you could get them to pay all the money they had. Men were so easy to control. I now feel that trying to identify who is controlled, and who is being controlled, is a six-five, pick 'em. And when I try sorting out who is the victim and who the perpetrator of manipulation, I can't tell the knife from the wound.

Dante describes Hell as a funnel-shaped cave descending to the center of the Earth. Circular ledges line the inside, Circles of Damnation. Descending into this "kingdom of eternal night,"[8] on each ledge he and Virgil find the damned souls of the perpetrators of increasingly grievous sins, each group tormented for Eternity by ironically fitting punishments. Carnal sinners, who in life betrayed reason by giving in to their every appetite and abandoning themselves to the wild sweep of their passions, are punished in kind, made to live on a dark ledge, swept 'round forever in the whirlwind of Hell's tempest. Gluttons who wallowed in food and drink, producing nothing but garbage, in Hell must wallow in "putrid slush,"[9] while being torn at by Cerebrus, the gluttonous, three-headed hound of the pit. Now it is they themselves who are slavered over.

Hoarders and Wasters are divided into two opposing groups, each of which must roll great Dead Weights of Mundanity at each other until they clash in the middle, each excess punishing the other. In the foul slime of the Marsh of Styx, the Wrathful attack one another. Up through the mud, bubbles rise from the places beneath in which the Sullen are entombed.

Heretics who denied immortality in life, believing instead that with the body dies the soul, must lie forever in open graves surrounded by the flames of God's wrath. In the River of Boiling Blood lie Murderers and Tyrants, who in life wallowed in the blood of others, doing violence to their neighbors. Panderers and Seducers, who used others for their own purposes, now are driven by whip-carrying, horned demons who force them to hurry along endlessly to serve the foul purposes of their own tormentors. Flatterers pay for having heaped false flattery on others, by living forever in "a river of excrement that seemed the overflow of the world's latrines . . . [forever] smeared with shit."[10]

Hypocrites march in a slow endless procession. Poetically, they are burdened with cloaks of lead, dazzlingly gilded on the outside, and dead-weighted on the inside. Falsifiers, who in life deceived the senses of their fellowmen, now in kind have their own senses offended by darkness and filth, by terrible sounds and smells. And those who betrayed people to whom they were bound by special ties are in the final pit of guilt, the pit of souls who denied love, and so denied God. In the dead center of the earth, they must endure the infernal ice frozen by the loss of all human warmth.

And at the very center is Satan, the King of Hell. The beating of his mighty wings sends out the icy Wind of Depravity, the chilling breath of evil. Once having come to the very center of Evil, having faced every sin and seen its consequences, only now can Dante hope to purify his soul. Only by facing life as it is can he find salvation.

Patients in therapy all begin by protesting, "I want to be good." If they cannot accomplish this, it is only because they are "inadequate," can't control themselves, are too anxious, or suffer from unconscious impulses. Being neurotic is being able to act badly without feeling responsible for what you do.

The therapist must try to help the patient to see that he is exactly wrong, that is, that he is lying when he says he wants to be good. He really wants to be bad. Mortality is an empirical issue. Worse yet, he wants to be bad but to have an excuse for his irresponsibility, to be able to say, "But I can't help it."

His only way out is to see that his pilgrimage to the heavenly City must be undertaken along the road through Hell. When we lay claim to the evil in ourselves, we no longer need fear its occurring outside of our control. For example, a patient comes into therapy complaining that he does not get along well with other people; somehow he always says the wrong thing and hurts their feelings. He is really a nice guy, just has this uncontrollable, neurotic problem. What he does *not* want to know is that his "unconscious hostility" is not his *problem,* it's his *solution.* He is really not a nice guy who wants to be good; he's a bastard who wants to hurt other people while still thinking of himself as a nice guy. If the therapist can guide him into the pit of his own ugly soul, then there may be hope for him. Once this pilgrim can see how angry and vindictive he is, he can trace his story and bring it to the light, instead of being doomed to relive it without awareness. Nothing about ourselves can be changed until it is first accepted. Jung points out that "the sick man has not to learn how to get rid of his neurosis but how to bear it. For the illness is not a superfluous and senseless burden, it is himself; he himself is that 'other' which we were always trying to shut out."[11]

If we flee from the evil in ourselves, we do it at our hazard. All evil is potential vitality in need of transformation. To live without the creative potential of our own destructiveness is to be a cardboard angel.

Much of the time I believe that we are all about as good and as bad as one another. A greater capacity for good, such as that to be found in the enlightened therapist, is matched by his increased capacity for even greater evil. As for the patient, "at best . . . [he] should come out of the analysis as he actually is, in harmony with himself, neither good nor bad, but as a man truly is, a natural being."[12]

Dante has descended into the Abyss of Evil; he has had to spend a season in Hell, before he could rise once more to be illumined by the Divine Light. There is no sin he could not find within himself. He is as good and as bad as the rest of us. But even if you should believe that some men are better than others, then I ask you in the name of myself and all of the others who find that we have never had a completely *pure* motive in our entire lives: "Even if a man is not good, why should he be abandoned?"[13]

·   ·   ·   ·   ·   ·   ·   ·

52 · THE BELLY OF THE WHALE

JOSEPH CAMPBELL

The idea that the passage of the magical threshold is a transit into a sphere of rebirth is symbolized in the worldwide womb image of the belly of the whale. The hero, instead of conquering or conciliating the power of the threshold, is swallowed into the unknown, and would appear to have died.

> *Mishe-Nahma, King of Fishes,*
> *In his wrath he darted upward,*
> *Flashing leaped into the sunshine,*
> *Opened his great jaws and swallowed*
> *Both canoe and Hiawatha.*[1]

The Eskimo of Bering Strait tell of the trickster-hero Raven, how, one day, as he sat drying his clothes on a beach, he observed a whale-cow swimming gravely close to shore. He called: "Next time you come up for air, dear, open your mouth and shut your eyes." Then he slipped quickly into his raven clothes, pulled on his raven mask, gathered his fire sticks under his arm, and flew out over the water. The whale came up. She did as she had been told. Raven darted through the open jaws and straight into her gullet. The shocked whale-cow snapped and sounded; Raven stood inside and looked around.[2]

The Zulus have a story of two children and their mother swallowed by an elephant. When the woman reached the animal's stomach, "she saw large forests and great rivers, and many high lands; on one side there were many rocks; and there were many people who had built their village there; and many dogs and many cattle; all was there inside the elephant."[3]

The Irish hero, Finn MacCool, was swallowed by a monster of indefinite form, of the type known to the Celtic world as a *peist*. The little German girl, Red Ridinghood, was swallowed by a wolf. The Polynesian favorite, Maui, was swallowed by his great-great-grandmother, Hine-nui-te-po. And the whole Greek pantheon, with the sole exception of Zeus, was swallowed by its father, Kronos.

The Greek hero Herakles, pausing at Troy on his way homeward with the belt of the queen of the Amazons, found that the city was being harassed by a monster sent against it by the sea-god Poseidon. The beast would come ashore and devour people as they moved about on the plain. Beautiful Hesione, the daughter of the king, had just been bound by her father to the sea rocks as a propitiatory sacrifice, and the great visiting hero agreed to rescue her for a price. The monster, in due time, broke to the surface of the water and opened its enormous maw. Herakles took a dive into the throat, cut his way out through the belly, and left the monster dead.

This popular motif gives emphasis to the lesson that the passage of the threshold is a form of self-Annihilation. Its resemblance to the adventure of the Symplegades is obvious. But here, instead of passing outward, beyond the confines of the visible world, the hero goes inward, to be born again. The disappearance corresponds to the passing of a worshiper into a temple— where he is to be quickened by the recollection of who and what he is, namely dust and ashes unless immortal. The temple interior, the belly of the whale, and the heavenly land beyond, above, and below the confines of the world, are one and the same. That is why the approaches and entrances to temples are flanked and defended by colossal gargoyles: dragons, lions, devil-slayers with drawn swords, resentful dwarfs, winged bulls. These are the threshold guardians to ward away all incapable of encountering the higher silences within. They are preliminary embodiments of the dangerous aspect of the presence, corresponding to the mythological ogres that bound the conventional world, or to the two rows of teeth of the whale. They illustrate the fact that the devotee at the moment of entry into a temple undergoes a metamorphosis. His secular character remains without; he sheds it, as a snake its slough. Once inside he may be said to have died to time and returned to the World Womb, the World Navel, the Earthly Paradise. The mere fact that anyone can physically walk past the temple guardians does not invalidate their significance; for if the intruder is incapable of encompassing the sanctuary, then he has effectually remained without. Anyone unable to understand a god sees it as a devil and is thus defended from the approach. Allegorically, then, the passage into a temple and the hero-dive through the jaws of the whale are identical adventures, both denoting, in picture language, the life-centering, life-renewing act.

"No creature," writes Ananda Coomaraswamy, "can attain a higher grade of nature without ceasing to exist."[4] Indeed, the physical body of the hero may be actually slain, dismembered, and scattered over the land or sea—as in the Egyptian myth of the savior Osiris: he was thrown into a sarcophagus and committed to the Nile by his brother Set,[5] and when he returned from the dead his brother slew him again, tore the body into fourteen pieces, and scattered these over the land. The Twin Heroes of the Navaho had to pass not only the clashing rocks, but also the reeds that cut the traveler to pieces, the cane cactuses that tear him to pieces, and the boiling sands that overwhelm him. The hero whose attachment to ego is already annihilated passes back and forth across the horizons of the world, in and out of the dragon, as readily as a king through all the rooms of his house. And therein lies his power to save; for his passing and returning demonstrate that through all the contraries of phenomenality the Uncreate-Imperishable remains, and there is nothing to fear.

And so it is that, throughout the world, men whose function it has been to make visible on earth the life-fructifying mystery of the slaying of the dragon have enacted upon their own bodies the great symbolic act, scattering their flesh, like the body of Osiris, for the renovation of the world. In Phrygia, for example, in honor of the crucified and resurrected savior Attis, a pine tree was cut on the twenty-second of March, and brought into the sanctuary of the mother-goddess, Cybele. There it was swathed like a corpse with woolen bands and decked with wreaths of violets. The effigy of a young man was tied to the middle of the stem. Next day took place a ceremonial lament and blowing of trumpets. The twenty-fourth of March was known as the Day of Blood: the high priest drew blood from his arms, which he presented as an offering; the lesser clergy whirled in a dervish-dance, to the sound of drums, horns, flutes, and cymbals, until, rapt in ecstasy, they gashed their bodies with knives to bespatter the altar and tree with their blood; and the novices, in imitation of the god whose death and resurrection they were celebrating, castrated themselves and swooned.[6]

And in the same spirit, the king of the south Indian province of Quilacare, at the completion of the twelfth year of his reign, on a day of solemn festival, had a wooden scaffolding constructed spread over with hangings of silk. When he had ritually bathed in a tank, with great ceremonies and to the sound of music, he then came to the temple, where he did worship before the divine. Thereafter, he mounted the scaffolding and, before the people took some very sharp knives and began to cut off his own nose and then his ears, and his lips, and all his members, and as much of his flesh as he was able. He threw it away and round about until so much of his blood was spilled that he began to faint whereupon he summarily cut his throat.[7]

. . . .

53 · THE USEFULNESS OF THE USELESS

GARY   TOUB

Over two thousand years ago Taoist philosopher Chuang Tzu wrote several parables extolling the virtues of useless, ugly, deformed human beings—hunchbacks, cripples, and lunatics—and knotted, gnarled, fruitless trees. One such story is the following.

Shih the carpenter was on his way to the state of Chi. When he got to Chu Yuan, he saw an oak tree by the village shrine. The tree was large enough to shade several thousand oxen and was a hundred spans around. It towered above the hill-tops with its lowest branches eighty feet above the ground. More than ten of its branches were big enough to be made into boats. There were crowds of people as in a marketplace. The master carpenter did not turn his head but walked on without stopping.

His apprentice took a long look, then ran after Shih the carpenter and said, "Since I took up my ax and followed you, master, I have never seen timber as beautiful as this. But you do not even bother to look at it and walk on without stopping. Why is this?"

Shih the carpenter replied, "Stop! Say no more! That tree is useless. A boat made from it would sink, a coffin would soon rot, a tool would split, a door would ooze sap, and a beam would have termites. It is worthless timber and is of no use. This is why it has reached such a ripe old age."

After Shih the carpenter had returned home, the sacred oak appeared to him in a dream, saying, "What are you comparing me with? Are you comparing me with useful trees? There are cherry, apple, pear, orange, citron, pomelo, and other fruit trees. As soon as their fruit is ripe, the trees are stripped and abused. Their large branches are split, and the smaller ones torn off. Their life is bitter because of their usefulness. That is why they do not live out their natural lives but are cut off in their prime. They attract the attentions of the common world. This is so for all things. As for me, I have been trying for a long time to be useless. I was almost destroyed several times. Finally, I am useless, and this is very useful to me. If I had been useful, could I have ever grown so large?

"Besides, you and I are both things. How can one thing judge another thing? What does a dying and worthless man like you know about a worthless tree?" Shih the carpenter awoke and tried to understand his dream.

His apprentice said, "If it had so great a desire to be useless, why does it serve as a shrine?"

Shih the carpenter said, "Hush! Stop talking! It is just pretending to be one so that it will not be hurt by those who do not know it is useless. If it had not become a sacred tree, it would probably have been cut down. It protects itself in a different way from ordinary things. We will miss the point if we judge it in the ordinary way."[1]

Similarly, there is Chuang Tzu's tale of the hunchback Shu who, despite his strange body took care of himself and lived to the end of his natural life.

These stories illustrate the importance the Taoists attributed to the seemingly useless—to those things that individuals and society shun due to their lack of utility. Even more, they are metaphors teaching the sage to honor and even cultivate his own uselessness (or useless qualities) in order to live a full, natural life.

Corresponding motifs exist in alchemy, fairy tales, and the dreams of modern-day indivduals. For instance, alchemists attached importance to obtaining the *prima materia,* the beginning substance of the transformation process. Yet the *prima materia* was described as poison, urine, and excrement—useless, despicable, and dangerous matter. In fairy tales, the useless is personified as the dummling—a stupid, lazy, and seemingly unlucky character who appears worthless. Yet in most tales, the dummling turns out to be the hero. This motif also appears in the symbolism of contemporary dreams. Take, for example, Carl's dream:

A young woman is frantically running along the balcony of an inner courtyard, trying to escape from someone. Suddenly she stumbles and falls over the railing, just managing to grab it as she goes over. Now she is in great danger, dangling precariously. Then along comes a horrible-looking, deformed, retarded man. His appearance is frightening to the woman. But the man reaches over and pulls her to safety. Later, I am walking into a large room where a religious celebration or ceremony is taking place. On one side of the room I see a row of identical, clean-cut, well-dressed young men. They are standing rigidly. On the other side there is a line of crippled, retarded people, dressed in rags. They look similar to the man who appeared earlier. I know I must choose which group to join. I decide to go with the latter group, whereupon they cheer and celebrate my decision.

This dream is remarkably similar to the Taoist stories lauding the useless, an archetypal motif essential to the individuation process.

THE RELATIVITY OF OPPOSITES

Stories of reverence for the useless express two basic features of Taoist thought: the relativity of values, and the principle of polarity. Taoism portrays the latter by the traditional Chinese symbolism of yin and yang, representing the shady and sunny sides of a mountain, and by extension, all paired existence. Like two sides of a coin, yin and yang, dark and light, useless and useful are complementary poles of nature that can never be separated. According to Chuang Tzu:

> Those who would have right without its correlative, wrong; or good government without its correlative, misrule—they do not apprehend the great principles of the universe nor the condition to which all creation is subject. One might as well talk of the existence of heaven without that of earth, or of the negative principle without the positive, which is clearly absurd. Such people, if they do not yield to argument, must be either fools or knaves. [2]

The Taoists realized that no single concept or value could be considered absolute or superior. If being useful is beneficial, then being useless is also beneficial. The ease with which such opposites may change places is depicted in a Taoist story about a farmer whose horse ran away.

> His neighbor commiserated only to be told, "Who knows what's good or bad?" It was true. The next day the horse returned, bringing with it a drove of wild horses it had befriended in its wanderings. The neighbor came over again, this time to congratulate the farmer on his windfall. He was met with the same observation: "Who knows what is good or bad?" True this time too; the next day the farmer's son tried to mount one of the wild horses and fell off, breaking his leg. Back came the neighbor, this time with more commiserations, only to encounter for the third time the same response, "Who knows what is good or bad?" And once again the farmer's point was well taken, for the following day soldiers came by commandeering for the army and because of his injury, the son was not drafted. [3]

According to the Taoists, yang and yin, light and shadow, useful and useless are all different aspects of the whole, and the minute we choose one side and block out the other, we upset nature's balance. If we are to be whole and follow the way of nature, we must pursue the difficult process of embracing the opposites.

INTEGRATING THE SHADOW

This was Jung's finding, too: the human psyche consists of light and dark, masculine and feminine, and countless other syzygies that coexist in a fluctuating state of psychic tension. Like the Taoists, Jung warned against resolving this tension by identifying with only one pole (for example, trying only to be productive in life). He felt that overvaluing or overdeveloping any single aspect of the psyche is dangerously one-sided, and often resulted in physical illness, neurosis, and psychosis. The alternative Jung recommended was to confront the opposites within ourselves—the *sine qua non* of the individuation process.

One of the major ways to integrate our inner opposites is by consciously confronting the shadow—the "dark" part of the personality that contains the undesirable qualities and attributes we refuse to "own." Facing and owning these attributes is a difficult and painful process, for although the shadow may contain positive elements of the personality, it primarily consists of our inferiorities—primitive, unadapted, and awkward aspects of our nature that we have rejected due to moral, aesthetic, and socio-cultural considerations.

Inasmuch as the shadow is generally viewed as despicable, lowly, and useless, it corresponds with the Taoist images of the gnarled tree and ugly hunchback. Like the shadow, neither appears to have any value. Therefore, one could say that within each of us there is a gnarled tree or hunchback Shu.

WHAT IS WRONG IS RIGHT

In addition to devaluing our shadow characteristics, we tend to view our physical and emotional problems as useless. We dislike what is wrong with us, be it a minor headache or upset stomach, or a severe case of cancer or depression. We see little value in our illnesses. They get in our way and we try to eliminate them.

This attitude toward illness is a causal reductive one that reflects our Western medical model. This model assumes that a disease is bad or wrong and that once the cause is removed, the patient will recover. While this approach facilitates healing, its pervasive application in Western culture creates a fundamentally negative attitude toward symptoms and illness corresponding to the way Chuang Tzu's carpenter initially felt toward the gnarled, old tree.

Chuang Tzu's parables offer us another way to view our problems. Just as the crippled hunchback and crooked tree benefited from their conditions, we can find some good in our ailments. In fact, what is wrong is usually absolutely right for us in the sense of carrying meaning or serving some unseen purpose.

That there is something positive in our symptoms and problems is fundamental to Jung's finalistic psychology. Jung proposed that we should not only look at our maladies in a causal reductive fashion, but seek their direction and meaning as well. According to Jung, our neurotic symptoms and complexes are elaborate arrangements designed by the unconscious as part of an urge toward self-realization. In *Two Essays on Analytical Psychology,* he wrote:

> I myself have known more than one person who owed his entire usefulness and reason for existence to a neurosis, which . . . *forced* him to a mode of living that developed his valuable potentialities.[4]

The tie between illness and self-realization was further developed in Esther Harding's *The Value and Meaning of Depression* (1970), in which she showed how depressive states are often creative attempts by the Self to drive us into deeper communication with our wholeness. Arnold Mindell found the same true for somatic symptoms. In an article in *Quadrant,* he stated:

> The more I work with the body, keeping my assumptions in a temporary state of reservation, the more I appreciate and sympathize with a given "disease." When a final philosophy coupled with clear observation replaces causal therapies and fears based on ignorance, the body no longer appears as a sick or irrational demon but as a process with its own inner logic and wisdom.[5]

Imbedded in our neuroses and physical illnesses are unconscious values and patterns that are essential for wholeness. In order to discover their meaning, we need to ally ourselves with our illnesses. This means paying close attention to the symptoms without making a priori assumptions or trying to change them. Basic to this approach is the idea that what is happening is somehow right and that we should assist it.

Mindell compares this way of working on symptoms and problems with the alchemical opus, which begins with an impure, incomplete body in need of transformation. The "impure body," or *prima materia,* is equivalent to our everyday pains, disorders, and problems that need to be alchemically cooked and transformed to reveal their meaning. This cooking process involves "heating up" what is already happening by intensely focusing on and amplifying it. The following examples illustrate how this works in practice.

USELESSNESS AND INDIVIDUALITY

In addition to teaching us to value our sicknesses, Chuang Tzu's stories tell us that to develop our full potential, we must become useless to the world.

Otherwise, we will live bitter, dissatisfied lives, abused and stripped of precious parts of our personalities. In his exaggerated way, Chuang Tzu is telling us to live as individuals.

Jung also emphasized the importance of living one's unique life. The key element in individuation is to develop one's own personality as opposed to living collectively. Jung was particularly concerned about the plight of the individual in modern society, for he observed that the moment the individual combines with the mass, his or her uniqueness is diminished and blurred. As Jolande Jacobi pointed out in *The Way of Individuation*:

> All too many people do not live their own lives, and generally they know next to nothing about their real nature. They make convulsive efforts to "adapt," not to stand out in any way, to do exactly what the opinions, rules, regulations, and habits of the environment demand as being "right." They are slaves of "what people think," "what people do," etc.[6]

This is increasingly the case the more we attempt to live as average members of society by marrying, having children, establishing a secure profession, and so forth. Such norms are especially deadly for those whose inner pattern deviates tremendously from the average, such as artists, geniuses, priests, and nuns.

The more we align ourselves with our own individual paths, the less we can live strictly according to collective norms and values. To realize our wholeness, we must free ourselves from the suggestive power of the collective psyche and the surrounding world and be willing to appear useless or stupid. As Lao Tzu said:

> *When the wise man learns the Way*
> *He tries to live by it.*
> *When the average man learns the Way*
> *He lives by only part of it.*
> *When the fool learns the Way*
> *He laughs at it.*
> *Yet if the fool did not laugh at it,*
> *It would not be the Way.*
> *Indeed; if you are seeking the Way*
> *Listen for the laughter of fools.*[7]

Lieh Tzu took the idea of being useless even further, suggesting that we refrain from sacrificing even a single hair for the benefit of the world. Only in this way will the world be in order. This, again, is an exaggeration; Lieh Tzu did not mean that we should abandon the world and become hermits. The true sage aims to follow his own nature in the world. In the words of Chuang Tzu:

> Only the perfect man can transcend the limits of the human and yet not withdraw from the world, live in accord with mankind and yet suffer no injury him-

self. Of the world's teachings he learns nothing. He has that which makes him independent of others.[8]

In other words, we should aim at becoming ourselves and bring *what we are* into the world.

· · · · · · ·

54 · WORKING WITH WOMEN'S DREAMS

KAREN   SIGNELL

"Who knows what evil lurks in the hearts of men? The Shadow knows." This introduction to the popular 1940s radio show, *The Shadow,* has a ring of truth to it. We sometimes glimpse, lurking in the dark corners of our awareness, mysteries that are part of the human conditon. We see and feel certain socially unacceptable things we would rather not acknowledge or experience. The term shadow usually refers to those negative qualities, all the bad things that don't fit our conscious picture of ourselves that we banish from the daylight of ego-consciousness.

In daily life, you may catch only a fleeting notion of your own shadow's existence in your avoidance of certain topics or your vague feelings of guilt, self-doubt, discontent, or discord. You may suddenly notice vague worries and feelings in a flush of embarrassment, in an awkward moment of nervous laughter, in a burst of tears, in a flare of anger. When a dream uncovers your shadow, you must be firm of mind enough to get past your resistance to understanding the dream's message and taking it to heart. This is a humbling experience, but it can also be healing and give you integrity.

The first dream shows how useful finding your own personal shadow can be, for by admitting your dark side, you can take better care of yourself and others.

> *A Rat in a Trap.* I smell something bad. It's a rat or mouse in my kitchen, caught in a trap, though still alive, writhing. I kill it or dispose of it. I take care of it somehow.

The dreamer, Peg, wondered, What's *my* rat—my shadow? Rats are sneaky, selfish, and stealthy. Peg's first association concerned her old boyfriend and her relief that he was not coming to town as he had planned. Suddenly it came to her—what she had caught herself at. She had been unconsciously planning to have sex with him even though she was currently in a monogamous relationship with someone else. Peg had uncovered the shadow many people have in their double standard toward affairs: It feels so innocent and understandable when you do it yourself, but so awful when your partner does it! This dream corrected that and called Peg a "dirty rat" if she did such a thing to her own partner. So the feeling of "I smell a rat" usually indicates the shadow in yourself or in someone else.

Dreams have many meanings, like layers of an onion, each true. You might wonder why the rat was writhing and needed to be killed, and why it was found in the kitchen—the place of nurturance. Peg had been unable to shake a flu for a long time; perhaps the dream could tell her what was wrong in her current life. Could the dream be a poetic metaphor for Peg's current relationship? It occurred to Peg that, indeed she had been writhing in a trap and had to bring herself, sooner or later, to do the ruthless, but merciful act of ending the relationship. She had been unconsciously drawn toward an affair because of her anger and dissatisfaction with her mate. This was something Peg had known, and yet had not known. The dream, with its strong imagery, snapped it into focus.

Even though the shadow brings unwelcome realizations—that we are not so fine as we think ourselves to be—finding it often releases lots of energy that has been languishing in the unconscious. In her next dreams, Peg danced in meadows with beautiful flowers in full bloom. Undoubtedly, the work on this dream—making her shadow more conscious—contributed to her flu clearing up soon afterward, too.

When a dream brings up your shadow, or a friend points out a fault, the natural impulse is to deny it and defend yourself, "I'm not that bad," or to shrug your shoulders, "That's just the way I am," or else take a breath and try to be better than you really are. These are mistakes. The shadow needs to be acknowledged and given its place. You must invite it to the dinner table, this dubious guest, civilize it as best you can, and see what it has to offer. You cannot leave it outside the door raising a rumpus or sneaking around and causing worry.

Our intense and prolonged experience in the family, with all its members vying for attention and power, with its alliances, secrets, and resentments, has a profound effect on our expectations of ourselves and other people in society. These are often unconscious expectations shared by the family, and thus we can speak of a "family unconscious" and a "family shadow." Some of our strongest shadow feelings are revealed in our relations with our siblings. For example, we built up an unconscious claim to the kind of position, whether beneficial or detrimental, we occupied in our family and we expect to have a similar position in other social settings. We slip into these expectations unconsciously because they are familiar.

Dreams can reveal unconscious positions and attitudes, specifically, those typical of sibling order: the oldest, middle, youngest, the only child without siblings, or a twin.

As a case in point, the oldest child is in a position to carry strong envy. The world changes for the oldest, who is bound to feel unfairly displaced by younger siblings, who appear to get part of what seems to belong rightfully to the eldest—the whole pie. This contrasts with the experience of the younger ones, who are born into a world where others already exist—they each expect only one slice. The oldest are usually told to suppress their negative feelings because the others are younger. This is a classic situation for a shadow problem of jealousy, which a person needs to sniff out later.

Sometimes the shadow is so far from consciousness and so frightening that the door must not be opened until one is ready to face it. One may be opening the door to the whole swamp of the unconscious and can be flooded with archetypal anxiety. In a tide of enthusiasm, as in group workshops, a person can be swept up into "uncovering it all," the deeper the better, but a person's real vulnerability must be taken into account.

Deeper is not always better. After all, defenses serve a purpose. In your curiosity, if you tear off a scab you may leave a raw wound if it is too early. The natural process of healing takes time. Once you have grown a protective coating for a deep wound, then you are safe and can look.

A woman, Carolyn, had the following dream:

> *Spooks.* It's like sitting in an audience watching a movie. The scene is a beach at night. There's an evil child, blood all over, and slashed bodies.
>
> I'm sitting near an open door, a closet, and I hasten to close and lock it. But there's a young woman named *Verité* sitting near me wanting me to open the door again. We argue about it and I have to fight her physically to keep the door locked for now. Then we're reconciled and we hug.
>
> A voice says, "You're fighting to keep something secret about a woman." People come to the beach. There are dead people there, zombies, looking at us menacingly. I throw a thick liquid at them and it anesthetizes some of them; but the others, whom I can't reach with the liquid, either run or remain to menace us. I need something else for them.

Carolyn's first thought was that she herself was the "evil child." She was reminded of a dream the previous month:

> [Earlier dream] *Mother Doesn't Remember Unpleasant Things.* My mother is watching a horror movie and turns her face away, saying, "I don't remember unpleasant things," but the daughter, watching her, knows that the mother *does* remember! It's as if both mother and daughter have vague memories of terrible things happening in the daughter's first years.

This is how a child catches the projection of archetypal evil. When there is a dark secret in a family, a child feels at fault—feels like the evil child. Carolyn said, "When I start to go to sleep at night, then the spooks come out."

What is the secret? The Spook dream has some clues. The fight with Verité, Truth—to keep the door closed to an awful secret about a woman—seemed to the dreamer her unconscious need at the time to keep believing that her mother was good, so she could keep a "good mother" in her memory and feel safe. In outer reality, it was maintaining her mother's prohibition against talking about certain things, keeping the "family unconscious" intact—in this case, the capacity to mistreat a child. Verité was fighting her to make her reveal the truth, but she wasn't ready yet.

What is the liquid that pacifies? Carolyn said it was alcohol, that she drinks beer or wine to relax. But, as in the dream, it only works once in a while to dispel the images, like spooks, that have haunted her all her life. As it says in the dream, not all could be anesthetized, that is, remain in the unconscious. The truth is restless, the ghosts are restless and want to reveal themselves and be laid to rest.

Since Verité, the Truth, didn't win out in the dream, Carolyn didn't try to find out more details at this time. She was not ready. Years later, when she herself could turn her face toward the truth, Carolyn found that she had been physically abused by her mother when she was an infant and small child, and then sexually molested by her father when she was about four, and that she had probably experienced those incidents "like in a movie," in a trance state or dissociated state, as children under five often do. The "zombies" in the dream were the images Carolyn had retained of her parents at the time. Her mother had been on a tranquilizer those early years and seemed strangely absent, like a zombie, yet sometimes suddenly intense as she lashed out in unconscious anger. Her father, during the molestation, had not seemed like his usual self, but strangely detached and unreal, probably in an unconscious state of compulsion himself, perhaps a re-living of a molestation he had been subjected to as a young child.

How did the dream apply to Carolyn's life at the time of the dream? Why did the dream come up at the time it did? Carolyn wondered if her own shadow—what she was afraid to let out of "the closet" in her current life— was her lesbianism. She felt great anxiety about it. Carolyn's real life struggle with Verité, then, whether to let this truth be known, undoubtedly raised the spectre deep inside her of a more frightening archetypal shadow that had been projected onto her as a physically abused infant and sexually molested young child, and her early image of herself as an "evil child." No wonder the dreamer had a struggle with Verité in the dream! And no wonder it was terrifying to Carolyn to imagine coming out of the closet as a lesbian, for any cultural disapproval would touch her deep personal and archetypal wound.

Carolyn respected what the dream implied: She was too anxious at this time to explore the exact nature of her early wounds and heal them; she was too anxious, still, to be open about her lifestyle. First, she needed to differentiate her real fears and her archetypal fears. Carolyn said she felt some pressure from herself and others to be open, but she said, "Those who feel invulnerable don't know cruelty." So she needed to go down the road a while longer, alongside her "good mother" who couldn't yet hear unpleasant things, before she could face the cruel truth of her early years and face the various reactions to her lifestyle that she might expect in her contemporary world with its ranges of rejection and acceptance.

In all these dreams, opening the door to your own negative shadow, frightening and humbling as it may seem—knowing your own sneaky rat, lemon-scented rivalry, your family's spooks, and your own secrets—can help you soften your heart toward yourself and others, as kindred spirits in human foibles, and can also help you keep a cautious eye on the shadow in order to protect yourself and others.

. . . .

55 · EMERGENCE OF THE SHADOW IN MIDLIFE

JANICE BREWI AND ANNE BRENNAN

The turning point that begins with the transition from the first to the second half of life summons up the more-or-less unconscious, hitherto neglected sides of the psyche. In this process the Shadow plays its great creative role.

By the time that mid-life comes, a person has usually settled into familiar psychological patterns and is ensconced in work and family. And then suddenly, a crisis! You wake up one day and you are unexpectedly out of gas. The atmosphere of personal ownership sinks; the sweet milk of achievement is sour; the old patterns of coping and acting pinch your feet. The ability to prize your favorite objects—your works; children, possessions, power positions, accomplishments—has been stolen and you are left wondering what happened last night? Where did it go? (Murray Stein)

It is the Shadow who is responsible for such a shocking theft. It is the Shadow who has come when the mid-life person begins to experience himself or herself in such a whole new way. Jung calls the realizations of the Shadow an "eminently practical problem." This growing awareness of the inferior part of the personality cannot be twisted into an intellectual activity.

At mid-life, this great unknown, this Shadow, has a sufficiently developed ego personality to engage, without immediately swallowing, that ego consciousness whole. However, at this same time in life the ego personality is in danger of closing it on itself and getting stuck, precisely because of this same strength. It is the Shadow, then, as the unconscious parts of the personality that the conscious ego has tended to reject or ignore, which begins to emerge as a kind of number-two personality. It is friend or foe? This is the mid-life question. Answering that question in fidelity to my Self, as the unique image of God that I am called to be, as I wrestle with it in each real situation that presents the question, is the spirituality of mid-life. Mid-life spirituality is lived on the stage of life, not in the auditorium. One acts integration and holiness. Here one cannot be a spectator.

These encounters with the Shadow are never an easy or simplistic affair. Yet, the word *Shadow* may give a name to all kinds of inexpressible new experiences of oneself that are totally individual. Trying to capture these very complex and subtle experiences in a word necessarily reduces them. However, having a word does place these sometimes frightening and always disturbing experiences within the horizon of human experience and, it is often infinitely comforting to know that one has had many Shadow experiences and is not "simply losing one's mind."

The experiences of Shadow, however, necessarily overflow the word and so the word can be a kind of catch-all term in a psychology of the second half of life.

The journey into the unconscious—encountering, befriending, and integrating the Shadow—is not to be undertaken lightly. Nor can it be undertaken at all until one's ego development is strong enough and consciousness truly valued and secure. Here is the great paradox and irony. It is only when we so believe in our consciousness that we almost see it as all there is that we can come to see, respect, and value the Shadow for its danger and its treasure. With each encounter with the Shadow, consciousness needs both to hold its own and surrender only when sufficiently convinced. The dance of bearing the tensions of opposites is always intricate, the goal is always the widening of consciousness, integrating what was formerly unconscious and possibly seen as evil. This is never done directly. It happens through an intermediary. The opposites unite in a third, a child of both, a symbol of transcendence. The lion and the lamb come together in the Kingdom; black and white come together in gray. The integration of the Shadow and consequent growth in consciousness will take time. It will happen in stages.

This is precisely the reality and meaning of the Shadow: Each of us could imagine and could commit any atrocity or achieve any greatness of which humanity is capable; the Shadow is the rest of who we are. For every virtue we have espoused, the opposite has had to remain undeveloped, unconscious. While we have the right to consider the murderer, thief, adulterer, terrorist, prostitute, blasphemer, drug dealer, extortionist, or racist in us sinister and evil, we do not have the right to consider any one of them absolutely nonexistent in us. We cannot deny the possibility; we cannot "forget our tail." We dare not forget that we have, as Christ said, a "least one" inside as well as outside: it is this least one and all the other primitive, inferior, undeveloped parts of each of us that have paid the price of neglect for the virtuous, capable, superior, skillful parts. Their neglect, suppression, and repression made possible the cultivation of their opposites.

> No wonder that many bad neuroses appear at the onset of life's afternoon. It is a sort of second puberty, another storm and stress period; not infrequently accompanied by tempests of passion—the "dangerous age." But the problems that crop up at this age are no longer to be solved by the old recipes: the hand of the clock cannot be put back. What youth found and must find outside, the man [or woman] of life's afternoon must find within himself [or herself]. (Jung, *Two Essays in Analytical Psychology*)

The first half of life is, as it were, for the growth and differentiation of the Shadow. The whole second half of life is for the greater and greater integration of the Shadow.

. . . .

56 · FOR THE MAN AT MIDLIFE

DANIEL J. LEVINSON

In the Mid-life Transition, as a man reviews his life and considers how to give it greater meaning, he must come to terms in a new way with destruction and creation as fundamental aspects of life. His growing recognition of his own mortality makes him more aware of destruction as a universal process. Knowing that his own death is not far off, he is eager to affirm life for himself and for the generations to come. He wants to be more creative. The creative impulse is not merely to "make" something. It is to bring something into being, to give birth, to generate life. A song, a painting, even a spoon or toy, if made in a spirit of creation, takes on an independent existence. In the mind of its creator, it has a being of its own and will enrich the lives of those who are engaged with it.

Thus, both sides of the Destruction/Creation polarity are intensified at mid-life. The acute sense of his own ultimate destruction intensifies a man's wish for creation. His growing wish to be creative is accompanied by a great awareness of the destructive forces in nature, in human life generally, and in himself.

For the man who is ready to look, death and destruction are everywhere. In nature, each species eats certain others and is eaten by still others. The geological evolution of the earth involves a process of destruction and transformation. To construct anything, something else must be destructured and restructured.

No man can get to age forty without some experience of human destructiveness. Other persons, including those closest to him, have in some ways damaged his self-esteem, hindered his development, kept him from seeking and finding what he wanted most. Likewise, he himself has at times caused great hurt to others, including his loved ones.

In reappraising his life during the Mid-life Transition, a man must come to a new understanding of his grievances against others for the real or imagined damage they have done him. For a time he may be utterly immobilized by the helpless rage he feels toward parents, wife, mentors, friends and loved ones who, as he now sees it, have hurt him badly. And, what is even more difficult, he must come to terms with his guilts—his grievances against himself—for the destructive effects he has had on others and himself. He has to ask himself: "How have I failed my adult responsibilities for loved ones and for enterprises that affect many persons? How have I failed myself and destroyed my own possibilities? How can I live with the guilt and remorse?"

His developmental task is to understand more deeply the place of destructiveness in his own life and in human affairs generally. Much of the work on this task is unconscious. What is involved, above all, is the reworking of painful feelings and experiences. Some men articulate their new awareness in words, others in the esthetic terms of music, painting or poetry. Most men simply live it out in their daily lives. In any case, a man must come to terms with his grievances and guilts—his view of himself as victim and as villain in the continuing tale of man's inhumanity to man. If he is burdened excessively by his grievances or guilts, he will be unable to surmount them. If he is forced to maintain the illusion that destructiveness does not exist, he will also be impaired in his capacity for creating, loving and affirming life.

It is necessary that a man recognize and take responsibility for his own destructive capabilities. Even without hostile intentions, he will at times act in ways that have damaging consequences for others. As a father, he may discipline his children for the best of reasons and to the worst of effects. In a love relationship, his feelings cool unexpectedly and he withdraws from the relationship; it makes no sense to marry, yet the other person feels abandoned and betrayed. As a boss, he must demote someone who is worthy but incompetent, damaging that person's self-esteem and future prospects. No act can be totally benign in its consequences. To have the power to do great good, we must bear the burden of knowing that we will cause some harm—and in the end, perhaps, more harm than good.

It is hard enough to acknowledge that we can be unwittingly destructive. It is most painful of all to accept that we have destructive wishes toward others, even loved ones. There are times when a man feels hatred and revulsion, when he would like to leave or assault his loved ones, when he finds them intolerably cruel, disparaging, petty, controlling. He often feels an intense rage or bitterness without knowing what brought it on or toward whom it is directed. Finally, he has actually done hurtful things to loved ones on purpose— with the worst of intentions, and in some cases with the worst of consequences.

Men at forty differ widely in their readiness to acknowledge and take responsibility for their own destructiveness. Some have no awareness that they have done harm to others or might wish to do so. Others are so guilty about the real or imagined damage they have inflicted that they are not free to consider the problems of destructiveness more dispassionately and place it in broader perspective. Still others have some understanding that a person may feel both love and hate toward the same person, and some awareness of the ambivalence in their own valued relationships. In each case, the developmental task is to take a further step toward greater self-knowledge and self-responsibility.

Even the most mature or knowledgeable man has a great deal to learn at mid-life about the workings of destructiveness in himself and in society. He has to learn about the heritage of anger, against others and against himself, that he has carried within himself from childhood. He has to learn, also, about the angers he has accumulated over the course of adulthood, building on and amplifying the childhood sources. And he has to place these internal destructive forces within the wider context of his ongoing adult life, setting them against the creative, life-affirming forces and finding new ways to integrate them in middle adulthood.

The learning I have just referred to is not purely conscious or intellectual. It cannot be acquired simply by reading a few books, taking a few courses, or even having some psychotherapy, though all of these may contribute to a long-term developmental process. The main learning goes on within the fabric of one's life. During the Mid-life Transition, we often learn by going through intense periods of suffering, confusion, rage against others and ourselves, grief over lost opportunities and lost parts of the self.

One possible fruit of a man's labors on this polarity is the "tragic sense of life." The tragic sense derives from the realization that great misfortunes and failures are not merely imposed upon us from without, but are largely the result of our own tragic flaws. A tragic story is not merely a sad story. In a sad story the hero dies or fails in his enterprise or is rejected by his special love; the unfortunate outcome is brought on by enemies, poor conditions, bad luck, or some unexpected deficiency in the hero.

The tragic story has a different character. Its hero is engaged with extraordinary virtue and skill in a noble quest. He is defeated in this quest. The defeat is due in part to formidable external difficulties, but it stems above all from an internal flaw, a quality of character that is an intrinsic part of the heroic striving. The flaw usually involves hubris (arrogance, ego inflation, omnipotence) and destructiveness. The nobility and the defect are two sides of the same heroic coin. But genuine tragedy does not end simply in defeat. Although the hero does not attain his initial aspirations, he is ultimately victorious: he confronts his profound inner faults, accepts them as part of himself and of humanity, and is to some degree transformed into a nobler person. The personal transformation outweighs the worldly defeat and suffering.

. . . .

57 · HOW TO DEAL WITH EVIL

LILIANE FREY-ROHN

Although it is possible for evil to be transformed into good, we must not overlook the fact that this is only a possibility. Man's highest virtues are called upon when he is confronted with evil. The most subtle problem of the psychology of evil is how one should deal with this adversary—this numinous and dangerous opponent in the psyche—so as not to be destroyed by it.

One can make a wide circle around evil, and assert that it must be sublimated, or suppressed. On the other hand, as Nietzsche suggested, one can ally oneself with it—with the reverse side of morality—and help the blind will to live to achieve realization. These two attempts at a solution, which are those which occur to one first, have directly opposite goals. The psychologist who follows the first method aims at making evil ineffective, by reuniting the individual with the collective morality, or by getting him to limit his own desires for self-development. In his later writings, Freud pointed out the curative effect of "education to reality," and the training of the intellect.[1] He attempted to achieve both these ends by strengthening Logos against the powers of Ananke (ominous fate). Nietzsche took the opposite position, the second method. In contradistinction to Freud's pessimism, he proclaimed a Dionysian affirmation of the world, and a passionate *amor fati*.[2] He praised not only the superman but also the evil of the subhuman, of the blond beast. Both these attempted solutions are one-sided, and bring about a dissociation between conscious good and unconscious evil. For, as we have tried to demonstrate, "too much morality" strengthens evil in the inner world, and "too little morality" promotes a dissocation between good and evil.

In this connection I should like again to refer to William James, who—consistently following up his insights into the function of evil—saw spiritual health in the completion of human personality to form a harmonious whole.[3] Not moral perfection but the promotion of the rejected complementary attitude is the basis of a religiously stable personality. James saw the deeper secret of the conquest of good and evil in the unconditional acceptance of the dictates of the unconscious self.[4] Although he did not overlook the risk of being placed at the mercy of the inner voice—since one can never be sure whether it is the voice of God or the voice of the Devil—he maintained that the individual's surrender to the transpersonal and the unconscious was the only way to salvation.

As Jung's investigations show, dealing with evil is in the end an individual secret, which one can only describe in broad outline. Experience constantly demonstrates that there is no guarantee that the individual can meet the challenge and no objective criterion for what is "right" in each situation. The experience of the archetypal shadow leads into the utterly "unknown," where one is exposed to unforeseeable dangers. It is equivalent to an experience of the God-image itself, in all its sublimity and depth, its good and evil. Such an event transforms the whole man; not only his ego-personality, but also his inner adversary.

Coming to terms with the unconscious always entails the risk that one may give the Devil too much credit. One is indeed trusting him too far, if one overlooks the fact that confrontation with the archetype can result in error and corruption as well as in guidance and truth. A message from the unconscious is not *eo ipso* to be equated with the voice of God. It is always necessary to question whether the author of the message is God or the Devil. This encounter can just as well result in a dissolution of the personality as in guidance on the path of wisdom. Therefore, mere surrender to, or blind faith in the unconscious powers is no more satisfactory than a stubborn resistance to the "unknown." Just as an attitude of complete trust can be the expression of childishness, so an attitude of critical resistance can be a measure of self-protection. Not only in the art of medicine, but also in psychology, caution is important in the "dosage" of poison. Everything depends upon "how" one deals with the adversary. Too close an approach to the numinous—no matter whether it appears as good or evil—inevitably carries with it the danger of an inflation, and the danger of being overwhelmed by the powers of light or of darkness.

We can see in *The Devil's Elixir,* by E. T. W. Hofmann,[5] what being overcome by the demonic can lead to. The author describes how the monk Medardus became possessed by the "mana personality" of Saint Anthony, and then in compensation fell victim to the unholy Antichrist. Intoxicated by his own eloquence and seduced by his lust for power, he was tempted to increase his effectiveness by taking a drink out of the Devil's bottle. By drinking the Devil's elixir he gained the secret of rejuvenation, but at the same time he fell into the Devil's power. His greed for love and the things of this world overpowered him and lured him to his destruction. As a result of this entanglement with the other side of his personality, his soul split into two autonomous systems, the body soul, and the spirit soul. Hofmann goes on to develop in a most impressive way the problem of what he calls the "double"—that is, the part of the soul which, though dissociated from the ego, nevertheless is its close companion. Equally impressive is the method he suggests for bringing the two parts of the soul together. It begins with Medardus' return to the loneliness of the monastery. There penance, insight, and remorse clear his beclouded senses, and for the first time, by realizing that moral goodness in nature is dependent on evil, he finds peace and release from his compulsive drives. This relativization of good and evil, which depended upon a partial acceptance of the heathen adversary, also meant a change in his Christian consciousness. The body-soul, however, understands only slowly what the spirit-soul already comprehends, so that the problem arises again with the greatest intensity. As with Faust, so also with Medardus: it is only in the twilight zone between life and death that he finds the longed-for reconciliation of spirit and nature; then he experiences the reconciliation as the pure beam of eternal love.

I now want to touch upon the most important problem in dealing with the shadow. As Jung always emphasizes, the shadow is "the moral problem par excellence." This holds good for the personal as well as for the archetypal shadow: it is a reality which challenges the highest effort of consciousness. Consciousness of the shadow is decisive for the stability not only of the individual life but also in large measure of the collective life. To be conscious of evil means to be painstakingly aware of what one does and of what happens to one. "If indeed thou knowest what thou doest, thou art blessed; but if thou knowest not, thou art cursed, and a transgressor of the law."[6] This is one of Jesus' apocryphal sayings. He said it to a Jew whom he saw working on the Sabbath.

Becoming conscious of the shadow sounds like a relatively simple demand. In reality, however, it is a moral challenge which is extremely difficult to meet. The task requires, first of all, the recognition of individual evil— that is, of those contra-values which the ego has rejected; and a simultaneous recognition of the conscious values of individual good; in other words, making the unconscious conflict conscious. This can mean (1) that a moral point of view, previously based on tradition, is now supplemented by subjective reflection, or (2) that the rights of the ego are given the same authority as the rights of the "thou," or (3) that the rights of instinct are recognized along with the rights of reason. Becoming conscious of the conflict is naturally experienced as an almost irreconcilable collision of incompatible impulses, as a civil war within oneself. *The conscious conflict between good and evil takes the place of an unconscious dissociation. As a result, unconscious instinctive regulation is supplemented by conscious control.* One gains the ability to estimate more correctly one's effect on other people, as well as to recognize the shadow projections and perhaps even to withdraw them. And, finally, one is forced to consider revising one's views about good and evil. One realizes that the secret of a better adjustment to reality often depends upon being able to give up "the wish to be good" and allowing evil a certain right to live. As Jung rightly remarks, it appears that "the disadvantages of the lesser good" are balanced against "the advantage of the lesser evil."[7] Contrary to the general opinion that consciousness of the shadow constellates and strengthens evil, one finds repeatedly that just the opposite is true: knowledge of one's own personal shadow is the necessary requirement for any responsible action, and consequently for any lessening of moral darkness in the world. This holds good to an even greater extent in relation to the collective shadow, to the archetypal figure of the adversary, who compensates the collective consensus of the time. Consciousness of the archetypal shadow is essential not only for individual self-realization, but also for that transformation of creative impulses within the collective upon which depends the preservation of both individual and collective life. The individual cannot detach himself from his connection with society; *responsibility toward oneself always includes responsibility toward the whole.* One can perhaps even risk the statement: Whatever consciousness the individual struggles for and is able to transmit benefits the collective. By coming to terms with the archetypal adversary he is able to sense collective moral problems and anticipate emerging values.

But awareness of the moral conflict is not enough. Dealing with the shadow requires a choice between two mutually exclusive opposites as well as a realization in conscious life. There are three ways in which the individual can attempt to solve the problem. He can renounce one side in favor of the other; he can retire from the conflict altogether; or he can seek a solution that will satisfy both sides. The first two possibilities need no further discussion. The third seems at first impossible. How can contradictory opposites like good and evil ever be reconciled? According to the rules of logic, *tertium non datur.* Reconciliation of the opposites, therefore, can only be achieved by "transcending" them; that is, by raising the problem to a higher level where the contradictions are resolved. If a person is successful in detaching himself from identification with specific opposites, he can often see, to his own astonishment, how nature intervenes to help him. Everything depends upon the individual's attitude. The freer he can keep himself of hard and fast principles and the readier he is to sacrifice his ego-will, the better are his chances of being emotionally grasped by something greater than himself. He will

then experience an inner liberation, a condition—to use Nietzsche's phrase—
"beyond good and evil." In psychological terms, the sacrifice of the ego-will
adds energy to the unconscious, and leads to an activation of its symbols.
This corresponds to the religious experience, in which the resurrection follows the crucifixion and the ego-will becomes one with the will of God.
From either standpoint, the acceptance of sacrifice is the *sine qua non* of salvation. A transformation takes place in the symbols of both good and evil.
Good loses some of its goodness, and evil some of its evil. As doubt of the
"light" of consciousness increases, so the "darkness" of the soul appears less
black. A new symbol emerges in which the opposites can be reconciled. I am
thinking here of the symbols of the Cross, of the *T'ai-Chi-Tu,* and of the
Golden Flower. For the individual, the emergence of such a symbol often
brings a new understanding of the conflict, a neutralization of the opposites,
and a transformation of the God-image. It always has a liberating effect on
the soul; the conscious personality and the inner adversary both appear transformed. Whether it attacks us in the form of illness, external disorder, inner
emptiness, or as a shattering invasion from within of an immoral demand,
evil can finally prove to be a means of healing, which reconciles the individual with the central core of his being, with the self, the image of the Godhead. Whoever attains such a reconciliation will not only feel open to the creative, he will also experience again the tension of the opposites—this time in
a positive manner—and so he will finally recover his powers of decision and
action.

· · · · · · ·

Put what salve you have on yourself.
Point out to everyone the disease you are.
That's part of getting well.
When you lance yourself that way,
you become more merciful and wiser.
Even if you don't have some particular
fault at the moment, you may soon
become the one who makes that very act
not notorious.

RUMI

· · · · · · ·

OWNING YOUR DARK SIDE THROUGH INSIGHT, ART, AND RITUAL

If a way to the better there be, it lies in taking a full
look at the worst.

THOMAS HARDY

So the person who has eaten his shadow spreads calm-
ness, and shows more grief than anger. If the ancients
were right that darkness contains intelligence and
nourishment and even information, then the person
who has eaten some of his or her shadow is more
energetic as well as more intelligent.

ROBERT BLY

I dreamt last night,
oh marvelous error,
that there were honeybees in my heart,
making honey out of my old failures.

ANTONIO MACHADO

If you bring forth what is within you, what you
bring forth will save you. If you do not bring forth
what is within you, what you do not bring forth
will destroy you.

JESUS

INTRODUCTION

. . . .

The goal of shadow-work—to integrate the dark side—cannot be accomplished with a simple method or trick of the mind. Rather, it is a complex, ongoing struggle that calls for great commitment, vigilance, and the loving support of others who are traveling a similar road.

Owning your shadow does not mean gaining enlightenment by banishing the dark, as some Eastern traditions teach. Nor does it mean gaining endarkenment by embracing the dark, as some practitioners of black magic or Satanism teach.

Instead, it involves a deepening and widening of consciousness, an ongoing inclusion of that which was rejected. The late analyst Barbara Hannah tells us that Jung said our consciousness is like a boat that floats on the surface of the unconscious.

> Each piece of the shadow that we realize has a weight, and our consciousness is lowered to that extent when we take it into our own boat. Therefore, one might say that the main art of dealing with the shadow consists in the right loading of our boat: if we take too little, we float away from reality and become, as it were, a fluffy white cloud without substance in the sky, and if we take too much we may sink our boat.

In this way, shadow-work forces us again and again to take another point of view, to respond to life with our undeveloped traits and our instinctual sides, and to live what Jung called the tension of the opposites—holding both good and evil, right and wrong, light and dark, in our own hearts.

Doing shadow-work means peering into the dark corners of our minds in which secret shames lie hidden and violent voices are silenced. Doing shadow-work means asking ourselves to examine closely and honestly what it is about a particular individual that irritates us or repels us; what it is about a racial or religious group that horrifies or captivates us; and what it is about a lover that charms us and leads us to idealize him or her. Doing shadow-work means making a gentleman's agreement with one's self to engage in an internal conversation that can, at some time down the road, result in an authentic self-acceptance and a real compassion for others.

In a personal letter written in 1937, Jung says that dealing with the shadow "consists solely in an attitude. First of all one has to accept and to take seriously into account the existence of the shadow. Secondly, it is necessary to be informed about its qualities and intentions. Thirdly, long and difficult negotiations will be unavoidable."

Simply to take the first small step, to acknowledge the darkness lying inside every human heart, can be sobering and humbling. It may be initiated by a betrayal by a loved one; a lie by a trusted friend; a deceit by an honored teacher; a rape or mugging by a total stranger. In every case, meeting the shadow robs us of our innocence.

If the mirror turns about and we see these behaviors in ourselves, recognizing the deeper truth that the lover and the liar, the saint and the sinner live in every one of us, we may be stunned, paralyzed at the gap between who we are and who we thought we were.

If we can allow this insight to penetrate us deeply, we may no longer act like the person in the popular tale who loses his key in the darkness by a doorway but insists on looking for it by the lamppost, where the light is better. We may learn, slowly, inexorably, that the key lies in the dark, that if we could embrace that very thing we most despise in ourselves or others, it might make us whole.

Like Beauty embracing the Beast, our beauty is deepened as our beastliness is honored. The poet Rainer Maria Rilke realized this when he said he feared that if his devils left him, his angels would take flight.

So we begin, perhaps timidly, to take Jung's second step—to discover the qualities of our own shadows by closely watching our reactions to other people and admitting that they are not the *other,* or the *enemy,* but that an impulse within ourselves makes them appear in this negative guise. In this way, we can learn to re-own our projections, to repossess the energy and power that, as Robert Bly puts it, belong in our own treasury.

In *The Spectrum of Consciousness,* transpersonal philosopher Ken Wilber also explores the projection of negative qualities onto others. In Chapter 58, he describes how to take responsibility for them by recognizing that "the shadow is not an affair between you and others, but between you and you."

In Chapter 59, from *A Little Book on the Human Shadow,* poet Robert Bly suggests that in order to "eat the shadow" we need to do more than identify it; we need to ask others to give us back our disowned traits, as well as use creativity to integrate them.

Psychologist and author Nathaniel Branden, who popularized the term *disowned self,* tells stories of clients taking back their childhood feelings of pain and power.

Psychologists Hal Stone and Sidra Winkelman apply the Voice Dialogue Method to integrating disowned energies such as sensuality and demonic feelings. In this piece from *Embracing Our Selves,* they tell client stories that illustrate their method.

In a piece from *Healing the Shame That Binds You,* best-selling author/ seminar leader John Bradshaw explores the inner voice that is shaming and critical. As Jungian analyst Gilda Frantz said, "Shame is the gristle we must chew on to integrate the shadow complex."

Opening a short series of pieces on active imagination, analyst Barbara Hannah offers a general introduction to the practice as it was taught to her by Jung. Readers will gain practical advice on how to use creative energies for owning the shadow.

In two pieces written especially for this volume, Los Angeles artist Linda Jacobson teaches exercises that use visualization to evoke images for drawing the shadow; and psychotherapist/novelist Deena Metzger explores writing about the *other* as a self-revealing form of shadow-work.

Even with great effort to own the shadow involving prolonged internal negotiations, the outcome is uncertain. We have no vision of a complete or perfected human being who has made conscious all shame, greed, jealousy, rage, racism, and enemy-making tendencies. There is no human being who has stopped projecting onto others his dark inferiorities or his light heroic longings.

Instead, as each layer of shadow is uncovered, as each fear is faced, each revulsion repossessed, we continuously uncover yet another dirt-encrusted nugget. Mining the dark recesses of the human psyche is endless. But at a certain point, in some strange turnabout, those qualities that before seemed so alluring, so full of light, are cast into darkness—and those that seemed wicked or weak appear somehow attractive. When a woman's sensuality and feminine wiles are in the shadow, voluptuous women seem gaudy and manipulative to her. But when her sensuality has been awakened, these same women seem to her like sisters.

Likewise, a man who abhors big business for its greedy, competitive, goal-oriented values and then achieves his own success will not so quickly judge his more materialistic brothers. In each case, our identities expand to include those characteristics that had been exiled onto others.

In this war between the opposites, there is only one battleground—the human heart. And somehow, in a compassionate embrace of the dark side of reality, we become bearers of the light. We open to the other—the strange, the weak, the sinful, the despised—and simply through including it, we transmute it. In so doing, we move ourselves toward wholeness.

· · · · · · ·

58 · TAKING RESPONSIBILITY FOR YOUR SHADOW

KEN WILBER

Like the projection of negative emotions, the projection of negative qualities is very common in our society, for we have been duped into equating "negative" with "undesirable." Thus instead of befriending and integrating our negative traits, we alienate and project them, seeing them in everybody else but ourselves. As always however, they nevertheless remain ours. As an example, nine out of a particular group of ten girls love Jill, but the tenth girl, Betty, can't stand her because, as Betty explains it, Jill is a prude. And Betty hates prudes. So she will go to lengths to try to convince her other friends of Jill's supposed prudishness, but nobody seems to agree with her, which further infuriates Betty. It is perhaps obvious that Betty hates Jill only because Betty is unconscious of her own prudish tendencies; and projecting them onto Jill, a conflict between Betty and Betty becomes a conflict between Betty and Jill. Jill, of course, has nothing to do with this argument—she simply acts as an unwanted mirror of Betty's own self-hatred.

All of us have blind spots—tendencies and traits that we simply refuse to admit are ours, that we refuse to accept and therefore fling into the environment where we muster all of our righteous fury and indignation to do battle with them, blinded by our own idealism to the fact that the battle is within and the enemy is much nearer home. And all it takes to integrate these facets is that we treat ourselves with the same kindness and understanding that we afford to our friends. As Jung most eloquently states:

> The acceptance of oneself is the essence of the moral problem and the epitome of a whole outlook upon life. That I feed the hungry, that I forgive an insult, that I love my enemy in the name of Christ—all these are undoubtedly great virtues. What I do unto the least of my brethren, that I do unto Christ. But what if I should discover that the least among them all, the poorest of all the beggars, the most impudent of all offenders, the very enemy himself—that these are within me, and that I myself stand in the need of the alms of my own kindness—that I myself am the enemy who must be loved—what then?[1]

The consequences are always twofold: one, we come to believe that we totally lack the quality which we are projecting, and thus it is unavailable to us—we do not act upon it, utilize it, or in any way satisfy it, which causes a chronic frustration and tension. Two, we see these qualities as existing in the environment, where they assume awesome or terrifying proportions, so that we end up clobbering ourselves with our own energy.

Projection on the Ego Level is very easily identified: if a person or thing in the environment *informs* us, we probably aren't projecting; on the other hand, if it *affects* us, chances are that we are a victim of our own projections. For instance, Jill might very well have been a prude, but was that any reason for Betty to hate her? Certainly not; Betty was not just *informed* that Jill was a prude, she was violently *affected* by Jill's prudishness, which is a sure sign that Betty's hatred of Jill was only projected or extroverted self-contempt. Similarly, when Jack was debating whether or not to clean the garage, and his wife inquired how he was doing, Jack over-reacted. Had he really not desired to clean the garage, had he really been innocent of that drive, he would have simply answered that he had changed his mind. But he did not—instead he snapped back at her—"imagine, *she* wants him to clean the garage!" Jack projected his own desire and then experienced it as pressure, so that his wife's innocent inquiry did not just *inform* Jack, it strongly *affected* Jack: he felt unduly pressured. And *that* is the crucial difference—what I see in other people is more-or-less correct if it only *informs* me, but it is definitely a projection if it strongly *affects* me emotionally. Thus if we are overly attached to somebody (or something) on the one hand, or if we emotionally avoid or hate someone on the other, then we are respectively either shadow-hugging or shadow-boxing, and the quaternary dualism-repression-projection has most definitely occurred.

The undoing of a projection represents a move or a shift "down" the spectrum of consciousness (from the Shadow to the Ego Level), for we are enlarging our area of identification by re-owning aspects of ourselves that we had previously alienated. And the first step, the primary step, is always to realize that what we thought the environment was mechanically doing to us is really *something we are doing to ourselves—we are responsible.*

Thus, if I am feeling anxiety, I would usually claim that I am a helpless victim of this tension, that people or situations in the environment are *causing* me to become anxious. The first step is to become fully aware of anxiety, to get in touch with it, to shake and jitter and gasp for air—to *really feel it,* invite it in, express it—and thus realize that I am responsible, that I am tensing, that I am blocking my excitement and therefore experiencing anxiety. I am doing this to myself, so that anxiety is an affair between me and me and not me and the environment. But this shift in attitude means that where formerly I alienated my excitement, split myself from it and then claimed to be a *victim* of it, I now am *taking responsibility for what I am doing to myself.*

If the first step in the "cure" of shadow projections is to take responsibility for the projections, then the second step is simply to *reverse* the direction of the projection itself and gently do unto others what we have heretofore been unmercifully doing unto ourselves. Thus, "The world rejects me" freely translates into "I reject, at least at this moment, the whole damn world!" "My parents want me to study" translates into "I want to study." "My poor mother needs me" becomes "I need to be close to her." "I'm afraid of being left alone" translates into "Damned if I'll give anybody the time of day!" "Everybody's always looking at me critically" becomes "I'm an interested critic of people."

We will return to these two basic steps of responsibility and reversal in just a moment, but at this point let us note that in all these cases of shadow projection we have "neurotically" tried to render our self-image acceptable by making it inaccurate. All of those facets of our self-image, our ego, which are incompatible with what we superficially believe to be our best interests, or all those aspects which do not mesh with the philosophic bands, or all those facets which are alienated in times of stress, impasse, or double-bind—all of that self-potential is abandoned. As a result we narrow our identity to only a fraction of our ego, namely, to the distorted and impoverised *persona.* And so by the same stroke are we doomed to be haunted forever by our own Shadow, which we now refuse to give even the briefest conscious hearing. But the Shadow always has its say, for it forces entry into consciousness and anxiety, guilt, fear, and depression. The Shadow becomes symptom, and fastens itself to us as a vampire battens on its prey.

To speak somewhat figuratively, it may be said that we have split the *concordia discors* of the psyche into numerous polarities and contraries and opposites, all of which for convenience sake we have been referring to collectively as the quaternary dualism, that is, the split between the persona and the Shadow. In each of these cases, we associate ourselves with only "one-half" of the duality while casting the banished and usually despised opposite to the twilight world of the Shadow. The Shadow, therefore, exists precisely as the *opposite* of whatever we, as persona, consciously and deliberately believe to be the case.

Thus it stands to good reason that if you would like to know just how your Shadow views the world, then—as a type of personal experiment— simply *assume exactly the opposite of whatever you consciously desire, like, feel, want, intend, or believe.* In this way you may consciously contact, express, play, and ultimately re-own your opposites. After all, you will own them, or they will own you—the Shadow always has its say. This, if anything, is what we have learned from every example in this chapter: we may wisely *be aware* of our opposites, or we will be forced to *beware* of them.

Now to play the opposites, to be aware of and eventually re-own our Shadows, is not necessarily to *act* on them! It seems that nearly every person is most reluctant to confront his opposites for fear they might overpower him. And yet it's rather just the other way round: we end up, totally against our will, following the dictates of the Shadow only when it's unconscious.

To make any valid decision or choice we must be fully aware of both sides, of both opposites, and if one of the alternatives is unconscious, our decision will probably be a less than wise one. In all areas of psychic life, as this and every example in this chapter has shown, we must confront our opposites and re-own them—and that doesn't necessarily mean to *act* on them, just to be *aware* of them.

By progressively confronting one's opposites, it becomes more and more obvious—and this point can hardly be repeated too often—that since the Shadow is a real and integral facet of the ego, all of the "symptoms" and discomforts that the Shadow seems to be inflicting on us are really symptoms and discomforts which we are inflicting on ourselves, however much we may consciously protest to the contrary. *It is very, very much as if I, for instance, were deliberately and painfully pinching myself but pretending not to!* Whatever my symptoms on this level may be—guilt, fear, anxiety, depression—all are strictly the result of my "mentally" pinching myself in one fashion or another. And this directly implies, incredible as it may seem, that *I want this painful symptom, whatever its nature, to be here just as much as I want it to depart!*

Thus, the first opposite you might try confronting is your secret and shadowed desire to keep and maintain your symptoms, your unawares desire to pinch yourself. And may we be impudent enough to suggest that the more ridiculous this sounds to you, the more out of touch you might be with your Shadow, with that side of you that *is* doing the pinching?

Hence, to ask, "How can I get rid of this symptom?" is to goof immediately, for that implies that it is not *you* who are producing it! It is tantamount to asking, "How can I stop pinching myself?" As long as you are asking how to stop pinching yourself, or as long as you are *trying* to stop pinching yourself, then you quite obviously have not seen that it is *you* who are doing the pinching! And so the pain remains or even increases. For if you clearly see that you are pinching yourself, you don't ask how to stop—you just stop, instantly! To put it bluntly, the reason the symptom doesn't depart is that you are trying to make it depart. This is why Perls stated that as long as you fight a symptom, it will get worse. Deliberate change never works, for it excludes the Shadow.

Thus, the problem is *not* to get rid of any symptom, but rather to deliberately and consciously try to increase that symptom, to deliberately and consciously experience it fully! If you are depressed, try to be more depressed. If you are tense, make yourself even tenser. If you feel guilty, increase your feelings of guilt—and we mean that literally! For by so doing you are, for the very first time, acknowledging and even aligning yourself with your Shadow, and hence are doing consciously what you have heretofore been doing unconsciously. When you, as a personal experiment, consciously throw every bit of yourself into actively and deliberately trying to produce your present symptoms, you have in effect *thrown your persona and Shadow together.* You have consciously contacted and aligned yourself with your opposites, and, in short, re-discovered your Shadow.

So, deliberately and consciously increase any present symptom to the point where you consciously see that *you* are and always have been doing it, whereupon, for the first time, you are spontaneously free to cease. If you can make yourself *more* guilty, it dawns on you that you can make yourself *less* guilty, but in a remarkably spontaneous way. If you are free to depress yourself, you are free not to. My father used to cure hiccups instantly by producing a twenty-dollar bill on the spot and demanding in return that the victim immediately hiccup just one more time. So also, allowed anxiety is no longer anxiety, and the easiest way to "un-tense" a person is to challenge him to be as tense as he possibly can. In all cases, conscious adherence to a symptom delivers you from the symptom.

But you mustn't worry about whether the symptom disappears or not—it will but don't worry about it. To play your opposites for the sole reason of trying to erase a symptom is to fail miserably at playing your opposites. In other words, don't play the opposites half-heartedly and then anxiously check to see whether or not the symptom has vanished. If you hear yourself saying, "Well, I tried to make the symptom worse, but it still didn't go away and I wish like hell it would!" then you have not contacted the Shadow at all, but merely rifled off some quick-fire lip service to placate the gods and demons. You must become those demons, until with the entire force of your conscious attention you are deliberately and purposefully producing and holding on to your symptoms.

So in contacting my symptoms and deliberately trying to identify with them, I will want to keep in mind that any particular symptom—if it has an emotional nucleus—is the visible form of a Shadow which contains not only the opposite quality but also the opposite direction. Thus, if I feel terribly hurt and mortally wounded "because of" something Mr. X said to me, and I consequently am in agony—although I consciously harbor nothing but good will toward X—the first step is to realize that I am doing this to myself, that literally I am hurting myself. Taking responsibility for my own emotions, I am now in a position to reverse the direction of the projection and to see that my feelings of being hurt are precisely my own desire to hurt X. "I feel hurt by X" finally translates correctly into "I want to hurt X." Now this doesn't mean that I go out and thrash X to a pulp—the awareness of my anger is sufficient to integrate it (although I might like to brutalize a pillow instead). The point is that my symptom of agony reflects not only the opposite quality, but also the opposite direction. Hence, I will have to assume responsibility both for the anger (which is the opposite quality of my conscious goodwill toward X) *and* for the fact that the anger itself is *from* me *toward* X (which is the opposite of my conscious direction).

In a sense, then, we have *first*—in the case of projected emotions—to see that what we thought the environment was doing to us is really something we are doing to ourselves, that we are literally pinching ourselves; and then, as it were, to see that this is actually *our own disguised desire to pinch others!* And for the "desire to pinch others," substitute—according to your own projections—the desire to love others, hate others, touch others, tense others, possess others, look at others, murder others, contact others, squeeze others, capture others, reject others, give to others, take from others, play with others, dominate others, deceive others, elevate others. You fill in the blank, or rather, let your Shadow fill it.

Now this *second* step of reversal is absolutely essential. If the emotion is not fully discharged in the correct direction, you will very quickly slip back into the habit of turning that emotion back on yourself. So as you contact an emotion, such as hatred, every time you start to turn the hatred back on yourself, then play the opposite direction! Turn it out! That is now your choice: to pinch or to be pinched, to look or to be looked at, to reject or to be rejected.

Taking back our projections is somewhat simpler—but not necessarily easier—when it comes to projected qualities, traits, or ideas, because they do not themselves involve a direction, at least not one as pronounced and as moving as that of the emotions. Rather, positive or negative traits, such as wisdom, courage, bitchiness, wickedness, stinginess, and so on, seem to be relatively much more static. Thus we have only to worry about the quality itself, and not so much about any direction of the quality. Of course, once these qualities are projected, we may react to them in a violently emotional manner—and then we may even project these reactive emotions, and then react to them, and so on in a dizzying whirl of shadow-boxing. And it may well be that no qualities or ideas are projected unless emotionally charged. Be all that as it may, considerable re-integration can nevertheless be accomplished if we simply consider the projected qualities by themselves.

As always, the projected traits—just like the projected emotions—will be all those items we "see" in others that don't merely inform us but strongly affect us. Usually these will be the qualities which we imagine another to possess and which we utterly loathe, qualities we are always itching to point out and violently condemn. Never mind that we are but flinging our condemnations at our own little black heart, hoping thereby to exorcise it. Occasionally the projected qualities will be some of our own virtues, so that we cling to those onto whom we hang our goodies, frequently attempting to feverishly guard and monopolize the chosen person. The fever comes, of course, from the powerful desire to hold onto aspects of our own selves.

In the last analysis, projections come in all flavors. In any case, these projected qualities—just like the projected emotions—will always be the opposite of those we consciously fancy ourselves to possess. But unlike the emotions, these traits themselves do not have a direction, and thus their integration is straightforward. In the very first step of playing your opposites, you will come to see that what you love or despise in others are only the qualities of your own Shadow. It is not an affair between you and others but between you and you. Playing your opposites you touch the Shadow, and in so understanding that you are pinching yourself, you stop. There is no direction to the projected traits themselves, and so their integration does not demand the second step of reversal.

And so it is that through playing our opposites, through giving the Shadow equal time, that we eventually extend our identity, and thus our responsibility, to all aspects of the psyche, and not just to the impoverished persona. In this fashion, the split between the persona and Shadow is "wholed and healed."

. . . .

59 · EATING THE SHADOW

ROBERT   BLY

It is proper to ask then, "How does one go about eating the shadow or retrieving a projection, practically?"

In daily life one might suggest making the sense of smell, taste, touch, and hearing more acute, making holes in your habits, visiting primitive tribes, playing music, creating frightening figures in clay, playing the drum, being alone for a month, regarding yourself as a genial criminal. A woman might try being a patriarch at odd times of the day, to see how she likes it, but it has to be playful. A man might try being a witch at odd times of the day, and see how it feels, but it has to be done playfully. He might develop a witch laugh and tell fairy stories, as the woman might develop a giant laugh and tell fairy stories.

For the man, when he figures out which woman or women are holding his witch, he can go to that woman, greet her cordially, and say, "I want my witch back. Give it to me." A curious smile will come over her face, and she may hand it back or she may not. If she does the man should excuse himself, turn to the left, facing the wall, and eat it. A woman might go to her mother with a similar request, for mothers often hold a daughter's witch, as a form of power. A woman might go to her father and say, "You have my giant. I want it back." Or she may go to an old teacher or ex-husband (or husband) and say,

"You have my negative patriarch. I want him back." Even if the person who carries the witch or giant or dwarf is dead, the encounter is often helpful.

There are many other ways to eat the shadow, or retrieve the projection, or lessen the length of the bag we drag behind us, and we all know dozens of them. I'll mention the use of careful language, by which I mean language that is accurate and has a physical base. Using language consciously seems to be the most fruitful method of retrieving shadow substance scattered out on the world. Energy we have sent out is floating around beyond the psyche; and one way to pull it back into the psyche is by the rope of language. Certain kinds of language are nets, and we need to use the net actively, throwing it out. If we want our witch back we write about her; if we want our spiritual guide back we write about the spiritual guide rather than passively experience the guide in another person. Language contains retrieved shadow substance of all of our ancestors, as Isaac Bashevis Singer or Shakespeare makes clear. If language doesn't seem right at the moment, painting or sculpture may be right, or making images with watercolors. When we paint the witch with conscious intention, we soon find out whose house she's in. So the fifth stage involves activity, imagination, hunting, asking. "Always cry for what you want."

People who are passive toward their projected material contribute to the danger of nuclear war, because every bit of energy that we don't actively engage with language or art is floating somewhere in the air above the United States, and Reagan can use it. He has a big energy sweeper that pulls it in. No one should make you feel guilty for not keeping a journal, or creating art, but such activity helps the whole world. What did Blake say?—"No person who is not an artist can be a Christian." He means that a person who refuses to approach his own life actively, using language, music, sculpture, painting, or drawing is a caterpillar dressed in Christian clothes, not a human being. Blake himself engaged his shadow substance with three disciplines: painting, music, and language. He illuminated his own poems, and set them to music. There was no energy around him that politicians could use to project onto another country. One of the things we need to do as Americans is to work hard individually at eating our shadows, and so make sure that we are not releasing energy which can then be picked up by the politicians, who can use it against Russia, China, or the South American countries.

· · · · · · ·

60 · TAKING BACK THE DISOWNED SELF

NATHANIEL BRANDEN

How does a person arrive at the state of being disconnected from his own emotional experience, of being unable to feel what things mean to him?

To begin with, many parents *teach* children to repress their feelings. A little boy falls and hurts himself and is told sternly by his father, "Men don't cry." A little girl expresses anger at her brother, or perhaps shows dislike toward an older relative, and is told by her mother, "It's terrible to feel that way. You don't really feel it." A child bursts into the house, full of joy and excitement, and is told by an irritated parent, "What's wrong with you? Why do you make so much noise?" Emotionally remote and inhibited parents tend to produce emotionally remote and inhibited children—not only by the parent's overt communications but also by the example they set; their own behavior announces to the child what is "proper," "appropriate," "socially acceptable." Parents who accept the teachings of religion are very likely to infect their children with the disastrous notion that there are such things as "evil thoughts" or "evil emotions"—and thus fill the child with moral terror of his inner life.

Thus a child can be led to the conclusion that his feelings are potentially dangerous, that sometimes it is advisable to deny them, that they must be "controlled."

What the effort at such "control" amounts to practically is that a child learns to *disown* his feelings, which means: he ceases to experience them. Just as emotions are a psychosomatic experience, a mental and physical state, so the assault on emotions occurs on two levels. On the psychological level, a child ceases to acknowledge or recognize undesired feelings; he super-rapidly deflects his awareness away from them. On the physical level, he tenses his body, he induces muscular tensions, which have the effect of partially anesthetizing him, of making him numb, so that he is no longer readily able to feel his own inner state—as in the case of a child who tenses the muscles of his face and chest, and curtails his breathing, so as to wipe out the knowledge that he is hurt. Needless to say, this process does not take place by conscious, calculated decision; to some extent it is subconscious. But the process of self-alienation has begun; in denying his feelings, in nullifying his own judgments and evaluations; in repudiating his own experience, the child has learned to disown parts of his personality. (It must be understood that the process of learning to regulate behavior in a rational manner is a different issue entirely. Here we are concerned with *the censoring and denying of inner experience*.) There is more, however, to the story of how emotional repression develops.

For the majority of children, the early years of life contain many frightening and painful experiences. Perhaps a child has parents who never respond to his need to be touched, held and caressed; or who constantly scream at him or at each other; or who deliberately invoke fear and guilt in him as a means of exercising control; or who swing between over-solicitude and callous remoteness; or who subject him to lies and mockery; or who are neglectful and indifferent; or who continually criticize and rebuke him; or who overwhelm him with bewildering and contradictory injunctions; or who present him with expectations and demands that take no cognizance of his knowledge, needs or interests; or who subject him to physical violence; or who consistently discourage his efforts at spontaneity and self-assertiveness.

A child does not have a conceptual knowledge of his own needs nor does he have sufficient knowledge to comprehend the behavior of his parents. But at times his fear and pain may be experienced as overwhelming and incapacitating. And so, in order to protect himself, in order to remain able to function—in order to survive, it may seem to him—he often feels, wordlessly and helplessly, that he must escape from his inner state, that contact with his emotions has become intolerable. And so he denies his feelings. The fear and the pain are not permitted to be experienced, expressed and thus discharged; they are frozen into his body, barricaded behind walls of muscular and physiological tension, and a pattern of reaction is inaugurated that will tend to recur again and again when he is threatened by a feeling he does not wish to experience.

It is not only negative feelings that become blocked. The repression extends to more and more of his emotional capacity. When one is given an anesthetic in preparation for surgery, it is not merely the capacity to experience pain that is suspended; the capacity to experience pleasure goes also—because what is blocked is the capacity to experience *feeling*. The same principle applies to the repression of emotions.

It must be recognized, of course, that emotional repression is a matter of degree; in some individuals it is far more profound and pervasive than in others. But what remains true for everyone is that to diminish one's capacity to experience pain is to diminish also one's capacity to experience pleasure.

It is not difficult to establish that the average person carries within him the burden of an enormous quantity of unacknowledged and undischarged pain—not only pain originating in the present, but pain originating in the early years of his life.

One evening, discussing this phenomenon with some colleagues, I was challenged by a young psychiatrist who felt I was exaggerating the magnitude of the problem in the general population. I asked him if he would be willing to cooperate in a demonstration. He was an intelligent but somewhat diffident person; he spoke quietly, almost reticently, as though he doubted that anyone present could really be interested in his opinion. He said he would be glad to volunteer, but he warned me that if I were proposing to explore his childhood I might be disappointed and defeat my purpose, even if my general thesis was correct, because he had had an exceptionally happy childhood. His parents, he said, had always been marvelously responsive to his needs, so perhaps he was not a good subject for my demonstration and it might be better to ask for another volunteer. I replied that I would like to work with him; he laughed and invited me to proceed.

I explained that I wanted him to do an exercise that I had developed for use with my clients in therapy. I asked him to sit back in his chair, relax his body, let his arms rest at his sides, and close his eyes.

"Now," I said, "I want you to accept the following situation. You are lying on a bed in a hospital and you are dying. You are your present age. You are not in physical pain, but you are aware of the fact that in a few hours your life will end. Now, in your imagination, look up and see your mother standing at the side of the bed. Look at her face. There is so much unsaid between you. Feel the presence of all the unsaid between you—all the things you have never told her, all the thoughts and feelings you have never expressed. If ever you would be able to reach your mother, it is now. If ever she would hear you, it is now. Talk to her. Tell her."

As I was speaking, the young man's hands clenched into fists, blood rushed to his face, and one could see the muscular tension around his eyes and forehead that was aimed at suppressing tears. When he spoke, it was a younger voice and much more intense, and his words were a rising moan, as he said: "When I spoke to you, *why didn't you ever listen to me? . . .Why didn't you ever listen?"*

At that point, I stopped him from continuing, although it was obvious he had much more to say. I did not wish to carry the demonstration further because to do so would have meant invading his privacy. This was not the occasion to do psychotherapy and I had not been requested to do it; but it would have been interesting to point out to him the possible relationship between the frustration of his need to be listened to as a child and his over-reserved personality as an adult. After a moment he opened his eyes, shook his head, looked astonished and a bit sheepish, and glanced at me with an expression that conceded the point.

Let me mention that the full use of this technique involves having the subject or client confront *both* of his parents, one after the other. Sometimes, in addition, he is requested to imagine the presence of an ideal mother or father, in contrast with his actual parents, and to ask that ideal mother or father for whatever he wants. This can be very helpful in putting a person in touch with early frustrated needs that have been denied and repressed. (Further, the exercise is usually conducted with the person lying on the floor, legs uncrossed and arms spread wide, because it has been found that when a person lies in a position of physical defenselessness there is a tendency for psychological defenses to weaken.)

Returning to the young psychiatrist, I want to draw attention to the fact that there was no question of his consciously lying about his childhood. It was obvious that he had been speaking sincerely when he spoke of it as happy; but in repressing his early pain, he was disowning certain of his own legitimate needs, disowning important feelings, therefore disowning a part of himself. The consequence for him as an adult was not only emotional impairment but also a thinking impairment, since any attempt he might have made to relate his past to his present, or to understand his reticent personality, would be hampered by distorted judgments; and further, distorted judgments necessarily obstruct his present effectiveness in human relationships.

In repressing significant memories, evaluations, feelings, frustrations, longings and needs, a person denies himself access to crucial data; in attempting to think about his life and his problems he is sentenced to struggle in the dark—because key items of information are missing. Further, the need to *protect* his repression, to *maintain* his defenses, operates subconsciously to keep his mind away from "dangerous" avenues of thought—avenues of thought that might lead to a "stirring up" or a re-activating of submerged and feared material. Distortion and rationalization are virtually inevitable.

Sometimes a client exhibits considerable resistance in working with this exercise; he fears to enter into it completely. But observing the particular form of a client's resistance can itself be illuminating.

I recall an occasion when I was invited to demonstrate this technique at a group therapy session conducted by a colleague. At first the woman with whom I was working addressed her father in a detached, impersonal voice; she was quite cut off from the emotional meaning of her own words. Gradually this defense began to dissolve, as I pressed her with such questions as, "But how does a five-year-old girl *feel* when her daddy treats her like this?" Then as she descended deeper into her emotions, she began to cry; one could see the hurt and anger on her face. However, just when she seemed prepared to let go completely, she abruptly pulled back to a more impersonal manner, obviously frightened by what she was experiencing, and said in a tone of self-reproach, "But actually it's silly of me to blame you—you couldn't help it—you had your own problems and you just didn't know how to handle children." When I explained that no issue of "blame" was involved, that all that mattered was for us to know what had happened and what she had felt about it, she seemed reassured and began again to descend into her emotions, and she spoke more forcefully about what had happened to her and what she had been made to feel; but always, just when she seemed about to explode with anger, it was as though some cut-off mechanism was activated, her impersonal voice returned and she again offered "excuses" to justify the treatment she had received. She was not yet ready to let go of her defenses.

To permit herself fully to experience her anger would have been unbearably threatening. It would have made her feel guilty to harbor such rage against her parents. It would have caused her to feel that if they somehow learned of her feelings, she would lose them forever. And further, if she permitted herself to follow her anger down to the bottom of her emotions, she would have had to face the enormity of the hurt and frustration lying there— and she was not yet prepared to face that, not only because the pain was so excruciating, but also because she would then have to confront the full reality of her *aloneness,* the full reality of the fact that the little girl who had been herself had not had, and now would never have, the parents she wanted and needed.

I can recall another instance when a client's block, at a certain point in the exercise, was as eloquent as anything that could have been revealed. The event took place about a month after the client—a man in his middle twenties— entered group therapy. He was one of the most physically tense and rigid persons with whom I have ever worked. His chief complaint was his utter incapacity to feel, or to know what he wanted out of life, or to know what career he wished to pursue. He informed me that he was incapable of crying. As we began the exercise, he spoke of his father in a soft, timid voice, describing the fear he had always felt at his father's remoteness and unyielding severity. Then I suggested that perhaps at times a young boy would feel rage toward a parent who treated him so cruelly. Then his whole body shuddered, and he shouted, "I can't talk about that!" "What would happen," I asked, "if you told him about your anger?" Tears suddenly streaming down his face, he screamed, "I'm afraid of him! I'm afraid of what he'll do to me! He'll kill me!"

His father had died nearly twenty years ago, when my client was six years old.

During the weeks that followed, I did not call upon him to perform this particular exercise again. Predominantly, I merely let him watch while I worked with others in his group. But now he cried at nearly every session, as he watched one client after another reconfront early traumatic experiences. He became more and more able to remember and talk about events in his childhood, and to do so with emotional involvement. As the weeks went by, one could observe the growing relaxation of his body, the gradual dissolving of tensions, and the reawakening of his capacity to feel. As he permitted himself to experience his formerly disowned needs and frustrations, he discovered within himself desires, responses and aspirations of which he had had no knowledge. Within a few months his passion for a particular career, which he had repressed long ago, was reborn.

· · · · · · ·

61 · DIALOGUE WITH THE DEMONIC SELF

HAL STONE AND SIDRA WINKELMAN

In learning to deal with demonic energies, one basic principle should be followed: The way to work with disowned instinctual energies that have become demonic is to *wait before working with them*. It is essential to first work for a considerable period of time with the primary selves who fear and are opposed to demonic energies. They have been protecting the individual since early childhood from these energies because they perceived them as dangerous. Demonic energies continue to be dangerous until such time as an aware ego is able to handle them as well as the more controlled, rational selves. It is also crucial to avoid being seduced by a subject who says: "I want to work with my demonic." These are not energies to be tampered with.

It is a paradox, we realize, to say that the key to exploring demonic energies is to not explore them, but this approach keeps the work safe and grounded. Having prepared by working with the primary selves, at the right moment the facilitator and subject can begin to explore some of these disowned instinctual energies. The role of the vulnerable child must not be overlooked, either. This self often fears the expression of demonic energies because it either fears abandonment or envisions some catastrophic retaliation.

Aside from the primary selves and the vulnerable child, many other parts of the personality have been conditioned by society to negate demonic energies, including the rational voice, the pleaser, and the spiritual voice. With such a well-developed barricade of selves to face, it is no wonder that demonic energies constitute one of the most profoundly negated psychic systems we will encounter in the evolution of consciousness.

The more energy we invest in holding back these energies, the more drained we become, physically and psychically. The African Bushmen have a saying that one should never go to sleep on the veldt because it means there is a large animal nearby. When we first heard Laurens van der Post make this statement, we were struck by its psychological implications. Exhaustion and fatigue, more often than not, are a function of strong instincts (animals) that are being disowned.

We worked with a woman who found the Bushmen's statement to be literally true. She discovered she had disowned her anger so totally that when she was deeply irritated by her husband, she experienced not anger but overwhelming desire to go to sleep. When she learned her drowsiness was a substitute for natural aggression, she began to search for the anger concealed by her overwhelming fatigue. As soon as she became aware of her anger voice and learned what it wanted, the drowsiness dissappeared.

If the lion in us wishes to roar but the goat bleats instead, we must pay for this substitution in one way or another. Payment will vary: For some, it will be experienced as depression, a loss of energy and enthusiasm, or a growing unconsciousness. For others, it can be uncontrollable, seemingly irrational behavior, during which life, fortune, profession, or marriage may be risked. In its most extreme form, the price may be a physical breakdown that can lead to illness or even death.

On a broader, more planetary level, disowning demonic energies contributes to the pain and darkness in the world. But the darkness of our world cannot be lit by love unless that love is an expression of an aware ego that can also encompass these demonic energies.

If an animal is kept locked in a cage for many years, it will become wild. If the door is opened inadvertently, the animal comes out raging. From this, its keeper accurately concludes that the animal is inherently dangerous. But this is not necessarily so. The danger is, at least in part, a result of the long imprisonment.

So it is with our instinctual life—those selves who fear instinct help lock our instinctual energies in a cage where they eventually become demonic. Periodically these energies erupt in vicious ways. The "keeper of instincts" within us tells us that this viciousness is proof that the animals inside us are bad. If we listen to the keeper, we will force our animal/instinctual nature back into the cage.

It requires great courage to allow the voice of the demonic to speak, for so much of what it has to say is unacceptable to our traditional values. We are challenged to allow this power energy to speak while we honor that part of ourselves that is fearful. The protector/controller's fear of the demonic is legitimate, for it possesses an enormous potential for destruction. The longer and more powerfully the demonic is negated, the greater its capacity to destroy.

Entering into a Voice Dialogue session involving demonic energies requires real choice. The following are possible leads for entering into Voice Dialogue with demonic energies.

May I talk to the part of Sue who would like to be able to do what she wants whenever she wants?

May I speak with the not-nice Ruth?

May I speak with the part of Ralph that would like to rule the world?

May I talk to the part of Lorna that would like to be a hooker?

Might I talk to the part of you that would like to be all-powerful?

Might I talk to the part of you that feels like killing insensitive people?

All of these are lead-ins to disowned energy patterns that are usually related to repressed instinctual energies. They are difficult voices for the vast majority of people. Facilitators must be flexible and alert enough to ask for the self that a particular subject is comfortable to bring out. The way the voice is invited to speak must be strong enough to evoke the disowned energies but not so strong that it threatens the subject's protector/controller.

SENSUALITY

For years, Sandra was plagued by a repetitive nightmare of being chased by wild animals, particularly feline animals. She began therapy and in an early dialogue session the facilitator asked to talk with her cat nature.

CAT VOICE:
She doesn't know me or like me.

FACILITATOR:
Why not?

CAT VOICE:
She's afraid of what would happen if I were around.

FACILITATOR:
Well, let's imagine that you were around all the time. What would you do? What would happen?

CAT VOICE:
I'd preen a lot. I'd take hot baths all the time—hot sudsy baths with smelly things in them. I'd eat when I wanted, not when others wanted. I'd never, never cook for anyone, unless I wanted to cook. Then I'd make sure the man

was with me while I was cooking, and I'd make sure he was making love to me all the time. That's another thing. I'd make love all the time. I'd never stop. I'd use all kinds of exotic oils and I'd massage myself all over.

Sandra had grown up conditioned to identify with being a proper lady. In her marriage, she was identified with being a good mother and a pleasing daughter. Her sensual Aphrodite nature had long been eradicated from her awareness. She was not allowed to be selfish, sensual, or self-indulgent. Fortunately for Sandra, her unconscious maintained its pressure. Over and over again, her feline nature appeared in her nightmares, chasing her like the aggressive demon it had become. A few nights after this dialogue session, she had the following dream:

> I'm again walking down the street; it feels very familiar. I'm aware again of the fear reaction and the sense of being followed. I know the cat is there. I start to run. Then I stop. I am tired of running. I turn around to face my pursuer. It is a lion. It comes racing up to me and then stops and licks my face. Why have I always been so afraid . . . ?

Because Sandra had been identified with a good girl/pleaser psychology all her life, it is no wonder that her natural instincts were negated. Having been rejected, they are now enraged; because she refused to look at them, they grew in power and authority. This made it even harder and more frightening for her to face them and listen to their demands.

What is remarkable about this whole process is that when we have the courage to look at our disowned parts, they change. The raging lion licks our face. He does not need to take over our personality; he only needs to be honored, to be heard, to be allowed to speak.

THE DEMONIC VOICE

John was considering a serious career change after practicing as an attorney for twelve years. Following the rather nasty breakup of his marriage, he became involved in a spiritual process that led him to feel he should give up his law practice. His spiritual self, with the support of a spiritual teacher John had become involved with, told him he needed more time for his spiritual development. His meditations inspired a number of profound experiences, but he felt an inner doubt about so radical a change. A number of his friends felt he had become too one-sided, so he sought help to find more of a balance in his life.

After an initial period of discussion, John's therapist asked to talk to John's spiritual voice. This voice spoke at great length about John's spiritual process, how much he had changed, and his need for time to devote to more introverted pursuits. The voice was quite positive and supportive and pointed out a clear direction for John's life. The therapist then asked John if another voice was available to speak with, one that would be the opposite of the spiritual self. What emerged was the voice of power, an energy John referred to as his demonic side.

THERAPIST (TO DEMONIC VOICE):
How do you feel about John's decision to give up his law practice?

DEMONIC:
I resent it and reject it. That son of a bitch has rejected me all his life. Then he gets into this spiritual trip and I go down another 2,000 feet into the earth.

THERAPIST:
Why are you so angry at the spiritual side? It has some very good ideas and John has been helped considerably by it.

DEMONIC:
I'm angry because I'm left out. Whatever I'm not part of is crap. His marriage was bullshit because I wasn't a part of it. I'm glad his wife nailed him. He deserved it. He was always the angel and she was the bitch. That's because I was buried. I'm telling you something—his blood is made of saccharin.

THERAPIST:
Have you always been this angry with John?

DEMONIC:
Look, wise up. I'm angry because he ignores me. He's Mr. Nice Guy. So long as he tries to act like Jesus Christ, I will do everything I can do to defeat him. All I want is to be acknowledged.

THERAPIST:
What would it mean for John to acknowledge you? I mean this in a very practical way. What does acknowledgment mean?

DEMONIC:
Right now he thinks I don't exist—that I'm not real. Before he got into this spiritual stuff he just rejected me. Now he's learned that I'm supposed to be transmuted. How would you feel if every time you expressed yourself someone tried to transmute you into something better or higher? It's insulting.

THERAPIST:
Well, I'm still not sure what it would mean on a very practical level.

DEMONIC:
I don't like his passivity with his wife. She controls everything in regard to the children. He thinks that by being nice, everything will get better. Well, it's not getting better. It's getting worse. And before he signs the final property settlement I suggest he listen to me. Mr. Nice Guy is giving her ten times too much. I also don't like some of the people in his group. I'd like him to listen to me, to take me seriously, to honor what I have to say.

John's demonic voice was like a caged animal—filled with the power and energy of being rejected for a lifetime. His marriage ended in disaster, in part because he forced his wife to carry the demonic side of himself. Because John had been unable to show his anger, negativity, or selfishness, it became necessary for her to express these points of view. Conversely, as she became more identified with these patterns, he was thrown ever more deeply into an identification with his peaceful and loving selves. It soon became apparent to everyone that his wife was the demon and he was the good guy. How often our mates and partners live out our disowned selves in this same manner.

John had slipped very easily into the spiritual mode. It was a natural way of expressing his very loving and positive nature. Unfortunately, his awareness was identified with these spiritual energies. Furthermore, the spiritual voices were identified with his previous "nice guy" mode, which precluded all expressions of power, anger, negativity, and selfishness. No wonder this voice was enraged!

It takes great courage to face our disowned demonic patterns. The energies of these selves have lived in isolation for years, like lepers shunned by regular society. When we see people who embody these qualities, we avoid them if possible. They are reprehensible to us. How easy, and yet how difficult, it is to take the next step to recognize that those people whom we cannot stand are clear reflections of our negated parts.

· · · · · · ·

62 · TAMING THE SHAMEFUL INNER VOICE

JOHN   BRADSHAW

As a formerly shame-based person, I have to work hard at total self-acceptance. Part of the work of self-acceptance involves the integration of our shame-bound feelings, needs and wants. Most shame-based people feel ashamed when they need help; when they feel angry, sad, fearful or joyous; and when they are sexual or assertive. These essential parts of us have been split off.

We try to act like we are not needy. We pretend we don't feel what we feel. I think of all the times I've said I feel fine when I was sad or hurting. We either numb out our sexuality and act very puritanical, or we use sexuality to avoid all other feelings and needs. In all cases we are cut off from vital parts of ourselves. These disowned parts appear most commonly in our dreams and in our projections. This is especially true of our sexuality and natural instincts.

Jung called these disowned aspects of ourselves our shadow side. Without integrating our shadow, we cannot be whole.

THE INNER VOICE

Negative self-talk is the internal dialogue that Robert Firestone calls the "inner voice." The inner voice has been described by others in different ways. Eric Berne referred to it as a set of parental recordings that are like cassette tapes. Some have estimated that there are 25,000 hours of these tapes in a normal person's head. Fritz Perls and the Gestalt school call these voices "introjected parental voices." Aaron Beck calls them "automatic thoughts." Whatever you call them, all of us have some voices in our heads. Shame-based people especially have dominant negative shaming, self-depreciating voices.

The voice basically tells a shame-based person that they are unlovable, worthless and bad. The voice supports the bad child image. The voice may be experienced consciously as a thought. Most often it is partially conscious or totally unconscious. Most of us are unaware of the habitual activity of the voice. We become aware of it in certain stressful situations of exposure when our shame is activated. After making a mistake, one might call oneself a "stupid fool." Or say, "There I go again. I'm such a blundering klutz." Before an important job interview, the voice might torment you with thoughts like, "What makes you think you could handle the responsibility of a job like this? Besides, you're too nervous. They'll know how nervous you are."

Actually getting rid of the voices is extremely difficult because of the original rupturing of the interpersonal bridge and the resulting fantasy bond. As children are abandoned, and the more severely they are abandoned (neglected, abused, enmeshed), the more they create the illusion of connection with the parent. The illusion is what Robert Firestone calls the "Fantasy Bond."

In order to create the fantasy bond the child has to idealize his parents and make himself "bad." The purpose of this fantasy bonding is survival. The child desperately relies on his parents. They can't be bad. If they are bad or sick, he can't survive. So the fantasy bond (which makes them good and the child bad) is like a mirage in the desert. It gives the child the illusion that there is nourishment and support in his life. Years later when the child leaves the parent, the fantasy bond is set up internally. It is maintained by means of the voice. What was once external, the parent's screaming, scolding and punishing voice, now becomes internal. For this reason the process of confronting and changing the inner voice creates a great deal of anxiety. But as Firestone points out, "There is no deep-seated therapeutic change without this accompanying anxiety."

The voice is mostly constituted by the shame-based shut-down defenses of the primary caretakers. Just as the shame-based parents cannot accept their own weakness, wants, feelings, vulnerability and dependency needs, they cannot accept their children's neediness, feelings, weakness, vulnerability and dependency. Firestone writes that the voice is the result of the "parents' deeply repressed desire to destroy the aliveness and spontaneity of the child whenever he or she intrudes on their defenses."

Robert Firestone has done pioneering work in identifying the origins and destructiveness of the voice. He has developed some powerful ways to bring these hostile thoughts into the patient's awareness. He writes that the "process of formulating and verbalizing negative thoughts acts to lessen the destructive effect of the voice on the patient's behavior."

In voice therapy patients are taught to *externalize* their inner critical thoughts. By so doing they expose their self-attacks and ultimately develop ways to change their negative attitude into a more objective, nonjudgmental view. As the voice is externalized through verbalization, intense feelings are released which result in powerful emotional catharsis with accompanying insight.

OVER-REACTION DIARY

The first method I would suggest flows directly from the early work Firestone did in testing the triggering of the obsessive critical voice process. It involves keeping a diary of your defensive over-reactions. It is best done when you are involved in some kind of feedback share group. But it can also be done simply in the context of your daily interpersonal life.

Each evening before retiring, think back over the events of the day. Where were you upset? Where did you over-react? What was the context? Who was there? What was said to you? How does what was said to you compare with what you say to yourself?

For example, on December 16th my wife and I were talking about remodeling rooms in our house. At one point in the conversation, I felt my voice tone accelerating and intensifying. Soon I was ranting about the stresses that my current work entails. I heard myself saying, "Don't expect me to supervise this job. I can just barely keep up with my basic obligations." Later, I entered this outburst into my diary. I used the following form:

> *Date:* Wednesday, December 16, 8:45 p.m.
> *Content:* Discussion of improvement of a room in our house
> *Over-reaction:* After she said, "I'm going to need some help from you," I said in an increasingly agitated tone, "Don't expect me to supervise this job, etc."
> *Underlying Voices:* You're a rotten husband. You don't know how to fix anything. You're pathetic. Your house is falling apart. What a phony! Real men know how to fix things and build. Good fathers take care of their homes.

It's crucial to take time with the voices. I recommend you get in a relaxed state when it's quiet all around. Really let yourself listen to what you're saying to yourself. Write it down and then say it out loud. Be spontaneous about the expression of the voices. Once you start saying it out loud, you may be surprised at the automatic outpouring.

In Firestone's group work he encourages the person to express the sentiments aloud and emotionally. He will tell him, "Say it louder," or "Really let go." I encourage you to do the same. Blurt out spontaneously anything that comes to mind. Say it in the second person. Let yourself enter into the emotional voltage triggered by the voice.

ANSWERING THE VOICE

Once you've expressed the voice, you can start answering the voice. You challenge both the content and the dictates of the voice. In my diary entry I answered that I am a good husband and I've provided a fine home. My manhood doesn't depend on my doing anything. I work hard and I can afford to pay someone to fix my house. I would hire someone even if I knew how. I've better things to do with my time. Many fine men are carpenters and builders. Many are not.

I repeat this dialogue the next day. I always answer both emotionally and matter of factly (logically). *Firestone recommends that one take action by consciously not complying with the voice, or by directly going against it.* In my example, I called a carpenter I knew and told him exactly what I wanted and left him alone. I played golf and exulted that I could afford to hire someone to fix my house.

TRACKING DOWN THE INNER CRITIC

A second way to expose the shaming voices comes from Gestalt therapy. I simply call it *Tracking Down The Inner Critic.* An inner self-critical dialogue goes on in all shame-based people. This game has been called the "self-torture" game. It is almost always so habitual that it is *unconscious.* The following exercise will help you make it more conscious, and give you tools to become more self-integrating and self-accepting. I've taken this exercise from the book, *Awareness,* by John O. Stevens.

Sit comfortably and close your eyes . . . Now imagine that you are looking at yourself, sitting in front of you. Form some kind of visual image of yourself, sitting there in front of you, perhaps as if reflected in a mirror. How is this image sitting? What is this image of yourself wearing? What kind of facial expression do you see?

Now silently criticize this image of yourself as if you were talking to another person. (If you are doing this experiment alone, talk out loud.) Tell yourself what you should and shouldn't do. Begin each sentence with the words, "You should_____," "You shouldn't_____" or their equivalent. Make a long list of criticisms. Listen to your voice as you do this.

Now imagine that you change places with this image. Become this image of yourself and silently answer these criticisms. What do you say in response to these critical comments? And what does the tone of your voice express? How do you feel as you respond to these criticisms?

Now switch roles and become the critic again. As you continue this internal dialogue, be aware of what you say, and also how you say it, your words, your tone of voice, and so on. Pause occasionally to just listen to your own words and let yourself experience them.

Switch roles whenever you want to, but keep the dialogue going. Notice all the details of what is going on inside you as you do this. Notice how you feel, physically, in each role. Do you recognize anyone you know in the voice that criticizes you and says, "You shouldn't_____?" What else are you aware of in this interaction? Continue this silent dialogue for a few minutes longer. Do you notice any changes as you continue the dialogue?

Now just sit quietly and review this dialogue. Probably you experience some kind of split or conflict, some division between a powerful, critical, authoritative part of you that demands that you change, and another less powerful part of you that apologizes, evades and makes excuses. It is as though you are divided into a parent and a child. The parent or "topdog" always trying to get control to change you into something "better," and the child or "underdog" continually evading these attempts to change. As you listened to the voice that criticized and made demands on you, you may have recognized that it sounded like one of your parents. Or it might have sounded like someone else in your life who makes demands on you, i.e., your husband or wife, a boss, or some other authority figure who controls you.

This critical voice can be activated in any situation of vulnerability or exposure. Once activated, a shaming spiral is set in motion. And once in motion, this spiral has a power of its own. It is imperative to externalize this internal dialogue, since it is one of the major ways you keep yourself nonself-accepting and divided. This exercise helps make the critical dialogue conscious. This is a first step in externalizing the voice.

The second step is to take each of the critical messages and translate them into a concrete specific behavior. Instead of "You are selfish," say, "I didn't want to do the dishes." Instead of "You are stupid," say, "I do not understand algebra." Each critical statement is a generalization. As such, it is untrue. There are some times when everyone wants his own way. There are areas in life in which everyone is confused. By translating these generalizations (judgments, conditions or worth) into concrete specific behaviors, you can see a real picture of yourself and accept yourself in a more balanced and integrated way.

The third step is to take these generalizations (judgments, conditions of worth) and make positive statements that contradict them. For example, instead of saying, "I am selfish," say, "I am unselfish." It is important to verbalize this and hear yourself saying it. I recommend going to someone, a person in your support group, your best friend, your husband or wife and verbalizing the positive self-affirming statement to him/her. Be sure that the person you go to is a nonshaming person.

. . . .

63 · LEARNING ACTIVE IMAGINATION

BARBARA HANNAH

I remember a very wise woman telling me that, on a long tour through countries she had always wanted to visit, she was forced to share a room with another woman who was completely uncongenial to her. At first she felt this would inevitably spoil the tour. Then she realized that she would waste one of the most interesting and pleasurable times of her life if she allowed her dislike to spoil it. Therefore, she set herself to accept her uncongenial companion, detaching herself from her negative feelings and from the woman herself, while being friendly and kind toward her. This technique worked marvelously, and she managed to enjoy the tour immensely.

It is just the same with elements from the unconscious that we dislike and which we feel are very uncongenial to us. We spoil our own tour through life if we allow ourselves to resent them. If we can accept them for what they are and be friendly toward them, we often find they are not so bad after all; and at least we are spared their hostility.

The first figure we usually meet in the confrontation with the unconscious is the personal shadow. Since she (or he) mainly consists of what we have rejected in ourselves, she is usually quite as uncongenial to us as the woman's traveling companion was to her. If we are hostile to the unconscious, however, it will become more and more unbearable, but if we are friendly—realizing its right to be as it is—the unconscious will change in a remarkable way.

Once, when I had a dream of a shadow who was especially obnoxious to me but which, from previous experience, I was able to accept, Jung said to me, "Now your consciousness is less bright but much wider. You know that as an indisputably honest woman, you can also be dishonest. It may be disagreeable, but it is really a great gain." The further we go, the more we realize that every widening of consciousness is indeed the greatest gain we can make. Almost all of our difficulties in life come from our having too narrow a consciousness to meet and understand them, and nothing helps us more in understanding these difficulties than learning to contact them in active imagination.

The greatest use of active imagination is to put us into harmony with the Tao, so that the right things may happen around us instead of the wrong. Although speaking of the Chinese Tao may perhaps impart a rather exotic flavor to what is really a simple matter of everyday experience, we find the same meaning in our most colloquial language: "He got out of bed on the wrong side this morning" (or, as the Swiss say, "with the left foot first"). This expression aptly describes a psychological condition in which we did not arise in harmony with our own unconscious. We are ill-tempered and disagreeable, and—it follows as the night follows the day—we have a disintegrating effect on our environment.

We have all experienced the fact that our conscious intentions are constantly crossed by unknown—or relatively unknown—opponents in the unconscious. Perhaps the simplest definition of active imagination is to say that it gives us the opportunity of opening negotiations, and in time, coming to terms, with these forces or figures in the unconscious. In this aspect, it differs from the dream, for we have no control over our own behavior in the latter. Of course, with the majority of cases in practical analysis, the dreams are sufficient to reestablish a balance between conscious and unconscious. It is only in certain cases that more is required. But, before we proceed, I will provide a short description of the actual techniques that can be used in active imagination.

The first thing is to be alone, and as free as possible from being disturbed. Then one must sit down and concentrate on seeing or hearing whatever comes up from the unconscious. When this is accomplished, and often it is far from easy, the image must be prevented from sinking back again into the unconscious, by drawing, painting or writing down whatever has been seen or heard. Sometimes it is possible to express it best by movement or dancing. Some people cannot get into touch with the unconscious directly. An indirect approach that often reveals the unconscious particularly well is to write stories, apparently about other people. Such stories invariably reveal the parts of the storyteller's own psyche of which he or she is completely unconscious.

In every case, the goal is to get into touch with the unconscious, and that entails giving it an *opportunity to express itself* in some way or other. (No one who is convinced that the unconscious has no life of its own should even attempt the method.) To give it this opportunity it is nearly always necessary to overcome a greater or lesser degree of "conscious cramp" and to allow the fantasies, which are always more or less present in the unconscious, to come to consciousness. (Jung once told me that he thought the dream was always going on in the unconscious, but that it usually needs sleep and the complete cessation of attention to outer things for it to register in consciousness at all.) As a rule, the first step in active imagination is to learn, so to speak, to see or hear the dream while awake.

In other places, Jung includes movement and music among the ways through which it is possible to reach these fantasies. He points out that with movement—although sometimes of the greatest help in dissolving the cramp of consciousness—the difficulty lies in registering the movements themselves and, if there is no outer record, it is amazing how quickly things that come from the unconscious disappear again from the conscious mind.

Jung suggests the repetition of the releasing movements until they are really fixed in the memory and, even then, it is my experience that it is as well to draw the pattern made by the dance or movement, or to write a few words of description, to prevent it from disappearing altogether in a few days.

There is another technique in dealing with the unconscious by means of active imagination which I have always found of the greatest possible help: conversations with contents of the unconscious *that appear personified.*

It is, of course, very important to know *to whom* one is speaking, and not to take every voice as uttering the inspired words of the Holy Ghost! With visualization, this is comparatively easy. But it is also possible when there is no visualization, for one can learn to identify the voices, or the way of speaking, so that one never need make a mistake. Moreover, these figures are very paradoxical: they have positive and negative sides, and one will often interrupt the other. In this case, you can judge best by what is said.

There is one very important rule that should always be retained in every technique of active imagination. In the places where we enter it ourselves, we must give our full, conscious attention to what we say or do, just as much—or even more—than we would in an important outer situation. This will prevent it from remaining passive fantasy. But when we have done or said all that we want, we should be able to make our minds a blank, so that we can hear or see what the unconscious wants to say or do.

The technique for both the visual and the auditory methods consists first of all in being able to let things happen. But images must not be allowed to change like a kaleidoscope. If the first image is a bird, for instance, left to itself it may turn with lightning rapidity into a lion, a ship on the sea, a scene from a battle, or what not. The technique consists of keeping one's attention on the first image and not letting a bird escape until it has explained why it appeared to us, what message it brings us from the unconscious, or what it wants to know from us. Already we see the necessity of entering the scene or conversation ourselves. If this is omitted after we have once learned to let things happen, the fantasy will either change as just described, or—even if we hold onto the first image—it will remain a sort of passive cinema, or we listen as if it were the radio that speaks. To be able to let things happen is very necessary, but it soon becomes harmful if indulged in too long. The whole purpose of active imagination is to come to terms with the unconscious, and for that we must have it out with the unconscious, for which it is necessary to have one's own firm viewpoint.

. . . .

64 · DRAWING THE SHADOW

LINDA JACOBSON

A huge, dark figure appears in my idyllic garden. I
am terrified by him. Quaking, I realize that I am at his
disposal. I am his possession. It is my father, the man
who raped me repeatedly as a young girl. Barely able
to contain my tears, I draw an image of that leering
man in the doorway about to devour me unless I do his

> bidding. Then I draw the shadow of this figure—he
> who has haunted my years and cast a pall over my
> entire life.

One of my students, N.R., had this experience during a guided visualization on drawing the shadow. The visualizations are designed so that images will erupt spontaneously from the unconscious, the source of much artwork.

Exploring Jung's techniques of active imagination, you can use the images you "see" during guided visualization to gain access to parts to yourself that have been closed to conscious awareness. These images include imaginary characters and dream personalities, or people from daily life who symbolize those parts of yourself that feel uncomfortable or look unattractive. Typically they seem to be the opposite of your self-image. Not only negative, they represent those qualities that we have been conditioned to believe should remain unexpressed.

In making these images conscious through drawing, you can better visualize your disowned parts by seeing them first within someone else, as a safe and objective image on a piece of paper. When you can recognize these shadow qualities, then you also can incorporate more positive hidden qualities—such as power, sexuality, assertiveness, gentleness—and expand your sense of self in this way.

Before doing this visualization, create a supportive environment through a simple ritual with candles, flowers, or music. Then, close your eyes, follow your breath, and tell yourself:

> You are in a beautiful garden, either a place you have been before or a completely imaginary place. You feel the texture of a stone path beneath your feet as you walk. You notice the bright colors of flowers and plants, the clear blue sky, the soft white clouds, and the feeling of the gentle wind. Is the temperature cool or warm? Notice other sensory details.
>
> Then let yourself feel the sacredness of this place, its safety and power. You are full of a radiant light, a fulfilled human being.
>
> Next, you see a person who is the very one you don't want to see. (Pause) This individual pushes all your buttons and upsets you terribly. You don't even know why. This person is your opposite in every way. Is this a dream figure, someone you know, or a composite of different characters? What does he or she look like? What colors and moods surround him or her? Do you feel anger, fear, awe? hatred or respect? love or disgust?
>
> What is so offensive to you? When this person speaks, what is the sound of his or her voice? What does this person say? Is he or she critical? selfish? cruel? timid? sexy? arrogant?
>
> Take a moment to fully experience this shadow figure. Let your feelings permeate every cell of your body so that this being is clear in your mind. (Pause)
>
> Then, with your eyes closed, begin to draw the feeling. When you are ready, slowly open your eyes and continue your drawing for fifteen minutes.

After the guided visualization, you can create drawings of your experience with materials that are quick and easy to use, such as oil or chalk pastels.

Be spontaneous. Allow the images to surface without critical editing of your inner vision. Try to stay with the feeling of the visualization as you draw, not becoming interested in the formal concerns of art, not judging the quality of the work, but going for emotional expression.

You may draw either abstractly or representationally, allowing the images to change as you draw. It is not necessary to understand the significance of the image. The simple act of drawing is healing because you now have a conscious image of your shadow to work with.

If a frightening image appears, such as an abused victim or an angry tyrant, try to keep drawing. The point of pain may offer the greatest opportunity for renewal and can be used as raw creative energy.

From this initial drawing, you can develop a series of images of your shadow. The image and colors may change, taking many forms, reflecting the healing process.

Like many of my students, N.R. found that confronting her father's shadow side and her victimized inner child led to a growing realization of her own strength and self-confidence. Here are a few other exercises for working with the shadow:

- Do a drawing that integrates your shadow into the rest of your persona.
- Do a written dialogue with your shadow drawing to find out what it needs.
- Do a drawing of yourself from the shadow's point of view.

You, too, may find drawing the shadow to be a rich creative experience.

. . . .

65 · WRITING ABOUT THE OTHER

DEENA METZGER

The shadow—that darkness which is ours, which we cannot escape, but which is most difficult to contact because it is by its nature elusive—is the reflection of ourselves that occurs when there is no light. Therefore, to contact the shadow, we must be willing to go into the dark, for that is where it lives, in order to make a partnership with the unknown. If we do not move toward it, we run the risk that the shadow will come to us in a meeting that will be furtive and violent; yet moving toward it, we are overwhelmed by the fear of being engulfed. In the dark, we often feel as if we ourselves *are* the dark.

How, then, do we meet the shadow? By conceding that there are parts of ourselves that we consider absolutely foreign and alien, that we abhor, disdain, or deny, and admitting that these parts, horrific as they are, are still ourselves. To allow that there is a part of self that is both stranger and kin to us is to enter into one of the great mysteries of the psyche. This act in itself becomes a peace offering that encourages the shadow to emerge.

We are all aware that the shadow lengthens as day falls, that toward the moment of twilight it is at its fullest. There is a moment in writing that resembles this twilight, the time when the noon light of reason has diminished. Under these conditions, the shadow is likely to respond to a call to manifest itself because here it can hold its own against that light which could annihilate it altogether and which, therefore, it avoids, refusing to appear, perhaps retreating even further.

With these ideas in mind, I formulated a series of questions, imaginal exercises, to engage the shadow through writing and developing characters and stories. Because these questions put the self and the shadow at equal risk, I have found that they coax the shadow into revealing itself.

The first questions begin to define the territory in which the shadow resides, in which we acknowledge that the shadow is a continuum of ourselves, that which we become when we go to the other side. It is our other face.

What are those qualities or attributes in others that you find least like yourself? Remember a time when you felt hate. Are there others who may hate you? What are your most intractable prejudices? With what group do you feel least affinity? Who are the people you could not and would not imagine being because they revolt, offend, terrify, or enrage you or are beneath you, are grotesque? Under what circumstances would you feel too humiliated to continue living? What horror within yourself would you find unbearable?

When we examine our responses, we see that some aversions are based upon moral or ethical principles, but other disaffinities are charged with repugnance, contempt, loathing, revulsion, nausea. The latter live in the realm of the shadow. From these qualities, then, allow a character to formulate itself, someone with a name, a personality, and a history. Enter into dialogue with this person, allowing intimacy, confidence, and revelation to occur, until you seemingly know everything about the person—where he lives, what her house looks like, what he eats for lunch, what she thinks, what he fears, what she wants, dreams. Be as truthful and forthcoming as you wish the shadow to be.

Here is another entryway to meeting this inner character: Imagine that your life is threatened and in order to escape the threat, you must create another identity, a false cover.

The cover must be perfect, an identity so like yourself and yet so different that you can be perfectly disguised while living the life of this other. As you take on this life, it will have qualities of being completely alien to you, yet comfortable and familiar. Who is the character you become in order to disguise yourself and thereby save your life? Imagine yourself invisible and follow through every moment of the character's day or week, observing him or her alone and with others. What does this other think when unable to sleep at 3:00 AM? What secrets, griefs, insights are you privy to? What essential part of your self is covered by this persona?

You can be assured that if you are scrupulous and kind, the shadow will emerge. Therefore, question, observe, be curious about everything, and accept everything that you see and come to know. Be careful not to make judgments or allow your biases and fears to contaminate or destroy the revelations that occur.

When you think that perhaps you know everything, that you know as much about the shadow as you know about yourself—or more—then imagine that this character is your sibling, born from the very same father and mother. Describe your relationship to this sibling. "Remember" your early years together; describe a moment when you had great affinity for each other. When did you begin to part, to pursue such different lives? Tell a story that may reveal the moment of differentiation. Imagine your mother and father looking at their two children and reminiscing about each, speaking of your similarities and differences.

Finally, allow your sibling/other/enemy/cover to look at you. Allow this character to speak in his or her own voice, to create a portrait of you. Whom do you become when seen from this perspective? As the other has developed a voice, enter into dialogue with each other. What is it you each want to know?

As you bring this sibling, this other, this shadow into your life, into your family so to speak, allow your imagination and your real life history to merge. Beware of the need to be literal, for this often shrouds deeper knowledge. On the other hand, don't permit the imagination to distract or distance you from the ways in which the shadow is, in fact, your family, your other, your self.

This shadow self is not separate from you, not even as separate as a sibling. This is the shadow you cast, the one who is always with you. Examine the portrait of this person, consider the life that he or she is living, from the outside but also from within. Enter into this irony: the one with whom you have created an island of communality and mutual understanding is utterly other; or, the one who is utterly other is the one whom you can understand perfectly. Imagine yourself living the other's life.

Lastly, imagine the death of the shadow self. Given the life he or she led, how does the shadow self die?

The shadow, of course, never dies; we always cast a shadow. But how we relate to it, and it to us, depends on whether it is known. Once known, we have inevitably lost an innocence that can never be recovered. What replaces it is a knowledge of the complexity of our nature. Sometimes we are fortunate, and this knowledge elicits a kindness and tolerance in us for others—even, perhaps, for ourselves.

In the end, what remains is what we can only come to know when we are alone, naked, and the light is behind us.

· · · · · ·

I go among trees and sit still.
All my stirring becomes quiet
around me like circles on water.
My tasks lie in their places

where I left them, asleep like cattle.
Then what is afraid of me comes
and lives a while in my sight.
What it fears in me leaves me,
and the fear of me leaves it.
It sings, and I hear its song.

Then what I am afraid of comes.
I live for a while in its sight.
What I fear in it leaves it,
and the fear of it leaves me.
It sings, and I hear its song.

WENDELL BERRY

· · · · · · ·

EPILOGUE

JEREMIAH ABRAMS

If the fool would persist in his folly he would
become wise

WILLIAM BLAKE

I am by nature an autodidact. I value learning from experience. Often, when I give thought and attention to a subject, synchronicities occur. A meaningful but not causally related event will happen in my outer experience or to other people I know. Always, I feel renewed and comforted by such immediate feedback. These events confirm for me what is real and true.

When I trained as a therapist I would frequently find that whatever was holding my attention on a given day would inevitably show up in my consulting room—invariably that very day! Early in my work, this was so disconcerting that I would disregard these coincidences as the products of my own selective perception (the pickpocket walking down the street seeing only pockets). But through the persistence of these events over time, I have come to trust them.

Today, for example, while I was writing this epilogue, I received a call from a young woman in distress about a dream she had had the night before. She wanted my help. I analyze dreams, so we spent some time on the phone working with her dream. This is the salient fragment:

In the dream, she is stooping over at her job when she feels several sharp pains in the middle of her back. She stands up and turns around to find a dark-haired woman throwing darts at her!

Here was her shadow, symbolized by a same-sex person of opposite coloring (the dreamer is a strawberry blonde), coming at the dreamer from behind, from the unconscious (symbolically, what is behind us, out of conscious sight), targeting her with darts of painful awareness.

I got the point too! Focusing can bring the shadow into our immediate sphere. When we attend to the disowned part of ourselves, it comes alive, responds.

During the creation of *Meeting the Shadow,* this became a living, conscious dialogue for me. The process has given me added confirmation of many of my own personal observations and experiences of the shadow. More importantly, it has forced me to do shadow-work myself. For more than a year I have peered into the dark face of things and carried these ideas around until they have become real for me. My sleep has been punctuated by shadow dreams, strange meetings with mysterious men, nocturnal struggles, and discoveries made with unlikely companions. I now know these effects person-ally and acknowledge more easily my own soul's imperfections. Decreasingly, I dedicate energy to my former pretense and posturing.

We each contain the potentials to be both destructive and creative. Ad-mitting to the dark enemies within us is really a confessional act, the begin-ning of psychological change. Nothing about ourselves can change unless we first accept it and grant it reality. Shadow-work is the initiatory phase of mak-ing a whole of ourselves.

But for all the talk about wholeness, none of us can really contain the whole, at least in a conscious way. We cannot be aware of everything at all times. Fragmentation is built into our way of knowing.

Trying to know the shadow is like wanting to know the mysteries of creation: our knowledge is always incomplete. We can only serve a reality principle, aspire to an unhypocritical life, and continue to conscientiously seek the deepest levels of truth. This often takes a bit of the trickster—the fool in ourselves—in order to recover what has been repressed or denied and then find personal meaning in it. In our willingness to be foolish, we find wisdom.

I find that humor works wonders in supporting others to see their shadows. Any stand-up comedian knows intuitively that humor releases these confusing and potentially dangerous shadow contents in a harmless way. Humor can shake loose our repressed fears and emotions and take the bite out of the embarrassment and shame we may feel about our weaknesses. Through the comic, we can get at the underbelly of things and see what we are unwilling to admit. If we don't have a sense of humor, it probably means that we have little connection to our shadow, that we have a strong need to service the charade of appearances. In laughter, we loosen and free the energy from those places inside where we are trapped, hiding, and afraid. "If we couldn't laugh," as the country-and-western tune goes, "we would all go insane."

My work is most enjoyable and effective when I can laugh with others, even about the most serious matters. I seek that edge of inappropriateness. This is the territory most worth taking risks to find. For it is here, on the borders of awareness, that we can discover the "Great Way" of Zen, the path where the deep meaning of things is undisturbed by the conscious mind's tendency to make distinctions. "To set up what you like against what you dis-like," says the third Zen Patriarch Sengstan, "is the disease of the mind."

I would suggest to you, the reader, that this selection of essays and ideas can bring into your sphere a growing awareness of the ubiquitous shadow in your life. It will come easily. Read a few pages here and go out into your life and look. The gifts of shadow-work will benefit you and the world.

Shadow-work is good medicine! It leads to a practice I refer to as *the pur-suit of the unhypocritical life,* which some might call living with integrity. To draw up and challenge my own hypocritical self (my shadow), I evaluate my questionable actions with this query: When on my deathbed and about to meet my maker, I wonder if I will still be able to say that I did the best job I could? As Gandhi said, "The only devils in the world are those running around in our own hearts. That is where the battle should be fought."

We can *choose* to be a person whom we can respect, we can choose behavior we can stand by and which produces no remorse. It is possible, but only if the choices are clear and we make them consciously. Awareness of the shadow personality can dissolve its unconscious power over our choices.

Here is the golden opportunity in realizing the shadow: the gold is in the awareness of choice, made possible by mediating the tension between our shadow and our ego. If we have choice about who we enact in the world, then it follows that we can take responsibility for the kind of world we create.

. . . .

To go in the dark with a light is to
*   know the light.*
To know the dark, go dark.
Go without sight, and find that the dark, too,
*   blooms and sings,*
and is traveled by dark feet and dark wings.

WENDELL BERRY

NOTES

· · · · · · · ·

Chapter 12/Downing

1. C. G. Jung, "Symbols of the Mother and Rebirth," *Collected Works* vol. 5, p. 259; (New York: Pantheon, 1959) C. G. Jung, *Two Essays on Analytical Psychology, C. W.* vol. 7, pp. 38, 75.

2. C. G. Jung, "Concerning Rebirth," *C. W.,* vol. 9.1, p. 131.

3. Otto Rank, *The Double* (Chapel Hill: University of North Carolina Press, 1971); *Beyond Psychology* (New York: Dover, 1941).

Chapter 16/Conger

1. C. G. Jung, *Symbols of Transformation: An Analysis of the Prelude to a Case of Schizophrenia,* 2d ed., trans. R. F. C. Hull, Bollingen Series XX, vol. 5 (Princeton, N.J.: Princeton University Press, 1956), p. 71.

2. C. G. Jung, *Analytical Psychology: Its Theory and Practice* (New York: Vintage, 1968), p. 23 (italics added).

3. Wilhelm Reich, *The Function of the Orgasm,* trans. Theodore P. Wolfe (New York: Meridian, 1970), p. 241.

4. Wilhelm Reich, *Ether, God, and Devil,* trans. Mary Boyd Higgins and Therese Pol (New York: Farrar, Straus & Giroux, 1973), p. 91.

5. C. G. Jung, *The Structure and Dynamics of the Psyche,* 2d ed., trans. R. F. C. Hull, Bollingen Series XX, vol. 8 (Princeton, N.J.: Princeton University Press, 1969), p. 215.

6. C. G. Jung, *The Archetypes and the Collective Unconscious,* trans. R. F. C. Hull, ed. Sir Herbert Read, Michael Fordham, and Gerhard Adler, Bollingen Series XX, vol. 9 (Princeton, N. J.: Princeton University Press, 1980), p. 284.

7. Wilhelm Reich, *The Mass Psychology of Fascism,* trans. Vincent R. Carfagno (New York: Farrar, Straus & Giroux, 1970), p. xi.

8. Hans Christian Andersen, "The Shadow," in *Hans Christian Andersen: Eighty Fairytales* (New York: Pantheon Press, 1982), p. 193. Also see Otto Rank, *The Double: A Psychoanalytic Study,* trans. and ed. Harry Tucker, Jr. (New York: Meridian, 1971), pp. 10–11.

9. Reich, *Mass Psychology of Fascism,* p. xi.

10. C. G. Jung, *Two Essays on Analytical Psychology,* 2d ed., trans. R. F. C. Hull, Bollingen Series XX, vol. 7 (Princeton, N.J.: Princeton Univesity Press, 1972), p. 192.

11. Reich, *Mass Psychology of Fascism,* p. xi.

Chapter 25/Glendinning

1. Lewis Mumford, *My Works and Days: A Personal Chronicle* (New York: Harcourt Brace Jovanovich, 1979), p. 14.

2. Paul Brodeur, *Outrageous Misconduct: The Asbestos Industry on Trial* (New York: Pantheon, 1985), p. 14.

Chapter 26/Bishop

1. R. Metzner, *Maps of Consciousness* (New York: Collier Macmillan, 1979), p. 2.

2. See B. E. Fernow, "Applied Ecology," *Science* 17 (1903); V. M. Spalding, "The Rise and Progress of Ecology," *Science* 17 (1903).

3. E. g., A. Chisholm, *Philosophers of the Earth: Conversations with Ecologists* (London: Sidgwick and Jackson, 1972).

4. In Chisholm, *Philosophers.* See also G. Sessions, "Ecophilosophy, Utopias, Education," *The Journal of Environmental Education* 15, no. 1 (Fall 1983).

5. The quotations are from Robinson Jeffers and Buckminster Fuller, in R. Buckminster Fuller, *Earth Inc.* (New York: Anchor Press, 1973), p. 69.

6. Quoted in M. Douglas and A. Wildavsky, *Risk and Culture: An Essay on the Selection of Technical and Environmental Dangers* (Berkeley: University of California Press, 1982), p. 64. They suggest there is little difference between the way industrial society views environmental issues and the supposedly "magical" world view of pre-literate societies. See also B. Weisberg, *Beyond Repair: The Ecology of Capitalism* (Boston: Beacon Press, 1971) on the unholy unity.

7. J. Schell, *The Fate of the Earth* (London: Picador, 1982), pp. 62–65.

8. J. Hillman in "Going Bugs" (one of his lectures on "Animals in Dreams" at the Dallas Institute of Humanities and Culture, Spring, 1982) also referred to *The Lord of the Flies,* the chorus of insects in *Faust,* and Kafka's *Metamorphosis.*

9. See R. Sardello, "The Suffering Body of the City," *Spring 1983*: pp. 145–64.

10. The ecologist Dr. N. Moore in Chisholm, *Philosophers;* see also I. Barbour, *Earth Might Be Fair: Reflections on Ethics, Religion, and Ecology* (New York: Prentice-Hall, 1972), pp. 56, 153. Douglas (*Risk and Culture,* p. 131) directly relates the form of organization of the environmental activist groups with their images of disaster.

11. L. Gallonedec, "Man's Dependence on the Earth," *Popular Science Monthly* 53 (May 1898), read in the Congress of Scientific Societies, France.

12. L. Eiseley, *The Star Thrower* (London: Wildwood House, 1978), p. 179.

13. C. G. Jung, *Collected Works,* trans. R. F. C. Hull, Bollingen Series XX, vol. 10 (Princeton, N.J.: Princeton University Press, 1970), section 615.

14. H. B. Hough, in D. Day, *The Doomsday Book of Animals* (London: Ebury Press, 1981), p. 10.

15. J. and P. Philips, *Victorians at Home and Away* (London: Croom Helm, 1978), p. 18. Nineteenth-century nationalism provided idealized images of unification, coherence and identity, which belied the intense internal fragmentation and conflict. Through imperial imaginings, for example of the Orient, attempts were made to categorize, organize, and control the globe.

16. J. Hillman, "Anima Mundi," *Spring 1982*: pp. 71–93; and R. Sardello, "Taking the Side of Things, *Spring 1984*: pp. 127-35.

17. See R. Nash's comprehensive *Wilderness and the American Mind* (New Haven, Conn.: Yale University Press, 1973).

18. See A. Portmann's reflections on beauty in nature, in "What Living Form Means to Us," *Spring 1982*: pp. 27-38; also, J. Hillman, "Natural Beauty without Nature," *Spring 1985*: pp. 50-55.

19. See A. Ziegler, "Rousseauian Optimism, Natural Distress, and Dream Research," *Spring 1976*: pp. 54-65; Eiseley, *Star Thrower*, p. 231; Nash, *Wilderness*, p. 165; F. Young-husband, *Wonders of the Himalayas* (1924) (Chandigarh: Abhishek Publications, 1977).

20. S. Larsen, *The Shaman's Doorway* (New York: Harper & Row, 1977), p 169.

21. The celebration of a generalized, aesthetic and realistic interpretation of natural landscape by Western lovers of wilderness is almost unique. While the Far East also had a long tradition of aesthetic landscape appreciation, it was highly idealized and formalized. Most traditional cultures have revered *specific* geographical places (rather than *views*) through the sacred stories that are associated with them (see M. Eliade, *Sacred and Profane* [New York: Harcourt, Brace and World, 1959]). Traditional cultures generally view sacred sites with a mixture of reverence, awe, caution, and fear. Similarly, the unknown land beyond their own territory is usually treated with considerable circumspection. In a previous paper ("Geography of Imagination: Tibet," *Spring 1984*: pp. 195-209), I have discussed the consequences of the Western attempt to remove imaginative paradox from its fantasies of Tibet.

22. See the important essay by L. White, Jr., "The Historical Roots of Our Ecological Crisis," in *The Environmental Handbook*, ed. G. de Bell (New York: Ballantine Books, 1970). For a less one-sided analysis that shows a far greater complexity in Western attitudes toward nature, see K. Thomas, *Man and the Natural World: Changing Attitudes in England, 1500–1800* (London: Allen Lane, 1983). See also S. Fox, *John Muir and His Legacy* (Boston: Little Brown & Co., 1981), chap. 11. See also Yi Fu-Tuan's "Discrepancies Between Environmental Attitudes and Behaviour: Examples from Europe and China," for an attempt to go beyond classic texts and correct the naive reification of Eastern ecological practices (P. English and R. Mayfield, *Man, Space and Environment* [New York: Oxford University Press, 1972]).

23. See Nash, *Wilderness,* and also K. Thomas, *Natural World.*

24. E.g., R. Kaplan, "Some Psychological Benefits of an Outdoor Challenge Program," *Environment and Behaviour,* no. 6 (1974); J. Swan, "Sacred Places in Nature," *The Journal of Environmental Education* 15, no. 4 (1983); W. Hammit, "Cognitive Dimensions of Wilderness Solitude," *Environment and Behaviour,* no. 14 (1982).

25. Douglas, *Risk and Culture,* p. 151.

26. Ibid., pp. 131-40 for a discussion of this relation between global fears and global strategies. A thoughtful example of this approach is R. Higgins, *The Seventh Enemy: The Human Factor in the Global Crisis* (London: Hodder and Stoughton, 1978). Kern, for example, relates the emergence of the concept of "open space" with the rise of nineteenth-century imperialism, exploration and the Western domination of the globe (*Culture of Time and Space,* p. 164).

27. Eiseley, *Star Thrower,* p. 262.

28. G. Bachelard, *The Poetics of Reverie* (Boston: Beacon Press, 1971), p. 127.

29. Eiseley, *Star Thrower,* p. 262. These dark murmurs from the environment and nature are also subject to political manipulation, and we have to ask why there are fluctuations in the focus of concern—pollution one year is displaced by energy crisis, overpopulation by nuclear war, and so on.

Chapter 33/Nichols

1. Alan McGlashan, *The Savage and Beautiful Country* (London: Chatto and Windus, Ltd., 1967).

2. C. G. Jung, *Psychological Reflections,* ed. Jolande Jacobi (Princeton, N.J.: Princeton University Press, 1970).

3. Ibid.

Chapter 35/Jung

1. C. W. Jung, *Aion, Collected Works,* trans. R. F. C. Hull, Bollingen Series XX, vol. 9, ii (Princeton, N.J.: Princeton University Press, 1980), pp. 82ff.

Chapter 37/Peck

1. Although so frequently and even evilly abused, perhaps the greatest beauty of Christian doctrine is its understanding approach to sin. It is a two-pronged approach. On the one hand, it insists upon our sinful human nature. Any genuine Christian, therefore, will consider himself or herself to be a sinner. The fact that many nominal and overtly devout "Christians" do not in their hearts consider themselves sinners should not be perceived as a failure of the doctrine but only a failure of the individual to begin to live up to it. More will be said later about evil in Christian guise. On the other hand, Christian doctrine also insists that we are forgiven our sins—at least as long as we experience contrition for them. Fully realizing the extent of our sinfulness, we are likely to feel almost overwhelmed by hopelessness if we do not simultaneously believe in the merciful and forgiving nature of the Christian God. Thus the Church, when in its right mind, will also insist that to endlessly dwell on each and every smallest sin one has committed (a process known as "excessive scrupulosity") is itself a sin. Since God forgives us, to fail to forgive ourselves is to hold ourselves higher than God—thereby indulging in the sin of a perverted form of pride.

2. Gerald Vann, *The Pain of Christ and the Sorrow of God* (Springfield, Ill.: Temple Gate Publishers, copyright by Aquin Press, 1947), pp. 54–55.

3. Ernest Becker, in his final work, *Escape from Evil* (Macmillan, 1965), pointed out the essential role of scapegoating in the genesis of human evil. He erred, I believe, in focusing exclusively on the fear of death as the sole motive for such scapegoating. Indeed, I think the fear of self-criticism is the more potent motive. Although Becker did not make the point, he might have equated the fear of self-criticism with the fear of death. Self-criticism is a call to personality change. As soon as I criticize a part of myself I incur an obligation to change that part. But the process of personality change is a painful one. It is like a death. The old personality pattern must die for a new pattern to take its place. The evil are pathologically attached to the status quo of their personalities, which in their narcissism they consciously regard as perfect. I think it is quite possible that the evil may perceive even a small degree of change in their beloved selves as representing total annihilation. In this sense, the threat of self-criticism may feel to one who is evil synonymous with the threat of extinction.

4. Buber, *Good and Evil,* p. 111. Since the primary motive of the evil is disguise, one of the places evil people are most likely to be found is within the church. What better way to conceal one's evil from oneself, as well as from others, than to be a deacon or some other highly visible form of Christian within our culture? In India I would suppose that the evil would demonstrate a similar tendency to be "good" Hindus or "good" Moslems. I do not mean to imply that the evil are anything other than a small minority among the religious or that the religious motives of most people are in any way spurious. I mean only that evil people tend to gravitate toward piety for the disguise and concealment it can offer them.

Chapter 38/Diamond

1. Liliane Frey-Rohn, "Evil from the Psychological Point of View," in *Evil* (Evanston, Ill: Northwestern University Press, 1967), p. 167.

2. Ibid., p. 160.

3. Carl Jung, *Memories, Dreams, Reflections* (New York: Pantheon Books, 1961), p. 153.

4. Rollo May, "Reflections and Commentary," in Clement Reeves, *The Psychology of Rollo May: A Study in Existential Theory and Psychotherapy* (San Francisco: Jossey-Bass, 1977), p. 304.

5. M. Scott Peck, *People of the Lie: The Hope for Healing Human Evil* (New York: Simon and Schuster, 1983), pp. 67, 78, 183. (For a critique of Peck's book, see Stephen Diamond, "The Psychology of Evil," *The San Francisco Jung Institute Library Journal* 9, no. 1 [1990]: pp. 5-26.)

6. Sigmund Freud, "Totem and Taboo," in *The Basic Writings of Sigmund Freud* (New York: Random House, 1938), p. 848.

7. Ibid.

8. Carl Jung, "Psychological Types," in *The Collected Works of C. G. Jung,* vol. 6 (Princeton, N. J.: Princeton University Press, 1971, p. 109.

9. Rollo May, *Man's Search for Himself* (New York: W. W. Norton, 1953), pp. 72-73.

10. Jung, *Memories, Dreams, Reflections,* p. 347.

11. Rollo May, *Love and Will* (New York: W. W. Norton, 1969), p. 121.

12. Marie-Louise von Franz, "Daimons and the Inner Companions," *Parabola* 6, no. 4 (1981): p. 36.

13. May, *Love and Will,* pp. 136-37.

14. Ibid., p. 129.

15. Ibid., p. 137.

16. Jung, *Memories, Dreams, Reflections,* p. 387.

17. May, "Reflections and Commentary," p. 305.

18. James Hillman, *Healing Fiction* (New York: Station Hill Press, 1983), p. 68.

19. von Franz, "Daimons and the Inner Companions," p. 39.

Chapter 39/Becker

1. Wilhelm Reich, *The Mass Psychology of Fascism,* 1933 (New York: Farrar, Straus, 1970), pp. 334ff.

2. Ibid., p. 339.

3. Erich Neumann, *Depth Psychology and a New Ethic* (London: Hodder & Stoughton, 1969), p. 40.

4. Carl Jung, "After the Catastrophe," *Collected Works,* vol. 10 (Princeton, N.J.: Bollingen, 1970), p. 203.

5. Ibid.

6. Neumann, *Depth Psychology,* p. 50

7. Jung, "After the Catastrophe," p. 216.

Chapter 40/Schmookler

1. M. Scott Peck, *People of the Lie: The Hope for Healing Human Evil* (New York: Simon & Schuster, 1983), p. 69.

2. M. Esther Harding, *The "I" and the "Not-I": A Study in the Development of Consciousness* (Princeton, N.J.: Princeton University Press, 1965), p. 91.

3. Quoted in *Tarrytown Letter,* April 1983, p. 16.

4. Quoted in Robert G. C. Waite, *The Psychopathic God: Adolf Hitler* (New York: Basic Books, 1977), p. xvii.

5. Ibid.

6. See Erik Erikson, *Gandhi's Truth: On the Origins of Militant Non-violence* (New York: W. W. Norton, 1969). It is interesting that something similar is to be found in the life of Leo Tolstoy. In the later years of his life, just as Tolstoy was exhorting the world toward the perfection of Christian love and peace, he was apparently ruling over his wife and his household with a rather cruel tyranny.

7. Erikson, *Gandhi,* p. 251.

8. George Orwell, *Collected Essays* (London: Heinemann, 1966), p. 456.

9. Erikson, *Gandhi,* p. 234.

10. Erich Neumann, *Depth Psychology and a New Ethic* (London: Hodder & Stoughton, 1969), p. 111.

11. Erikson, *Gandhi,* p. 433.

12. Quoted in Peck, *Lie,* p. 11.

Chapter 46/Lifton

1. Paul W. Pruyser, "What Splits in Splitting?," *Bulletin of the Menninger Clinic* 39 (1975): pp. 1-46.

2. Melanie Klein, "Notes on Some Schizoid Mechanisms," *International Journal of Psychoanalysis* 27 (1946): pp. 99-110; and Otto F. Kernberg, "The Syndrome," in *Borderline Conditions and Pathological Narcissism* (New York: Jason Aronson, 1973), pp. 3-47.

3. Henry V. Dicks, *Licensed Mass Murder: A Socio-Psychological Study of Some SS Killers* (New York: Basic Books, 1972).

4. See, for example, Erik H. Erikson, *Identity: Youth and Crisis* (New York: W. W. Norton, 1968); Heinz Kohut, *The Restoration of the Self* (New York: International Universities Press, 1977); Henry Guntrip, *Psychoanalytic Theory, Therapy and the Self* (New York: Basic Books, 1971); and Robert Jay Lifton, *The Broken Connection: On Death and the Continuity of Life* (New York: Basic Books, 1983 [1979]).

5. William James, *The Varieties of Religious Experience: A Study in Human Nature* (New York: Collier, 1961 [1902]), p. 144.

6. Rank's two major studies of this phenomenon are *The Double: A Psychoanalytic Study* (Chapel Hill: University of North Carolina Press, 1971 [1925]); and "The Double as Immortal Self," in *Beyond Psychology* (New York: Dover, 1958 [1941]), pp. 62-101.

7. Rank, *Double,* pp. 3-9; Rank, *Beyond Psychology,* pp. 67-69. On "Der Student von Prag," see Siegfried Kracauer, *From Caligari to Hitler: A Psychological History of the German Film* (Princeton, N.J.: Princeton University Press, 1947), pp. 28-30. Rank's viewing of *The Student of Prague,* during a revival in the mid-1920s, was the original stim-

ulus for a lifelong preoccupation with the theme of the double. Rank noted that the screenplay's author, Hanns Heinz Ewers, had drawn heavily on E. T. A. Hoffmann's "Story of the Lost Reflection." (See E. T. A. Hoffmann, "Story of the Lost Reflection," in J. M. Cohen, ed., *Eight Tales of Hoffmann* (London, 1952).

8. Rank, *Beyond Psychology*, p. 98.

9. In his early work, Rank followed Freud in connecting the legend with the concept of "narcissism," of libido directed toward one's own self. But Rank gave the impression that he did so uneasily, always stressing the issue of death and immortality as lurking beneath the narcissism. In his later adaptation, he boldly embraced the death theme as the earlier and more fundamental one in the Narcissus legend and spoke somewhat disdainfully of "some modern psychologists [who] claimed to have found a symbolization of their self-love principle" in it. (See Rank, *Beyond Psychology*, pp. 97-101.) By then he had broken with Freud and established his own intellectual position.

10. Rank, *Double*, p. 76.

11. Ibid.

12. Rank, *Beyond Psychology*, p. 82.

13. Michael Franz Basch speaks of an interference with the "union of affect with percept without, however, blocking the percept from consciousness." See Michael Franz Basch, "The Perception of Reality and the Disavowal of Meaning," *Annual of Psychoanalysis,* vol. 11 (New York: International Universities Press, 1982), p. 147. In that sense, disavowal resembles psychic numbing, as it alters the *valencing* or emotional charge of the symbolizing process.

14. Ralph D. Allison, "When the Psychic Glue Dissolves," *HYPNOS-NYTT* (December 1977).

15. The first two influences are described in George B. Greaves, "Multiple Personality: 165 Years After Mary Reynolds," *Journal of Nervous and Mental Disease* 168 (1977): pp. 577–96. Freud emphasized the third in *The Ego and the Id,* in the *Standard Edition of the Works of Sigmund Freud,* James Strachey, ed. (London: Hogarth Press, 1955 [1923]), vol. XIX, pp. 30–31.

16. Margaretta K. Bowers et al., "Theory of Multiple Personality," *International Journal of Clinical and Experimental Hypnosis* 19 (1971): p. 60.

17. See Lifton, *Broken Connection,* pp. 407–9; and Charles H. King, "The Ego and the Integration of Violence in Homicidal Youth," *American Journal of Orthopsychiatry* 45 (1975): p. 142.

18. Robert W. Rieber uses the term "pseudopsychopathy" for what he describes as "selective joint criminal behavior" within the kinds of subculture mentioned here. See Robert W. Rieber, "The Psychopathy of Everyday Life" (unpublished manuscript).

19. James S. Grotstein speaks of the development of "a separate being living within one that has been preconsciously split off and has an independent existence with independent motivation, separate agenda, etc.," and from which can emanate "evil, sadism, and destructiveness" or even "demoniacal possession." He calls this aspect of the self a "mind parasite" (after Colin Wilson) and attributes its development to those elements of the self that have been artificially suppressed and disavowed early in life. (See James S. Grotstein, "The Soul in Torment: An Older and Newer View of Psychopathology," *Bulletin of the National Council of Catholic Psychologists* 25 (1979): pp. 36–52.

Chapter 51/Kopp

1. Dante Alighieri, *The Inferno,* trans. John Ciardi (New York and Toronto: The New American Library, A Mentor Classic, 1954).

2. Francis Fergusson, *Dante's Dream of the Mind: A Modern Reading of the Purgatorio* (Princeton, N.J.: Princeton University Press, 1953), p. 5.

3. T. S. Eliot, "Dante," in *The Sacred Wood: Essays on Poetry and Criticism* (New York: Barnes and Noble, 1960, and London: Methuen & Co., Ltd., University Paperbacks), p. 170 ff.

4. Dante, *Inferno,* p. 42.

5. *Ibid.,* p. 43.

6. *Ibid.,* ff.

7. C. G. Jung, *Wirklichkeit der Seele* (Zurich: Ascher, 1934), p. 52. Quoted in *Psychological Reflections: An Anthology of the Writings of C. G. Jung,* ed. Jolande Jacobi (New York: Harper and Row, Harper Torch-books, The Bollingen Library, 1961), p. 75.

8. Dante, *Inferno,* p. 54.

9. *Ibid.,* p. 66.

10. *Ibid.,* p. 161.

11. C. G. Jung, "Versuch einer Darstellung der psycho-analytischen Theorie," *Jahrbuch für psychoanalytische und psychopathologische Forschungen* (Liepzig and Vienna: Deuticke, v 1913), p. 106. Quoted in *Psychological Reflections, p. 75.*

12. C. G. Jung, "Zur gegenwartigen Lage der Psychotherapie," *Zentralblatt für Psychotherapie und ihre Grenzgebiete,* VII (1934) 2. p. 12ff. Quoted in *Psychological Reflections, p. 73.*

13. Lao Tzu, *Tao Tê Ching* (Harmondsworth, Middlesex, England: Penguin Books, Ltd., Penguin Classics, 1963), p. 123.

Chapter 52/Campbell

1. Longfellow, *The Song of Hiawatha,* VIII. The adventures ascribed by Longfellow to the Iroquois chieftain Hiawatha belong properly to the Algonquin culture hero Manabozho. Hiawatha was an actual historical personage of the sixteenth century.

2. Leo Frobenius, *Das Zeitalter des Sonnengottes* (Berlin, 1904), p. 85.

3. Henry Callaway, *Nurse Tales and Traditions of the Zulus* (London, 1868), p. 331.

4. Ananda K. Coomaraswamy, "Akimcanna: Self-Naughting," in *New Indian Antiquary,* vol. 3 (Bombay, 1940), p. 6, note 14, citing and discussing Thomas Aquinas, *Summa Theologica,* I, 63, 3.

5. The sarcophagus or casket is an alternative for the belly of the whale. Compare Moses in the bulrushes.

6. Sir James G. Frazer, *The Golden Bough* (one-volume edition), pp. 347–49. Copyright 1922 by The Macmillan Company and used with their permission.

7. Duarte Barbosa, *A Description of the Coasts of East Africa and Malabar in the Beginning of the Sixteenth Century* (London: Hakluyt Society, 1866), p. 172; cited by Frazer, op cit., pp. 274–75. Reprinted by permission of The Macmillan Company, publishers. This is the sacrifice that King Minos refused when he withheld the bull from Poseidon. As Frazer has shown, ritual regicide was a general tradition in the ancient world. "In Southern India," he writes, "the king's reign and life terminated with the

revolution of the planet Jupiter round the sun. In Greece, on the other hand, the king's fate seems to have hung in the balance at the end of every eight years. . . . Without being unduly rash we may surmise that the tribute of seven youths and seven maidens whom the Athenians were bound to send to Minos every eight years had some connection with the renewal of the king's power for another octennial cycle" (ibid., p. 280). The bull sacrifice required of King Minos implied that he would sacrifice himself, according to the pattern of the inherited tradition, at the close of his eight-year term. But he seems to have offered, instead, the substitute of the Athenian youths and maidens. That perhaps is how the divine Minos became the monster Minotaur, the self-annihilate king, the tyrant Holdfast, the hieratic state, wherein every man enacts his role, and the merchant empire, wherein each is out for himself. Such practices of substitution seem to have become general throughout the antique world toward the close of the great period of the early hieratic states, during the third and second millenniums B.C.

Chapter 53/Toub

1. Chuang Tsu, *Chuang Tse,* edited by G. F. Feng and J. English (New York: Vintage Books, 1974), pp. 80–82.

2. Chuang Tzu, *Chuang Tzu,* translated by H. Giles (London: Unwin Paperbacks, 1980), p. 164.

3. H. Smith, *The Religions of Man,* (New York: Harper & Row, 1958), p. 212.

4. C. Jung, *Two Essays on Analytical Psychology,* (Princeton, N.J.: Princeton University Press, 1966), par. 68.

5. A. Mindell, "Somatic Consciousness," *Quadrant* 14 (1/1981): pp. 71–73.

6. J. Jacobi, *The Way of Individuation,* (New York: Harcourt, Brace & World, 1967), p. 82.

7. Lao Tsu, *Tao Te Ching,* edited by G. F. Feng & J. English (New York: Vintage Books, 1972), Chap. 41.

8. Chuang Tzu, *Chuang Tzu,* translated by H. Giles (London: Unwin Paperbacks, 1980), pp. 263–264.

Chapter 57/Frey-Rohn

1. Sigmund Freud, *The Future of an Illusion,* trans. W. D. Robson-Scott, International Psycho-Analytical Library, vol. 15 (London: The Hogarth Press, Ltd., 1949), p. 86.

2. Friedrich Nietzsche, *The Case of Wagner,* in *Selected Aphorisms in Works,* vol. VIII, p. 59.

3. William James, p. 176.

4. Ibid., p. 488 note. "Evil is not evaded, but sublated in the higher religious cheer of these [twice-born] persons."

5. E. T. W. Hoffman (Amadeus), *The Devil's Elixir,* trans. anon. (Edinburgh, 1824).

6. Code Bezae ad Luc. 6.4.

7. C. G. Jung, *Mysterium Coniunctionis, Collected Works,* trans. R. F. C. Hull, Bollingen Series XX, vol. 14 (Princeton, N.J.: Princeton University Press, 1963), p. 428.

Chapter 58/Wilber

1. C. G. Jung, *Modern Man in Search of a Soul* (London: Harcourt Brace Jovanovich, 1955), pp. 271–272.

BIBLIOGRAPHY

. . . .

The following list includes the sources for this collection, as well as other relevant titles.

Andersen, Hans Christian. "The Shadow." *Eighty Fairy Tales.* New York: Pantheon Books, 1976.

Babbs, John. "New Age Fundamentalism." *Critique,* Spring, 1990.

———. "You Are So Wonderful." *Critique,* Spring, 1990.

Bach, George R., and Herb Goldberg. *Creative Aggression.* New York: Doubleday, 1974.

Bauer, Jan. *Alcoholism and Women.* Toronto: Inner City Books, 1982.

Becker, Ernest. *The Denial of Death.* New York: Free Press, 1973.

———. *Escape from Evil.* New York: Free Press, 1975.

Bernstein, Jerome S. *Power and Politics: The Psychology of Soviet-American Partnership.* Boston: Shambhala (for the C. G. Jung Foundation, New York), 1989.

Berry, Patricia. *Echo's Subtle Body.* Dallas: Spring Publications, 1982.

Berry, Wendell, *Sabbaths.* San Francisco: North Point Press, 1987.

Berzin, Alexander (trans.). *The Mahamudra of the Ninth Karmapa, Wang-Ch'ug dor-je: Eliminating the Darkness of Ignorance.* Dharamsala, India: Library of Tibetan Works and Archives, 1978.

Birkhauser-Oeri, Sibylle. *The Mother: Archetypal Image in Fairy Tales.* Toronto: Inner City Books, 1988.

Bishop, Peter. "The Shadows of the Wholistic Earth." *Spring,* 1986.

Bleakley, Alan. *Fruits of the Moon Tree.* London: Gateway Books, 1984.

———. *Earth's Embrace: Facing the Shadow of the New Age.* Bath, England: Gateway Books, 1989.

Bly, Robert. *A Little Book on the Human Shadow.* New York: Harper & Row, 1988.

Boer, Charles. "In The Shadow of the Gods: Greek Tragedy." *Spring,* 1982.

Bolen, Jean Shinoda. *Gods in Everyman.* New York: Harper & Row, 1989.

Borysenko, Joan. *Guilt Is the Teacher, Love Is the Lesson.* New York: Warner Books, 1990.

Bradshaw, John. *Healing the Shame That Binds You.* Deerfield Beach, Fla.: Health Communications, 1988.

Branden, Nathaniel. *The Disowned Self.* New York: Bantam Books, 1978.

Brewi, Janice, and Anne Brennan. *Celebrate Mid-Life: Jungian Archetypes and Mid-Life Spirituality.* New York: Crossroad, 1989.

Buber, Martin. *The Writings of Martin Buber.* New York: Meridian Books, 1956.

————. *Good and Evil.* Magnolia, Mass.: Peter Smith, 1984.

Bulfinch, Thomas. *Myths of Greece and Rome.* New York: Penguin, 1981.

Butler, Katy. "Encountering the Shadow in Buddhist America." *Common Boundary,* May/June, 1990.

Campbell, Joseph. *The Hero with a Thousand Faces.* Princeton, N.J.: Princeton University Press, Bollingen Series, 1973.

Castellanos, Rosario. *The Selected Poems of Rosario Castellanos,* St. Paul, Minn.: Graywolf Press, 1988.

Chuang Tsu. *Chuang Tse.* (G.–F. Feng and J. English, ed.). New York: Vintage Books, 1974.

Chuang Tzu. *Chuang Tzu.* (H. Giles, trans.). London: Unwin Paperbacks, 1980.

Chernin, Kim. *The Hungry Self.* New York: Random House, 1985.

Conger, John P. *Jung and Reich: The Body as Shadow.* Berkeley, Calif.: North Atlantic Books, 1985.

D'Aulaire, Ingri and Edgar. *Book of Greek Myths.* Garden City, N.Y.: Doubleday, 1962.

Diamond, Stephen A. "The Psychology of Evil." *The San Francisco Jung Institute Library Journal* 9, no. 1, 1990.

Dodds, E. R. *The Greeks and the Irrational.* Berkeley: University of California Press, 1951.

Dossey, Larry. *Beyond Illness.* Boston: Shambhala, 1984.

Downing, Christine. *Psyche's Sisters.* New York: Harper & Row, 1988.

————— (ed.). *Archetypes of the Self.* Los Angeles: Jeremy P. Tarcher, 1991.

Edinger, Edward F. *The Anatomy of the Psyche.* La Salle, Ill.: Open Court, 1986.

Eichman, William Carl. "Meeting Darkness on the Path." *Gnosis,* no. 14, Winter, 1990.

Ekman, Paul. *Why Kids Lie.* New York: Charles Scribners, 1988.

Eliot, T. S. *Four Quartets.* London: Faber and Faber, 1949.

Feinstein, David, and Stanley Krippner. *Personal Mythology: The Psychology of Your Evolving Self.* Los Angeles: Jeremy P. Tarcher, 1988.

Ferrucci, Piero. *What We May Be.* Los Angeles: Jeremy P. Tarcher, 1982.

Fjerkenstad, Jerry. "Alchemy and Criminality." *Inroads,* Spring, 1990.

Frazer, James G. *The Golden Bough.* New York: St. Martin's Press, 1977.

Frey-Rohn, Liliane. "Evil from the Psychological Point of View." *Spring,* 1965.

————. "The Shadow Revealed in the Works of Friedrich Neitzsche." *The Well Tended Tree* (Hilde Kirsch, ed.). New York: G. P. Putnam's Sons (for the C. G. Jung Foundation, New York), 1971.

————. *From Freud to Jung: A Comparative Study of the Psychology of the Unconscious.* Boston: Shambhala, 1990.

Fromm, Erich. *Anatomy of Human Destructiveness.* New York: Henry Holt & Co., 1973.

Gallard, Martine Drahon. "Black Shadow/White Shadow." *The Archetype of the Shadow in a Split World* (Mary Ann Mattoon, ed.). Zurich: Daimon, 1987, pp. 199–213.

Gerzon, Mark. *Act II: How to Turn Your Midlife Crisis Into a Quest.* (forthcoming: Delacorte).

Gibran, Kahlil. *The Prophet.* New York: Alfred A. Knopf, 1923.

Glendinning, Chellis. *When Technology Wounds: The Human Consequences of Progress.* New York: William Morrow, 1990.

Goldberg, Jane. *The Dark Side of Love.* Los Angeles: Jeremy P. Tarcher, 1991.

Goleman, Daniel. *Vital Lies, Simple Truths.* New York: Simon & Schuster, 1986.

———. "The Dark Side of Charisma." *New York Times,* April 1, 1990.

Greene, Liz, and Stephen Arroyo. *The Juniper/Saturn Conference Lectures.* Sebastapol, Calif.: CRCS Publications, 1984.

Griffin, Susan. *Pornography and Silence: Culture's Revenge Against Nature.* New York: Harper & Row, 1981.

Grof, Christina and Stanislov. *The Stormy Search for the Self.* Los Angeles: Jeremy P. Tarcher, 1990.

Guggenbühl-Craig, Adolf. "Quacks, Charlatans and False Prophets." *The Reality of the Psyche* (Joseph Wheelright, ed.). New York: G. P. Putnam's Sons, 1972.

———. *Marriage Dead or Alive.* Dallas: Spring Publications, 1977.

———. *Power in the Helping Professions.* Dallas: Spring Publications, 1978.

———. *Eros on Crutches.* Dallas: Spring Publications, 1980.

Hannah, Barbara. "Ego and Shadow." Guild of Pastoral Psychology, *lecture no.* 85, March, 1955.

———. *Encounters with the Soul: Active Imagination.* Boston: Sigo Press, 1981.

Harding, Esther M. "The Shadow." *Spring,* 1945.

———. *The I and the Not I.* Princeton, N.J.: Princeton University Press, Bollingen Series, 1965.

Henderson, Joseph L. *Shadow and Self: Selected Papers in Analytical Psychology.* Wilmette, Ill.: Chiron Publications, 1989.

Hendrix, Harville. *Getting the Love You Want.* New York: Harper & Row, 1988.

Hill, Michael Ortiz. "Healing the Dream of Apocalypse" and "Out of My Father's House: A Fairy Tale." Unpublished papers.

Hillman, James. "Friends and Enemies: The Dark Side of Relationship." *Harvest,* no. 8, 1962, pp. 1–22.

———. *Insearch: Psychology and Religion.* New York: Charles Scribners, 1967.

———. *The Dream and the Underworld.* New York: Harper & Row, 1979.

———. "Notes on White Supremacy." *Spring,* 1986, pp. 29–59.

———. (ed.). *Puer Papers.* Dallas: Spring Publications, 1979.

———. (ed.). *Soul and Money.* Dallas: Spring Publications, 1982.

Hopcke, Robert H. *A Guided Tour of the Collected Works of C. G. Jung.* Boston: Shambhala, 1989.

Irwin, Jolen T. *Doubting and Incest—Repetition and Revenge: A Speculative Reading of Faulkner.* Baltimore and London: Johns Hopkins, 1975.

Jacobi, Jolande. *The Psychology of C. G. Jung.* New Haven: Yale University Press, 1951.

———. *Masks of the Soul.* Grand Rapids, Mich.: William B. Eerdmans, 1967.

————. *The Way of Individuation.* New York: Harcourt, Brace & World, 1967.

Jaffé, Aniela (ed.). *C. G. Jung: World and Image.* Princeton, N.J.: Princeton University Press, Bollingen Series XCVII: 2, 1979.

Johnson, Robert A. *Inner Work.* New York: Harper & Row, 1986.

————. *Ecstasy: Understanding the Psychology of Joy.* New York: Harper & Row, 1987.

————. *Owning Your Shadow.* New York: Harper & Row, forthcoming.

Joy, W. Brugh. *Avalanche: Heretical Reflections on the Dark and the Light.* New York: Ballantine Books, 1990.

Jung, Carl Gustav. "The Fight with the Shadow." *Listener,* November 7, 1946.

————. *Answer to Job.* London: Routledge & Kegan Paul, 1952.

————. *Collected Works, vols. 1–20,* (R. F. C. Hill, trans., and H. Read, M. Fordham, G. Adler, and William McGuire, eds.). Princeton, N.J.: Princeton University Press, Bollingen Series XX, 1953–1990.

————. *Memories, Dreams, Reflections.* New York: Pantheon Books, 1973.

————, and M.-L. von Franz, Joseph L. Henderson, Jolande Jacobi, and Aniela Jaffé. *Man and His Symbols.* Garden City, N.Y.: Doubleday, 1964.

————. *Two Essays on Analytical Psychology.* Princeton, N.J.: Princeton University Press, 1966.

Keen, Sam. *Faces of the Enemy.* New York: Harper & Row, 1986.

————, and Anne Valley-Fox. *Your Mythic Journey.* Los Angeles: Jeremy P. Tarcher, 1989.

Kelsey, Morton. *Discernment: A Study in Ecstasy and Evil.* New York: Paulist Press, 1978.

Keppler, Carl F. *The Literature of the Second Self.* Tucson, Ariz.: Books Demand UMI, 1972.

Koestler, Arthur. *Janus: A Summing Up.* New York: Vintage Books, 1978.

Kopp, Sheldon B. *If You Meet the Buddha on the Road, Kill Him.* Palo Alto, Calif.: Science & Behavior Books, 1976.

Kunkel, Fritz. *Selected Writings.* New York: Paulist Press, 1984.

Lao Tsu. *Tao Te Ching.* (G.–F. Feng and J. English, eds.). New York: Vintage Books, 1972.

Le Guin, Ursula K. *The Wizard of Earthsea.* New York: Parnassus Press, 1975.

Leonard, Linda Schierse. *Witness to the Fire.* Boston: Shambhala, 1989.

Lessing. Doris. *The Marriages Between Zones Three, Four and Five.* New York: Vintage Books, 1981.

Levinson, Daniel, J. *The Seasons of a Man's Life.* New York: Random House, 1979.

Lifton, Robert Jay. *The Nazi Doctors: Medical Killing and the Psychology of Genocide.* New York: Basic Books, 1986.

Lorde, Audre. *Sister Outsider.* New York: Crossing Press, 1984.

Lowen, Alexander. *The Betrayal of the Body.* New York: Macmillan, 1967.

Lowinsky, Naomi. *Stories from the Motherline.* Los Angeles: Jeremy P. Tarcher, forthcoming.

Martin, P. W. *Experiment in Depth.* London: Routledge & Kegan Paul, 1955.

May, Rollo. *Power and Innocence.* New York: W. W. Norton, 1972.

McWhinney, Will. "Evil in Organizational Life: Faustians, Professionals, Bureaucrats & Humanists." Unpublished paper.

Metzger, Deena. "Personal Disarmament: Negotiating with the Inner Government." *Re-vision* 12, no. 4, Spring, 1990.

Metzner, Ralph. *Opening to Inner Light.* Los Angeles: Jeremy P. Tarcher, 1986.

Miller, Alice. *For Your Own Good: Hidden Cruelty in Child-Rearing and the Roots of Violence.* New York: Farrar, Straus, Giroux, 1983.

————. *Banished Knowledge: Facing Childhood Injuries.* New York: Doubleday, 1990.

Miller, Patrick D. "What the Shadow Knows: An Interview with John A. Sanford." The *Sun,* no. 137, 1990.

Miller, William A. *Your Golden Shadow.* New York: Harper & Row, 1989.

Mindell, Arnold. "The Golem." *Quadrant* 8, no. 2, Winter, 1975.

————. "Somatic Consciousness." *Quadrant* 14:1 (1972), pp. 66–67.

————. *City Shadows: Psychological Interventions in Psychiatry.* London: Routledge, 1989.

Moffitt, Phillip. "The Dark Side of Excellence." *Esquire.* December, 1985.

Monick, Eugene. *Phallos: Sacred Image of the Masculine.* Toronto: Inner City Books, 1987.

Moreno, Antonio. *Jung, Gods and Modern Man.* South Bend, Ind.: University of Notre Dame Press, 1970.

Morrish, Ivor. *The Dark Twin: A Study of Evil & Good.* Essex, England: L. N. Fowler, 1980.

Murdock, Maureen. *The Heroine's Journey.* Boston: Shambhala, 1990.

Nebel, Cecile. *The Dark Side of Creativity.* Troy, N.Y.: Whitston Publishing, 1988.

Neumann, Erich. *Depth Psychology and a New Ethic.* New York: Putnam, 1969.

Nichols, Sallie. *Jung and Tarot.* York Beach, Me.: Samuel Weiser, 1980.

O'Flaherty, Wendy Doniger. *Dreams, Illusion, and Other Realities.* Chicago: University of Chicago, 1984.

O'Neill, John. *The Dark Side of Success.* Los Angeles: Jeremy P. Tarcher, forthcoming.

Peavey, Fran. "Us and Them." *Whole Earth Review* no. 49, Winter, 1985.

Peck, M. Scott. *People of the Lie.* New York: Simon & Schuster, 1983.

Perera, Sylvia Brinton. *The Scapegoat Complex: Toward a Mythology of Shadow and Guilt.* Toronto: Inner City Books, 1986.

Pierrakos, John C. *Anatomy of Evil.* New York: Institute for the New Age of Man, 1974.

————. *Core Energetics: Developing the Capacity to Love and Heal.* Mendocino, Calif.: LifeRhythm, 1988.

Raine, Kathleen. "The Inner Journey of the Poet." *In the Wake of Jung* (Molly Tuby, ed.). London: Coventure, 1986.

Rank, Otto. *Beyond Psychology.* New York: Dover, 1958 [1941].

————. *The Double* (Harry Tucker, Jr., trans. and ed.). New York: New American Library, 1977.

Rilke, Rainer Maria. *The Sonnets to Orpheus* (Stephen Mitchell, trans.). New York: Simon & Schuster, 1985.

Robb, Christina. "Shadows Loom in the Stuart Case." *Boston Globe,* January 16, 1990.

Rosen, David. *Depression, Ego, and Shadow.* Los Angeles: Jeremy P. Tarcher, forthcoming.

Samuels, Andrew, et al. *A Critical Dictionary of Jungian Analysis.* London: Routledge & Kegan Paul, 1986.

Sandner, Donald F. "The Split Shadow and the Father-Son Relationship." *Betwixt & Between* (Louise Mahdi, et al., eds.). La Salle, Ill.: Open Court, 1988.

Sanford, John A. *Evil: The Shadow Side of Reality.* New York: Crossroad, 1984.

———. *The Strange Trial of Mr. Hyde.* New York: Harper & Row, 1987.

Scarf, Maggie. *Intimate Partners: Patterns in Love and Marriage.* New York: Random House, 1982.

Schmookler, Andrew Bard. *Out of Weakness: Healing the Wounds that Drive Us to War.* New York: Bantam, 1988.

Sharp, Daryl. *The Survival Papers: Anatomy of a Mid-Life Crisis.* Toronto: Inner City Books, 1988.

Sidoli, Mara. "The Shadow Between Parents and Children." *The Archetype of the Shadow in a Split World* (Mary Ann Mattoon, ed.). Zurich: Daimon, 1987.

———. "Shame and Shadow." *The Journal of Analytical Psychology,* no. 33.

Signell, Karen A. *Wisdom of the Heart: Working with Women's Dreams.* New York: Bantam, 1990.

Sinetar, Marsha. *Do What You Love, The Money Will Follow.* New York: Dell Books, 1987.

Singer, June. *Boundaries of the Soul.* New York: Doubleday, 1972.

Slater, Philip. *Earthwalk.* Garden City, N. Y.: Anchor Press/Doubleday, 1974.

Smith, Huston. *The Religions of Man.* New York: Harper & Row, 1958.

Solzhenitsyn, Alexander. *The Gulag Archipelago.* New York: Harper & Row, 1978.

Stein, Robert M. *Incest and Human Love: The Betrayal of the Soul in Psychotherapy.* Dallas: Spring Publications, 1973.

Stevens, Anthony. *Archetypes: A Natural History of the Self.* New York: Quill, 1983.

———. *The Roots of War: A Jungian Perspective.* New York: Paragon House, 1989.

Stillings, Dennis. "Invasions of the Archetypes." *Gnosis,* no. 10, Winter, 1989.

Stone, Hal, and Sidra Winkelman. *Embracing Our Selves.* San Rafael, Calif.: New World Library, 1989.

Te Paske, Bradley A. *Rape and Ritual: A Psychological Study.* Toronto: Inner City Books, 1982.

Toub, Gary. "The Usefulness of the Useless." *Psychological Perspectives* 18, no. 2, Fall, 1987.

Tuby, Molly. "The Shadow." The Guild of Pastoral Psychology, *Guild lecture* no. 216, London, 1963.

Tucher, Harry, Jr. "The Importance of Otto Rank's Theory of the Double." *Journal of the Otto Rank Association.* Winter 1977–78.

Tymes, Ralph. *Doubles in Literary Psychology.* Cambridge, England: University of Oxford Press, 1949.

Van Over, R., ed. *Taoist Tales.* New York: New American Library, 1973.

Ventura, Michael. *Shadow Dancing in the USA.* Los Angeles: Jeremy P. Tarcher, 1985.

von Franz, Marie-Louise. *Shadow and Evil in Fairytales.* Dallas: Spring Publications, 1974.

———. *C. G. Jung: His Myth in Our Time.* New York: G. P. Putnam's Sons (for the C. G. Jung Foundation, New York), 1975.

———. *Projection and Re-collection in Jungian Psychology.* La Salle, Ill.: Open Court Publishing, 1980.

———, and James Hillman. *Jung's Typology.* Dallas: Spring Publications, 1971.

Wakefield, Joseph. "Analysis in Revolution: Shadow and Projection in El Salvador." *Spring,* 1987.

Washburn, Michael. *The Ego and the Dynamic Ground.* New York: State University of New York Press, 1988.

Whitmond, Edward C. *The Symbolic Quest.* Princeton, N.J.: Princeton University Press, 1978.

———. "Individual Transformation and Personal Responsibility." *Quadrant* 18, no. 2, Fall, 1985, pp. 45–56.

Wilber, Ken. *The Spectrum of Consciousness.* Wheaton, Ill.: Theosophical Publishing House, 1982.

Wilmer, Harry A. *Practical Jung: Nuts and Bolts of Jungian Psychotherapy.* Wilmette, Ill.: Chiron Publications. 1987.

Woodman, Marion. *The Pregnant Virgin.* Toronto: Inner City Books, 1985.

Woodruff, Paul, and Harry Wilmer (eds.). *Facing Evil at the Core of Darkness.* La Salle, Ill.: Open Court, 1986.

Yandell, James. "Devils on the Freeway." "This World," *San Francisco Chronicle,* July 26, 1987.

Ziegler, Alfred J. *Archetypal Medicine.* Dallas: Spring Publications, 1983.

PERMISSIONS AND COPYRIGHTS

. . . .

Chapter 1 consists of an excerpt, "The Long Bag We Drag Behind Us," from *A Little Book on the Human Shadow* by Robert Bly. Copyright © 1988 by Robert Bly. Reprinted by permission of HarperCollins Publishers, Inc.

Chapter 2 is composed of excerpts from the book *The Symbolic Quest* by Edward C. Whitmont. Copyright © 1969 by the C. G. Jung Foundation of Analytical Psychology. Reprinted by permission of Princeton University Press.

Chapter 3 is composed of excerpts from *What the Shadow Knows: An Interview with John A. Sanford* by D. Patrick Miller. Copyright © 1990 by D. Patrick Miller. Reprinted by permission of the author.

Chapter 4 is composed of excerpts from *Archetypes: A Natural History of The Self* by Anthony Stevens. Copyright © 1982 by Dr. Anthony Stevens. Reprinted by persmission of William Morrow & Company.

Chapter 5 is an excerpt from *Evil: The Shadow Side of Reality* by John A. Sanford. Copyright © 1981 by John A. Sanford. Reprinted by permission of The Crossroad Publishing Company.

Chapter 6 consists of excerpts from *Man and His Symbols,* Carl G. Jung (ed.). Copyright © 1964 Aldus Books, Ltd. Permission granted by J. G. Ferguson Publishing Co.

Chapter 7 consists of an excerpt from *Your Golden Shadow: Discovering and Fulfilling Your Undeveloped Self* by William A. Miller. Copyright © 1989 by William A. Miller. Reprinted by permission of HarperCollins Publishers, Inc.

Chapter 8 consists of an excerpt from *Getting the Love You Want* by Harville Hendrix. Copyright © 1988 by Harville Hendrix. Reprinted by permission of Henry Holt & Company.

Chapter 9 consists of an excerpt from *Incest and Human Love: The Betrayal of the Soul in Psychotherapy* by Robert M. Stein. Copyright © 1973 by Robert M. Stein. Reprinted by permission of the author and Spring Publications, Inc.

Chapter 10 consists of an excerpt from *The Hungry Self: Women, Eating, and Identity* by Kim Chernin. Copyright © 1985 by Kim Chernin. Reprinted by permission of Times Books, a division of Random House, Inc.

Chapter 11 consists of an excerpt from *Evil: The Shadow Side of Reality* by John A. Sanford. Copyright © 1981 by John A. Sanford. Reprinted by permission of The Crossroad Publishing Company.

Chapter 12 consists of excerpts from *Psyche's Sisters: ReImagining the Meaning of Sisterhood* by Christine Downing. Copyright © 1988 by Christine Downing. Reprinted by permission of HarperCollins Publishers, Inc.

Chapter 13 consists of an excerpt from *The Survival Papers: Anatomy of A Midlife Crisis (Studies in Jungian Psychology by Jungian Analysts,* no. 35) by Daryl Sharp. Copyright © 1988 by Daryl Sharp. Reprinted by permission of the author and Inner City Books, Toronto.

Chapter 14 consists of excerpts from *Intimate Partners: Patterns in Love and Marriage* by Maggie Scarf. Copyright © 1987 by Maggie Scarf. Reprinted by permission of Random House, Inc.

Chapter 15 consists of an excerpt from *Shadow Dancing in the USA* by Michael Ventura. Copyright © 1985 by Michael Ventura. Reprinted by permission of Jeremy P. Tarcher, Inc.

Chapter 16 is an excerpt from *Jung & Reich: The Body as Shadow* by John P. Conger. Copyright © 1988 by John P. Conger. Reprinted by permission of the author.

Chapter 17 consists of an excerpt from *Anatomy of Evil* by John C. Pierrakos. Copyright © 1974 by John C. Pierrakos, M.D. Reprinted by permission of the author.

Chapter 18 consists of an excerpt from *Beyond Illness: Discovering the Experience of Health* by Larry Dossey. Copyright © 1984 by Larry Dossey, M.D. Reprinted by permission of Shambhala Publications, Inc., 300 Massachusetts Avenue, Boston, MA 02115

Chapter 19 is composed of excerpts from *Archetypal Medicine* by Alfred J. Ziegler, M.D., translated from the German by Gary V. Hartman. Copyright © 1983 by Spring Publications, Inc. Reprinted by permission of Spring Publications, Inc.

Chapter 20 is an excerpt from *Marriage Dead or Alive* by Adolf Guggenbühl-Craig. Copyright © 1977 by Adolf Guggenbühl-Craig. Translated by Murray Stein. Reprinted by permission of Spring Publications, Inc.

Chapter 21 is an original essay created especially for this volume by Bruce Shackleton, Ed.D. Copyright © 1990 by Bruce Shackleton. Used by permission of the author.

Chapter 22 is an original essay based on the *The Dark Side of Success,* by John R. O'Neill (forthcoming, Jeremy P. Tarcher, Inc.). Copyright © 1990 by John R. O'Neill. Reprinted by permission of the author.

Chapter 23 is an essay by Adolf Guggenbühl-Craig, excerpted from *The Reality of the Psyche,* edited by Joseph B. Wheelright. Copyright © 1972 C. G. Jung Foundation. Reprinted by permission of the C. G. Jung Foundation.

Chapter 24 consists of excerpts from *Do What You Love, The Money Will Follow* by Marsha Sinetar. Copyright © 1987 by Dr. Marsha Sinetar. Used by permission of Dell Books, a division of Bantam, Doubleday, Dell Publishing Group, Inc.

Chapter 25 consists of excerpts from *When Technology Wounds,* by Chellis Glendinning. Copyright © 1990 by Chellis Glendinning. Reprinted by permission of William Morrow & Co., Inc

Chapter 38 is an essay, "Redeeming Our Devils and Demons," by Stephen A. Diamond, based upon an essay/review published in The San Francisco Jung Institute Library *Journal* 9, no. 1, 1990, under the title "The Psychology of Evil." Copyright © 1990 by Dr. Stephen A. Diamond. Used by permission of the author and the San Francisco Jung Institute Library *Journal.*

Chapter 39 is a chapter excerpted from *Escape from Evil* by Ernest Becker. Copyright © 1975 by Marie Becker. Reprinted by permission of The Free Press, a division of Macmillan Publishing Company, Inc.

Chapter 40 is composed of excerpts from *Out of Weakness* by Andrew Bard Schmookler. Copyright © 1988 by Andrew Bard Schmookler. Used by permission of Bantam Books, a division of Bantam, Doubleday, Dell Publishing Group, Inc.

Chapter 41 consists of excerpts from *Faces of the Enemy* by Sam Keen. Copyright © 1986 by Sam Keen. Reprinted by permission of HarperCollins Publishers Inc.

Chapter 42 consists of an excerpt from *Heart Politics* by Fran Peavey. Copyright © 1984 by Fran Peavey. Reprinted by permission of New Society Publishers, Philadelphia, PA., Santa Cruz, CA, and Gabriola Island, BC, Canada (800-333-9093).

Chapter 43 consists of excerpts from *Pornography and Silence* by Susan Griffin. Copyright © 1981 by Susan Griffin. Reprinted by permission of Harper-Collins Publishers Inc.

Chapter 44 is an excerpt from *Sister Outsider* by Audre Lorde. Copyright © 1984 by Audre Lorde. Reprinted by permission of The Crossing Press, California, and excerpted by permission of the Charlotte Sheedy Agency, Inc.

Chapter 45 consists of an excerpt from *Power and Politics: The Psychology of Soviet-American Partnership* by Jerome S. Bernstein. Copyright © 1989 by Jerome S. Bernstein. Reprinted by arrangement with Shambhala Publications, Inc., 300 Massachusetts Avenue, Boston, MA 02115.

Chapter 46 consists of an excerpt from *The Nazi Doctors: Medical Killing and the Psychology of Genocide* by Robert Jay Lifton. Copyright © 1986 by Robert J. Lifton. Reprinted by permission of Basic Books, Inc., Publishers, New York.

Chapter 47 consists of an excerpt from *Eros on Crutches: Reflections on Amorality and Psychopathy* by Adolph Guggenbühl-Craig. Copyright © 1980 by Adolf Guggenbühl-Craig. Reprinted by permission of Spring Publications, Inc.

Chapter 48 is composed of excerpts from an essay, "Alchemy and Criminality," by Jerry Fjerkenstad, which first appeared in *Inroads: Men, Creativity, Soul,* Spring 1990. Copyright © 1990 by Jerry Fjerkenstad. Reprinted by permission of *Inroads,* Minneapolis, MN 19901.

Chapter 49 is an article, originally titled *Devils and Angels Play the Merging Game,* by James Yandell, which appeared in the *San Francisco Chronicle* July 26, 1987. Copyright © 1987 by James Yandell. Used by permission of the author.

CONTRIBUTORS

. . . .

JOHN BABBS writes and teaches in Boulder, Colorado.

ERNEST BECKER (1924–1974) taught at the University of California, Berkeley, San Francisco State University, and Simon & Fraser University in Canada. He won the Pulitzer Prize for general nonfiction in 1974 for his book *The Denial of Death*. His other works include *Birth and Death of Meaning; Revolution in Psychiatry; Angel in Armor; The Structure of Evil;* and *Escape from Evil*.

JEROME S. BERNSTEIN is a Jungian analyst and clinical psychologist in private practice in Washington, D.C. Former vice-chairman of the C. G. Jung Institute of New York, he also was an official in the U.S. Office of Economic Opportunity and a consultant to the mayor of New York City and the governor of New Jersey. He is the author of *Power and Politics: The Psychology of Soviet-American Partnership*.

PETER BISHOP is lecturer in sociology at the South Australian College for Advanced Education. He is the author of *The Myth of Shangri-La (Tibet, Travel Writing and the Western Creation of Sacred Landscape)* and *The Greening of Psychology: The Vegetable World in Myth, Dream, and Healing*.

ROBERT BLY, an outstanding poet and translator, is the author of many books and the National Book Award winner for poetry for *The Light Around the Body*. His work includes *Loving a Woman in Two Worlds; News of the Universe: Poems of Twofold Consciousness; A Little Book on the Human Shadow,* and *Iron John: A Book About Men*. Based in Minnesota, Bly is currently writing on men's mythology and leading workshops for men around the country.

JOHN BRADSHAW is a Houston-based family counselor, lecturer, and workshop leader. His popular PBS television series has resulted in the best-selling books *Bradshaw: On the Family; Healing the Shame that Binds You;* and *Homecoming: Reclaiming and Championing Your Inner Child*.

NATHANIEL BRANDEN is a Los Angeles psychologist, teacher, and popular author. His books include *The Disowned Self; Honoring the Self; How to Raise your Self-Esteem;* and *The Psychology of Romantic Love*.

JANICE BREWI and ANNE BRENNAN are the founders of Mid-life Directions in Vailsburg, New Jersey, and coauthors of *Celebrate Mid-Life: Jungian Archetypes and Midlife Spirituality* and *Midlife: Psychological and Spiritual Perspectives*.

KATY BUTLER is a California-based freelance writer who has written about Buddhism for *The New Yorker, Mother Jones, Yoga Journal,* and *Common Boundary*.

JOSEPH CAMPBELL (19??–1987) taught comparative mythology at Sarah Lawrence College for forty years. He was the subject and narrator of the popular PBS series with Bill Moyers "The Power of Myth." A prolific author, his works include *The Hero with a Thousand Faces; The Masks of God* (4 vols.), *The Mythic Image; Myths to Live By; The Atlas of World Mythology; The Power of Myth;* and the posthumous interview transcripts *An Open Life* (with Michael Toms).

ROSARIO CASTELLANOS (1925–1974), born in Mexico City, was a writer of plays, novels, stories, and poetry. She published eight volumes of poetry, which were anthologized in 1972 as *Poesia No Eres Tu (Poetry Is Not You)*. The *Selected Poems of Rosario Castellanos* was assembled from that anthology.

KIM CHERNIN is the author of *The Obsession; In My Mother's House;* and *The Hungry Self;* as well as the poetry collection *The Hunger Song* and the novel *The Flame Bearers.* She lives in Berkeley, California, where she counsels women with eating disorders and in developmental crisis.

JOHN P. CONGER is a clinical psychologist in private practice, a trainer with the Bioenergetic Society of Northern California, and an associate professor in graduate psychology at John F. Kennedy University in Orinda, California.

STEPHEN A. DIAMOND is a licensed psychologist practicing in Los Altos, Californa. His written work includes the articles "The Psychology of Evil," "Rediscovering Rank," and "Finding Beauty," a review of Rollo May's work.

LARRY DOSSEY is a physician in Santa Fe, New Mexico, and the author of *Space, Time and Medicine; Beyond Illness: Discovering the Experience of Health;* and *Recovering the Soul: A Scientific and Spiritual Search.*

CHRISTINE DOWNING is professor and chairwoman of Religious Studies at San Diego State University and the author of *The Goddess; Psyche's Sisters; Journey through Menopause;* and *Myths and Mysteries of Same-Sex Love.*

WILLIAM CARL EICHMAN is a teacher and student of esoteric knowledge at State College, Pennsylvania.

GEORG FEUERSTEIN has published a dozen books on Indian philosophy, including *Yoga: The Technology of Ecstasy* and *Holy Madness: The Outer Limits of Religion and Morality.*

JERRY FJERKENSTAD is a psychologist in private practice in Minneapolis. He also works in sex-offender treatment and is artistic director of the Dream Guild Threatre.

LILIANE FREY-ROHN, one of C. G. Jung's closest collaborators, is a senior training analyst in Zurich, Switzerland, who has written extensively on the subject of evil. She is the author of *Friedrich Nietzsche: A Psychological Interpretation of His Life and Work* and *From Freud to Jung: A Comparative Study of the Psychology of the Unconscious.*

CHELLIS GLENDENNING is a psychologist living in Tesque, New Mexico, and author of *Waking Up in the Nuclear Age* and *When Technology Wounds.*

LIZ GREENE is a Jungian analyst, astrologer, and writer in London. Her publications include novels and children's books, as well as *The Astrology of Fate; Relating: An Astrological Guide to Living with Others on a Small Planet; Saturn: A New Look at an Old Devil;* and *The Jupiter/Saturn Conference Lectures* (with Stephen Arroyo).

SUSAN GRIFFIN is the feminist author of *Voices; Rape: The Power of Consciousness; Woman and Nature: The Roaring Inside Her; Pornography and Silence: Culture's Revenge Against Nature,* and the forthcoming *A Course of Stones: The Private Life of War.* She lives and writes in Berkeley, California.

ADOLF GUGGENBÜHL-CRAIG is a psychiatrist and Jungian analyst in Zurich, Switzerland. He is former president of the Curatorium of the C. G. Jung Institute, Zurich, former president of the International Association of Analytical Psychology, and the author of *Power in the Helping Professions; Marriage Dead or Alive;* and *Eros on Crutches.*

BARBARA HANNAH was born in England and lived in Switzerland, as a practicing psychotherapist, analyst, and teacher at the C. G. Jung Institute. She is the author of *Striving Towards Wholeness; Jung: His Life and Work, a Biographical Memoir;* and *Encounters with the Soul.*

HARVILLE HENDRIX lives in New York City, where he is the director of the Institute for Relationship Therapy, which he founded in 1984. He is a diplomate in the American Association of Pastoral Counselors, a trainer of relationship therapists, and author of the best-seller *Getting the Love You Want: A Guide for Couples.*

JAMES HILLMAN, Jungian analyst, lectures widely and is a prolific writer. Hillman is the founder of Archetypal Psychology, a third generation of thought based on the work of C. G. Jung. He is the former editor and publisher of the journal *Spring* and of the respected small press Spring Publications. His own titles include *The Myth of Analysis; Suicide and the Soul; Insearch: Psychology and Religion; Re-Visioning Psychology; The Dream and the Underworld; Loose Ends; Anima: An Anatomy of a Personified Notion; Healing Fiction; Blue Fire;* the interview book, *Inter Views;* and *Puer Papers* (ed.).

LINDA JACOBSON is a Los Angeles artist who teaches at UCLA extension.

W. BRUGH JOY, a physician turned healer, conducts residential workshops in northern Arizona and is the author of *Joy's Way* and *Avalanche: Heretical Reflections on the Dark and the Light.*

CARL GUSTAV JUNG (1875–1961) is probably best known as one of the founders of psychoanalysis. Jung's overriding interest was the mystery of consciousness and personality and the spiritual dilemma of the modern individual. His many books include *The Collected Works* (20 volumes); *Modern Man in Search of a Soul; Man and His Symbols;* and his popular autobiography, *Memories, Dreams, Reflections.*

SAM KEEN, philosopher and former editor of *Psychology Today,* is the author of *To a Dancing God; The Passionate Life: Stages of Loving; Your Mythic Journey* (with Anne Valley-Fox); *Faces of the Enemy: Reflections of the Hostile Imagination* and *Fire in the Belly: On Being A Man.*

SHELDON B. KOPP is a psychotherapist in Washington, D.C., and author of *Even a Stone Can Be a Teacher* and *If You Meet the Buddha on the Road, Kill Him.*

DANIEL J. LEVINSON is a professor of psychology in the Department of Psychiatry at Yale University School of Medicine, New Haven, Connecticut, and author of *The Seasons of a Man's Life* and coauthor of *The Authoritarian Personality.*

ROBERT JAY LIFTON is a distinguished professor of psychiatry and psychology at the City University of New York. His widely acclaimed works include *Death in Life; Home from the War; The Future of Immortality;* and *The Nazi Doctors.*

AUDRE LORDE is a black lesbian feminist poet and essayist and the mother of two sons. Her books include *Sister Outsider; The Black Unicorn; A Burst of Light; Cancer Journals;* and many books of poetry.

ROLLO MAY, esteemed psychotherapist and lecturer, is the author of many books, including *The Meaning of Anxiety; Man's Search for Himself; Love and Will; The Search for Beauty;* and *Power and Innocence.*

DEENA METZGER is a Los Angeles psychotherapist, poet, teacher, and novelist whose books include *Tree; The Woman Who Slept with Men to Take the War Out of Them; What Deena Thought,* and *Looking for the Faces of God.*

D. PATRICK MILLER is a freelance writer in Encinitas, California, investigating psychological and spiritual subjects. He serves as contributing editor to *Yoga Journal* and has written for the *Sun, New Age Journal, Free Spirit of New York City,* and *The Columbia Journalism Review.*

WILLIAM A. MILLER, a Jungian analyst in Plymouth, Minnesota, is author of *The Joy of Feeling Good; Make Friends with Your Shadow; When Going to Pieces Holds You Together;* and *Your Golden Shadow.*

SALLIE NICHOLS, author of *Jung and Tarot: An Archetypal Journey,* studied at the C. G. Jung Institute in Zurich, taught symbolism of the tarot to trainees at the C. G. Jung Institute in Los Angeles, and lectures frequently on this subject.

JOHN R. O'NEILL is president of the California School of Professional Psychology and President of the California NEXUS Foundation. He has had a long career in business and education, and consulting and venture-capital activities since leaving the American Telephone and Telegraph Company in 1970. He is also former vice-president of Mills College in Oakland, California.

FRAN PEAVEY has a background ranging from taxi driving and furniture design to political activism and doctoral work in innovation theory and technological forecasting. She is the author of the book *Heart Politics.*

M. SCOTT PECK is a best-selling author and psychiatrist practicing in Connecticut. He is the author of *The Road Less Traveled; People of the Lie; The Different Drum;* and the novel *A Bed by the Window.*

JOHN C. PIERRAKOS studied with Wilhelm Reich in the 1940s. He is co-creator, with Alexander Lowen, of Bioenergetics Therapy, creator of Core Energetics Therapy, and director of the Institute for the New Age of Man in New York City. He lectures and teaches throughout the world and is the author of *Core Energetics.*

JOHN A. SANFORD is an Episcopal priest and Jungian analyst in San Diego. His books include *Dreams: God's Forgotten Language; The Kingdom Within; Dreams and Healing; Healing and Wholeness; Invisible Partners;* and *Evil: The Shadow Side of Reality.*

MAGGIE SCARF is the author of *Intimate Partners: Patterns in Love and Marriage* and *Unfinished Business: Pressure Points in the Lives of Women.*

ANDREW BARD SCHMOOKLER is senior policy advisor to Search for Common Ground in Washington, D.C., and author of *The Parable of the Tribes* and *Out of Weakness: Healing the Wounds That Drive Us to War.*

BRUCE SHACKLETON is a psychologist in private practice in Boston, an organization consultant, and a staff member at the Occupational Health Clinic of Massachusetts General Hospital and Harvard Medical School.

DARYL SHARP is a Jungian analyst in Toronto and the publisher of Inner City Books. He is the author of *The Secret Raven; Personality Types;* and *The Survival Papers.*

KAREN SIGNELL is a Jungian analyst in San Francisco and author of *Wisdom of the Heart: Working with Women's Dreams.*

MARSHA SINETAR is an organizational psychologist and the author of *Do What You Love, The Money Will Follow* and *Ordinary People as Monks and Mystics.*

ROBERT M. STEIN is a senior training analyst at the C. G. Jung Institute of Los Angeles and has a private practice in Beverly Hills. He is the author of numerous articles and the book *Incest and Human Love: The Betrayal of the Soul in Psychotherapy.*

BROTHER DAVID STEINDL-RAST is a Benedictine monk who was inspired to study Eastern traditions by his mentor Thomas Merton. He spends most of the year in seclusion but travels regularly to give lectures.

ANTHONY STEVENS was born and educated in the west of England and studied psychology and medicine at Oxford University. He practices as a psychotherapist and psychiatrist in London and in Devon, England, and combines his clinical work with writing and lecturing. He is the author of *Archetypes: A Natural History of the Self* and *The Roots of War: A Jungian Perspective.*

HAL STONE is a clinical psychologist, teacher, and the director of the Academy of Delos in Northern California, where he and his wife, Sidra Winkelman, offer training groups in the Voice Dialogue Process. He is the author of *Embracing Heaven and Earth* and coauthor of *Embracing Our Selves* and *Embracing Each Other.*

GARY TOUB is a psychologist and Jungian analyst in private practice in Denver, specializing in dreamwork and bodywork.

MICHAEL VENTURA is a columnist for the *L.A. Weekly,* a screenwriter, novelist, and author of *Shadow Dancing in the USA* and the novel *Night Time, Losing Time.*

MARIE-LOUISE VON FRANZ, eminent Swiss psychoanalyst, is probably Carl Jung's most important living disciple, having worked directly with him for thirty-one years. Her work embodies the essence of his thought, though she is in her own right an original and provocative thinker. Her books include *Number and Time; The Grail Legend* (with Emma Jung); *Puer Aeternus; Projection and Re-collection in Jungian Psychology; The Feminine in Fairytales; Interpretation of Fairytales; Shadow and Evil in Fairytales; On Dreams and Death;* and the transcript book from the filmed interview, *The Way of the Dream.*

EDWARD C. WHITMONT is a psychiatrist and founding member of the C. G. Jung Institute of New York and author of *The Symbolic Quest; Psyche and Substance;* and *Return of the Goddess.*

KEN WILBER is a transpersonal philosopher and the prolific author of *No Boundary; The Spectrum of Consciousness; Atman Project; Up from Eden; Eye to Eye; Quantum Questions;* and *Grace and Grit: Sprituality and Healing in the Story of Treya Killam-Wilber* (forthcoming).

SIDRA WINKELMAN is a psychotherapist, mother, and cocreator of the Voice Dialogue Process, which she and her husband, Hal Stone, teach in the United States and abroad. She is coauthor of *Embracing Our Selves* and *Embracing Each Other.*

JAMES YANDELL is a psychiatrist and Jungian analyst practicing in Berkeley, California.

ALFRED J. ZIEGLER is a physician, Jungian analyst, and psychosomatic consultant. He is the author of *Archetypal Medicine.*

ABOUT THE EDITORS

. . . .

CONNIE ZWEIG is a freelance writer and book editor living on a ridgetop in Topanga Canyon, California. She is the former executive editor of *Brain/Mind Bulletin,* a former columnist for *Esquire,* and currently senior editor for Jeremy P. Tarcher, Inc. She has a long-standing interest in psychology and, as a meditation student and teacher, has been devoted to the spiritual journey. She is author of the collected volume *To Be A Woman: The Birth of the Conscious Feminine.*

JEREMIAH ABRAMS has worked for the past twenty years as a Jungian therapist, dream analyst, writer, counselor, and consultant. He is currently the director of the Mount Vision Institute, a Center for Individuation, in Sausalito, California. He lives with his wife and two children in Northern California. He is author of the collected volume *Reclaiming the Inner Child.*

New Consciousness Reader Series

. . . .

Dreamtime and Dreamwork. The definitive book on the worldwide use of dreams as a special source of knowledge, dream interpretation, problem solving, and healing through dreams, shared dreaming, lucid dreaming, forming dream groups, and new brain research.

Healers on Healing. Reveals the common thread that unites healers from a wide range of approaches and techniques. Thirty-seven original essays by leading physicians, therapists, and writers in alternative and mainstream healthcare. Over 35,000 copies in print.

Meeting the Shadow. This collection of sixty-five essays explores the hidden power of the dark side of human nature in families, intimate relationships, sexuality, work, spirituality, politics, and psychotherapy, and how to use it creatively through "shadow-work."

Reclaiming the Inner Child. The best writing on the most current topic in psychology and recovery by the world's leading experts. Thirty-seven wide-ranging articles offer a comprehensive overview of the inner-child concept and its application to healing, creativity, and daily joy. Highlights many applications for people in all forms of recovery.

Spiritual Emergency. Leading experts explore the relationship between spirituality, madness, and healing. Edited by Stan and Christina Grof, this ground-breaking work reveals that within the crisis of spiritual emergency lies the promise of spiritual emergence and renewal.

To Be a Woman. A striking collection of original writing by the best-selling authorities in women's psychology. In twenty-three essays this book reveals the next stage of development in women's awareness: conscious femininity. For all women who long to feel strong, yet fully feminine.

What Survives? This thought-provoking collection of twenty new essays examines emerging evidence and developments in the fields of parapsychology, near-death studies, consciousness research, new-paradigm biology, and physics, helping the reader to arrive at an optimistic, yet informed and rational, answer to the question "what survives the body after death?"